Going to the Source
The Bedford Reader in American History

Going to the Source

The Bedford Reader in American History

VOLUME 2: SINCE 1865

Victoria Bissell Brown

Grinnell College

Timothy J. Shannon

Gettysburg College

Bedford/St. Martin's   Boston ◆ New York

To our students, who have taught us so much

For Bedford/St. Martin's
Publisher for History: Patricia A. Rossi
Director of Development for History: Jane Knetzger
Executive Editor for History: Elizabeth M. Welch
Developmental Editor: Laura W. Arcari
Production Editor: Arthur Johnson
Senior Production Supervisor: Nancy Myers
Marketing Manager: Jenna Bookin Barry
Editorial Assistants: Elizabeth Wallace, Rachel L. Safer
Production Assistants: Kristen Merrill, Amy Derjue
Copyeditor: Richard Steins
Text Design: Claire Seng-Niemoeller
Indexer: Steve Csipke
Cover Design: Billy Boardman
Cover Art: Photograph of Stanford historian Carl Degler, © Ressmeyer/CORBIS. *Nineteenth-Century Blackfoot Chief Mu-Nahxk-Wai-yo,* c. 1876–1896, © CORBIS. WPA Mural at Coit Tower, © Robert Holmes/CORBIS. "Infantry Company Poses beside Train," 1894, © Bettmann/CORBIS; the 15th United States Infantry Company C, called in by President Cleveland to help break up a railroad strike against the Pullman Palace Car Company, pose beside a special Rock Island Railroad patrol train. "U.S. Paratrooper Reading a Letter, Vietnam, 1969," © Tim Page/CORBIS; a U.S. paratrooper from the 1st Air Cavalry receives mail while stationed in a blocking position north of the Michelin Plantation.
Composition: Pine Tree Composition, Inc.
Cartography: Mapping Specialists
Printing and Binding: R.R. Donnelley & Sons Company

President: Joan E. Feinberg
Editorial Director: Denise B. Wydra
Director of Marketing: Karen Melton Soeltz
Director of Editing, Design, and Production: Marcia Cohen
Managing Editor: Elizabeth M. Schaaf

Library of Congress Control Number: 2003112719

For information, write: Bedford/St. Martin's, 75 Arlington Street, Boston, MA 02116
(617-399-4000)

ISBN: 0–312–40205–8

Acknowledgments

CHAPTER 2
Page 37 (Source 1): "Greetings from Glacier National Park," c. 1920. Great Northern Railway Company Advertising & Publicity Department Photos, Minnesota Historical Society.
Page 38 (Source 2): "Great Northern Railway Calendar," 1923. Great Northern Railway Company Advertising & Publicity Department Photos, Minnesota Historical Society.
Page 39 (Source 3): "Blackfeet and Park Golfers," c. 1930. Great Northern Railway Company Advertising & Publicity Department Photos, Minnesota Historical Society.

Preface for Instructors

The scene is familiar: you have only one class period in which to discuss a topic—say, anti-Irish nativism in the 1840s. The reader you are using includes a half-dozen or more documents—two newspaper editorials, a petition, a sermon excerpt, a cartoon, a letter, several job advertisements. What to do with such a wealth of material? All of it points to anti-Irish prejudice, so you focus the class meeting around that historical development, hoping the students will walk away from all those documents with a general impression of how nativism operated in the 1840s. But there are some bumps along the way. The students have a hard time distinguishing the utility of one document from another, but you lack the time to introduce and discuss the differences between these types of sources. Ultimately, the level of discussion suffers because the students focus on recalling the content of the varied materials they read rather than analyzing them as historical evidence. You end the class wishing you had the time and teaching instrument necessary to talk directly to students about how historians would actually turn such sources over in their hands and heads, assessing the advantages and disadvantages of each, before using them to write a history of anti-Irish nativism.

Our purpose in *Going to the Source* is to provide you with both the time and the instrument for coupling a discussion of historical content with a discussion of a specific type of historical source. As teachers, we have often felt uncomfortably stuffed by the smorgasbord servings of different primary and secondary documents typically offered in U.S. history readers. Our goal in writing this reader is to provide a streamlined focus on a particular topic while blending in a healthy portion of historical thinking about the nature of different types of sources, be they newspapers, letters, paintings, statistical data, or scholars' secondary writing. To achieve this, we've designed each chapter around one historical topic and one type of source in order to allow for more focused student reading and assignments, as well as an enriched classroom discussion, on the various processes that go into researching and reconstructing the past.

In the course of writing *Going to the Source,* we have read numerous discussions of how to employ primary and secondary documents in the teaching of history. Most of those discussions focus on the worthy goal of enlivening historical content; they tend to emphasize the way in which a letter from a Lowell mill worker, for example, can illuminate that particular historical experience. We were looking, however, for a method that would allow us to combine more explicitly a lively study of the past with equally lively classroom discussion of the challenges and rewards historians face in reconstructing the past with primary and secondary sources.

We have been encouraged in this endeavor by the work of Sam Wineburg, a cognitive psychologist at Stanford University, whose research reveals the difference between the way that trained historians approach a historical document and the way nonhistorians, especially undergraduate students, approach the same document.[1] Wineburg has found that historians have so absorbed their discipline's way of handling a document—looking first at its provenance and making instantaneous calculations about the date, the author, the proximity to the event discussed, the authenticity of the document, and the reliability of the document's creator—that they have difficulty describing a reading process that is as natural to them as breathing.

Wineburg has also found that students most successfully travel out of the present and into the past if their teachers can explain and demonstrate that the pathway to the past is often a rutted road comprised of more and less reliable documents that every historian must pick up, examine, and evaluate. Wineburg calls on historians to "bring this messier form of expertise into the classroom" so that students can become conscious of both the distance between now and then and the logical processes historians use to traverse that distance via their sources.

The organization of each chapter in *Going to the Source* is designed to expose historians' processes and reveal to students how historians utilize sources. The seven-part organization of each chapter includes an introduction that sets the stage for the case study that will unfold in the documents, a "Using the Source" section that examines the advantages and disadvantages inherent in the particular type of source utilized in that chapter, and a section called "Working with the Source" that provides students with tools to aid them in their analysis of the documents. The longest portion of each chapter is "The Source," a section consisting of documents that draw from a single source or single type of source. It is followed by "Analyzing the Source," which offers questions suitable for written assignments or class discussion. An epilogue entitled "Beyond the Source" provides closure on the case study, and "Finding and Supplementing the Source" suggests additional sources for further study. In addition, this book features an "Introduction for Students" that discusses the principles and practices of working with sources and a "Documenting the Source" appendix that shows students how to document the sources included in these volumes according to *The Chicago Manual of Style*.

Taken as a whole, the fourteen chapters in each volume offer documents that are personal and documents that are public; the sources included here run the gamut from popular to official, from obvious to obscure. In satisfying our own interest in Americans' struggle to realize democratic ideals out of undemocratic realities, we have provided sources from the margins of society as well as the centers of power. By including documents that balance a bottom-up with a top-down approach to U.S. history, we seek to remind students that the nation's conflicts over democratic ideals have not been confined to marginal communities or anonymous voices. Historians seeking to trace these conflicts

[1] Sam Wineburg, *Historical Thinking and Other Unnatural Acts: Charting the Future of Teaching the Past* (Philadelphia: Temple University Press, 2001), and "Teaching the Mind Good Habits," *The Chronicle of Higher Education* 49 (April 11, 2003), B20.

look high and low, examining congressional speeches along with the oral reports of obscure witnesses to the American scene. By exposing students to elite or official documents as well as private or anonymous ones, we seek to remind them that influence can arise from humble communities in America, that centers of power cannot be ignored when writing the history of American democracy, and that marginal people have had to learn about elite institutions in order to influence the powerful. We also seek to remind students of the span of sources a historian can draw upon to capture U.S. history and to convince them of their ability to understand—and their right to access—a vast array of documentary material.

ACKNOWLEDGMENTS

We would like to thank the following reviewers who guided us in our revisions with their suggestions and comments: James Beeby, West Virginia Wesleyan College; Jamie Bronstein, New Mexico State University; William Cario, Concordia University; John R. Chávez, Southern Methodist University; Edward J. Davies, University of Utah; Douglas W. Dodd, California State University Bakersfield; Bruce Dorsey, Swarthmore College; Chris Erickson, Indiana State University; Jim Farmer, University of South Carolina at Aiken; Gayle Fischer, Salem State College; Andrew Frank, Florida Atlantic University; Susan E. Gray, Arizona State University; Emily Greenwald, University of Nebraska–Lincoln; Bradley J. Gundlach, Trinity College; Steven Hahn, Northwestern University; Barbara Handy-Marchello, University of North Dakota; Päivi Hoikkala, Cal State Polytechnic University; Kathleen Kennedy, Western Washington University; Todd Kerstetter, Texas Christian University; David Krugler, University of Wisconsin–Platteville; Molly Ladd Taylor, York University; Charlene Mires, Villanova University; Susan Rugh, Brigham Young University; John Sacher, Emporia State University; Rebecca S. Shoemaker, Indiana State University; Michael Topp, University of Texas at El Paso; Robert Wolff, Central Connecticut State University; and David E. Woodard, Concordia University.

We extend our thanks to the editorial staff at Bedford/St. Martin's: Joan E. Feinberg, president, and her predecessor, Charles H. Christensen; Patricia A. Rossi, publisher for history; Heidi H. Hood, our first developmental editor, and her successor, Laura W. Arcari, who, in addition to working with us to bring this book to publication, was responsible for writing the "Documenting the Source" appendix; Jane Knetzger, director of development for history; our editorial assistants, Rachel Safer and Elizabeth Wallace; our production editor, Arthur Johnson, and production assistants Kristen Merrill and Amy Derjue. Thanks also to our copyeditor, Richard Steins, and to the book's designer, Claire Seng-Niemoeller. We give special thanks to Katherine Kurzman, our original sponsoring editor, who started us on our journey. This book never would have happened without her impetus.

We were greatly aided in our endeavors by the librarians at Gettysburg College, including Chris Amadure, Karen Drickamer, Linda Isenberger, and Susan Roach, as well as the Government Documents librarians at the University of

Iowa, Marianne Mason and John Elson; the collections manager at the Pennsylvania State Museum, Janet Johnson; and the staff in the archives section of the Minnesota Historical Society. Staff assistance from Carla Pavlick and Linda Price is gratefully acknowledged, as is the advice we received from colleagues who answered questions and read drafts of chapters. We are particularly grateful to Gabor Boritt, Joe Coohill, Brendan Cushing-Daniels, William Farr, Keith Fitzgerald, Matt Gallman, Tom Hietala, Jim Jacobs, Shawna Leigh, Ann Lesch, Karl Lorenz, Gerald Markowitz, Barbara Sommer, Mark Weitz, and Robert Wright. The assistance of students and former students was invaluable in this project, and we owe much to Maggie Campbell, Katie Mears, Posey Gruener, Amy Scott, Jason Stohler, Matthew Raw, and Lauren Rocco. Finally, of course, we owe thanks to our families, who encouraged us throughout this process and regularly offered much-needed relaxation from our labors. Thanks to Jim, Colleen, Caroline, Daniel, and both of our Elizabeths.

Introduction for Students

In the debate over going to war with Iraq in 2003, the American people were asked to examine and interpret different kinds of evidence from multiple sources: the United Nations' evidence on Iraqi weapons programs, Amnesty International's evidence on the Iraqi government's torture of its own citizens, the Pentagon's evidence of Iraqi ties to international terrorist organizations, British prime minister Tony Blair's evidence of Iraqi interest in obtaining nuclear weapons. Some of this evidence was unverified when the United States launched its preemptive war against Iraq in March 2003, but none of it was easily dismissed. American citizens had the responsibility of reading and listening to the evidence as it was presented by both disinterested experts and partisan analysts and reaching their own conclusions about the case for war. That process did not end when U.S. troops occupied Baghdad. The debate over the Iraq evidence continues to influence American citizens' support for their government's policies, and the debate over the evidence will be aired among historians for decades to come. The Iraq war is only the most obvious recent example of the importance of evidence, data, sources, intelligence, information, and, yes, values, beliefs, and opinion in making decisions that shape our lives. It is also the most prominent example of a contemporary story that will be told and retold in history books, drawing on evidence we have available today as well as evidence that is bound to emerge in the coming years.

Going to the Source intends to sharpen your skills at reading, evaluating, and interpreting evidence. To achieve that goal, we ask you to put yourself in the position of a historian who is interrogating different kinds of sources from the past, trying to determine what is reliable in the testimony that each type of source provides. In the end, it is our hope that your work with *Going to the Source* will leave you with a set of practices and principles that you can just as easily apply to reading your local newspaper as to examining a grandmother's letter found in the attic, an eighteenth-century oil painting, or a Vietnam war intelligence report. These principles and practices have guided our writing of every story and exercise included here, and though we do not ask that you memorize our guidelines, we offer them here as a preview of concepts that will become quite familiar to you while working with this volume.

PRINCIPLES AND PRACTICES OF WORKING WITH SOURCES

- Every tangible object that human beings produce, whether it be a piece of clothing or a laundry list, is a kind of "document" and as such has the potential to serve as a historical "source."

- Every document is created in a particular context—a particular place, a particular time, a particular culture, a particular political situation—and must be examined with that context in mind. No document can be understood on its own, in a vacuum.

- Once placed in context, the first questions we must ask of a document are: Who created it? When? Why? What was the document creator's purpose? What end was this document intended to serve? What was this document doing?

- Because all documents are human creations, all documents have a bias. That is to say, all documents are produced by someone with a particular point of view. This is not an unfortunate flaw of historical sources, it is what makes them rich with meaning.

- As human creations with a point of view, historical sources are complex witnesses to the past. Moreover, different documents from different creators are likely to present diverging angles of vision if not outright contradictions.

- The historian's job is neither to dismiss nor to adopt the bias of the source but rather to figure out what the bias is and use it as evidence of one viewpoint operating in that place, at that time. This is what we mean by "interpreting" a document: figuring out the viewpoint of a particular source and positioning that viewpoint among all the others in that historical moment.

LIMITATIONS, LOGIC, AND ETHICS IN HISTORICAL ANALYSIS

In the work you will be undertaking in *Going to the Source,* you will have multiple opportunities to see these principles and practices in operation and to apply them to your own examination and interpretation of historical documents. As you engage in these activities, which replicate the daily work of every historian, you will confront the limitations, logic, and ethics of historical source analysis. The limitations are the root of all frustration and creativity in historical work and derive from the simple fact that we do not have access to everything humans created in any time or place. We are left with what has survived, and no single piece of the surviving evidence can tell a whole story. Historians must piece together different kinds of surviving sources the way you would piece together a broken vase, hoping that the shards you have to work with are sufficient to hold water.

Logic is vital to this process because historians must consider what arguments a source can be used to support. For example, the written opinion of a majority of Supreme Court justices cannot be used as evidence of the attitudes of the majority of Americans, but it can be used as evidence of the law that ruled those Americans. The anti–woman suffrage speeches of a sexist legislator in 1910 cannot be used as evidence of the views of every male in the United States, but they can be used as evidence of the attitudes the woman suffrage movement was combating. As you work with the sources in this volume, you often will have to consider how a particular source can legitimately and logically be used in piecing together the past and what parts of the puzzle that source simply cannot address.

Ethics come into play in this process because the effectiveness of historians rests on their readers' trust that no sources were unearthed and then hidden because those sources complicated or contradicted a preconceived interpretation. For example, historians who set out to tell the story of male opposition to woman suffrage are likely to come across speeches, editorials, letters, and meeting minutes that indicate some men's active support of woman suffrage. The historians then have a choice: either they expand the parameters of their story to compare the views of those men who opposed woman suffrage with the views of men who supported it, or they tell their readers up front that their particular story focuses only on male opponents of woman suffrage and not on the other story to be told about male supporters of suffrage. Ethics do not dictate that every historian tell every story; rather, they dictate that none of us cover up evidence of the stories we are not telling and of the viewpoints we are not representing. Historians use logic and ethics to carefully and explicitly define the scope of their stories because the limitations of the surviving evidence make that a practical necessity.

THE ORGANIZATION OF *GOING TO THE SOURCE*

You will immediately notice, in your work in the first chapter of *Going to the Source*, that we are not asking you to juggle multiple types of sources on each topic. Instead, you will focus on just one type of source in the context of each chapter's story. The source types will range from archaeological findings of seventeenth-century Indian-European encounters to freed slaves' testimony before a post–Civil War congressional committee to U.S. Census Bureau data on modern immigration. We make no claim that our one-source-at-a-time approach will expose you to everything there is to know about each story told in this volume; no history text could make such a claim. Instead, we propose that this approach puts the spotlight on the nature of the sources themselves, illuminating the challenges and the opportunities a historian faces when analyzing any newspaper report, memoir, photograph, or set of song lyrics.

In order to give you a chance to apply the practices and principles that guided the creation of *Going to the Source*, we have organized every chapter into seven sections, each with a specific purpose. These sections give you a predictable framework in which to explore the historical issues, problems, and advantages unique to each type of source.

- An **introduction** at the start of each chapter provides you with historical context and tells you the broader story you need to know in order to interpret the sources in the chapter.
- **"Using the Source"**   Here we introduce the type of source you will be working with and alert you to the particular advantages and disadvantages that historians confront when using that type of source, be it magazine advertisements or child-rearing literature. An annotated example models how historians approach the source featured in the chapter, showing you how to unpack the evidence in a document. We also raise issues

here about the logical application of the particular source type, noting the questions that this type of source can address and the questions that must be answered by other types of sources.

- **"Working with the Source"**   This section offers you some strategies for pulling the chapter's documents apart and reorganizing the evidence into meaningful patterns. These strategies reflect the kinds of simple categorizing tools that historians invent in the course of sorting through mountains of documentary material.

- **"The Source"**   Each chapter will offer for your examination a single, coherent set of documents from a single source or from a single type of source. For example, all of the documents will come from one court case, or all of the documents will be individuals' autobiographical accounts. In a number of cases, these sources will be excerpts from much longer documents; you will recognize the use of ellipses—three dots that look like periods—to signal when words have been omitted. In every excerpt, we have endeavored to retain the author's purpose while remembering that you have limited time for reading and analyzing long historical documents.

- **"Analyzing the Source"**   In this section, you will encounter specific questions that build on your notes and reflections while "Working with the Source." These questions are meant to help you and your classmates explore further the nature of the source, interpret the source in the historical context of the chapter's story, and suggest ways in which this source might be combined with other sources to expand the story even further.

- **"Beyond the Source"**   There is no final word on any historical story, but this section offers information on later developments in the chapter's story and draws connections between this one story and larger themes in U.S. history.

- **"Finding and Supplementing the Source"**   Even if you do no further research on the chapter's topic, reading through this section will serve as a reminder that any topic in history attracts the attention of multiple historians, who devise new and interesting approaches and interpretations because they draw on varying sources or discover wholly new documents that shed an entirely different light on the topic. We invite you to peruse this section to enhance your awareness of the different books, articles, and Web sites that one historical topic can generate.

Going to the Source was created by human beings; therefore, it is a document with its own biases or point of view. We have already listed the principles and practices that guided our design and discussion in this book, but in the course of writing the book we became aware of another set of assumptions operating in these pages. As American historians who specialize in Native American history, women's history, and immigration history, we are acutely conscious of the contradictions in America's historical promises of equality and liberty. We are equally conscious of some Americans' historical struggle to preserve those contradictions and other Americans' equally determined struggle to eliminate them. We knew when we began this project that the stories we would choose to tell would illuminate this central theme in American life, the conflict over how to be true to American principles. We also knew that we wanted to represent that conflict with sources that came from the most humble corners of American life as well as the most elite centers. The mix of very popular, prominent, and private documents in *Going to the Source* is meant to convey two messages: historians must seek out and carefully assess a wide variety of sources when telling any story about the past; and the American struggle over equality and liberty has not been confined to only one tier of society — it must be examined in many sites and in multiple sources.

Contents

11 Speaking of Equality: The Senate Debate on the Civil Rights Act of 1964   227

Analyzing the Source   324

Beyond the Source   324

Finding and Supplementing the Source   326

CHAPTER 1

Political Terrorism during Reconstruction

Congressional Hearings and Reports on the Ku Klux Klan

Elias Thomson was an old man in 1871. Born a slave in Spartanburg County, South Carolina, he had lived his entire life on the plantation of Dr. and Mrs. Vernon. When he gained his freedom in 1865, he continued to live there, farming land he rented from his former masters. Thomson's daily life after the war must have gone on much the same as it did before, but freedom did bring some opportunities he was anxious to seize, even at his advanced age. In particular, the ratification of the Fifteenth Amendment in March 1870 guaranteed him the right to vote. Thomson exercised that right in the fall of 1870, casting his ballot in the state and congressional elections for the Republican ticket.

Late one night the following May, a group of men disguised in hoods appeared on his doorstep. They dragged him from his home and told him to start praying, for "your time is short." When Thomson refused, they pointed pistols at his head and asked him, "Who did you vote for?" Thomson responded that he had voted for Claudius Turner, a neighbor whom he held in high esteem. The disguised men told him he had made the wrong choice and whipped him. They told Thomson to remain silent about what had happened and left him with a final warning: "We will have this country right before we get through."

Elias Thomson was one of many Southern men and women to suffer at the hands of the Ku Klux Klan between 1867 and 1871. In fact, his home in Spartanburg, South Carolina, was at the center of one of the most violent and prolonged outbreaks of Klan violence during Reconstruction. The Klan had first appeared there in 1868, using intimidation, arson, whippings, sexual assault, and murder to keep potential Republican voters away from the polls in that year's election. Despite such efforts, the state government remained in the hands of the Republicans, and the Klan temporarily receded as a public threat. Klan violence rose again, however, with the next election in 1870 and became more intense as white and black Republicans tried to mobilize the vote. In addition to intimidation and physical assaults on potential black voters, Klansmen burned black churches, schools, and homes and murdered black men who had enrolled in the state militia. In several counties of the Carolina up-country, where white and black populations were roughly equal or whites held a slight majority, the Klan conducted these crimes without fear of prosecution. Local sheriffs failed to make arrests, and if they did, white juries refused to render guilty verdicts. In some up-country counties, such as Spartanburg, state Republican officials estimated that practically all of the white adult male population belonged to the Klan or sympathized with it.

The Ku Klux Klan was of very recent origins in 1871 but had spread quickly throughout the former Confederate states. It was founded in 1867 by a group of Confederate veterans in Pulaski, Tennessee, who initially intended for it to be nothing more than a social club, similar in purpose and organization to the Freemasons and other secret fraternal orders popular with American males in the nineteenth century. Like the Freemasons, early Klan members created their own ritual, costume, and hierarchy from a mishmash of precedents in ancient mythology: the name "Ku Klux" was derived from the Greek word *kuklos*, meaning circle, and one of the titles in the organization was "Grand Cyclops." As the Klan spread, however, it acquired a different purpose. In Tennessee and the Carolinas in 1868, local "dens" of the Klan began acting as vigilantes, calling themselves "regulators" or "night riders" who enforced law and order according to local custom rather than the dictates of the postwar state governments created by Congress and the Republican Party. Never a centralized organization to begin with, local Klansmen operated autonomously and rarely cooperated with each other beyond the county level. Regardless of that fragmentation, the primary targets of their terrorism remained the same: any blacks who challenged white supremacy by daring to vote, teach, or acquire land, and "carpetbaggers," white Northerners who came to the South after the war to seek their fortunes or to assume office in the Reconstruction state governments.

The violence and intimidation the Klan visited upon freedmen and women and white Republicans seriously challenged the federal government's plans for the postwar South. After passing the Civil Rights Act of 1866, congressional Republicans had pegged their hopes for Reconstruction on enfranchising the former slaves as full and equal U.S. citizens. In this manner, the freedmen would become a core constituency for the Republican Party in the South and prevent the defeated Confederates from reassuming control of government and society there. The ratification of the Fourteenth Amendment in 1868 made this plan part of the Constitution by granting the freedmen and women U.S. citizenship and guaranteeing them equal protection under the law. When some Southern states failed to extend their franchise to the freedmen, Republicans in Congress responded with the Fifteenth Amendment, which prohibited states from denying the right to vote to any citizen because of "race, color, or previous condition of servitude."

Republicans had great success in passing their legislative agenda for Reconstruction in Washington, D.C., but the enforcement of those laws in the South remained very much in question. The twenty thousand federal troops stationed in the South in 1867 were not nearly enough to pacify regions such as the Carolina up-country, where the Klan was at its greatest strength. Furthermore, military officers were reluctant to assume control over matters of law enforcement without specific requests from civilian authorities to do so, lest they alienate the defeated Southern white population even further. As news of the Klan's expansion and pervasive influence in the South made its way to the nation's capital, Republican leaders agreed that further legislation to counteract it was necessary.

In a special message to Congress in December 1870, President Ulysses S. Grant noted that the Klan and similar organizations were using violence to prevent citizens from voting in the Southern states. Acting on a request he had received from the governor of North Carolina for assistance, he asked Congress to investigate the matter. Congress formed a committee to review affairs in North Carolina, and then in April 1871, it created another, much larger committee to expand the investigation into other states. This group, titled the Joint Select Committee to Inquire into the Condition of Affairs in the Late Insurrectionary States, was composed of seven senators and fourteen representatives, thirteen of whom were Republicans and eight of whom were Democrats.

At approximately the same time that it formed the Joint Select Committee to investigate the Klan, Congress also passed the Ku Klux Klan Act. This law gave the president the power to use federal troops and courts to protect the lives, property, and rights of U.S. citizens in the South. For the first time, crimes committed by private persons against other citizens became eligible for prosecution under federal rather than state law. Provisions included in the Ku Klux Klan Act effectively gave the president the ability to declare martial law in any state or region he deemed under Klan influence. The most controversial of these provisions concerned suspension of the writ of habeas corpus, a cornerstone of American civil liberties. The writ of habeas corpus protects citizens from unlawful imprisonment by requiring that any person placed under arrest be charged with a specific crime and placed on trial. By allowing the president to suspend it, Congress made it possible for suspected Klansmen to be jailed indefinitely. Many congressmen, even some Republicans, questioned the constitutionality of this provision and of the Ku Klux Klan Act in general, but the majority who supported the law believed the Klan could not be defeated without such a powerful weapon.

Congressmen formulated and debated this legislation in Washington while freedmen and women in the South confronted the Klan face to face. Casting a ballot or even expressing an interest in voting could put a former slave's life in jeopardy. Those who joined militias, held office, or tried to improve their economic circumstances faced similar reprisals, while the promise of assistance from Washington must have seemed far off indeed. In 1871, a showdown was brewing between the Ku Klux Klan and the federal government that placed people like Elias Thomson squarely in the middle of the battle to determine Reconstruction's fate in the postwar South.

Using Congressional Hearings and Reports as a Source

The Joint Select Committee undertook one of the most far-reaching congressional investigations ever conducted up to that time. During the summer and fall of 1871, it heard testimony from witnesses in Washington, D.C., and sent subcommittees to interview witnesses throughout the South. Most of its work was concentrated on North Carolina and South Carolina, where the activities and impact of the Klan were reported to be most severe, but committee members also visited Alabama, Florida, Georgia, Mississippi, and Tennessee, compiling a record of testimony that numbered in the thousands of pages. In February 1872, the Joint Select Committee submitted this testimony and its reports to Congress. The majority report, signed by every Republican on the committee, endorsed the Ku Klux Klan Act of 1871 and recommended continuing the president's powers to combat the Klan through the use of federal troops, courts, and suspension of the writ of habeas corpus. The minority report, signed by every Democrat on the committee, did not deny the existence of Klan-related violence but blamed it on misguided federal Reconstruction policy, which had left the Southern states in the hands of carpetbaggers and former slaves.

Advantages and Disadvantages of Working with Congressional Hearings and Reports

Since its publication in 1872, historians have found the thirteen volumes of the Joint Select Committee's report a remarkably detailed and comprehensive source for studying Reconstruction in the South. One of its chief advantages as a source is its sheer size. The committee conducted its work thoroughly, and the hundreds of witnesses who testified before it represented a broad spectrum of Southern society: white and black, rich and poor, male and female, Republican and Democrat. One historian has called their testimony "the richest single source" for understanding Southern society during the Reconstruction era. In the case of freedmen and women, testimony before the committee provides invaluable first-person narratives of what the transition from bondage to freedom was like.

Another advantage of working with this source has to do with the methods by which the Joint Select Committee collected its evidence. Its procedures resembled legal hearings: oaths were administered to witnesses, and witnesses were subjected to cross-examination, all in meetings open to the public. No witnesses appeared anonymously or gave secret testimony. While those procedures may have prevented many from testifying for fear of reprisals, they nevertheless lent an air of authenticity to the witnesses' descriptions of the Klan that was not necessarily accorded to rumors or sensationalistic stories reported in the press. The Klan conducted its terrorism under cover of night and in disguise. By its very nature, it did not submit willingly to public scrutiny. For the most part, however, the witnesses who appeared before the committee in Southern towns and counties were eyewitnesses to the Klan's activities, making their testimony the most complete and reliable account of this secret organization's operations during Reconstruction.

The disadvantages associated with using the Joint Select Committee's report stem mostly from its inherent political biases. The Republicans who dominated the Joint Select Committee by a two-to-one margin were most interested in finding evidence that the Klan was a conspiratorial organization bent on depriving black and white Republicans of their civil and political liberties. Such evidence could be used to justify imposing martial law in those regions affected by the Klan. Democrats accused the Republicans of using the committee to drum up stories of Klan brutality and lawlessness that could be publicized to Republican advantage in the upcoming election of 1872. While the Democrats on the committee could not deny the violence of the Klan, they used their questioning of witnesses to cast doubt on its political motives, depicting Klansmen instead as isolated, ill-advised characters pushed to extremes by desperation and offended honor. It is important to remember that Congress had already passed the Ku Klux Klan Act when the Joint Select Committee conducted its work. Given that the committee's majority was made up of the same Republicans who had passed that piece of legislation, how likely was it that the committee's findings would challenge its enforcement? By passing the Ku Klux Klan Act *before* its investigation of the Klan, Congress clearly anticipated the outcome of the Joint Select Committee's work.

As you read the testimony, you will quickly realize that neither the Republicans nor the Democrats on the Joint Select Committee resembled neutral fact finders. Each side brought an agenda to the proceedings that influenced the nature of the testimony before the committee. Consider, for example, these excerpts from the testimony of D. H. Chamberlain, the Republican attorney general of South Carolina, given before the committee in Washington, D.C., on June 10, 1871. A good historian quickly learns to read between the lines of such evidence, looking carefully at the questions as well as the answers to determine what biases and ulterior motives shaped the construction of this source.

D. H. Chamberlain, sworn and examined.

By the Chairman:

An oath to tell the truth similar to that given in a court of law

Republican senator John Scott of Pennsylvania chaired the committee and typically initiated the questioning

Question: How long have you been a resident of the State?

Answer: I have been a resident there since December, 1865.

Question: Please go on and state to the committee the knowledge you have acquired, from your official position, as to the efficiency with which the laws are executed throughout the State of South Carolina, and the protection afforded to life and property in the State. Make your statement in general terms.

Invites Chamberlain to speak freely about law enforcement

Answer: The enforcement of the law has, from time to time, been very much interrupted and disturbed from special causes; lately by what are popularly known as Ku-Klux operations. . . .

By Mr. Van Trump:

Philadelph Van Trump, a Democratic representative from Ohio, typically led the cross-examination

Question: You say you went to South Carolina in 1865?

Answer: Yes, sir.

Question: How long after the termination of the war; what part of the year?

Answer: I went in December, 1865.

Question: From where did you go?

Returns to the subject of Chamberlain's background, seeking to discredit him as a carpetbagger

Answer: From Massachusetts. I had been in the Union army during the war. I settled at Charleston in December, 1865, and remained there, and my residence is there now, although I have to be at the capital of the State most of the time.

One other disadvantage to bear in mind about the Joint Select Committee's report is that while the committee's hearings had the appearance of legal proceedings, they did not work with the same standards of evidence as a court of law. In particular, the Republican majority of the committee was willing to accept hearsay, what someone had heard but not personally witnessed, as evidence. Democrats on the committee objected mightily to this, likening it to accepting rumors and gossip as facts. They equated the two-dollars-a-day allowance the committee paid to witnesses with bribery and accused the local Republican officials of coaching witnesses as well. In the thousands of pages of testimony in the Joint Select Committee's report, some witnesses do appear more reliable than others. As a historian, you face a twofold task in dealing with this source. First, you have to keep track of the information it provides you about the persons and events involved in the Klan's activities. Second, you must judge whether the evidence you are reading is reliable, by establishing your own measures for assessing its truthfulness: Is the testimony hearsay or an eyewitness account? Does the witness contradict himself or herself under cross-examination? What evidence is there, if any, of outside pressure or influence on the witness's testimony?

Working with the Source

As you read the sources in the next section, use the tables on page 8 to organize your notes on what they tell you about the Klan's operations in South Carolina and the federal government's response to them. For Sources 1 through 5, summarize what the witnesses said about the Klan's actions and the purposes behind them in the first column of the first table. In the second column, note the type of evidence each witness presented: was it a firsthand account? hearsay? personal opinion? For Sources 6 and 7, summarize how each report described the Klan in the first column, and in the second column, note each report's assessment of the federal response to it.

	Description of the Klan's Actions and Purposes	Type of Evidence Provided
1. Samuel T. Poinier		
2. D. H. Chamberlain		
3. Elias Thomson		
4. Lucy McMillan		
5. Mervin Givens		

	Description of the Klan	Assessment of Federal Response to the Klan
6. Majority Report		
7. Minority Report		

The Source: Testimony and Reports from the Joint Select Committee to Inquire into the Condition of Affairs in the Late Insurrectionary States

All of the testimony that follows is taken from the Joint Select Committee's investigation of the Ku Klux Klan in South Carolina. Sources 1 and 2 come from testimony heard in Washington, D.C., while Sources 3, 4, and 5 are from testimony heard in Spartanburg, South Carolina. Sources 6 and 7 are excerpts from the committee's majority and minority reports, which were completed after the investigation was over.

1 *Testimony of Samuel T. Poinier,*
Washington, D.C., June 7, 1871

Poinier was a Republican newspaper editor and a federal tax collector in South Carolina at the time of his testimony.

Samuel T. Poinier sworn and examined.

By the Chairman:[1]

> *Question:* Please state in what part of South Carolina you reside.
> *Answer:* In Spartanburg County, the most northern county in the State.
> *Question:* How long have you resided there?
> *Answer:* Since February, 1866; a little over five years.
> *Question:* From what part of the United States did you go to South Carolina?
> *Answer:* I went there from Louisville, Kentucky. . . . I went there in 1866 with no intention whatever of remaining. I went entirely for social reasons, to marry, and I was persuaded to stay there. My wife was a native of Charleston, and I found her up in Spartanburg after the war, where a large number of Charleston people went during the bombardment of the city. . . .
> *Question:* Were you in the Union Army?
> *Answer:* Yes, sir: I went out from Kentucky.
> *Question:* Proceed with your statement.

---

[1] Republican senator John Scott from Pennsylvania.

Source: United States Congress, *Report of the Joint Select Committee to Inquire into the Condition of Affairs in the Late Insurrectionary States,* vol. 2, *South Carolina, Part I* (Washington, D.C.: Government Printing Office, 1872), 25–28, 33–34.

9

Answer: Just before our last campaign,[2] it was May a year ago, I . . . identified myself publicly with the republican party. I made my paper a republican paper. I did everything I could in the last State election for the reelection of Governor Scott[3] and our other State officers. From that time I have been in very deep water. . . . I was ordered away last fall, immediately after our last election, in November. It was soon after the first appearance of this Ku-Klux organization, or whatever it is. Soon after these outrages occurred in our county I received a note ordering me away from there, stating that I must leave the county; that all the soldiers of the United States Army could not enable me to live in Spartanburg. . . . two days prior to our election, a party of disguised men went, at night, and took out two white men and three negroes, one of them a colored woman, and whipped them most brutally. Two of them were managers of the box[4] at that election; and the men told them that if they dared to hold an election at that box they would return and kill them. That was the first appearance of any trouble in the State. . . .

Question: Were those people of whom you spoke in disguise?

Answer: They were all in disguise. One of the colored men who were whipped swore positively as to the identity of some of them, and the parties were arrested, but nothing could ever be done with them; they proved an *alibi*, and some of them have since gone to Texas. . . .

Question: Go on and state any similar occurrences in that county since that time . . .

Answer: Since that time outrages of that nature have occurred every week. Parties of disguised men have ridden through the county almost nightly. They go to a colored man's house, take him out and whip him. They tell him that he must not give any information that he has been whipped. They tell him, moreover, that he must make a public renunciation of his republican principles or they will return and kill him. . . .

Question: Do the facts that have transpired and the manner in which they have occurred satisfy you of the existence of the organization in that portion of South Carolina?

Answer: Yes, sir; I have no doubt of it in the world. I have received anonymous communications signed by the order of "K.K.K.," directing me to leave the county, stating that I could not live there; that I was a carpet-bagger. But personally I have never met with any trouble.

By Mr. Van Trump:[5]

Question: You have a connection with the partisan press there?

Answer: Yes, sir. I am editing a republican paper.

Question: Do you advocate the cause of the negro in your paper?

---

[2] The election of 1870.

[3] Robert K. Scott was the Republican governor of South Carolina.

[4] Ballot box.

[5] Democratic representative Philadelph Van Trump from Ohio.

Answer: Not the negro especially. I advocate the general principles of republicanism.

Question: You support the whole republican doctrine in your paper?

Answer: So far as general principles go, I do. I do not approve or uphold the State government in many of its acts; but, so far as the general principles of republicanism are concerned, I uphold it very strongly. I advocate the right of the colored people to vote and to exercise their civil and political privileges. . . .

Question: These men who assert that their object is to put down the negro and get possession of the Government are prominent men, are they not?

Answer: Yes, sir.

Question: Can you name a single man?

Answer: Well, I cannot name anybody specially who has made such a remark, but I hear it in the hotels.

Question: Have you yourself heard them make the remark?

Answer: I have heard the remark made; it is a common thing.

Question: Is it not rather an uncommon remark?

Answer: It is not, there.

Question: You cannot recollect the name of a single person who has made that declaration?

Answer: No sir, I cannot recall any now.

2   *Testimony of D. H. Chamberlain,*
Washington, D.C., June 10, 1871

Chamberlain was a Republican and the attorney general of South Carolina.

D. H. Chamberlain, sworn and examined.

By the Chairman:

Question: How long have you been a resident of the State?

Answer: I have been a resident there since December, 1865.

Question: Please go on and state to the committee the knowledge you have acquired, from your official position, as to the efficiency with which the laws are executed throughout the State of South Carolina, and the protection afforded to life and property in the State. Make your statement in general terms.

Answer: The enforcement of the law has, from time to time, been very much interrupted and disturbed from special causes; lately by what are popularly known as Ku-Klux operations. There have been a great many outrages committed, and a great many homicides, and a great many whippings. I speak

Source: Report of the Joint Select Committee, vol. 2, South Carolina, Part I, 48–51.

now, of course, of what I have heard; I have never seen any outrages committed myself; I am simply stating what I believe to be fact. . . .

Question: In what part of the State are these offenses committed which you attribute to the influence of this organization?

Answer: Notably in Spartanburg, Newberry, Union, and York Counties; those are the principal counties that have been the scenes of these disturbances. But they have extended into Laurens, Chester, and Lancaster Counties.[1] . . .

Question: Have there been any convictions for these offenses in the State, so far as your information goes; offenses committed by these organized bands?

Answer: No sir, no convictions, and no arrests, except in the case of this wounded Ku-Klux.[2] . . .

By Mr. Van Trump:

Question: You say you went to South Carolina in 1865?
Answer: Yes, sir.
Question: How long after the termination of the war; what part of the year?
Answer: I went in December, 1865.
Question: From where did you go?
Answer: From Massachusetts. I had been in the Union army during the war. I settled at Charleston in December, 1865, and remained there, and my residence is there now, although I have to be at the capital of the State most of the time.

By Mr. Stevenson:[3]

Question: When did it first come to your knowledge that this organization existed in the State of South Carolina?

Answer: It would be difficult to say. My conviction that there is such an organization has grown up very gradually. . . . I cannot fix the date exactly.

Question: Had you any knowledge of the fact that there were acts of violence and disorders in that State about the time of the election in 1868?

Answer: Yes, sir.

Question: Had you any information of the sending of arms at that time into that State?

Answer: O, I remember that a great many arms were purchased by private individuals, if you refer to that. I know that at the time, during the canvass,[4] there was considerable excitement when it was understood that the democrats,

---

[1] All seven of these counties were in the piedmont or up-country region of South Carolina, where the black and white populations were roughly equal.

[2] Chamberlain is referring to a Klansman wounded during a raid on the Newberry County Courthouse. He was jailed and then released on bail and subsequently either died while in the care of a friend or was spirited away by friends to avoid prosecution.

[3] Republican representative Job Stevenson from Ohio.

[4] Campaigning for votes.

as we call them, were arming themselves with Winchester and Henry rifles, or something of the kind.

    Question: Repeating rifles?

    Answer: Yes, sir. . . .

By Mr. Blair:[5]

    Question: Did you have any actual knowledge of the fact that the democrats were then arming?

    Answer: No, sir.

    Question: Then you make this statement as a rumor merely?

    Answer: Well, yes, sir; I should use, perhaps, a little stronger term than rumor. I had heard it so often that it came to be a belief with me, but it was hearsay. . . .

    Question: Was it a common report that those arms all went into the hands of democrats?

    Answer: As I heard it, it was understood that those arms were imported into the State upon order of individuals. I do not know but a republican might have had his order filled, but the belief was that they were generally ordered by democrats.

By Mr. Stevenson:

    Question: You have no knowledge of any general arming among the republicans at that time?

    Answer: No, sir.

    Question: You were a republican, then, were you not?

    Answer: Yes, sir.

By Mr. Blair:

    Question: Did not the republicans have arms?

    Answer: O, yes.

By Mr. Van Trump:

    Question: Did not the negroes have arms?

    Answer: Yes, sir; it is very common for people to have their shot-guns, to have some kind of arms. I suppose that in this instance people thought that there was an unusually large number brought in at a particular time, and that they were not for sporting purposes. They were repeating rifles.

    Question: Have you been a politician for any part of your life?

    Answer: No, sir; I do not think I have ever been a politician.

    Question: Have you never heard a thousand rumors during an election that had no foundation in fact?

    Answer: Yes, sir; many of them.

    Question: Got up for excitement merely?

    Answer: Yes, sir.

---

[5] Democratic senator Frank Blair from Michigan.

3   *Testimony of Elias Thomson,*
Spartanburg, South Carolina, July 7, 1871

Elias Thomson (colored) sworn and examined.

By the Chairman:

> *Question:* Where do you live?
> *Answer:* Up on Tiger River, on Mrs. Vernon's plantation.[1]
> *Question:* What do you follow?
> *Answer:* Farming.
> *Question:* Do you live on rented land?
> *Answer:* Yes, sir.
> *Question:* How much have you rented?
> *Answer:* I think about fifty acres.
> *Question:* How long have you been living there?
> *Answer:* Ever since the surrender; I never left home.
> *Question:* Have you ever been disturbed any up there?
> *Answer:* Yes, sir.
> *Question:* How?
> *Answer:* There came a parcel of gentlemen to my house one night — or
men. They went up to the door and ran against it. My wife was sick. I was lying
on a pallet, with my feet to the door. They ran against it and hallooed to me,
"Open the door, quick, quick, quick." I threw the door open immediately, right
wide open. Two little children were lying with me. I said, "Come in gentlemen." One of them says, "Do we look like gentlemen?" I says, "You look like
men of some description; walk in." One says, "Come out here; are you ready to
die?" I told him I was not prepared to die. "Well," said he, "Your time is short;
commence praying." I told him I was not a praying man much, and hardly ever
prayed; only a very few times; never did pray much. He says, "You ought
to pray; your time is short, and now commence to pray." I told him I was not a
praying man. One of them held a pistol to my head and said, "Get down and
pray." I was on the steps, with one foot on the ground. They led me off to a
pine tree. There was three or four of them behind me, it appeared, and one on
each side, and one in front. The gentleman who questioned me was the only
one I could see. All the time I could not see the others. Every time I could get a
look around, they would touch me on the side of the head with a pistol, so I
had to keep my head square in front. The next question was, "Who did you
vote for?" I told him I voted for Mr. Turner — Claudius Turner, a gentleman in
the neighborhood. They said, "What did you vote for him for?" I said, "I
thought a good deal of him; he was my neighbor." I told them I disremembered
who was on the ticket besides, but they had several, and I voted the ticket.
"What did you do that for?" they said. Says I, "because I thought it was right."

---

[1] The Vernons were Thomson's former masters.
Source: Report of the Joint Select Committee, vol. 2, South Carolina, Part I, 410–15.

They said, "You thought it was right? It was right wrong." I said, "I never do anything hardly if I think it is wrong; if it was wrong, I did not know it. That was my opinion at the time and I thought every man ought to vote according to his notions." He said, "If you had taken the advice of your friends you would have been better off." I told him I had. Says I, "You may be a friend to me, but I can't tell who you are." Says he, "Can't you recognize anybody here?" I told him I could not. "In the condition you are in now, I can't tell who you are." One of them had a very large set of teeth; I suppose they were three-quarters of an inch long; they came right straight down. He came up to me and sort of nodded. He had on speckled horns and calico stuff, and had a face on. He said, "Have you got a chisel here I could get?" I told him I hadn't, but I reckoned I could knock one out, and I sort of laughed. He said, "What in hell are you laughing at? It is no laughing time." I told him it sort of tickled me, and I thought I would laugh. I did not say anything then for a good while. "Old man," says one, "have you got a rope here, or a plow-line, or something of the sort?" I told him, "Yes; I had one hanging on the crib." He said, "Let us have it." One of them says, "String him up to this pine tree, and we will get all out of him. Get up, one of you, and let us pull him up, and he will tell the truth." I says, "I can't tell you anything more than I have told. There is nothing that I can tell you but what I have told you and you have asked me." One man questioned me all this time. One would come up and say, "Let's hang him a while, and he will tell us the truth"; and another then came up and said, "Old man, we are just from hell; some of us have been dead ever since the revolutionary war." . . . I was not scared, and said, "You have been through a right smart experience." "Yes," he says, "we have been through a considerable experience." One of them says, "we have just come from hell." I said, "If I had been there, I would not want to go back." . . . Then they hit me thirteen of the hardest cuts I ever got. I never had such cuts. They hit me right around my waist and by my hip, and cut a piece about as wide as my two fingers in one place. I did not say a word while they were whipping, only sort of grunted a little. As quick as they got through they said, "Go to your bed. We will have this country right before we get through; go to your bed," and they started away. . . .

Question: Who is Claudius Turner?

Answer: He is a gentleman that run for the legislature here. He was on the ticket with Mr. Scott.

Question: The republican ticket?

Answer: Yes, sir; the radical[2] ticket. . . .

By Mr. Van Trump:

Question: Explain to me, if you can, if the object of this Ku-Klux organization is to intimidate the colored people, why they were so particular as to make you promise, under penalty of death, that you would never disclose the fact that you had been visited; do you understand why that is?

---

[2] Radical Republicans were known for their support of black suffrage and the disenfranchisement of former Confederate military and civilian officers.

Answer: I can explain this fact this far: You know when they said to me to not say anything about this matter, I asked them what I must say, and when I asked, "What must I say? I will have to say something," they said, "What are you going to say?" I said, "What must I say?" He said, "Are you going to tell it?" I told them, "I have to say something, of course, and what must I say; what can I say?" Then they said, looking straight at me—

Question: Why is it that so often in giving your testimony you have to get up and make gesticulations like an orator? Have you been an orator?

Answer: No, sir, but I was showing the way they did me, and what they said to me. They said, "You just let me hear of this thing again, and we will not leave a piece of you when we come back."

Question: To whom have you talked lately about this case, or consulted here in town?

Answer: I have not consulted much about it.

Question: How long have you been waiting to be examined?

Answer: Since Tuesday about 10 o'clock.

Question: Have any white republicans been to see you?

Answer: No, sir; nobody at all.

Question: Did you see them?

Answer: I don't know who the republicans are here. I may have seen some.

Question: Do you pretend to say that since Tuesday you have not talked with any white about your case?

Answer: With none about the Ku-Klux matter.

4   *Testimony of Lucy McMillan,*
Spartanburg, South Carolina, July 10, 1871

Lucy McMillan (colored) sworn and examined.

By the Chairman:

Question: Where do you live?

Answer: Up in the country. I live on McMillan's place, right at the foot of the road.

Question: How far is it?

Answer: Twelve miles.

Question: Are you married?

Answer: I am not married. I am single now. I was married. My husband was taken away from me and carried off twelve years ago.

Question: He was carried off before the war?

Answer: Yes, sir; the year before the war; twelve years ago this November coming.

Source: Report of the Joint Select Committee, vol. 3, South Carolina, Part 2, 604–7.

Question: How old are you now?

Answer: I am called forty-six. I am forty-five or six.

Question: Did the Ku-Klux come where you live at any time?

Answer: They came there once before they burned my house down. The way it happened was this: John Hunter's wife came to my house on Saturday morning, and told they were going to whip me. I was afraid of them; there was so much talk of Ku-Klux drowning people, and whipping people, and killing them. My house was only a little piece from the river, so I laid out at night in the woods. The Sunday evening after Isham McCrary[1] was whipped I went up, and a white man, John McMillan, came along and says to me, "Lucy, you had better stay at home, for they will whip you anyhow." I said if they have to, they might whip me in the woods, for I am afraid to stay there. Monday night they came in and burned my house down; I dodged out alongside of the road not far off and saw them. I was sitting right not far off, and as they came along the river I knew some of them. I knew John McMillan, and Kennedy McMillan, and Billy Bush, and John Hunter. They were all together. I was not far off, and I saw them. They went right on to my house. When they passed me I run further up on the hill to get out of the way of them. They went there and knocked down and beat my house a right smart while. And then they all got still, and directly I saw the fire rise.

Question: How many of these men were there?

Answer: A good many; I couldn't tell how many, but these I knew. The others I didn't. . . .

Question: What was the reason given for burning your house?

Answer: There was speaking down there last year and I came to it. They all kept at me to go. I went home and they quizzed me to hear what was said, and I told them as far as my senses allowed me.

Question: Where was this speaking?

Answer: Here in this town. I went on and told them, and then they all said I was making laws; or going to have the land, and the Ku-Klux were going to beat me for bragging that I would have land. John Hunter told them on me, I suppose, that I said I was going to have land. . . .

Question: Was that the only reason you know for your house being burned?

Answer: That is all the reason. All the Ku-Klux said all that they had against me was that I was bragging and boasting that I wanted the land. . . .

By Mr. Van Trump:

Question: Do you mean to say that they said they burned the house for that reason?

Answer: No sir; they burned the house because they could not catch me. I don't know any other reason. . . .

Question: Who was John Hunter?

Answer: He is a colored man. I worked for him all last summer. I worked with him hoeing his cotton and corn.

---

[1] Another freedman who testified before the committee in Spartanburg.

Question: What was he doing with these Ku-Klux?

Answer: I don't know. He was with them. . . .

Question: How did you come to be named Lucy McMillan?

Answer: I was a slave of Robert McMillan. I always belonged to him.

Question: You helped raise Kennedy and John?[2]

Answer: Not John, but Kennedy I did. When he was a little boy I was with him.

Question: Did he always like you?

Answer: Yes, sir. They always pretended to like us.

Question: That is while you were a slave?

Answer: Yes, sir, while I was a slave, but never afterward. They didn't care for us then.

[2] Sons of Robert McMillan.

5 *Testimony of Mervin Givens,* Spartanburg, South Carolina, July 12, 1871

Mervin Givens (colored) sworn and examined.

By Mr. Stevenson:

Question: Your name in old times was Mery Moss?

Answer: Yes, sir; but since freedom I don't go by my master's name. My name now is Givens.

Question: What is your age?

Answer: About forty I expect. . . .

Question: Have you ever been visited by the Ku-Klux?

Answer: Yes, sir.

Question: When?

Answer: About the last of April.

Question: Tell what they said and did.

Answer: I was asleep when they came to my house, and did not know anything about them until they broke in on me.

Question: What time of night was it?

Answer: About twelve o'clock at night. They broke in on me and frightened me right smart, being asleep. They ordered me to get up and make a light. As quick as I could gather my senses I bounced up and made a light, but not quick enough. They jumped at me and struck me with a pistol, and made a knot[1] that you can see there now. By the time I made the light I catched the voice of them, and as soon as I could see by the light, I looked around and saw by the

[1] Bump.

Source: Report of the Joint Select Committee, vol. 2, South Carolina, Part 2, 698–700.

size of the men and voice so that I could judge right off who it was. By that time they jerked the case off the pillow and jerked it over my head and ordered me out of doors. That was all I saw in the house. After they carried me out of doors I saw nothing more. They pulled the pillow-slip over my head and told me if I took off they would shoot me. They carried me out and whipped me powerful.

Question: With what?

Answer: With sticks and hickories. They whipped me powerful.

Question: How many lashes?

Answer: I can't tell. I have no knowledge at all about it. May be a hundred or two. Two men whipped me and both at once.

Question: Did they say anything to you?

Answer: They cursed me and told me I had voted the radical ticket, and they intended to beat me so I would not vote it again.

Question: Did you know any of them?

Answer: Yes, sir; I think I know them.

Question: What were there names?

Answer: One was named John Thomson and the other was John Zimmerman. Those are the two men I think it was.

Question: How many were there in all?

Answer: I didn't see but two. After they took me out, I was blindfolded; but I could judge from the horse tracks that there were more than two horses there. Some were horses and some were mules. It was a wet, rainy night; they whipped me stark naked. I had a brown undershirt on and they tore it clean off. . . .

By Mr. Van Trump:

Question: There were, then, two men who came to your house?

Answer: Yes, sir; that was all I could see.

Question: Were they disguised?

Answer: Yes, sir.

Question: How?

Answer: They had on some sort of gray-looking clothes, and much the same sort of thing over their face. One of them had a sort of high hat with tassel and sort of horns.

Question: How far did John Thomson live from there?

Answer: I think it is two or three miles.

Question: Were you acquainted with him?

Answer: Yes, sir.

Question: Where?

Answer: At my house. My wife did a good deal of washing for them both. I was very well-acquainted with their size and their voices. They were boys I was raised with. . . .

Question: Did you tell anybody else it was John Thomson?

Answer: I have never named it.

Question: Why?

Answer: I was afraid to.

Question: Are you afraid now?

Answer: I am not afraid to own the truth as nigh[2] as I can.

Question: Is there any difference in owning to the truth on the 12th of July and on the 1st of April?

Answer: The black people have injured themselves very much by talking, and I was afraid.

Question: Are you not afraid now?

Answer: No, sir; because I hope there will be a stop put to it. . . .

Question: Do you think we three gentlemen can stop it?

Answer: No, sir; but I think you can get some help.

Question: Has anybody been telling you that?

Answer: No, sir; nobody told me that. . . .

Question: Why did you not commence a prosecution against Thomson and Zimmerman?

Answer: I am like the rest, I reckon; I am too cowardly.

Question: Why do you not do it now; you are not cowardly now?

Answer: I shouldn't have done it now.

Question: I am talking about bringing suit for that abuse on that night. Why do you not have them arrested?

Answer: It ought to be done.

Question: Why do you not do it?

Answer: For fear they would shoot me. If I were to bring them up here and could not prove the thing exactly on them, and they were to get out of it, I would not expect to live much longer.

[2] Near.

Majority Report of the Joint Select Committee to Inquire into the Condition of Affairs in the Late Insurrectionary States, February 19, 1872, Submitted by Luke P. Poland

Poland was a Republican representative from Vermont.

The proceedings and debates in Congress show that, whatever other causes were assigned for disorders in the late insurrectionary States, the execution of the laws and the security of life and property were alleged to be most seriously

Source: Report of the Joint Select Committee, vol. 1, Reports of the Committee, 2–3, 98–99.

threatened by the existence and acts of organized bands of armed and disguised men, known as Ku-Klux. . . .

The evidence is equally decisive that redress cannot be obtained against those who commit crimes in disguise and at night. The reasons assigned are that identification is difficult, almost impossible; that when this is attempted, the combinations and oaths of the order come in and release the culprit by perjury either upon the witness-stand or in the jury-box; and that the terror inspired by their acts, as well as the public sentiment in their favor in many localities, paralyzes the arm of civil power. . . .

The race so recently emancipated, against which banishment or serfdom is thus decreed, but which has been clothed by the Government with the rights and responsibilities of citizenship, ought not to be, and we feel assured will not be left hereafter without protection against the hostilities and sufferings it has endured in the past, as long as the legal and constitutional powers of the Government are adequate to afford it. Communities suffering such evils and influenced by such extreme feelings may be slow to learn that relief can come only from a ready obedience to and support of constituted authority, looking to the modes provided by law for redress of all grievances. That Southern communities do not seem to yield this ready obedience at once should not deter the friends of good government in both sections from hoping and working for that end. . . .

The law of 1871[1] has been effective in suppressing for the present, to a great extent, the operations of masked and disguised men in North and South Carolina. . . . The apparent cessation of operations should not lead to a conclusion that community would be safe if protective measures were withdrawn. These should be continued until there remains no further doubt of the actual suppression and disarming of this wide-spread and dangerous conspiracy.

The results of suspending the writ of *habeas corpus* in South Carolina show that where the membership, mysteries, and power of the organization have been kept concealed this is the most and perhaps only effective remedy for its suppression; and in review of its cessation and resumption of hostilities at different times, of its extent and power, and that in several of the States where it exists the courts have not yet held terms at which the cases can be tried, we recommend that the power conferred on the President by the fourth section of that act[2] be extended until the end of the next session of Congress.

For the Senate:	For the House of Representatives:
JOHN SCOTT, Chairman	LUKE P. POLAND, Chairman
Z. CHANDLER[3]	HORACE MAYNARD[4]

[1] The Ku Klux Klan Act.

[2] To suspend the writ of habeas corpus.

[3] Republican senator from Michigan.

[4] Republican representative from Tennessee.

BENJ. F. RICE[5]   GLENNI W. SCOFIELD[6]

JOHN POOL[7]   JOHN F. FARNSWORTH[8]

DANIEL D. PRATT[9]   JOHN COBURN[10]

                                 JOB E. STEVENSON

                                 BENJ. F. BUTLER[11]

                                 WILLIAM E. LANSING[12]

[5] Republican senator from Arkansas.
[6] Republican representative from Pennsylvania.
[7] Republican senator from North Carolina.
[8] Republican representative from Illinois.
[9] Republican senator from Indiana.
[10] Republican representative from Indiana.
[11] Republican representative from Massachusetts.
[12] Republican representative from New York.

 ## Minority Report of the Joint Select Committee to Inquire into the Condition of Affairs in the Late Insurrectionary States, February 19, 1872, Submitted by James B. Beck

Beck was a Democratic representative from Kentucky.

The atrocious measures by which millions of white people have been put at the mercy of the semi-barbarous negroes of the South, and the vilest of the white people, both from the North and South, who have been constituted the leaders of this black horde, are now sought to be justified and defended by defaming the people upon whom this unspeakable outrage had been committed. . . .

There is no doubt about the fact that great outrages were committed by bands of disguised men during those years of lawlessness and oppression. The natural tendency of all such organizations is to violence and crime. . . . It is so everywhere; like causes produce like results. Sporadic cases of outrages occur in every community. . . . But, as a rule, the worst governments produce the most disorders. South Carolina is confessedly in the worst condition of any of the States. Why? Because her government is the worst, or what makes it still worse,

Source: Report of the Joint Select Committee, vol. 1, *Reports of the Committee,* 289, 463–64, 514–16, 588.

her people see no hope in the future. . . . There never was a Ku-Klux in Virginia, nobody pretends there ever was. Why? Because Virginia escaped carpet-bag rule. . . .

The Constitution was trampled under foot in the passage of what is known as the Ku-Klux law; a power was delegated to the President which could be exercised by the legislative authority alone; whole communities of innocent people were put under the ban of executive vengeance by the suspension of the writ of *habeas corpus* at the mere whim and caprice of the President; and all for what? For the apprehension and conviction of a few poor, deluded, ignorant, and unhappy wretches, goaded to desperation by the insolence of the negroes, and who could, had the radical authorities of South Carolina done their duty, just as easily have been prosecuted in the State courts, and much more promptly and cheaply, than by all this imposing machinery of Federal power, through military and judicial departments. . . .

. . . The antagonism, therefore, which exists between these two classes of the population of South Carolina does not spring from any political cause, in the ordinary party sense of the term; but it grows out of that instinctive and irrepressible repugnance to compulsory affiliation with another race, planted by the God of nature in the breast of the white man, perhaps more strongly manifested in the uneducated portion of the people, and aggravated and intensified by the fact that the Negro has been placed as a *ruler* over him. . . .

We feel it would be a dereliction of duty on our part if, after what we have witnessed in South Carolina, we did not admonish the American people that the present condition of things in the South cannot last. It was an oft-quoted political apothegm, long prior to the war, that no government could exist "half slave and half free." The paraphrase of that proposition is equally true, that no government can long exist "half black and half white." If the republican party, or its all-powerful leaders in the North, cannot see this, if they are so absorbed in the idea of this newly discovered political divinity in the negro, that they cannot comprehend its social repugnance or its political dangers; or, knowing it, have the wanton, wicked, and criminal purpose of disregarding its consequences, whether in the present or in the future, and the great mass of American white citizens should still be so mad as to sustain them in their heedless career of forcing negro supremacy over white men, why then "farewell, a long farewell," to constitutional liberty on this continent, and the glorious form of government bequeathed to us by our fathers. . . .

The foregoing is a hurried, but, as we believe, a truthful statement of the political, moral, and financial condition of the State of South Carolina, under the joint rule of the Negro and the "reconstructive" policy of Congress.

Frank Blair

T. F. Bayard[1]

S. S. Cox[2]

---

[1] Democratic senator from Delaware.

[2] Democratic representative from New York.

JAMES B. BECK

P. VAN TRUMP

A. M. WADDELL[3]

J. C. ROBINSON[4]

J. M. HANKS[5]

[3] Democratic representative from North Carolina.
[4] Democratic representative from Illinois.
[5] Democratic representative from Arkansas.

Analyzing the Source

REFLECTING ON THE SOURCE

1. Using your notes from the first table on page 8, describe the actions and purposes witnesses attributed to the Ku Klux Klan in South Carolina. How did the descriptions of the Klan differ between witnesses examined in Washington, D.C. (Sources 1 and 2) and those examined in South Carolina (Sources 3, 4, and 5)? How would you explain those differences?

2. Briefly compare the nature of evidence presented in the testimony: How did it differ between black and white witnesses? In what ways did the Klan's attacks on blacks differ from those on white Republicans? What do you think accounts for such differences?

3. What patterns did you find in the cross-examination of witnesses? How did Van Trump and other Democrats on the committee seek to discredit or shape the testimony they heard, and do you think they succeeded in any instances? Which witnesses do you think were most successful in answering their cross-examinations? Did any of the witnesses contradict themselves?

MAKING CONNECTIONS

4. Consider whether the majority and minority reports (Sources 6 and 7) could have been written before the committee heard any witnesses. Using your notes from the second table on page 8, do you think any of the congressmen sitting on the committee had their minds changed about the Ku Klux Klan or the federal government's response to it by the testimony they heard? What specific examples or passages from the reports would you use to support your answer?

5. What does this source tell you about the limits of federal power during Reconstruction? According to the testimony and reports, what accounted for the breakdown of law and order in South Carolina, and how was it most likely to be restored? How did Republicans and Democrats differ in this regard?

6. Judging from the testimony of witnesses you have read here, how might you use this source to study the social and economic conditions of the freedmen

and women of the South during Reconstruction? What evidence does the testimony of Thomson, McMillan, and Givens (Sources 3, 4, and 5) provide of the ways in which African American men and women valued and acted on their freedom after 1865? Judging from this evidence, what limits did whites try to impose on that freedom?

Beyond the Source

As noted in the Joint Select Committee's majority report, the Ku Klux Klan Act of 1871 did succeed in suppressing the Klan's activities in those regions where it was enforced. In October 1871, while the Joint Select Committee was still at work, President Grant suspended the writ of habeas corpus in nine South Carolina counties, including Spartanburg, and sent in federal troops to arrest approximately 1,500 suspected Klansmen. Even more Klansmen fled the region to avoid prosecution. In a series of trials managed by U.S. Attorney General Amos Akerman in late 1871 and in 1872, about ninety Klansmen were sentenced to prison terms ranging from three months to ten years. Most of those given long sentences were released within a year or two, under amnesty offered by President Grant. Overall, very few Klansmen were ever brought to meaningful justice for their crimes, but by the election of 1872, reports of Klan terrorism had declined considerably and the organization's ability to intimidate black voters appeared to have been broken.

During the 1920s, the Ku Klux Klan was revived by whites who felt threatened by Catholic and Jewish immigrants as well as by African Americans. At its peak, this version of the Klan included three million members and spilled beyond the South into western and northern states. After ebbing in the 1940s, the Klan surged again during the civil rights movement of the 1950s and 1960s. This incarnation was much smaller than its predecessor in the 1920s but more violent in its resistance to racial equality. Today a number of white supremacist organizations continue to call themselves the Ku Klux Klan, but they are poorly organized and constantly at odds with each other and with similar hate groups on the far right of American politics.

In the larger story of Reconstruction, it would seem that the Ku Klux Klan Act and the congressional investigation of the Klan were shining examples of how the federal government and the freedmen and women of the South acted in partnership to advance the cause of racial justice and equality in the United States. Unfortunately, these successes were short-lived. During his second term, Grant reduced considerably the number of federal troops posted in the South, and the Republicans split between a liberal faction still committed to racial equality and a more conservative faction willing to jettison Reconstruction policies and black voters in return for political compromises with Democrats on other issues.

The third branch of the federal government did not help African Americans in their pursuit of equality either. In two cases from the 1870s, the

Supreme Court interpreted the Fourteenth Amendment in such a way that it severely restricted the federal government's ability to intervene on behalf of private citizens when their civil and political rights were violated. In the *Slaughterhouse Cases* (1873), the Court ruled that the Fourteenth Amendment protected only those rights that were derived directly from the federal government, most of which dealt with matters of interstate or foreign travel or business; the civil rights of most concern to blacks in the South still fell under the jurisdiction of state courts and law enforcement. In *U.S. v. Cruikshank* (1876), the Court ruled that the Fourteenth Amendment empowered the federal government only to prosecute violations of civil rights by the states, not by individual persons (violations in that category still fell under state jurisdiction). The combined effect of these two decisions was to place responsibility for protecting the rights of the South's African American population under the authority of the state governments, while making any federal intervention on their behalf similar to that pursued under the Ku Klux Klan Act unconstitutional.

After the last of the former Confederate states had fallen back into Democratic hands in 1877, Southern whites found new ways to confine blacks to second-class citizenship that were far more subtle than the Klan's political terrorism. Insulated from federal intervention by the Supreme Court's decisions and congressional indifference, Southern states passed laws that disenfranchised blacks by imposing poll taxes and literacy tests. They also erected a system of social segregation known as Jim Crow laws that limited black access to education and economic opportunity. When blacks challenged this system, mobs and night riders responded with the same methods used by the Klan, most notably lynching and arson, to prevent any sustained resistance to white rule. Not until the civil rights movement of the 1950s would the federal government again embrace the cause of racial justice in the South with the same vigor it had shown during its battle against the Klan in 1871.

Finding and Supplementing the Source

Like all federal government reports, the Joint Select Committee's report was published by the Government Printing Office in Washington, D.C. In every state, libraries designated as federal repositories receive copies of such publications, and your college or university library may in fact be one. The full citation for the report is *Report of the Joint Select Committee to Inquire into the Condition of Affairs in the Late Insurrectionary States*, 13 volumes (Washington, D.C.: Government Printing Office, 1872). It can also be found under the title *Senate Reports*, 42d Congress, 2d sess., no. 41 (serial 1484–96) or *House Reports*, 42d Congress, 2d sess., no. 22 (serial 1529–41). Some libraries may also catalogue it under the title printed on the spine of each volume, *The Ku Klux Conspiracy*. Volume 1 contains the majority and minority reports, and the subsequent volumes contain the verbatim testimony of witnesses before the committee.

For a more accessible selection of the testimony heard by the Joint Select Committee, see Albion W. Tourgée, *The Invisible Empire* (1880; repr., Baton Rouge: Louisiana State University Press, 1989). Tourgée was a disillusioned carpetbagger when he published his autobiographical novel about Reconstruction, *A Fool's Errand*, in 1879. A year later, he published *The Invisible Empire* as an exposé of the Ku Klux Klan. For the definitive modern study of the Ku Klux Klan during Reconstruction, see Allen W. Trelease, *White Terror: The Ku Klux Klan Conspiracy and Southern Reconstruction* (New York: Harper and Row, Publishers, 1971). The Klan's place in the wider current of political violence in the Reconstruction-era South is explained in George C. Rable, *But There Was No Peace: The Role of Violence in the Politics of Reconstruction* (Athens: University of Georgia Press, 1984). The best comprehensive history of Reconstruction, Eric Foner's *Reconstruction: America's Unfinished Revolution, 1863–1877* (New York: Harper and Row, Publishers, 1988), also provides a good summary of the Klan's origins and role in Reconstruction. For a study of the constitutional significance of the Ku Klux Klan Act and similar Reconstruction-era legislation, see Harold M. Hyman, *A More Perfect Union: The Impact of the Civil War and Reconstruction on the Constitution* (New York: Alfred A. Knopf, 1973). The film *Birth of a Nation* (1915), directed by D. W. Griffith and based on Thomas Dixon's popular novel *The Clansman* (1905), is a stunning example of how the Klan was mythologized during the Jim Crow era as an organization that defended white Southerners against the depredations of Northern carpetbaggers and black Republicans during Reconstruction.

CHAPTER 2

Picturing a Western Myth

Photography and the Blackfeet

When Glacier National Park in Montana opened its doors to the public in the summer of 1911, its advertising promised tourists that a visit to the park would include a "wilderness experience" replete with glimpses of the "vanishing" American Indian. Countless brochures, calendars, postcards, and magazine layouts featured photographs of the Blackfeet, the tribe that was native to the region in northwestern Montana that became Glacier Park. The Glacier Park publicity campaign was so successful that the image of the Blackfeet, with their feathered headdresses and buffalo-hide tipis, became a standard image of all American Indians, despite great variations in dress and housing among Native Americans.

Descriptions of the Blackfeet as "specimens of a Great Race soon to disappear" lent immediacy to Glacier Park's promotional campaign and tapped into the then-familiar idea that Native American cultures were wholly incompatible with modern life. The assumption was that if people maintained their native identities and cultures, then they were sadly stuck in the past and destined to be mowed down by modernity. If they adjusted themselves and their cultures to modern life, then they were no longer Indians; they had, in effect, "vanished."

The belief that people can be either modern or native, but not both, shapes the Native American story into a tale of unavoidable natural disaster, similar to a flood or an earthquake: no one was responsible, and Indians like the Blackfeet were helpless in its wake. There are two historical problems with this interpretation: first, it overlooks U.S. government policies that actively hindered natives' freedom to blend native culture with modern life; second, it ignores the ways in which people like the Blackfeet refused to let their cultures vanish and, despite government policies, found ways to accommodate native culture to modern culture. For example, the story of Glacier National Park is, in part, a story of Blackfeet adaptation to modern life. In accommodating to the park, the Blackfeet carved out a clever market niche: they sold back to white Americans, who were seeking a "wilderness experience," the mythic image of a "vanished people."

The Blackfeet signed their first treaty with the federal government in 1855, which made them one of the last native tribes to establish any treaty relations with the United States. According to that treaty, Blackfeet allowed whites to build roads, telegraph lines, military posts, missions, schools, and U.S. government agencies throughout their territory. In exchange, the U.S. government agreed to pay out $200,000 in "useful goods and services" and to provide $150,000 to promote the "civilization and Christianization" of the Blackfeet.

The terms of that 1855 treaty, and all subsequent treaties between the Blackfeet and the U.S. government, included the key feature limiting natives' power to design their own accommodation to modern life: all government payments for the land the United States bought from the Blackfeet were made in goods, services, and programs that the government deemed appropriate for civilizing and Christianizing the tribe, and all such payments were made according to the government's timetable. The government did not pay the natives directly for the lands it acquired, as would have been customary in any other European-American land deal, and the Blackfeet did not gain the economic resources from land sales that would have allowed them to invest in their own style of assimilation. While the government stated its desire to have natives assimilate into modern American life, it denied people like the Blackfeet the economic independence that was central to American identity. Compare this with the experience of immigrants to the United States in the nineteenth century. While immigrants struggled economically, they were not legally denied control over whatever wages or business profits they could earn. As a result, they were able to direct their earnings toward building an independent community base from which to influence the timing and the terms of their accommodation to American society. It was this economic autonomy that U.S. policy denied to native tribes.

In the four decades between 1870 and 1910, between the close of the Civil War era and the opening of Glacier National Park, the problems in federal Indian policy became clear for the Blackfeet, for in these decades the buffalo disappeared from the northern Montana grasslands. This happened, in part, because whites overhunted the buffalo for sport, but it also happened because supplying buffalo meat to the tribe and selling buffalo hides to whites were the only economic activities left to the Blackfeet. They, too, overhunted. At the same time that the buffalo were declining, over twenty thousand land-hungry white settlers poured into the Montana territory. They occasionally met with violent resistance from the Blackfeet, and the U.S. military helped the settlers fight off that resistance.

The combination of food shortages, smallpox, and conflict with whites reduced the Blackfeet population from eight thousand in 1855 to twenty-five hundred in 1880. Another 20 percent died of starvation in the winter of 1884 when the federal government failed to deliver food allotments owed in exchange for land. U.S. military reprisals against Blackfeet resistance were sufficiently harsh in these years that the *New York Times* questioned if the killing of women and children was necessary to achieve peace with the Blackfeet. Adding to these difficulties was a major change in U.S. policy in 1871 that declared that the government no longer regarded Native American tribal groups as independent, treaty-making nations. They were now defined as "wards" of the state.

It was as wards of the state that the starving remainder of the Blackfeet nation negotiated two major land sales to the government, one in 1887, the other in 1895. By the turn of the century, the two thousand residents of the Blackfeet reservation still owned 1.5 million acres of grazing land but had relinquished ownership of the western mountains, lakes, and streams that had traditionally been a vital source of spiritual and dietary nourishment. For the land, the Blackfeet received $3 million, half of what they had asked for. Again, payment never came as a direct infusion of capital for the tribe to control and invest; it was always in the form of goods and services controlled by the Bureau of Indian Affairs, a then-famously corrupt arm of the federal government.

At the time that white ranchers, farmers, and miners were moving onto Blackfeet lands, an emerging lobby of white conservationists were increasingly alarmed that uncontrolled development would destroy the West's natural beauty and resources. These conservationists figured out that they could protect precious pockets of the region by appealing to modern Americans' nostalgia for the vanishing wilderness. Thus it was, in 1910, that conservationists joined with the Great Northern Railway Company to win congressional approval for Glacier National Park, sixteen hundred square miles of alpine beauty that had once formed the "backbone" of the Blackfeet's world (see Map 2.1 on p. 31). The Great Northern, which stood to profit from a tourism trade in Montana, financed the construction of roads and trails, two magnificent hotels, and a series of smaller "chalets" and tourist-friendly camps around the park. In less than a decade, aggressive marketing increased tourism to Glacier National Park from four thousand in the summer of 1911 to almost twenty thousand in the summer of 1920.

To provide tourists with opportunities for contact with the supposedly vanishing natives, the Great Northern hired Blackfeet every summer to relocate from the reservation into designated areas of the park. There, they could be viewed in a living museum, occupying traditionally styled tipis and wearing costumes that twentieth-century whites thought of as authentic. Though publicity stills occasionally depicted a Blackfeet male spearing a fish or holding his bow and arrows, Glacier Park rules actually followed the national parks' prohibition on hunting rather than the Blackfeet's treaty rights to hunt and fish in their old territory. In devising means of economic survival in the modern world, the Blackfeet found that they could adapt native culture to U.S. culture as entertainers but not as hunters of game or fish.

For those Blackfeet who profited from their summertime performances as historical artifacts, this pragmatic use of their culture was layered with irony. Glacier Park's romantic myth of the "vanishing" Indian was reinforced by government policy on the Blackfeet reservation, where federal agents spent the money owed to the tribe on programs to transform Blackfeet hunters into the mythic American family farmer. The Dawes Severalty Act of 1887 had made it U.S. policy to encourage natives to divide tribally held lands into individually held, 160-acre plots and to farm independently from the tribe. The government would hold each plot of land in trust for twenty-five years and then grant the land and citizenship to the former tribe member. Hailed as a reform of the failed reservation system, the Dawes plan proved unsuited to the harsh western environment. White farmers at this time were concluding that western agriculture demanded substantial capital outlays for irrigation, planting, and harvesting technology applied to vast grain acreage, but Indian agents, implementing the Dawes plan, insisted that the Blackfeet could survive and assimilate by farming small plots of oats, barley, and vegetables.

Reports by the U.S. Commissioner of Indian Affairs indicate that the Blackfeet adopted some features of the government's assimilation program and resisted others. For example, the commissioner reported in 1900 that the number of reservation Blackfeet who wore "citizens' dress"—the clothing style of whites—had increased to 2,085 from only 40 in 1886. There were similar increases in Blackfeet use of "citizens'" household wares, wagons, and foodstuffs because the Blackfeet were paid for their land with all manner of modern, American goods. But in that same 1900 report, the commissioner admitted that

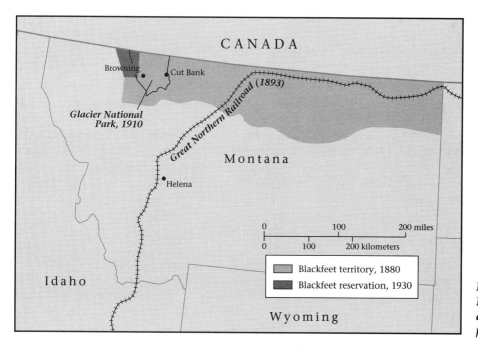

Map 2.1 Glacier National Park and the Black-feet, 1880–1930

only five hundred acres on the Blackfeet reservation were under farm cultivation. Denied the independent authority to invest the tribe's funds in livestock ranching, which was the endeavor that made the most economic and cultural sense to the Blackfeet, native men resisted federal efforts to turn them into vegetable gardeners in a grassland climate of hot, dry summers and long, cold winters. Indeed, the most prosperous Blackfeet were mixed-bloods whose white fathers had profited by bringing their livestock to graze for free on the Blackfeet wives' tribal grasslands.

In the first three decades of the twentieth century, right at the time that the Great Northern Railroad was eulogizing the passage of a "Great Race," the Blackfeet were not, in fact, vanishing, nor were they strictly adhering to the government's assimilation plan. Instead, they were struggling to create an alternative method of survival that retained native traditions while utilizing the opportunities presented by the surrounding white society. An excellent example of the Blackfeet's creativity in this regard is their adaptation of the Sun Dance. From the 1880s on into the twentieth century, Christian missionaries and federal agents opposed the Sun Dance as a blatant display of "heathen worship" that had to be eliminated if the Blackfeet were ever to assimilate. But other whites, including, eventually, those at Glacier National Park, were fascinated by the Blackfeet's elaborate ritual of sacred vows to the holy sun. By the turn of the century, the Blackfeet had rescheduled the Sun Dance to coincide with the Fourth of July, thereby turning it into a patriotic celebration that became a major tourist event that the church and the government did not dare oppose. In this way, as in other ways, the Blackfeet preserved their traditions while accommodating to the realities of life in white society.

Using Photographs as a Source

Photographs are one of the most modern types of documents available to students of history. For centuries, historians have consulted written texts, paintings, sculpture, music, and all sorts of manufactured artifacts to reconstruct human life in the past. But it was only in the 1840s that advances in camera design made it possible to capture and preserve an image of a physical object. This technological invention revolutionized human access to the past; permanent photographs gave every viewer a unique window on people and places long gone.

Native Americans became the subjects of photographs as early as the 1850s when Indian delegations to Washington, D.C., were regularly photographed as part of the official record of treaty negotiations. In photography's early years, the camera's shutter speed was too slow to capture the action of battle, but hundreds of native warriors went to portrait studios in the 1860s, where they sat motionless for the eighty seconds required to capture an image on a glass "plate." In the same era, dozens of intrepid photographers ventured out west with horses bearing cameras, tripods, glass plates, developing chemicals, and a tent "darkroom." Though burdened by the technology's requirement that they develop every photo within ten minutes of taking it, these early western photographers were determined to capture images of tribal people in their native environments.

Like other European Americans, photographers assumed that Native Americans were destined for oblivion and believed, therefore, that they were preserving on film the last survivors of a doomed people. Joseph Henry, the first secretary of the Smithsonian Institution, tried to raise government funds in 1867 to build a complete photographic record of the "principal tribes of the U.S." by arguing that "the Indians are passing away so rapidly that but few years remain within which this can be done, and the loss will be irretrievable . . . when they are gone."

Secretary Henry was not granted his funds, so photography of Indians proceeded in a haphazard way, driven by technology and influenced by commercial, cultural, and personal motives. Thanks to the introduction in 1888 of George Eastman's handheld "box" camera, photography became the pastime of amateurs as well as the business of professionals, and the "vanishing" Indian continued to be a favorite photographic subject into the twentieth century. There are today over ninety thousand photographs at the National Museum of the American Indian at the Smithsonian Institution in Washington, D.C. And the NMAI is just one of dozens of photographic archives in the United States that serve, according to one historian, as "a collective witness to Indian transitions."

Advantages and Disadvantages of Working with Photographs

Photographs are a valuable historical source for the obvious reason: they give us access to subtle and minute details on the natural world and social life. From the dusty look of a Blackfeet family's vegetable harvest to the jaunty swing of a golfer's club at Glacier National Park, photos can capture and preserve a wealth of information without even intending to. The lens that focused on a quartet of Blackfeet students also recorded useful information on reservation clothing, activities, and attitude. Indeed, the record of individuals' facial expressions, body poses, even their gestures and glances toward one another is one of photography's greatest contributions to our connection to people in the past.

There are disadvantages, however, to working with photographs. Everyone who has ever dug through a box of old, unmarked photographs knows that pictures cannot answer all of the questions they raise. The image itself cannot tell us why a man in a photo was smiling, whether his smile was genuine or an act for the camera, whether he owned the clothes he was wearing in the photo, or what his relationship was to the person taking the photo.

Consider, for example, the detail on page 34 from a photograph taken around 1930 at a traditional tribal dance on the reservation, where the audience included tourists from Glacier Park. (The photograph can be seen in its entirety on p. 43.) On the one hand, it provides a wealth of evidence on the blending of native culture with modern American culture. On the other hand, it raises a host of unanswererable questions about the thoughts and feelings of those who appear in the photo.

Important clue for dating the photo

Consider the meaning of the American flags

What is the significance of farm machinery next to a tipi?

Note the use of sunglasses

While this slice of a photograph offers valuable information on Blackfeet incorporation of American products into daily tribal life, it cannot tell us the attitude of the women toward the automobile in the background. Does the car signify the natives' own prosperity or is it a sign of white wealth derived from Blackfeet land? Do the American flags denote Blackfeet deference to governmental power or a calculated use of white icons in tribal rituals? Might the flags simply testify to Blackfeet patriotism?

Such questions remind us that photographs alone cannot reveal all we want to know about the objects in front of the camera. But this is not photography's only limitation in recording the past. For in addition to asking questions about who and what are in front of the camera, historians must also ask questions about who is behind the camera. We have been told that "the camera doesn't lie," yet we also know that every camera has an angle. More precisely, every camera has a photographer operating it, a person who brings some mix of cultural attitudes, personal emotions, economic motives, and artistic assumptions to the picture-taking process. When reading a photograph for evidence of the past, we cannot afford to regard the camera as a neutral technology or the photograph as purely an "objective" witness. We must regard every photograph as the creative product of a photographer's point of view and must attempt to put each photograph into the context in which it was taken.

The selection of photographs included in this chapter allows you to compare two very different types of photographs of Blackfeet. The first six photos were taken by commercial photographers who were hired by the Great Northern Railway to create advertising pictures for Glacier National Park. These commercial photos are representative of the vast majority of surviving images of Native Americans; they convey a romantic image of the Indian as the embodiment of a noble and pristine American past. The highly skilled, world-famous photographers, such as Edward S. Curtis and Roland Reed, who created these photographic myths for companies like the Great Northern Railway often manipulated the scene by dressing tribal people in anachronistic costumes, blocking out signs of modern life, and posing natives in a wistful or stoic stance. By contrast, the amateur photographers on the Blackfeet reservation, who were probably store merchants or U.S. Indian agents, did not block out modern life or natives' accommodation to that life. We know the economic motives of the commercial photographers, the economic purpose of their photos, and the economic reasons that the Blackfeet posed for those photos. But we are left to guess at the motives of the amateurs standing behind the camera on the reservation and at the attitudes of the Blackfeet whose images, shorn of mythic romance, were recorded for posterity.

Working with the Source

Historians of Native American life often trace tribal responses to the assumption that traditional tribal life among natives like the Blackfeet could not coexist with modern American life. As you examine the photographs in this chapter, take note of the Blackfeet response to this assumption, using the table on page 36. Where do you find evidence of tradition, of modernity, or of both?

	Evidence of Tradition	Evidence of Modernity
1. Greetings from Glacier National Park		
2. Great Northern Railway Calendar		
3. Blackfeet and Park Golfers		
4. Spearfishing in Glacier National Park		
5. Two Guns White Calf Reading		
6. Old Ration Place		
7. Blackfeet Performance		
8. Family at Sun Dance Encampment		
9. Students with Their Harvest		
10. Mad Plume Family Harvest		
11. Blackfeet Girl at Glacier National Park Switchboard		
12. Sewing Class at the Cut Bank Boarding School		

The Source: Photographs of the Blackfeet at Glacier National Park and on the Reservation, 1890–1930

PHOTOGRAPHS FROM GLACIER NATIONAL PARK

1   *Greetings from Glacier National Park,* c. 1920

The following photo was used on a wide variety of Glacier National Park publicity materials throughout the 1920s. This photo appeared at the top of park stationery and on the front of specialized brochures sent to convention participants. It was often accompanied by the words, "Ki-tuk-a, Stum-ik-Us-tsi-kai-yi" and "Ok-yi! Ik-so-ka-pi" along with the translation: "Us Indians will be glad to see you at Glacier Park this summer and next summer too" and "We shake hands with you!" Typically the photo's caption promised that the men in the photo would be at the Glacier Park train station to greet conventioneers when they arrived.

Source: Great Northern Railway Collection, Glacier Park Views, Minnesota State Historical Society. Photographer unknown.

Great Northern Railway Calendar, 1923

The Great Northern Railway Company made extensive use of commercial photographs of the Blackfeet in this popular form of advertising.

Source: Great Northern Railway Collection, Glacier Park Views, Minnesota State Historical Society. Photographer unknown.

3 *Blackfeet and Park Golfers,* c. 1930

Blackfeet sometimes served as caddies for Glacier Park golfers, but this undated publicity photo does not depict the natives in that role.

Source: Great Northern Railway Collection, Glacier Park Views, Minnesota State Historical Society. Photographer unknown.

4   *Spearfishing in Glacier National Park,* date unknown

Though it made for an impressive publicity shot, the Blackfeet art of spearfishing could not actually be pursued in Glacier National Park.

Source: Great Northern Railway Collection, Glacier Park Views, Minnesota State Historical Society. Tomer J. Hileman, photographer.

5 *Two Guns White Calf Reading,* **date unknown**

Two Guns White Calf often appeared in Glacier Park publicity shots. Here, Tomer Hileman posed him reading a book by Zane Grey, a famous writer of western stories.

Source: Great Northern Railway Collection, Glacier Park Views, Minnesota State Historical Society. Tomer J. Hileman, photographer.

PHOTOGRAPHS TAKEN ON BLACKFEET RESERVATION IN MONTANA

6 *Old Ration Place,* date unknown

Blackfeet sale of tribal lands to the U.S. government was paid for in food rations. After the buffalo disappeared, Blackfeet gathered each week for the one and one-half pounds of beef, half pound of flour, and small amounts of beans, bacon, salt, soda, and coffee allocated to each man, woman, and child.

Source: Montana Historical Society.

7   *Blackfeet Performance,* c. 1930

This photo from the Great Northern Railway's photo archives does not appear to have been used for Glacier Park publicity. It suggests that park visitors in the 1930s took day trips to the reservation to view Blackfeet performances. This may have been a combined celebration of the Blackfeet's Sun Dance and the Fourth of July.

Source: Great Northern Railway Collection, Glacier Park Views, Minnesota State Historical Society. Photographer unknown.

8   *Family at Sun Dance Encampment,* 1908

Blackfeet traveled to a central location on the reservation for the annual Sun Dance. This 1908 photo, taken at that year's Sun Dance encampment, shows one family's display of finery and prized possessions.

Source: Photo by Thomas Magee.

9   *Students with Their Harvest,* 1912 (above right)

Source: Photo by E. L. Chase.

10   *Mad Plume Family Harvest,* c. 1920 (below right)

Source: Photo courtesy of Mae Vallance.

These two photos reflect the government's effort to encourage Blackfeet vegetable farming in the decades following the 1887 Dawes Act. The students shown in Source 9 attended the Cut Bank Boarding School, where sailor suits were the regulation uniform. Albert and Susan Mad Plume and members of their family display their harvest for a photographer in Source 10. They were among the full-blooded Blackfeet who supported the government's plans for agricultural self-sufficiency.

11 *Blackfeet Girl at Glacier National Park Switchboard,* c. 1920

This photo, probably taken in the 1920s, is from the Great Northern Railway's photo archive but was not used for publicity. It suggests that some Blackfeet were hired into jobs at Glacier Park that gave them training in marketable skills.

Source: Great Northern Railway Collection, Glacier Park Views, Minnesota State Historical Society. Photographer unknown.

12 *Sewing Class at the Cut Bank Boarding School,* 1907

At government-sponsored boarding schools, Blackfeet were taught to use modern technology and encouraged to assimilate into American culture. Native recollections of these schooling experiences vary widely; some former students have very positive memories, while others report being made to feel inferior.

Source: Courtesy of the Sherburne Collection, University of Montana Archives.

Analyzing the Source

1. The table on page 36 had you look for evidence of traditional and modern life in the Blackfeet photographs. In your analysis, did you find more evidence of tradition or modernity in the Glacier Park photographs? Was the evidence different in the reservation photographs? What explanation do you have for the pattern of tradition and modernity that you were able to trace in these photos?

2. Every photograph, like every written text, invites multiple interpretations. Try to construct two entirely different interpretations for each of the following photographs: Source 1, Source 3, Source 7, and Source 9. What additional evidence would you seek to test out the validity of these varying interpretations?

3. If the publicity photos taken at Glacier National Park are inauthentic representations of Blackfeet life, then of what legitimate use are they to historians? Since there are few surviving photographs of Native Americans taken *by* Native Americans prior to the 1950s, should historians not use photographs as a source in Native American history?

MAKING CONNECTIONS

4. Some might argue that the Blackfeet cooperated with Glacier National Park officials in perpetuating anachronistic stereotypes of the unchanging, tradition-bound Native American. How might members of the Blackfeet tribe in the 1920s have responded to that argument?

5. Very few photographs that historians find, whether in archives or attics, are accompanied by complete information on the photographer, the subject of the photograph, or the circumstances under which the photo was taken. In the face of such common deficits, what principles would you devise to guard against faulty historical interpretation of photographs?

Beyond the Source

In 1996, Elouise Cobell, a Montana banker and a member of the Blackfeet tribe, filed a lawsuit to force the federal government to provide a full accounting of the Indian Trust Fund, which had been in place since passage of the Dawes Severalty Act in 1887. Cobell took this drastic action because, she says, she "got fed up" with the government's chaotic bookkeeping and evasive answers to questions she asked about the workings of the Indian Trust Fund. Cobell, a trained accountant with considerable business experience, runs a ranch and directs the Blackfeet Reservation Development Fund, Inc., in Browning, Montana.

Under the provisions of the Dawes Act, it was the Indian Trust Fund that held legal title to individual Indian's land plots. Cobell and many of her fellow Native Americans suspect that federal agents in charge of the fund swindled natives out of millions of acres and billions of dollars by failing to honor native ownership, selling off plots of land to whites, and not transferring the profits to natives. The suit further claims that the federal government has never paid Native Americans what they are owed for oil extraction and mineral mining on native lands. In essence, this landmark suit, which is still being argued in federal court, purports that the U.S. government "has stolen, lost or misallocated" close to $140 billion since the Dawes Act set up the Indian Trust Fund. The goal of Cobell's suit, which could affect five hundred thousand native beneficiaries, is to force the government to account for all trust funds and to reform the still-existing trust system.

Royce C. Lamberth, the U.S. district judge charged with the case, has been aggressive in pressing the Department of Interior, which manages Native American affairs, to produce an accounting method that can answer the questions raised by the suit. In September of 2002, Judge Lamberth declared that the Interior Department's conduct could serve as the "gold standard for mismanagement by the federal government for more than a century." He has underscored that view by finding Secretary of Interior Bruce Babbitt and, later, Secretary of Interior Gale Norton in contempt of court for failing to produce the accounting demanded in the suit.

For its part, the federal government points to a long history of charges of mismanagement of Indian lands, arguing that it cannot now reconstruct a record that everyone admits has been fraudulent. As far back as 1929, the General Accounting Office reported "numerous expenditures . . . made from these funds" that did not go to Indian landowners and that could only be justified by "using a very broad interpretation of what constitutes the benefit of the Indian." That same report conceded that the trust fund's accounting methods were so poor that it was impossible to certify that "the Indian received the full measure of benefit to which he was entitled." Over sixty years later, a 1992 congressional report again confirmed a history of inadequate accounting and payment practices at the fund. That report was titled "Misplaced Trust: The Bureau of Indian Affairs' Mismanagement of the Indian Trust Fund." Given this history, the federal government insists that even the best-faith effort could not reconstruct a valid account of all trust fund transactions. Plaintiffs in the case question the government's commitment to finding a solution, noting that the government continued to destroy hundreds of boxes of trust fund records after Judge Lamberth ordered that all surviving records be preserved.

However the case is settled, it certainly refutes all predictions that America's natives were destined to vanish. The nation's four million Native Americans, including its fifteen thousand Blackfeet, are still very much alive and often closely identified with their tribal cultures. Like Elouise Cobell, these natives are quite prepared to employ the tools of modern life, including the court system, to promote tribal prosperity and preserve their native communities.

Finding and Supplementing the Source

The commercial photographs of the Blackfeet used here can be found in the archives of the Great Northern Railway Company at the Minnesota State Historical Society in St. Paul, Minnesota. There are additional collections of Glacier Park photographs of the Blackfeet at the National Museum of the American Indian in Washington, D.C., and in the Sherburne family collection at the University of Montana. The reservation photographs of the Blackfeet were taken from *The Reservation Blackfeet, 1882–1945: A Photographic History of Cultural Survival* by William E. Farr (Seattle: University of Washington Press, 1984). This chapter was inspired by original research conducted at the Newberry Library in Chicago and the Minnesota State Historical Society by Amy E. Scott in 1996, when she was an undergraduate at Grinnell College.

Collections of Native American photographs are open for public view at the National Museum of the American Indian (NMAI) in Washington, D.C., and in archives in an array of state and local historical societies. The NMAI also has a Web site on which it presents "virtual exhibits" of photographs on various native tribes and topics. Two excellent published collections of Native American photographs are *Spirit Capture: Photographs from the National Museum of the American Indian,* edited by Tim Johnson (Washington, D.C.: Smithsonian Institution Press, 1998), and *The Photograph and the American Indian* (Princeton, N.J.: Princeton University Press, 1994), edited by Alfred L. Bush and Lee Clark Mitchell. For an intriguing discussion of the cultural meanings that now surround our approach to photographs, see Miles Orvell, *The Real Thing: Imitation and Authenticity in American Culture, 1880–1940* (Chapel Hill: University of North Carolina Press, 1989).

Among the many studies of the encounter between Native American and Euro-American cultures, two of the most useful are Brian W. Dippie, *The Vanishing American: White Attitudes and U.S. Indian Policy* (Middletown, Conn.: Wesleyan University Press, 1982), and Mark David Spence, *Dispossessing the Wilderness: Indian Removal and the Making of the National Parks* (New York: Oxford University Press, 1999). A useful reference book on Native American history and modern life is *The Native American Almanac: A Portrait of Native America Today,* edited by Arlen Hirschfelder and Martha Kreipe de Montano (New York: Prentice Hall General Reference, 1993).

For more specific historical background on the Blackfeet Indians, see John C. Ewers, *The Blackfeet: Raiders on the Northwestern Plains* (Norman: University of Oklahoma Press, 1967); Howard L. Harrod, *Mission Among the Blackfeet* (Norman: University of Oklahoma Press, 1971); and Paul Rosier, *Rebirth of the Blackfeet Nation, 1912–1954* (Lincoln: University of Nebraska Press, 2001). James Welch's highly praised novel, *Fools Crow* (New York: Viking Press, 1986), tells the story of the Blackfeet tribe through the eyes of a young male tribe member coming of age in the decades after the Civil War. For information on the Blackfeet tribe today, go to **blackfeetnation.com.**

CHAPTER 3

Reading the 1894 Pullman Strike

Chicago's Daily Papers Report the News

Victor Harding was working as a reporter for the *Chicago Times* in the summer of 1894 when the Pullman labor strike tied up rail lines from Lake Michigan to the Pacific Ocean. On the night of July 5, when federal troops had marched into Chicago to break the strike at its center, Harding mounted a horse and rode up and down the city's miles of railway track to witness the uprising of thousands of unemployed workers. He saw twenty rail cars overturned at Forty-third Street, saw gangs of boys with iron pipes destroy a railway switching mechanism, and watched the smoke billow up from rail cars set afire; Harding noted that few of the rioters were railroad workers and even fewer police were taking action to stop the rebellion. Chicago seemed headed for a conflagration, and the unions, the railway companies, the police, and the army seemed unable to stop it.

The Pullman strike had begun in May of 1894 as a peaceful labor protest against a single Chicago employer. On its face, there was nothing remarkable about this particular local strike against the Pullman Palace Car Company. Though all labor strikes were illegal in the United States, that fact did not silence the thousands of U.S. workers' protests staged in the three decades following the Civil War. The Pullman strike might have erupted and been put down like countless others. But uniquely combustible conditions in the early summer of 1894 ignited the local Pullman strike, causing it to explode first into a national boycott of more than twenty railroads and then into a violent confrontation between the federal government, the railroad companies, and American workers. A singular mix of employer intransigence, government aggression, worker bitterness, and general economic desperation transformed the Pullman strike into a pivotal event, galvanizing debates in America over the rights of employers and workers in an industrialized democracy and over the role of government in labor disputes.

Long before the strike, the Pullman Palace Car Company and its president, George Pullman, were famous. Pullman had perfected the passenger rail car, providing comfortable seats and sleeper cars to the traveling public in the 1870s and 1880s. Pullman's cars were so popular and his business dealings so shrewd that by 1890 three-quarters of the nation's railroads were under contract to carry only Pullman Company passenger cars, and the brand name "Pullman" had become synonymous with "passenger car." In addition to the fame of his product, George Pullman was well-known for creating the "model" industrial town of Pullman, Illinois, just fifteen miles south of Chicago.

Some observers admired Pullman town's array of fourteen hundred red brick rental units, which ranged from boardinghouses and two-bedroom tenements to four-bedroom homes. Others praised its modern systems of water, gas, and sewage. Some, however, criticized Pullman's town for its lack of elected government and the paternalistic nature of the company-owned schoolhouse, shopping "arcade," library (where borrowers had to pay a member's fee), and hotel—the fanciest place in town and the only place where alcoholic beverages could be sold. Still others worried that Mr. Pullman owned the only church building in town and set the rent too high for working-class congregations. But George Pullman was firm on the subject of rent in Pullman town: this real estate endeavor was no charity. Investors in the Pullman Land Association were assured of a steady 5 percent return on their shares in the town.

Pullman workers experienced both boom and bust in the year before their strike. The World's Columbian Exposition was staged in Chicago in 1893 to celebrate American industrial progress, and "the Fair" momentarily stimulated full employment and high wages in Pullman town. But a stock market crash in New York that same year led to the bankruptcy of sixteen thousand businesses nationwide—including hundreds of railroads.

In the town of Pullman itself, the depression caused layoffs, wage cuts, and increased resentment over the company's housing policies. During the Fair's boomtime, less than 40 percent of the forty-five hundred Pullman workers had chosen to live in the company town. Most chose to live in neighboring towns, with lower rents, greater independence, and the opportunity to buy their own home. When the depression began, the Pullman company laid off workers, cut wages by as much as 40 percent, and then gave rehiring preference to workers who took up residence in Pullman town, where the rents (unlike wages) had not been reduced at all. Bitterness over these practices grew because management salaries did not decline during the depression and because stockholders' guaranteed dividends of 8 percent were not reduced. That bitterness caused Pullman workers to join the American Railway Union (ARU) early in 1894 and culminated in a strike vote in May, after George Pullman and his managers refused to negotiate with the union.

The minute Pullman workers affiliated with the American Railway Union, their local labor conflict became part of a national struggle within the railway industry, the most important arm of transport and travel in the United States in the late nineteenth century. On one side of the struggle, the railroad owners affiliated in voluntary collectives like the General Managers' Association (GMA), which represented the twenty-four railroads with terminals in Chicago. GMA members secretly set wage scales and work rules for its lines and negotiated with a few craft unions of highly skilled workers while agreeing to blacklist all workers who attempted to form industry-wide unions. On the other side of the struggle was the ARU, a brand-new, national "industrial" union in which skilled, semiskilled, and unskilled railroad workers formed one industry-wide association. Railway owners feared the potential power of the ARU, which first appeared in 1893 and claimed 150,000 members by 1894. Just weeks before the Pullman strike began, the ARU won a strike against the Great Northern Railroad, and the members of the GMA understood that, on the field of labor, this new, industry-wide union was the player to beat.

The ARU, led by its charismatic president, Eugene V. Debs, gathered for its national convention in Chicago in late June 1894. The Pullman strike had been underway for six weeks, and the company had refused all invitations to arbitrate the dispute. At that moment, public sympathy lay with the workers, who appeared to be battling a stubborn, paternalistic employer. Debs and the ARU hoped for a great victory by refusing to handle any Pullman cars on the railway lines, thereby forcing George Pullman to the negotiating table. Members of the GMA saw the situation differently. The railway owners hoped for a victory over the ARU by insisting that their lines were contract-bound to carry Pullman cars and they would have to cease all service if workers would not attach Pullman cars to their trains. The GMA was betting that public sympathy would shift its way if the ARU appeared to be threatening America's vital arteries of trade and travel.

This showdown on the railroads lasted from June 26 to July 10, but those two weeks brought a bloody end to both the national boycott and the local Pullman strike. During the first week of the showdown, close to one hundred thousand railway workers refused to handle Pullman cars and twenty-four railways refused to run trains without Pullman cars. Even Eugene Debs was stunned by the strength and speed of the strike, which revealed railway workers' anger at their own employers as much as it showed support for Pullman workers. The ARU work stoppage tied up lines across the country. During that first week, vital trade arteries in twenty-seven states were stalled and snarled, which meant delays and disruptions for travelers, manufactured goods, fuel, livestock, produce, and—most important—the U.S. mail.

During the second week of the showdown, control of events shifted from the railway workers to the federal government, which used court injunctions and federal troops to quell the strike. The officials of President Grover Cleveland's administration were in no mood to negotiate. The GNP was down by almost 10 percent, national unemployment was climbing to over 15 percent, and the United Mine Workers had just rallied 125,000 miners to a nationwide coal strike. Moreover, the highest officials in the administration favored the railroads in this conflict since those officials had worked as lawyers for railway companies, and the federal government in 1894 had no formal mechanism for mediating disputes between labor and management. For all of these reasons, no one in the White House viewed arbitration of the strike as an option. Instead, on July 2, a federal judge issued sweeping injunctions forbidding the ARU from interfering with rail service, from interrupting mail service, or from inducing workers to cease working for the railroads. Working in cooperation with the GMA, the U.S. attorney general's office effectively declared all ARU activity to be illegal. It then dispatched over sixteen thousand federal troops to enforce the court orders.

The injunctions and the appearance of troops in cities like Chicago sparked the violence that reporter Victor Harding witnessed on the night of July 5. Street protests, attacks on railway property, fires in rail yards, and confrontations between demonstrators and authorities erupted all over the city. Armed but ill-trained federal marshals scuffled with the unemployed and disaffected, and no one in the government, the GMA, or the ARU could control the outcome. Fifty-one people died and over five hundred were arrested in street skirmishes. In the end, none of the violence occurred in Pullman town and only a handful of those arrested for violence were ARU members, but seventy-one union leaders—including Eugene Debs—were arrested on July 10 and charged with violating the federal injunctions. With its leaders in jail and troops on the streets, ARU members could not sustain their boycott and Pullman workers could not sustain their strike. By July 19, the trains were running and the Pullman Palace Car Company was ready to hire anyone who pledged not to join a union.

Using Newspapers as a Source

The old saying "newspapers are the day books of history" certainly holds true in the case of public events like the Pullman strike. While there exists an array of primary sources on the strike, including court proceedings, judicial rulings, government testimonies, speeches, pamphlets, and even novels, it is the daily newspaper articles on the strike that allow historians to watch events as they were unfolding and to feel the passions aroused at the moment. When incidents like the Pullman strike occur in today's world, we all gather around the television set and tune to the station we trust for news coverage. In 1894, people gathered around the pages of their favorite newspaper, where reactions were chronicled—and shaped. It is because of newspapers' central role in recording events and reflecting attitudes that historians so often include them among their sources.

By the time of the Pullman strike, urban American newspapers had become a vital part of the public life that they themselves covered. In the thirty years following the Civil War, the number of American cities with populations over fifty thousand had increased from sixteen to fifty-eight; by 1890, 19 percent of Americans lived in these sizable urban communities. Chicago alone had grown from almost three hundred thousand in 1870 to over a million in 1890. In this expanding sea of strangers, newspapers offered not only a basis for common knowledge about civic affairs and influential people but also a means by which urban residents could identify with (or against) strangers across town.

At the same time, urban newspapers in late nineteenth-century America had become big businesses that competed for a mass of readers by charging one or two cents for a ten-page daily. In the city of Chicago in 1890, there were twenty-six different daily newspapers with circulation rates between 10,000 and 230,000. Nine of those newspapers provided general news in English; ten offered the news in a foreign language; the rest provided financial or neighborhood news. Information was then, as it is now, the commodity that these newspapers sold. Then, as now, newspapers packaged their information in a story, but newspapers in the late nineteenth century were much less subtle than newspapers today when inserting editorial opinion into news stories. After all, in a city like Chicago, where the competition was fierce, a newspaper's editorial opinion was as important as its information in winning readers' loyalty.

Advantages and Disadvantages of Working with Newspapers

The best way to appreciate the value of newspapers as a historical source is to think about the difficulties that historians face when they must reconstruct an event in the past without the benefit of newspapers. In that situation, even the most basic information is hard to establish. With only recollections from individuals with no duty to "cover" an event, it is often impossible to determine with any accuracy when or where an event occurred or who exactly was present. Thus, in tracing events that took place before there was televised news footage, newspapers serve as the most immediate eyewitnesses to unfolding stories. In the case of the Pullman strike, for example, newspapers were competing to provide the most extensive coverage of daily developments all over the city and the country. The result for historians is a record of local skirmishes, fires, and arrests along with the names and affiliations of otherwise anonymous individuals. By gathering the bits and pieces of data from different news articles, a historian can trace patterns and make connections that reporters were too close to see and not paid to analyze.

The immediacy of daily newspapers provides an excellent gauge of the public climate at the time an event was actually occurring. Newspapers cannot tell us what readers were thinking, but they can tell us what information and opinions readers were being exposed to, and circulation figures can give us a sense of the popularity of different editorial positions on an event. In Chicago, eight of the city's nine daily English-language newspapers opposed the ARU's railway boycott. Only one newspaper, the *Chicago Times*, supported the ARU. And though the *Times* lost most of its commercial advertising during the strike, its circulation rose from just forty thousand to over one hundred thousand in the heat of the boycott, suggesting that its editorial stance temporarily won over new readers.

The advantages of newspapers—their provision of local details, their reflection of an immediate climate, and their investment in appealing to a particular readership—are the very reasons why historians are cautious in using newspapers as sources of information and never rely on a single story to reconstruct events. The key disadvantage to using newspapers as a source is that reporters are, by definition, "on deadline" and do not always have time to check and recheck their facts. Information gathered in the heat of the moment may be incomplete. A second disadvantage is that newspapers are supposed to offer an editorial position as well as report the news. Historians must be alert to the possibility that a newspaper's editorial position shaped its presentation of news events and must watch for the ways in which legitimate opinion on the editorial page often became slanted reporting on the news page.

In the case of the Pullman strike, the slippage between editorial position and news reporting is not difficult to detect. The 1894 strike coincided with the infamous period of "yellow journalism," when competitive newspapers violated their own boastful claims to accuracy by inflating, exaggerating, and even fabricating "facts" to increase their circulation; it was each newspaper's editorial stance that dictated how a story would be reported. To appreciate the role of editorial bias in shaping news reporting during the Pullman strike, consider these excerpts from the *Chicago Tribune* and the *Chicago Times,* on June 30, 1894—four days after the national railway boycott began and three days before U.S. troops were called up. Note the ways in which each reporter's language, as well as his choice of content, served to shape each story:

CHICAGO TRIBUNE, JUNE 30, 1894

"Law is Trampled On"

With the coming of darkness last night Dictator Debs' strikers threw off the mask of law and order and began the commission of acts of lawlessness and violence. A Pan Handle train carrying seven sleeper cars was flagged at Riverdale, and the engineer and fireman, under threat of being killed if they moved, were forced to hold the train while a mob of 800 men detached the Pullmans. . . . The mob grew in numbers and resisted efforts of the train men to recouple the Pullmans.

CHICAGO TIMES, JUNE 30, 1894

"Mail Trains Must Move"

At noon today United States Marshall Byington received telegraphic instructions . . . to move all mail trains that were being detained in this city on account of the Pullman boycott. He . . . notified the . . . American Railway Union . . . giving them until 2 p.m. to decide whether or not they would offer any interference. A committee of strikers called on [Byington] an hour later and informed him that the trains would be allowed to proceed. . . . Passenger trains on the Ohio & Mobile roads were allowed to go out this morning without sleepers.

It is easy to tell from these two paragraphs that the *Chicago Tribune* was opposed to the ARU boycott and the *Chicago Times* supported it. The more difficult task for the historian is to piece together a single, plausible version of events from such varying stories. It is not safe to assume that the version that appeared in the majority of papers is the most accurate, nor is it legitimate to assume that the story whose editorial bias we agree with is the most accurate. Newspapers can alert historians to obscure events, but historians then have to consult other sources such as police reports or court testimony to determine the validity of news reports.

In addition to sifting through the biased language of news articles to figure out what happened on a particular day, historians also utilize that biased language as evidence of the level of emotion surrounding an event. Passionate prose about the "Dictator Debs" acting in the "darkness" of night may not accurately depict the ARU's president during the Pullman strike, but it does suggest the heightened tempers in Chicago, and historians must consider how such hot language further intensified the climate. Just the fact that Chicago newspapers covered their front pages with strike stories in late June and early July constitutes historical evidence. The sheer quantity of coverage and size of headlines conveyed a sense of crisis. And the more frightening the boycott appeared, the more likely people were to turn against the ARU and support the federal troops. So while sensational coverage in newspapers has to be corroborated, it also serves as its own kind of historical evidence.

The newspaper stories you will be examining in this chapter are a seven-day sample from the sixty-six-day Pullman strike representing coverage in the *Chicago Tribune* and the *Chicago Times*. The *Tribune* was a staunchly Republican newspaper and a strong opponent of the ARU boycott. It was the oldest newspaper in the city in 1894, and its daily circulation of seventy-five thousand made it the third most popular paper in the city. The *Chicago Times,* a boycott supporter, was the second oldest newspaper in Chicago and had been a Republican newspaper until it was purchased by a Democratic politician in 1893. The *Times'* prolabor stance represented, therefore, a recent effort to improve its anemic circulation of forty thousand by reaching out to a new, more working-class audience.

Working with the Source

Any historian working with newspaper reports on the Pullman strike would be taking notes on two things: (1) factual claims about specific events that could be verified by checking other types of sources or, at least, a number of other Chicago newspapers and (2) evidence of editorial bias.

As you read through the following excerpts from the *Chicago Tribune* and the *Chicago Times*, use the table on page 58 to note one or two examples from each story of a factual claim a historian could use in telling the story of the strike, and one or two examples of each story's editorial bias.

	Factual Claims	Editorial Bias
May 12, 1894 *Chicago Tribune:* *Chicago Times:*		
May 15, 1894 *Chicago Tribune:* *Chicago Times:*		
June 26, 1894 *Chicago Tribune:* *Chicago Times:*		
June 28, 1894 *Chicago Tribune:* *Chicago Times:*		
July 1, 1894 *Chicago Tribune:* *Chicago Times:*		
July 7, 1894 *Chicago Tribune:* *Chicago Times:*		
July 15, 1894 *Chicago Tribune:* *Chicago Times:*		

The Source: Chicago Newspaper Articles on the Pullman Strike, May 12, 1894–July 15, 1894

FIRST FULL DAY OF THE LOCAL PULLMAN STRIKE

1 *Chicago Tribune*, May 12, 1894, page one

PULLMAN MEN OUT

DISCHARGES THE CAUSE

Committeemen Laid Off and Their Comrades Act.

Two thousand employees in the Pullman car works struck yesterday, leaving 800 others at their posts. This was not enough to keep the works going, so a notice was posted on the big gates at 6 o'clock . . . saying: "These shops closed until further notice."

Mr. Pullman said last night he could not tell when work would be resumed.

The American Railway Union, which has been proselyting for a week among the workmen, announces that it will support the strikers. Just exactly how, Vice-President Howard would not say. He intimated, however, that the trainmen on the railways on which are organized branches of the union might refuse to handle any of the Pullman rolling stock. It is not believed, however, that such action will be taken and it is equally impossible to see how the union can otherwise aid the strikers.

The walk-out was a complete surprise to the officials. . . . Mr. Pullman had offered to allow the men the privilege of examining the books of the company to verify his statement that the works were running at a loss. When the men quit work at 6 o'clock Thursday evening none of them had any idea of striking. . . . But the Grievance Committee of Forty-six held a session at the Dewdrop Saloon in Kensington which lasted until 4:30 o'clock in the morning. At that time a ballot was taken which resulted: 42 to 4 in favor of a strike. A second ballot was unanimous. So a messenger was sent to the freight car builders to order them to stop, and all seventy-five walked out of the big gate. One department at a time, the men went out so that by 10 o'clock 1500 men were out. Thirteen hundred and fifty men kept at work until noon, but only 800 came back after lunch. . . .

Included among the strikers were 400 girls from the laundry, sewing-rooms, and other departments. In the afternoon, everyone—men, women, and children—put on their best clothes and assembled on the ball grounds. They stood in groups or rolled around in the grass, making no demonstration and acting in a subdued manner.

Chicago Times, May 12, 1894, page one

PULLMAN MEN OUT

Nearly 4,000 Throw Down Their Tools and Quit

Refuse to Strike Another Link Till Wrongs are Righted

Firing Three Men Starts It

Almost the entire force of men employed in the Pullman shops went out on strike yesterday. Out of the 4,800 men and women employed in the various departments there were probably not over 800 at work at 6 o'clock last evening. The immediate cause of the strike was the discharge or laying off of three men in the iron machine shop. The real but remote cause is the question of wages over which the men have long been dissatisfied and on account of which they had practically resolved to strike a month ago.

The strike of yesterday was ordered by a committee of forty-six representing every department at the Pullman works. This committee was in session all night Thursday night, and finally came to the conclusion to order a strike 4:30 o'clock yesterday morning. The vote stood 42 in favor of a strike and 4 against.

The terms upon which the men insist before returning to work are the restoration of the wage scale of 1893, time and one-half for overtime, and no discrimination against any of those who have taken a prominent part in the strike.

The position of the company is that no increase in wages is possible under the present conditions. . . . The position of the men is that they are receiving less than a living wage, to which they are entitled. . . . President George M. Pullman told the committee that the company was doing business at a loss even at the reduced wages paid the men and offered to show his books in support of his assertion.

FOURTH DAY OF THE LOCAL PULLMAN STRIKE

3   *Chicago Tribune,* May 15, 1894, page eight

THEY MAY GO HUNGRY

Grocers Threaten to Cut Off Credit for Pullman Strikers

It will soon be a question of how to get food with the Pullman strikers if the strike continues much longer. A committee of the Kensington grocerymen, who furnish supplies for the men, told the Grievance Committee yesterday they were in a peculiar position. To extend credit to men on an indefinite strike meant ruin, while to refuse credit probably would mean a boycott when the men resumed work and began to earn money. So the grocers wanted to know how long the strike was going to last. . . . The strikers' committeemen said they had no means of knowing, so there the matter rests. The Arcade Mercantile Company [in Pullman], which ran a strictly cash concern in the market and a credit place in the Arcade, closed up the credit branch. . . . Eugene V. Debs, President of the American Railway Union, is certain that the strikers will win. He said so several times yesterday but absolutely refused to give reasons for his supreme confidence. He still hints darkly at what will happen if the union should refuse to handle Pullman cars.

"Why," he said, "the boys all over the country are clamoring to tie up the Pullman cars. They are in an inflammable mood and longing for a chance to take part in this affair. . . . The whole country is in an inflammable condition. . . . When a man gets $2 a day he can live and is therefore a coward—afraid to try to get more—but when he gets cut down to $1.40 or $1 he gets desperate. The difference between that and nothing is so slight he feels he has almost nothing to lose and everything to gain by a strike. . . ."

The strikers are following the advice of their leaders to stay at home and let whiskey alone. Morning, noon, and night the streets in Pullman and Kensington are as quiet and deserted as of a Sunday. There are no groups at the street corners; no loafers in the saloons. Even at the headquarters the crowd rarely exceeds 200 men, and these sometimes become bored and go home, leaving the hall empty. . . . John S. Runnells, general counsel for the Pullman company, said yesterday: "The statement made in some of the newspapers that after a while there would be a great number of evictions at Pullman and consequent scenes of excitement is entirely untrue."

4   *Chicago Times,* May 15, 1894, page one

SKIMS OFF THE FAT

Pullman Company Declares a Dividend Today

Quarterly 2 Per Cent Thrives at the Men's Expense

Full Pockets Swallow $600,000 While Honest Labor is Starving

Today the Pullman company will declare a quarterly dividend of 2 per cent on its capital stock of $30,000,000 and President George M. Pullman is authority for the statement that his company owes no man a cent. This despite the assertion of Mr. Pullman that the works have been run at a loss for eight months. Six hundred thousand dollars to shareholders, while starvation threatens the workman.

H. J. Pingrey, vestibule builder at the Pullman shops, has worked or reported daily for work since Jan. 1, till the strike, and during that time has been able to put in eighty days, for which he received $100. During that time he paid back to the company $40 for house rent and still owes $10 on that account.

The Rev. Mr. Oggel, who preaches in the beautiful green stone church on Watt Avenue, hard by the Pullman shops, marveled greatly in his sermon of Sunday night that Pingrey and his fellow workmen should have been so foolish as to go on a strike. The Rev. Mr. Oggel draws about $40 a week salary paid by Pullman workmen, and house rent free, to expound the gospel of Christ. . . .

Another matter which caused a ripple of excitement among the men was the announcement made by a committee representing the merchants . . . that under the existing circumstances . . . they could not give further credit to the strikers for goods. . . . Mr. Heathcoate [ARU local president] told the committee that . . . no individual merchant need hope to avert the certain boycott which would follow his refusal to give his customers credit. . . . "These are the merchants who have made a living out of the working men here for years and now when our time of trouble comes, they abandon us almost before we have a chance to ask for accommodation; we are not asking them for charity."

FIRST DAY OF THE NATIONAL ARU BOYCOTT OF PULLMAN CARS

 5   *Chicago Tribune,* June 26, 1894, page eight

BOYCOTT IS ON TODAY

American Railway Union Begins Its Fight on Pullman

The American Railway Union at noon today will begin a test of its strength with railways using the Pullman Palace Car company's sleeping and dining-room cars. At that hour the boycott of Pullman cars ordered by the union will go into effect. Though its purpose is to force the Pullman company to consent to an arbitration of the Pullman strike, its manifestation will be nothing more or less than a fight with the railways in which the Pullman company will take no part.

The railway lines have already been told through the press that they must haul no Pullman cars in their trains. They have accepted the implied challenge and yesterday their representatives in joint meeting voted to stand together as one and resist the union's demand. Their contracts with the Pullman company . . . impose a penalty for failure to haul the Pullman cars and they will certainly haul them, say the managers. Representative men among them declare the boycott will amount to but little. . . . George M. Pullman yesterday made a statement of his company's position. It contained no offer to arbitrate the strike.

6   *Chicago Times,* June 26, 1894, page one

UNITED TO FIGHT

Railway Managers Arrayed Against the A.R.U.

In the big fight which will open between the Pullman Palace Car company and the American Railway union at noon today, Mr. Pullman will have the concerted aid of all the railroad companies which use his cars. At a meeting of the board of general managers of the railroads running into Chicago, the following resolutions were adopted:

"... That it is the sense of this meeting that the said proposed boycott, being confessedly not in the interest of any employees of said railroad companies, or on account of any grievance between said railroad companies and said employees, is unjustifiable and unwarranted. ... That we hereby declare it to be the lawful right and duty of the said railway companies to protest against said proposed boycott; to resist the same in the interest of their existing contracts and for the benefit of the traveling public, and that we will act unitedly toward that end."

THIRD DAY OF THE NATIONAL RAILWAY BOYCOTT

7   *Chicago Tribune,* June 28, 1894, page one

DEBS IS A DICTATOR

His Warfare on the Railroads is Waged Effectively

The American Railway Union became aggressive yesterday in its efforts to force a settlement between Mr. Pullman and his striking employees. By calling out their switchmen, it threw down the gauntlet to the Erie, Grand Trunk, Monon, Eastern Illinois, Northern Pacific, Wisconsin Central, Chicago Great Western, Baltimore and Ohio, Pan-Handle, and Santa Fe railroads. It continued the warfare commenced the night before against the Illinois Central and continued it so successfully that the road had to abandon its suburban service at 9 o'clock. Its freight service was at a standstill all day and the same is practically true of other roads. In no case, however, did the strikers prevent the departure of any regular passenger trains from Chicago. ...

Debs' master stroke, however, occurred at midnight, when every employee on the Santa Fe belonging to the American Railway Union was ordered out. ... Whether the men will obey the mandate will be learned today. ...

So far no marked violence has been attempted. Two hundred policemen put in the day in various railroad yards, but their services were not needed. Chief Brennan says he has 2,000 men who can be massed at any point inside of an hour.

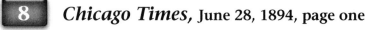

8   *Chicago Times,* June 28, 1894, page one

NOT A WHEEL TURNS IN THE WEST

**Complete Shutdown of All Roads in the Territory Beyond
the Missouri River**

Chicago Center of Eastern Trouble

It May Be the Biggest Tie-Up in All History

All the western half of the United States has begun to feel the paralysis of the
American Railway Union's boycott of Pullman. From the Missouri River to the
Pacific Coast, from the Canadian to the Mexican line, there is scarcely a railway
that has not been gripped by the boycott. At every important division point in
the west, southwest, and northwest, there are trains blockaded because the
American Railway Union men will not run them with Pullman cars attached
and the railway managers will not allow them to run otherwise. Some roads are
absolutely and utterly blockaded, others feel the embargo slightly yet, but it
grows in strength with every hour. It is spreading eastward from Chicago, too.
No man can tell what the end will be. . . . This is the end of the second day.
This, when so far the American Railway Union has done little beyond ordering
the withdrawal of switching crews, switch tenders, and towermen. By tomorrow, they promise that all conductors, engineers and firemen on freight and
passenger trains will join in the strike and then, well, nobody can tell.

General Manager Ainsley of the Wisconsin Central notified his men that
unless they go to work today he will supply their places with nonunion men.
Then there may be trouble. . . .

The six o'clock train on the Great Western started out with two Pullman
sleepers and one Pullman diner. It ran about two car lengths. The conductor
rang the bell, the train stopped, the whole crew got down and cut off those
three cars. This with a squad of policemen standing by and the company's officials looking on. The train pulled out without the Pullmans. It was the most decisive thing the boycotters have done yet.

SIXTH DAY OF THE NATIONAL RAILWAY BOYCOTT

9 *Chicago Tribune,* July 1, 1894, page one

MOBS BENT ON RUIN

Debs' Strikers Begin a Work of Destruction

Men Who Attempt to Work are Terrorized and Beaten

Dictator After the Managers

Continued and menacing lawlessness marked the progress yesterday of Dictator Debs and those who obey his orders in their efforts at coercing the railroads of the country into obeying the mandates of the American Railway Union. The Rock Island was the chief sufferer from the mob spirit which broke loose the moment its men struck. It was as much as a man's life was worth to endeavor to operate a train on that road to transact the business of the company, and at 6:20 o'clock the culmination was reached by the deliberate wrecking of a passenger train at Blue Island.[1] A striker named Murvin rushed to a switch over which an officer was standing guard, pushed him aside, threw the switch, and derailed the train. Strange to say, he was arrested. Fortunately, none of the passengers was hurt, but unfortunately for the road the cars were thrown across the track in such positions that they effectively blocked traffic. At 10 o'clock the officials threw up their hands and discontinued service for the night. At Blue Island, anarchy reigned. The Mayor and police force of that town could do nothing to repress the riotous strikers and they did their own sweet will. . . .

On the Illinois Central it was the same old story of destruction of the company's property without interference from the police. . . . Dictator Debs was as blatant as ever yesterday. He asserted . . . that the fight against Pullman was now a thing of the past. He is waging his warfare against the General Managers, who had committed the sin of combining against him.

---

[1] Blue Island was a close-knit community sixteen miles southwest of downtown Chicago. Many of the town's residents worked in local railway freight yards.

10   *Chicago Times,* July 1, 1894, page one

ONE IS DERAILED

Rock Island Engine Runs Off at Blue Island

It Almost Brings on a Riot

Rock Island train No. 19 for Kansas City and St. Paul was partly derailed at Blue Island at 6:30 o'clock last night. The switch was thrown by James Mervin,[1] a switchman, and the heavy engine and tender left the rails and stuck fast in the mud, completely blocking the track. The train fortunately did not go over the embankment. It was well filled with passengers. . . .

Mervin was arrested by Deputy Sheriff Leibrandt and will be brought to Chicago for examination.

The train was a mixed train and was composed of three Pullmans . . . and ran along without interference until it reached the crossover switch at the west end of the Blue Island yard. There were some fifty strikers standing in the pouring rain on the right of the track just at the switch. The front wheels passed over them, there was a lurch, and the powerful engine careened to the left. . . . Several passengers who were standing on the platform were violently thrown to the ground, and some of them bruised besides being bespattered with mud. The wildest consternation ensued among them. . . . For a few minutes it looked as if a bloody conflict would follow. All was excitement, but added to the demand of the deputies for the crowd to stand back came a similar demand from several of the American Railway Union to let the law take its course. . . .

Mayor John Zacharias rushed down . . . in the drenching rain in his shirt sleeves. The prisoner shook him by the hand, and it was not until then that anyone seemed to know who the prisoner was. His name is James Mervin, aged 32 years, a switchman, and has been employed in the Rock Island yards at Blue Island. Mervin seemed to have hosts of friends [who] demanded bail, and the mayor fixed it at $5,000. . . . scores of Mervin's friends proffered the small fortunes for the bond, but up to the latest hour they had not been able to subscribe the requisite amount. Mervin . . . denies, and his friends who were standing by him deny, that he touched the switch.

[1] The *Tribune* spelled the arrested man's name "Murvin"; the *Times* spelled it "Mervin."

FEDERAL TROOPS HAD BEEN IN CHICAGO FOR THREE DAYS

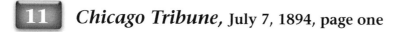

11   *Chicago Tribune,* July 7, 1894, page one

YARDS FIRE SWEPT

Hundreds of Freight Cars, Loaded and Empty, Burn

Rioters Prevent Firemen from Saving the Property.

From Brighton Park to Sixty-first street the yards of the Pan-Handle road were last night put to the torch by the rioters. Between 600 and 700 freight cars have been destroyed, many of them loaded. Miles and miles of costly track are in a snarled tangle of heat-twisted rails. Not less than $750,000—possibly a whole $1,000,000 of property—has been sacrificed to the caprice of a mob of drunken Anarchists and rebels. That is the record of the night's work by the Debs strikers in the Stock-Yards District.

They started early in the afternoon. . . . They were done by 10 o'clock; at that hour they had a roaring wall of fire down the tracks. . . . The flames of their kindling reddened the southwestern sky so that the whole city could know they were at work.

This work the rioters did calmly and systematically. They seemed to work with a deliberate plan. There was none of the wild howlings and ravings that marked their work of the night before.

12   *Chicago Times,* July 7, 1894, page one

MEN NOT AWED BY SOLDIERS

MOST OF THE ROADS AT A STANDSTILL

Railway Union Is Confident of Winning Against Armed Capital

Despite the presence of United States troops and the mobilization of five regiments of state militia, despite threats of martial law and total extermination of the strikers by bullet and bayonet, the great strike inaugurated by the American Railway Union holds three-fourths of the roads running out of Chicago in its strong fetters, and last night traffic was more fully paralyzed than at any time since the inception of the tie-up. . . . With the exception of an occasional car or two moved by the aid of the military, not a wheel is turning. . . .

In the southwest section of the city all railroad property is considered fair game for the attack of the mob. Apparently the police of this district think so, too, for they stand by and appear indifferent to the annihilation of property. Wholesale destruction by incendiarism yesterday succeeded to the train wrecking of the day previous. . . . Nothing pertaining to the railroads seems sacred to the crowd. A splendid new towerhouse, which operates the Pan-Handle's intricate interlocking switches . . . was only spared yesterday through the efforts of a party of striking tower operators of the railroad. . . . The strikers saw there was danger of the fire spreading from a burning toolhouse nearby, a plank walk connecting the two. They tore this sidewalk up and thus saved the towerhouse. . . .

If the soldiers are sent to this district, bloodshed and perhaps death will follow today, for this is the most lawless element in the city, as is shown by their riotous work yesterday. . . . But the perpetrators are not American Railway Union men. The people engaged in this outrageous work of destruction are not strikers, most of them are not even grown men. The persons who set the fires yesterday on the authority of the firemen and police are young hoodlums. . . . The setting fire to the cars yesterday was done openly where anyone could see it and when the slightest effort would have resulted in the apprehension of the guilty ones, but no such effort was made. The firemen were overwhelmed with the work of attending to a dozen different fires and could not, and the police on the scene apparently didn't care to or would not make arrests. . . . At six o'-clock, the police had not a single prisoner.

THE STRIKE DRAWS TO A CLOSE

On July 10, Debs and other ARU officers had been arrested for violating the federal court injunction of July 2 constraining ARU activity. They were held for several hours until posting $10,000 bail.

13   *Chicago Tribune*, July 15, 1894, page one

WITH A DULL THUD

The Strike Collapses with Wonderful Rapidity

DEBS' WILD ASSERTIONS

He is Still Defiant While His "Union" Crumbles About Him

Like the last flicker of a candle that is almost burned out is the "war to the knife" defiance hurled yesterday by Eugene V. Debs in the face of the railroad managers of Chicago. Deserted by the men who answered his first calls for help, denounced by many who followed his banner of revolt only to lose their positions . . .

with the very fabric of the American Railway Union falling upon his head and the support on which he stood slipping rapidly from under his feet, he declared that the strike was "on and would be fought to a successful issue."

The value of Mr. Debs' utterances at this stage of the game are shown conclusively by comparing threats and assertions he made yesterday . . . with the condition of affairs last night. . . . "The Northwestern will not be turning a wheel tonight," said Mr. Debs. At midnight not a wheel on the Northwestern had failed to turn. The Northwestern people are inclined to look upon Mr. Debs' declaration as a huge joke. . . . And so it was on the Chicago, Milwaukee and St. Paul, which, according to Debs, was to suffer the same fate as the Northwestern. The officials of the road regard his threats with derision.

14 *Chicago Times*, July 15, 1894, page one

DEBS SURE HE CAN WIN

Says the Battle is But Begun

More than 1,000 railroad men held an enthusiastic meeting at Uhlich's hall yesterday afternoon, the speakers being President Debs and Vice-President Howard.

President Debs then told the men that the situation was more favorable than it had been at any time since the men were called out. He said that telegrams from twenty-five points west of the Mississippi showed that the roads were completely tied up. . . . "I cannot stop now that defiance has been flung in our teeth by the General Managers' Association. I propose to work harder than ever and teach a lesson to those bigoted idiots. . . . The managers refuse to treat for peace. They say war to the end, and yet the law does not send them to jail. The law seems to be against us . . . but if the law makes it a crime to advise your men against the encroachments of capital by all the gods united I will rot in jail. . . .

"There are men who have returned to their work, but they are traitors. . . . We are better without them. Let them range themselves on the other side and we can then close up ranks and see where we stand. We must unite as strong as iron, but let us be peaceable in this contest. Bloodshed is unwarranted and will not win. It is not by blood that we want to win."

Analyzing the Source

REFLECTING ON THE SOURCE

1. Reviewing the evidence of factual claims you recorded in the table on page 58, where do you find enough agreement in the two newspapers' accounts to feel confident that you could corroborate specific events in the strike?

2. Reviewing your table's evidence of editorializing, do you find more evidence of bias in the basic word choice in the headlines and stories or in the different stories' overall emphases?

3. The two newspapers pointed to very different perpetrators when reporting on the strike's violence and arson. Which newspaper did you find more plausible on this point and why? How would you go about verifying whether strikers or hoodlums were responsible for the destruction?

MAKING CONNECTIONS

4. The Pullman strike can be told as a story of conflict between George Pullman and his workers or as a conflict between the General Managers' Association and the American Railway Union. But as you have observed, it can also be treated as a conflict between the *Chicago Tribune* and the *Chicago Times*. Using the news stories you have here, how would you describe the philosophical differences separating the two newspapers? How do those differences reflect the larger conflicts in the strike?

5. There is an air of crisis in the Pullman strike coverage in both newspapers. Given the context of the strike—rapid urbanization and industrialization as well as sudden economic depression—what deep fears did the *Tribune* convey to its readers? What fears did the *Times* transmit? How might these fears, appearing in the press, have influenced the course of the strike?

Beyond the Source

In the aftermath of the Pullman strike, the *Times* and the *Tribune* offered predictably different coverage of the single most surprising outcome of the whole event: the report issued by the presidentially appointed U.S. Strike Commission in mid-November 1894, just four months after the strike collapsed. This detailed government report, written by three well-respected men of America's ruling elite, was read with shock by both supporters and opponents of the strike because it was far more favorable to labor and far more critical of employers than anyone expected.

After interviewing 111 witnesses, the three commissioners criticized the ARU for tying up the nation's rail system over a local factory dispute, but it basically blamed the strike on George Pullman's stubborn refusal to negotiate with his workers. It then praised the Pullman workers for their "dignified, manly and conservative conduct" throughout the strike and, finally, and most unexpectedly, it rendered a very harsh judgement of the General Managers' Association for its "arrogant and absurd" claim to the right to collectively set wages and working conditions across the railway industry while denying workers the right to organize as a competitive body.

The *Chicago Times* headlined its November 13 story on the commission report, "All in Labor's Favor." That same day, the *Tribune* declared, "Report is a

Roast." The *Times* characterized the report as a "stroke on behalf of justice" and reprinted the report's argument that Pullman should have cut salaries, rents, and profits more—and wages less—in order to more fairly distribute the pain of the depression. The *Times* skipped over the commissioners' critique of the ARU for getting involved in the strike in the first place, focusing instead on their finding that the union was not responsible for the "disgraceful" violence in July. Not surprisingly, the *Times* applauded the commission's "bitter condemnation" of the "all-powerful" GMA.

In its editorial on the U.S. Strike Commission report, the *Tribune* called the dismissal of ARU responsibility for violence a "wild assertion." Focusing on George Pullman as one bad apple in the capitalist bin, the *Tribune* scoffed at the commission's "caustic view" of the GMA. So while the paper endorsed the commission's criticism of Pullman's stubbornness, it did not comment on the commission's more threatening notions that the employer should have distributed depression profits differently or that the GMA should allow unions. Instead, the *Tribune* chose to reprint an article from *Harper's Weekly* that fumed over the commissioners' "astonishing" radicalism and asked, "What is the state of mind of men who sign such a report?"

The U.S. Strike Commission's most historically significant recommendations were that unions be legitimized by government policy and that the government set up a system for labor arbitration in order to avoid "barbarous" and costly strikes in the future. The *Times* claimed that such ideas "may serve organized labor for a charter and a creed," but the *Tribune* was curiously quiet on the subject of these far-reaching policy recommendations. *Tribune* readers were left with only the reprint of the *Harper's Weekly* article, which warned that the commissioners' views were "the first stage in a socialistic revolution" and the end of "civilized society."

Six months later, the *Tribune* took solace in the Supreme Court judgment that Eugene Debs was guilty of violating a legitimate federal injunction and expressed pleasure that "Dictator Debs" would be spending six months in jail. As it turned out, however, Debs' sentence was less predictive of labor's future than the commission report. It would take forty years, until the New Deal of the 1930s, before the government fully implemented the report's recommendations for labor arbitration. But the Pullman strike—and the report that emanated from it—marked a significant shift in public support for government as a strike mediator, not a strike breaker.

Finding and Supplementing the Source

The 1894 issues of the *Chicago Tribune* and *Chicago Times* used for this chapter were accessed on reels of microfilm. Despite the availability of modern newspaper articles online, newspaper publishers are not storing entire issues digitally, so it is doubtful that historians in the future will be able to access today's newspapers electronically. Instead, there is a major effort being coordinated by the United States Newspaper Program (USNP) to "locate, catalog, and preserve on microfilm all newspapers published in the United States from the eighteenth century to the present." The existence of the USNP testifies to the importance that researchers and librarians attach to newspapers as a record of American society. Thanks to the USNP, a future researcher who is seeking a particular newspaper from a particular day will not be told that the newspaper he or she needs was never preserved and has literally disintegrated into the dustbin of history. This microfilming program means that researchers tomorrow, like researchers today, will read old newspapers on microfilm or microfiche. For more information on the USNP, see the program Web site at **neh.gov/ projects/usnp.html**. Public and university libraries can inform you of the availability of a newspaper you want to borrow on microfilm through interlibrary loan.

There are two classic works on the Pullman strike: Almont Lindsey's *The Pullman Strike: The Story of a Unique Experiment and a Great Labor Upheaval* (Chicago: University of Chicago Press, 1942) is an informative but very partisan defense of the Pullman workers and the American Railway Union, while Stanley Buder's *Pullman: An Experiment in Industrial Order and Community Planning, 1880–1930* (New York: Oxford University Press, 1967) is less lively but more balanced. More recent perspectives on the strike are available in *The Pullman Strike and the Crisis of the 1890s: Essays on Labor and Politics* (Urbana: University of Illinois Press, 1999), a collection of essays edited by Richard Schneirov et al. Two studies connecting the Pullman strike to popular urban culture in the 1890s are to be found in *Urban Disorder and the Shape of Belief: The Great Chicago Fire, the Haymarket Bomb, and the Model Town of Pullman* by Carl Smith (Chicago: University of Chicago Press, 1995) and *Perfect Cities: Chicago's Utopias of 1893* by James Gilbert (Chicago: University of Chicago Press, 1991). David Ray Papke provides a concise overview of the strike and clear discussion of the legal aspects of the event in *The Pullman Case: The Clash of Labor and Capital in Industrial America* (Lawrence: University Press of Kansas, 1999).

The history of newspapers includes very general and very particular studies. Among the general studies, *Discovering the News: A Social History of American Newspapers* by Michael Schudson (New York: Basic Books, 1978) offers an interesting discussion of "objectivity" in news reporting. For the newspapers and events related to the Pullman strike, see David Paul Nord, *Newspapers and New Politics: Midwestern Municipal Reform, 1890–1900* (Ann Arbor: University of Michigan Press, 1979), and *Communities of Journalism: A History of American Newspapers and Their Readers* (Urbana: University of Illinois Press, 2001).

CHAPTER 4

Immigrant to the Promised Land

Memory and Autobiography

When Hilda Satt thought back on her childhood in Wloclawek, Poland, she remembered Sabbath dinners in the family dining room, golden noodle soups, apple puddings, aromatic spices, holiday wines, copper pots, silver trays, and shiny brass candlesticks. Alongside those sweet memories lay Hilda's bitter recollections of persecution by the Russian officials who controlled Wloclawek, a city of some fifty thousand people located about ninety miles northwest of Warsaw. Wloclawek lay within the sizable territory between the Baltic Sea and the Black Sea known as the "Pale of Settlement." There, the ruling Russian government confined all of Russia's five million Jews and enforced a system of discrimination that fueled Christian residents' superstitions about Jewish life and faith.

Hilda's childhood in Wloclawek coincided with an especially harsh era in Russian treatment of Jews. After 1881, new legal restrictions on Jews' religious and economic life, coupled with violent attacks, known as pogroms, served to impoverish and terrorize Jewish communities within the Pale. The Satt family occupied a fortunate place among the ten thousand Jews living in Wloclawek because Hilda's father, Louis Satt, was a skilled artisan, a tombstone carver. "And since people died fairly regularly," Hilda later recalled in her autobiography, "and since their families felt a deep responsibility to mark every grave of a departed relative, Father was kept busy and earned considerable sums of money. In short, we were not poor" (Hilda Satt Polacheck, *I Came a Stranger: The Story of a Hull-House Girl,* ed. Dena Polacheck Epstein [Urbana: University of Illinois Press, 1989], 6).

Even though he owned a relatively spacious home and his own workshop, and though his wife, Dena, employed a cook and a nursemaid to help with their three sons and three daughters, still Louis Satt feared the possible effects of Russian oppression and economic depression on his family's future. So in 1891, Louis Satt set forth by himself to establish a new home in America. Connections with a *landsmann* (fellow countryman) took him to Chicago, where a population of almost fifty thousand eastern European Jews created a demand for tombstones with Hebrew, Yiddish, Polish, Russian, and German inscriptions. Within a year of his arrival in Chicago, Louis Satt's skills enabled him to open his own shop, to finance his family's trip to America, and to furnish a six-room flat in the heart of Chicago's Russian Jewish neighborhood. Hilda and her siblings were enrolled in the Jewish Training School nearby, and though Dena no longer had household servants, the Satts' future in America looked prosperous.

That picture changed overnight in 1894 when Hilda's father died. Dena moved the family into cheaper housing and tried to support her six children by working as a street peddler. Hilda later looked back on her widowed mother's fear "of hunger and cold, not so much for herself as for the rest of us. Food, coal, clothing, and shelter had become her only interests in life" (ibid., 60). Before Hilda reached the legal working age of fourteen, she left school and went to work with her older sister in a knitting factory. Four years later, she moved to a factory that manufactured ladies' "shirtwaist" dresses,[1] where she was paid according to the number of cuffs she could sew while sitting at a machine from eight in the morning until six at night. Until she discovered the evening classes and social clubs at the Hull-House settlement, a community center in her neighborhood, Hilda had little to break the "deadly monotony" of "a life that offered only food and warmth and shelter" (ibid., 60).

The hardships Hilda Satt faced as an immigrant to the United States in the 1890s have a familiar ring to them. The popular version of the immigrant experience in America is captured in the Statue of Liberty's poetic plea:

> Give me your tired, your poor,
> your huddled masses, yearning to breathe free,
> The wretched refuse of your teeming shore.
> Send these, the homeless, the tempest-tost to me,
> I lift my lamp beside the golden door!

But this well-intentioned picture of human misery, crafted by the immigrant poet Emma Lazarus in 1883 and added on a plaque at the base of the Statue in 1903, obscures the fact that most immigrants to America have not been the poor, wretched refuse of the world. They have often been people like the Satts, who possessed some resources in their homeland and made a careful, rational

---

[1] A shirtwaist was a woman's blouse with pleats in the front to resemble a man's dress shirt with buttons in the back. A shirtwaist dress combined that blouse style with a long, dark skirt. This style became popular as young women moved into sales and office jobs.

calculation that they could increase those resources for the family's benefit by moving to the United States. In the best of times and certainly in the worst of times—times of pogroms and famine—the poorest, most wretched people in nineteenth-century Europe lacked the means necessary for escape. Funds were needed to obtain passports or to bribe government officials at various borders, and even more funds were required for ship tickets, for travel expenses, for train travel beyond their U.S. port of entry, and for setting up accommodations in a new abode. We need not deny the terrible economic and political pressures that immigrants faced in their homelands (and in the United States) in order to grasp that the people who responded to those pressures by moving across the ocean to a strange land were the ones with skills, family backing, some resources, or a unique store of energy.

Hilda Satt's family is representative of many of the Jewish immigrants who came to America in the great wave of immigration that the United States experienced between 1880 and 1920. The vast majority of the Jews who arrived in these decades were from eastern Europe and defined themselves ethnically as Yiddish-speaking "Jews," rather than nationally as Russians or Poles or Lithuanians. Fathers often immigrated first, but Jews typically settled as family groups planning to stay permanently, not as individual workers planning to return home. They tended to be workers with urban skills or trades rather than farmers (since Jews were not allowed to own land in much of eastern Europe) or professionals, and they felt simultaneously pushed out of Europe by persecution and poverty and pulled to America by opportunity and optimism. For example, in 1891, the year Louis Satt came to the United States, there were rumors of impending new persecutions of Jews and, in response, immigration of eastern European Jews to America doubled. Just three years later, however, when an economic depression made jobs scarce in the United States, emigration of Jews from the still-oppressive Pale of Settlement declined. This tells us that Europe's "teeming masses" did not rush blindly to the United States in the late nineteenth century; they came when the balance of push and pull in their particular families made emigration to America a sensible, if risky, venture.

Hilda Satt's experience in Chicago also illustrates significant features of life for urban, working-class immigrant families. Her father's death produced the economic adversity common to many households in which parents, especially widows, could not earn enough for survival, and adolescents, even children, had to take low-paying, back-breaking factory jobs. Hilda's story is also a reminder that immigrants had to do more than merely survive the journey, the oppressive labor, the dirty streets, the filthy housing, the strange language, the new laws, the alien neighbors, and the unfamiliar shopkeepers. Hilda Satt, like every immigrant to the United States, had to shape a new identity that reconciled her homeland culture with her American experience. Some immigrants achieved this by joining labor unions, some by affiliating closely with ethnic societies or with ethnic synagogues or churches, still others by focusing on business or politics. Hilda's way of forging an American identity out of her roots as a middle-class Polish Jew was through education, a route she was able to pursue because of Hull-House, the settlement house in her Chicago neighborhood.

Hull-House, which opened its doors in 1889, was the second settlement house established in the United States. By 1900, there would be four hundred of these privately funded community centers in American cities. Hull-House was staffed by native-born, middle-class volunteer "residents" who lived at the settlement and dedicated themselves to providing education and recreation for their immigrant, working-class "neighbors." Hull-House was unique among settlements in the breadth and depth of its offerings; in its commitment to democratic reform on behalf of the poor, immigrants, and workers; and in its firm but delicate guidance under the hand of Jane Addams, the settlement's "head resident."

Hilda Satt Polacheck subtitled her memoir "The Story of a Hull-House Girl" because her decade there as a student, club member, and teacher shaped her future life in America. In fact, Hull-House influenced the lives of thousands of immigrant and working-class families in the neighborhood surrounding it at Halsted and Polk streets on Chicago's industrial west side. By the time Hilda became a regular at Hull-House, the settlement had expanded far beyond its original old wood mansion to include a dozen brick buildings circling a square block, with a playground in the center. It appealed to those neighbors who sought secular activities and wanted to learn English, read history and literature, or argue about politics. So, too, it attracted those looking for music lessons, dance classes, dramatic productions, a pottery workshop, a sewing machine, a basketball court, a daycare center—or just a hot bath. Every week at Hull-House, young Hilda Satt rubbed shoulders with literally thousands of her neighbors who had come to the settlement for a class or game, a debate or rehearsal, a club or a dance.

Satt's memoir is one of the few surviving ethnic testimonies of life at Hull-House. Her voice supports the claims made by volunteers that Hull-House offered immigrants an alternative to the disdain and exploitation they met elsewhere in Chicago. Her stories suggest that the settlement affirmed the status that she and other immigrants had enjoyed back home, reminded them of why they had come to America in the first place, and provided them with the practical tools they needed to achieve their economic, political, and cultural goals.

Using Autobiographies as a Source

"Autobiography" and "memoir" are twin terms referring to life stories written by the people who lived them. For readers who want their history up close and personal, there is something very attractive about memoirs. They seem unfiltered, untouched by an expert, unmediated by authorities. Whether discovered as yellowed sheets of paper in a box buried in the attic or cleanly bound between covers in a library, memoirs often appear to be the most authentic and transparent form of history.

Hilda Satt Polacheck's 170-page memoir, *I Came a Stranger: The Story of a Hull-House Girl,* is just the sort of engaging life story that readers turn to for an immediate sense of history. It is also a text that invites some consideration of the challenges autobiography poses as a historical source.

Advantages and Disadvantages of Working with Autobiographies

It is easy to understand why historians, like general readers, are drawn to autobiographies. The primary advantage of autobiographies is that they offer us unique access to the "feel" of a place and a time; they provide sounds, smells, tastes, attitudes, and emotions that only eyewitnesses can recall, and they often testify to the quality of relationships that we can only infer from a distance. For example, historians have long debated about whether the native-born, middle-class residents of Hull-House were patronizing toward their immigrant, working-class neighbors. Polacheck's eyewitness testimony does not end this debate, but the publication of her memoir in 1989 offers support to those who argue that Hull-House was more egalitarian than patronizing. After all, Polacheck was there, and Polacheck's memoir states that the settlement residents treated their neighbors with dignity and respect.

Autobiographies, however, are not without their disadvantages, and one must exercise caution when turning to a memoir as a historical source. If historians wanted to draw upon *I Came a Stranger* as a primary source of information about interactions at Hull-House, they would have to keep three basic principles in mind: first, human memory is a complex tool for retrieval, so we cannot presume that an individual's life stories provide an unfiltered image of the past; second, the overall emotional message conveyed by a memoir is often more reliable than the specific events recounted; and, third, independent information about a memoirist's life is valuable for corroborating autobiographical claims.

Historians have learned from cognitive psychologists that our memories are not stored in our minds like perfect reels of film. Instead, our minds hold, lose, regain, and reshape pieces of the incomplete puzzle that is our past. Typically, autobiographers arrange the puzzle pieces of their memory (and imagine the missing pieces) according to their current beliefs about what happened in the past. Those beliefs, and the stories that arise from them, have been shaped by intervening experiences and by the philosophical message that the autobiographer wishes to convey to the reader. Every autobiographer writes to convey some message, and that aim—not pure, unadulterated memory—shapes the memoir.

Hilda Satt Polacheck wrote her autobiography in the 1950s, when she was a widow in her early seventies. It was based "principally on her memory" because, as her daughter Dena Epstein explains, Polacheck "had no diary" (Polacheck 179). While some memoirists conduct their own historical research and consult piles of scrapbooks, letters, and personal artifacts to buttress their recollections, most, like Hilda Satt Polacheck, rely solely on memory. Any historian wishing to draw on Polacheck's autobiography as evidence of life at

Hull-House would have to treat it as a product of memory, not as a reel of documentary film. Thus, the historian could accurately report that Polacheck carried with her into her seventies a powerful memory of being treated at the settlement with unconditional positive regard. That same historian might not be able to affirm the accuracy of every story she tells in her memoir to illustrate this positive treatment, nor could that historian use Polacheck's experience to generalize about every settlement neighbor's experience. But the overall message in her memoir could be used as evidence that it was quite possible for a Jewish immigrant girl to have rewarding encounters at Hull-House at the turn of the last century.

Beyond that, the historian can seek out independent information on Polacheck's life to corroborate or put into historical context her sunny depiction of interactions at Hull-House. For example, we can verify independently that Hilda Polacheck was a democratic socialist throughout her life, and was, therefore, not inclined to defer to the rich and powerful. One historian might point to this information as proof that Polacheck's happy memories of egalitarian treatment at Hull-House were accurate; her socialist stance would have led her to criticize a settlement house that was elitist. But another historian might wonder if Polacheck filtered out of her memory or deliberately omitted from her memoir any patronizing scenes she witnessed at Hull-House simply because, for her, the settlement paved the way to a good life.

The many questions a historian can raise about a memoir do not invalidate memoirs as valuable sources of historical knowledge; they simply remind us to be cautious about what we conclude from them and encourage us to do as much independent research as possible to corroborate and contextualize a memoir.

In the case of Hilda Polacheck, the historian who conducted the independent research was her daughter, Dena Polacheck Epstein. Years after Hilda died in 1967, Epstein retrieved eight different, incomplete, handwritten versions of her mother's life story and set about trying to compile the most accurate version. Epstein sought independent documentation for every story in the memoir by checking old city directories, Chicago newspapers, Hull-House records, school records, and letters between Hilda and her husband, William Polacheck. She had to do detective work just to determine her mother's birthdate; some of Hilda's recollections indicated she was born in 1887, others pointed to 1888, and still others to 1889. It was the letters, combined with her mother's enrollment records at the Jewish Training School and the University of Chicago, that convinced Epstein that Hilda Satt was actually born in 1882.

So what? How does a trivial fact like birthdate contribute to our understanding of the memoir? Knowing that Hilda was born in 1882 tells us that she was fifteen years old in early 1898, and we know from her memoir and additional records that she had left school by that age and gone to work in the knitting factory. That independent knowledge casts a curious light on this passage from the memoir, where Hilda recalled the Spanish-American War:

Implies she was in school in 1898

What is her message?

In February 1898 I began to realize that America was at war. . . . now the children came to school wearing huge buttons pinned to their dresses and coats with the words "Remember the Maine; to hell with Spain." . . . That button bothered me. Why did I have to be profane to be patriotic? One day I asked Mrs. Torrance why she had told us not to use the word "hell" and then allowed us to wear the button with the word on it. I was told that in time of war things were different. I accepted her explanation, but I felt that I was giving up a certain decency on account of the war. (Polacheck 47)

How is she depicting war supporters?

Records show that she was Hilda's *first* teacher in Chicago

Since we know that Hilda Satt was not a schoolchild in Mrs. Torrance's room in 1898, and since Epstein tells us that her detective work turned up very few inaccuracies in Hilda's story, we could simply dismiss this bit of autobiographical fiction as a bizarre fluke. But most historians would want to combine this tale about the Spanish-American War with existing knowledge of Polacheck's life to strengthen our understanding of her motives in writing her memoir because it is often the case that inaccuracies in a memoir reveal larger truths about the author and the author's purpose.

Consider the fact that Polacheck concocted this uncharacteristically false story on a particular subject: war. Combine that with the fact that, throughout her autobiography, Polacheck explicitly aligned herself with Jane Addams's philosophy of antimilitarism, and throughout her adult life Polacheck was active in the Women's International League for Peace and Freedom, the organization Addams founded in protest against World War I. By taking into account Polacheck's peace activism, we can see her phony Spanish-American War story as quite "true" to the memoir's political purpose if not Polacheck's actual childhood experience. Remembering, too, that she wrote this memoir in the early 1950s, during the military buildup of the cold war, we can appreciate her sly invention of an innocent schoolgirl's voice to express antiwar views. This was just the sort of disarming rhetorical strategy that she might have learned from her mentor, Jane Addams, at Hull-House.

As you read through the excerpt from *I Came a Stranger: The Story of a Hull-House Girl,* keep in mind that memoirs are not transparent, unfiltered accounts of the past; they are complex constructions of memory and meaning. They can be enormously useful to historians in recreating the past, but they must be handled with care. Take note of those claims that a historian like Dena Polacheck Epstein could independently verify—enrollment at the University of Chicago, classes taken and taught at Hull-House, paid jobs in the city—and imagine the legwork involved in such corroboration. Consider, as well, the claims that cannot be verified, the reports of conversations held or feelings experienced. Where, for you, is the "truth" in such memories? What light do they shed on the values and ambitions of a seventy-year-old woman writing in the 1950s, and what do they tell us about that young Jewish immigrant she was remembering?

Working with the Source

1. As you read the excerpts from Hilda Polacheck's autobiography, make a list of specific examples of how immigrant neighbors were treated at Hull-House. When you are done reading, circle those items on your list that you feel a historian could use as strong evidence of good treatment at the settlement. What is the difference between the items you circled and those items on the list that you did not regard as equally strong?

2. Hilda Polacheck refers often in her memoir to her love of America. Keep track of those features of American life that she extols. How does her particular embrace of America fit with her socialist politics?

The Source: *I Came a Stranger: The Story of a Hull-House Girl* by Hilda Satt Polacheck

1   *I Discover Hull-House*

Several days before Christmas 1896 one of my Irish playmates suggested that I go with her to a Christmas party at Hull-House. I told her that I never went to Christmas parties.

"Why not?" she asked.

"I do not go anywhere on Christmas Day," I said.

"But this party will not be on Christmas Day. It will be the Sunday before Christmas Day," she said.

I repeated that I could not go and she persisted in wanting to know why. Before I could think, I blurted out the words: "I might get killed."

"Get killed!" She stared at me. "I go to Hull-House Christmas parties every year, and no one was ever killed."

I then asked her if there would be any Jewish children at the party. She assured me that there had been Jewish children at the parties every year and that no one was ever hurt.

The thought began to percolate through my head that things might be different in America. In Poland it had not been safe for Jewish children to be on the streets on Christmas. I struggled with my conscience and finally decided to accompany my friend to the Hull-House Christmas party. . . .

My friend and I arrived at Hull-House and went to the coffee shop where the party was being held. There were many children and their parents seated when we arrived. It was the first time that I had sat in a room where there was

Source: I Came a Stranger: The Story of a Hull-House Girl by Hilda Satt Polacheck, edited by Dena Polacheck Epstein (Urbana: University of Illinois Press, 1989).

a Christmas tree. In fact, there were two trees in the room: one on each side of the high brick fireplace. The trees looked as if they had just been brought in from a heavy snowstorm. The glistening glass icicles and asbestos snow looked very real. The trees were lighted with white candles and on each side stood a man with a pail of water and a mop, ready to put out any accidental fire.

People called to each other across the room. Then I noticed that I could not understand what they were saying. It dawned on me that the people in this room had come from other countries. Yet there was no tension. Everybody seemed to be having a good time. There were children and parents at this party from Russia, Poland, Italy, Germany, Ireland, England, and many other lands, but no one seemed to care where they had come from, or what religion they professed, or what clothes they wore, or what they thought. As I sat there, I am sure I felt myself being freed from a variety of century-old superstitions and inhibitions. There seemed to be nothing to be afraid of.

Then Jane Addams came into the room! It was the first time that I looked into those kind, understanding eyes. There was a gleam of welcome in them that made me feel I was wanted. She told us that she was glad we had come. Her voice was warm and I knew she meant what she said. . . .

The children of the Hull-House Music School then sang some songs, that I later found out were called "Christmas carols." I shall never forget the caressing sweetness of those childish voices. All feelings of religious intolerance and bigotry faded. I could not connect this beautiful party with any hatred or superstition that existed among the people of Poland.

As I look back, I know that I became a staunch American at this party. I was with children who had been brought here from all over the world. The fathers and mothers, like my father and mother, had come in search of a free and happy life. And we were all having a good time at a party, as the guests of an American, Jane Addams.

We were all poor. Some of us were underfed. Some of us had holes in our shoes. But we were not afraid of each other. What greater service can a human being give to her country than to banish fear from the heart of a child? Jane Addams did that for me at that party. . . .

2   *The Oasis in the Desert*

Four years passed before Hilda returned to Hull-House because, once she began factory work, she was too tired in the evenings to go out. When she was seventeen, Hilda could no longer stand a life confined to sewing cuffs during the day and reading romance novels at night.

One evening in 1900, after a particularly boring day at the factory, I decided to walk over to Hull-House three blocks from where I lived. I had not been there since that eventful Christmas party.

This event marked the beginning of a new life for me. . . .

After a span of fifty years, I look back and realize how much of my leisure time was spent at Hull-House and how my life was molded by the influence of Jane Addams. I was not only hungry for books, music, and all the arts and crafts offered at Hull-House, but I was starved for the social stimulus of people my own age. All this was to be found at the house on Halsted and Polk streets. . . .

Hull-House was in the Nineteenth Ward of Chicago. The people of Hull-House were astounded to find that while the ward had 1/36th of the population of the city, it registered 1/6th of the deaths from typhoid fever. Miss Addams and Dr. Alice Hamilton launched an investigation that has become history in the health conditions of Chicago.

. . . Many of the pipes supplying drinking water were found to be defective, so the polluted sewage would seep into the drinking water, spreading the germs of typhoid fever. . . .

The bathing problem in the neighborhood was no small matter. I still recall the huge kettles of water being heated on the stove and the washtub being dragged into the kitchen for our weekly baths. But we did get scrubbed once a week. There were, however, many people in the neighborhood who did not have the stamina for carrying kettles of hot water. This led to a discussion of public baths, one day. One of our German neighbors was telling my mother that in Germany she would go to a public bath whenever she wanted a bath. By this time I had the feeling that Hull-House was a place from which "all blessings flow," and I asked somebody if there were any public baths there. I was told where the public bath was. I found out later that it was through the efforts of Jane Addams that this public bath had been established. . . .

Yes, Hull-House was an oasis in a desert of disease and monotony. And monotony can become a disease. The work at the factory, the making of cuffs, and more and more cuffs, had a dulling effect on all my senses. The only variation in this deadly monotony was that some days the cuffs would be blue and other days they would be green or pink or yellow. But the thought of going to Hull-House in the evening made the day's work bearable.

And then there was the possibility of seeing Jane Addams in action, a woman with that supreme faith that the world could be made into a better place for the whole human race. One evil condition after another was brought to the attention of city authorities, in a patient, simple, but resolute manner. The problems of the immigrants, who were to play a significant part in the pattern of American life, were brought to the surface, waking the conscience of Chicago. . . .

Jane Addams was never condescending to anyone. She never made one feel that she was a "lady bountiful." She never made one feel that she was doling out charity. When she did something for you, you felt she owed it to you or that she was making a loan that you could pay back. . . .

I remember Miss Addams stopping me one day and asking me if I had joined the dancing class. She thought I worked too hard and needed some fun. So I joined the dancing class and learned the waltz, two-step, and schottische. By this time I was able to pay the dollar that paid for ten lessons.

. . . We danced once a week in this carefree class, all winter. In June, the class closed for the summer with a gay cotillion, every bit as gay, if not as elaborate, as the ones staged today to introduce debutantes to society. No matter where the members of the dancing class came from, dingy hovels, overcrowded tenements, for that one night we were all living in a fairyland.

My sister and I next joined the gymnasium. We managed to scrape together enough money to buy the regulation gymnasium suit—wide bloomers and blouse—though if anyone could not afford the suit, she could attend anyway. Miss Rose Gyles was the teacher, and she put us through the paces once a week.

The gymnasium was like an oasis in a desert on Halsted Street. Hundreds of boys, who had no other means of recreation, could go to the gymnasium and play basketball till they were so worn out that they could only go home and go to bed.

One evening, as I entered the reception room, Miss Addams called me into the residents' sitting room and asked me to join a class in English composition. The class was just being organized and the instructor was to be Henry Porter Chandler, of the University of Chicago. Not many students had applied, and Miss Addams asked me to register for the class as she did not want Mr. Chandler to feel that people were not interested in such a class.

I told Miss Addams that I had never written anything. But she insisted, and so I went into the dining room where four or five people were gathered. She introduced me to Mr. Chandler. Mr. Chandler outlined a course of work. He asked us if we had ever written anything. Most of us had not. He then told us that there were certain kinds of writing, such as book reviews, short stories, arguments, criticisms, and some others. He asked each of us to write anything that we wanted and to bring it to the class the following week. He then dismissed the class.

Mr. Chandler was the secretary to William Rainey Harper, the first president of the University of Chicago, and an instructor in English composition.

I could not sleep that night. Why was it that he did not tell us how to write? How could a person just write? Then the thought came to me that if you had something to say, perhaps you could write it down on paper. I kept thinking, Have I something to say?

3 *"The Ghetto Market"*

Hilda's first essay, "The Ghetto Market," described the filth she saw at the open market in her neighborhood. Precisely because she was an immigrant with actual experience in "the old world," she did not romanticize the market as a charming example of old-world customs. In the essay's first and last paragraphs, Hilda echoed many Hull-House attitudes.

During that week, I did not attend any classes at Hull-House. Every evening, as soon as I reached home from work, I would hurry through with supper and helping with the dishes and then would sit at the kitchen table and write. I still have that "masterpiece." Here it is:

"The Ghetto Market"

Sociologists who are studying and seeking to remedy conditions among the wretchedly poor have done vast good. The poor may now be clothed; they receive medical attention and surgical care which none but the very rich could afford to pay for. They need not be ignorant, for schools are free and there are many devoted women in the social settlements who are laboring night and day to make up for whatever deficiency may exist in the capacity of the city institutions. But there is one injustice untouched; one wrong which is crying for immediate remedy. This is the unsanitary, filthy food which the poor in certain quarters are forced to eat. Not until the city takes the matter in hand and orders all vegetables, meat and fish to be sold only in adequate and sanitary rooms will this condition be entirely overcome; for as long as the old market of the Ghetto district exists, so long will the inhabitants of the district patronize it. . . .

   Is this question not well worthy of consideration? Cannot the poultry shop, fish stall and cake stand be kept off the street, free from the dust and the flies? Why should this class of people who work harder than any other be compelled to eat inferior food when they might be supplied with good food for the same money? Are there not plenty of men employed in building houses, ice boxes and various appliances for keeping provisions? Yet these people eat food sold on the street under the filthiest conditions.

The next time the class met, I brought the masterpiece, over which I had sweated five nights and a whole day Sunday, to Mr. Chandler. Each member of the class had brought a composition. Mr. Chandler did not look at the papers. He told us he would let us know the following week what he thought of our efforts.

4   *The University*

After a miserable day at the factory, when everything seemed to happen, my machine had broken down and I had lost several hours of work, I arrived at Hull-House. The composition class was to meet that night. What would Mr. Chandler think of my composition? Would he pay any attention to it? He had probably thrown it into the wastebasket. It couldn't possibly be worth anything, I kept telling myself.

   The class assembled and Mr. Chandler opened his briefcase and pulled out a mass of papers. He handed them to the various authors, without any comment.

   My heart missed several beats.

   Then he handed me my paper and said: "Very good." I do not remember anything else that he said that night. But as the class was being dismissed, Miss

Addams came into the room and said that she wanted to talk to me, that I was to wait for her. She talked for a few minutes with Mr. Chandler, then she took me into the octagon[1] and said these magic words: "How would you like to go to the University of Chicago?" She was very calm, as if she had asked me to have a cup of tea.

She did not realize that she had just asked me whether I wanted to live. I just sat there looking at her.

"Did you say the University of Chicago?" I finally gasped.

"Yes," she said. "Mr. Chandler told me that your paper shows promise, and he will make all the arrangements."

"But that is impossible," I said.

"Nothing is impossible," said Jane Addams.

For some time I could not talk. I kept thinking, I did not graduate from grammar school. How could I hope to go to the great university?

Miss Addams, with her infinite patience, sat there holding my hand. I know she was living through my thoughts.

If this could happen, then all sorts of miracles could happen. But then, did not miracles happen in Hull-House all the time?

"But what about a high school diploma?" I asked. "I heard that no one can go to college without a high school diploma."

"Mr. Chandler said that you could come as an unclassified student," she said.

"But what about money?" I was beginning to lose hope.

"You will be granted a scholarship," she said. "It will cost you nothing."

"But I must contribute to the support of the family," I said. "My wages are needed at home."

"Well, I thought of that, too," she said smiling. "We will make you a loan of the amount that you would earn, and whenever you are able, you can pay it back."

By this time tears were running down my cheeks. What had I done to deserve all this? She took my hand and said: "I know how you feel, my dear. I want you to go home and talk this over with your mother, and let me know what you want to do. But I want you to go, remember that."

I went home and found Mother and my sister sitting at the kitchen table, drinking tea. I sat down without removing my coat. My sister looked at me.

"What's happened to you?" she said.

I just sat there staring—then I blurted out: "Miss Addams wants me to go to the University of Chicago."

"But how can you?" my sister asked.

Then I poured out my soul. I told them what Miss Addams had said about a loan, how my tuition would be free, how my life would be changed.

"This can happen only in America," Mother said.

"Yes," I said, "because in America there is a Jane Addams and Hull-House."

---

[1] The "octagon" was a small, eight-sided room in Hull-House that Jane Addams used as her more public office space.

The exciting events of the night before did not keep me from going to work the next day. I sewed cuffs all day. As soon as I had finished eating supper, I dashed off to Hull-House. I waited for Miss Addams to come out of the dining room.

She saw me at once and took me into the octagon. The walls were covered with the photographs of the great humanitarians of the world: Leo Tolstoy, Abraham Lincoln, Henry Demarest Lloyd, John Peter Altgeld, Susan B. Anthony, Peter Kropotkin, Eugene V. Debs, and a host of others. And while these faces were looking down at us, I told Miss Addams that my mother and sister had consented to my going.

It was with a great deal of satisfaction that I told the foreman of the shirt-waist factory that I was leaving.

Memories keep coming back. It must have been the winter term when I matriculated at the University of Chicago. I remember that it was very cold traveling to the university early in the morning.

I was told to go to Mr. Chandler's office. He took me to the registration office and I registered for three classes. I was to take English literature with Mr. Percy Boynton, German with Mr. Goettsch, and composition with Mr. Chandler.

. . . Since I did not have to worry about grades, being an unclassified student, I could drink in all the fabulous information that came from Mr. Boynton's mouth. And reading the assigned books became a tonic to my soul. I soon came to know Ben Jonson, Alexander Pope, Beaumont and Fletcher, Keats, Shelley, and Shakespeare.

In 1904 there were separate classes for men and women. Most of my classes met in Lexington Hall. It was a poorly constructed building and was drafty and often very cold. In the composition class, when we were told to write about anything, I became bold, and perhaps a little impudent, and wrote a paper on why women students were assigned to cold, drafty buildings while the men were in more solid ones.

I think I got a high mark on that paper, but Mr. Chandler made no comment.

The subject of the next assignment was a debate on "Woman Suffrage." We were asked to hand in an outline as to which side we would take. I don't know why, but I chose to be against woman suffrage. The next day Mr. Chandler asked me to stay for an interview and in short order he convinced me that I was not against woman suffrage and that there was no point in writing something that I did not believe. I am sure that he still remembered my previous paper on the discrimination shown to women students and he was not going to allow me to contradict myself as to woman's rights. He proved to be right.

When the university closed for the summer, I evaluated my work. The English literature course had opened all sorts of vistas to me. But I think I did not pass. The jump from the fifth grade in the grammar school to Chaucer was a little too much for me. But the course gave me an everlasting desire to read and study, so it was not a loss. I did pass in German and I think I fared well in the composition class.

That term at the University of Chicago opened a new life to me. And I have never stopped being grateful for having been given the opportunity to explore the treasures to be found in books.

I often wonder what sort of a life I would have lived if I did not have that short term in the university made possible by Jane Addams.

After the short but eventful term at the University of Chicago, I must confess I was at loose ends. I was determined not to go back to the factory to sew cuffs. But I knew that I had to earn my living and help support the family. I now felt prepared to do more interesting and stimulating work. The question was, What could I do?

The answer came sooner than I dared hope. Miss Addams was preparing to go to Bar Harbor for the summer and she suggested that I take the job of answering the doorbell and the telephone. . . .

Most of the classes were discontinued during the hot summer months. But there had been a great demand for English classes for adult foreigners. A delegation of the students called on Miss Addams and asked her to allow the classes to continue during the summer. Miss Addams agreed to try one class if a teacher could be found. I volunteered.

As I look back on that momentous event, I realize how presumptuous it was of me to offer to teach a class at Hull-House, where the standards were very high. I had no training in teaching. But English had fascinated me from the start; I had worked very hard to learn it, so why could I not teach the immigrants what I had learned? . . .

Here my training at the Jewish Training School became a blessing. Mrs. Torrance[2] had been very meticulous about pronunciation, and I used her method that summer with surprising and satisfactory results. Most of my students learned to speak without an accent. The great value of not having an accent, in those days, was that you could get a better job. And that was rewarding.

But the great reward came that fall, when Miss Addams told me that I could continue to teach the class for the winter. The day I picked up the *Hull-House Bulletin* and saw my name listed as a teacher of an English class equaled only the day when I was told that I could go to the University of Chicago.

---

[2] Mrs. Anna Torrance had been Hilda's teacher when she began school in Chicago.

5   *New Horizons*

Being allowed to teach English to immigrants at Hull-House did more for me than anything that I imparted to my students. It gave me a feeling of security that I so sorely needed. What added to my confidence in the future was that my class was always crowded and the people seemed to make good progress. From time to time Jane Addams would visit the class to see what I was doing, and she always left with that rare smile on her face; she seemed to be pleased.

There were no textbooks for adult beginners in English at that time. It soon became evident that it would be a waste of time to talk about cat, rat, mat, fat, sat to people who probably had been to high school in a foreign country.

This situation was emphasized for me one evening when Miss Addams brought a Greek professor to my class. He had come to America for the express purpose of learning English and had come to Chicago because he wanted to see relatives who were living near Hull-House. These relatives had suggested that he find out what Hull-House was doing about teaching English to adults. Miss Addams told me that the professor would stay one or two nights in my class to see what was being done. The crowning glory of my teaching was when he decided to join the class and attended all winter.

But to come back to the subject of textbooks, since there were none, I decided to use the Declaration of Independence as a text. It was a distinct success. The students did not find the words difficult; so in addition to learning English, we all learned the principles of Americanism.

I next introduced the manual on naturalization and the class learned English while studying how to become a citizen. It was all very exciting and stimulating.

My students were now beginning to confide in me. Classes at Hull-House were never just classes where people came to learn a specific subject. There was a human element of friendliness among us. Life was not soft or easy for any of them. They worked hard all day in shops and factories and made this valiant effort to learn the language of their adopted country. . . .

Hull-House had a unique arrangement for getting work done. No teachers or attendants were paid. It was all volunteer work. The residents of Hull-House were occupied with outside work during the day, and each gave a certain number of evenings to teaching and directing clubs. The only people who were paid were those who devoted their full time to the house.

So in the fall, when volunteers returned, I decided to look for a job. I had learned to use a typewriter, so I decided to look for more "genteel" work. I still shuddered when I thought of those cuffs.

I started scanning the want ads, but now I looked under the heading "Office Help."

A large mail-order house, which shall remain unnamed, advertised for bill clerks who could operate billing machines. Since the keyboard of a typewriter was the same as that of a billing machine, I decided to apply. I was pleasantly surprised when I was told to report for work on the following day.

Carrying my lunch, I set out for my new job. I was taken to a large room that was filled with long tables on which the billing machines had been placed. There were about three feet between the machines. I was assigned to a machine and an instructor came to show me how the work was done. She also told me the rules of the office. I was told that no talking was permitted during working hours. I could, however, do what I wanted during the lunch period, which was forty-five minutes, even talk. . . .

I had no difficulty learning to do the work and at first it was new and exciting. About the third day my mother noticed that my voice was husky, and she wanted to know what was wrong. I suddenly realized that I had not been using my vocal cords for three days and that my voice was beginning to show the lack of exercise. I suddenly realized that "genteel" work can be as deadly monotonous as factory work.

I made a feeble protest. I saw no reason why I could not speak to the girl next to me once in a while. The next day I was told that I was "too smart" for the job, and I was fired.

Several years later I went with a group of people on a sight-seeing tour that took us to the state penitentiary at Joliet. As I walked through the overall factory, I saw a spindle and several colored cards at each machine. I asked the guide what the cards meant and was told that when a prisoner needed supplies he had to use the cards to indicate what he needed, as no talking was permitted during working hours.

I often wondered whether the mail-order house got the idea from the prison, or the prison from the mail-order house.

I was again looking for a job. Miss Addams suggested that I might try A. C. McClurg & Co., a publishing house and at the time the largest bookstore in Chicago. With a letter of introduction from Jane Addams, I was given a very friendly interview and got the job.

Working among books was almost as good as taking a course in literature. It gave me the opportunity of knowing what books were being published. I was keenly interested in what books people were reading. And I had the great privilege of working at McClurg's when *The Quest of the Silver Fleece* was published. It was the first time that I came across the name of W. E. B. Du Bois. This book aroused a keen interest in the growth of cotton in the South and the part that the Negro played in the industry.

I still spent my evenings at Hull-House, and one evening Miss Addams asked me to help organize a social and literary club for young men and women about my age. We all needed an outlet for recreation. About thirty young people joined the club, which was named the Ariadne Club. . . .

I now had the opportunity to come into contact with young men. The club met once a week, and how I looked forward to those meetings. . . . Since this was a social and literary club, one week was devoted to dancing and the next to study. For the more serious evening, a member was usually assigned to write a paper and to read it before the club. This was followed by a discussion.

And what subjects we discussed.

Papers were written on the collection of garbage, grand opera, clean streets, single tax, trade unionism, and many others. I think our subjects were influenced by what was going on at Hull-House. . . .

It was about this time that I found a copy of *Uncle Tom's Cabin*. I was deeply moved by the misery of the slaves. For the first time I read about slavery. For the first time I found out that people could be bought and sold on the auction block; that children could be taken from parents; that fathers could be sold, never to see their families again. . . .

Most of the club members had no contact with Negroes. We even found that some of the members had never seen a Negro. Dr. James Britton, who was the club leader, told us that most of the Negroes had lived longer in America than any of us present and were fully entitled to anything and everything that the country offered. I thought of all the racial hatreds in Poland, Germany, and Russia, and I was thankful that I was being cured of this disease of intolerance.

In this connection, I recall that shortly after I had arrived in Chicago, one of my playmates told me that I must cross the street when I approached the Chinese laundry on Halsted Street. When I wanted to know why, she told me that if you pass the laundry, the "Chinaman" will come out with a long knife and kill you. I realize now that my playmate must have been told this fantastic tale by someone. Until I found out that the Chinese man who operated this laundry was the soul of kindness, I was afraid to pass the laundry.

We also had music in the Ariadne Club. The members who could play an instrument, or sing, would perform; we heard some very good concerts. Many of the members who worked all day would study music at night. I recall when a piano lesson could be had for twenty-five cents. Some of the members attended the Hull-House Music School, and I venture to say that not a few became successful musicians.

The Ariadne Club also produced plays. I recall taking part in *David Garrick*, in which I played a fussy and obnoxious old maid.

My interest in the theater was a direct outgrowth of the dramatics at Hull-House. It was a preparation for life.

Analyzing the Source

REFLECTING ON THE SOURCE

1. Hilda Polacheck was able to produce this memoir in the 1950s because she was literate in English, was in good health, and had the economic resources that allowed her time and space to write. Consider how these optimal circumstances might have influenced her memories of her experiences in Chicago.

2. Dena Polacheck Epstein said that her mother's "uncritical picture of Jane Addams was a sincere expression of her feelings toward the woman who sub-

stantially changed her life." How useful is such an affectionate portrait for our understanding of Addams and Hull-House?

3. What can one old woman's recollections add to our knowledge of immigrant life in Chicago that we cannot learn from government investigations, Hull-House reports, or journalists' observations? Why, given the well-known flaws in human memory, do historians still consult memoirs in constructing their picture of the past?

MAKING CONNECTIONS

4. Hilda Polacheck was a Jewish immigrant. But she was also a white immigrant, a female immigrant, and an immigrant whose parents had been middle-class back home in Poland. What does her story teach us about the relative importance of ethnicity, race, gender, and class in shaping an individual immigrant's opportunities in the United States?

5. Historians of immigration debate whether immigrants chose to assimilate into American culture or were forced to do so. How can evidence from Hilda Polacheck's memoir inform this debate? What factors account for her enthusiastic participation in the Americanizing activities at Hull-House?

Beyond the Source

Hilda Satt became Hilda Polacheck in 1912 when, at the age of thirty, she married William Polacheck, an American-born Jew of German ancestry from Milwaukee who prospered in the lighting fixture business. Hilda did not work for pay once she married but did continue to support her mother. In fact, Hilda's own life resembled her mother's life back in Poland: she had a comfortable home, nice belongings, and servants to help with the four healthy children she bore in ten years.

Like so many educated, socially conscious American women of her day, Hilda used her middle-class privilege to engage in social and political reform work. William shared the political views that Hilda had acquired at Hull-House and, together, they engaged in the sort of prosocialist, prolabor, proreform activities that were still quite respectable in the years before World War I and the Bolshevik Revolution. The lasting connection to Hull-House proved important when Hilda's life again mirrored her mother's and she suddenly became a widow at age forty-five, with four children between the ages of four and thirteen to support. Unlike her mother, however, Hilda had some financial resources to draw upon and was comforted by the thought that she was:

> . . . better prepared to meet hardship than my mother had been. The years I had spent at Hull-House, under the influence of Jane Addams, were now my strength and support. I had been taught to think clearly and meet events with

courage. I kept thinking of the many tragedies enacted day after day in the reception room at Hull-House. The immediate task before me was to earn enough money to care for the children. (Polacheck 167)

Hilda met her responsibilities during the Depression of the 1930s by working, first as the manager of a large apartment building back in Chicago, a position gained through Hull-House friends. Later, she was hired as a "reporter" for the Illinois branch of the Federal Writers' Project, a New Deal program to employ writers. During World War II, she ran a sewing room for Russian war relief. She had joined Jane Addams's peace organization, the Women's International League for Peace and Freedom, as a protest against World War I and and remained active in WILPF during the cold war and the early years of the Vietnam War. In the last twenty years of her life, Hilda was cared for by her children. She died in 1967 at the age of eighty-five, leaving her unpublished memoir in a pile of "loose sheets and revisions."

When Hilda wrote her memoir in the early 1950s, she was out of sync with the times. In those very conservative cold war years when many Americans feared communist subversion by foreigners and political leftists, Hilda wrote an immigrant memoir that proclaimed loyalty to both the Declaration of Independence and socialist ideals. At a time when many regarded Jane Addams and Franklin Delano Roosevelt as past collaborators with the leftist enemy, Hilda described them as patriots who instilled loyalty to American principles in the hearts of immigrants and workers. And in an era when women's capacities were disdained, Hilda documented women's accomplishments. Her memoir, like so many others, is a philosophical testament as much as it is a life story. Little wonder that publishers in the cold war years told Hilda that readers were not interested in the life of an obscure Jewish woman. It was the social movements in the last forty years of the twentieth century that created new interest in immigrants, women, and social activists and thus made it possible for the University of Illinois Press to publish *I Came a Stranger: The Story of a Hull-House Girl* as part of its series on women in American history. Once again, history shaped Polacheck's memoir.

Finding and Supplementing the Source

I Came a Stranger: The Story of a Hull-House Girl is readily available in your library or through interlibrary loan. There are many similar, published memoirs that are documented in the way Dena Epstein documented her mother's. These published memoirs provide explanatory endnotes that tell you if events reported are consistent with other historical sources. One very accessible, well-documented collection of American immigrant autobiographies is *Immigrant Voices: New Lives in America, 1773–1986,* edited by Thomas Dublin (Urbana: University of Illinois Press, 1993).

If you have a particular topic area in which you would like to find an individual's life story told in the first person, you can do a "subject" search in your library's electronic catalogue and ask, for example, for "Asian Americans—autobiography." Libraries are more likely to catalogue books as "autobiographies" than as "memoirs." If you want the experience of reading an unpublished, undocumented autobiography, you can visit your local historical society or a university's archives and ask the librarian there to assist you in your search. Or you can visit the Library of Congress on the Web by going to **memory.loc.gov** and sampling any one of that site's four hundred autobiographies, some as short as five pages and others as long as five hundred pages.

If you wish to read more about Hilda Polacheck or Jane Addams, see Hilda Satt Polacheck, *I Came a Stranger: The Story of a Hull-House Girl,* edited by Dena J. Polacheck Epstein (Urbana: University of Illinois Press, 1989), or Jane Addams, *Twenty Years at Hull-House*, edited by Victoria Bissell Brown (Boston: Bedford/St. Martin's, 1999). Among the many fine books available on American immigration and U.S. settlement houses, see John Bodnar, *The Transplanted: A History of Immigrants in Urban America* (Bloomington: Indiana University Press, 1985); Irving Howe, *World of Our Fathers: The Journey of Eastern European Jews to America and the Life They Found and Made* (New York: Simon and Schuster, 1976); and Mina Carson, *Settlement Folk: Social Thought and the American Settlement Movement, 1885–1930* (Chicago: University of Chicago Press, 1990).

CHAPTER 5

Selling Respectability

Advertisements in the
African American Press, 1910–1913

In 1910, 80 black American citizens were lynched—hanged by white mobs without benefit of trial—in the United States. That figure was lower than it had been in 1901, when 108 blacks were lynched, and it was higher than it would be in 1915, when 53 blacks were lynched. But the lynching rate in 1910 was consistent with the pattern of lynchings in the years between 1889 and 1918, when white Americans typically lynched 84 black citizens every year. 1910 was a notable year, however, because in that year a coalition of African Americans and progressive whites formed the National Association for the Advancement of Colored People (NAACP). The NAACP's purpose was to combat this violent terrorism against black citizens and to challenge, as well, the whole system of white supremacy that governed U.S. political, economic, and social life in these years. The organization's stated aim was "to make 11,000,000 Americans physically free from peonage, mentally free from ignorance, politically free from disenfranchisement, and socially free from insult."

The NAACP had its work cut out for it. In the three decades following the end of Reconstruction, white racists had successfully reversed the legal, political, and economic gains made by blacks in the 1870s and 1880s. Blacks who were children when slavery ended in 1865 had come of age in an optimistic moment: black men could vote and hold elective office, blacks and whites shared the same public facilities, and over thirty black colleges were opened. The 1870s and 1880s were not easy decades for African Americans, but young black men and women in those years could believe progress was possible. By the time that generation of blacks reached middle age in the 1890s and early 1900s, however, they had experienced a brutal cancellation of their rights as citizens and of their dignity as human beings.

The founders of the NAACP had witnessed the disenfranchisement of black men in every southern state, starting with Florida in 1889 and ending with Georgia in 1908, through the use of such stratagems as the poll tax, the literacy test, and the grandfather clause. They had seen, too, the introduction of laws throughout the South mandating the strict segregation of blacks from whites in all public facilities, from railway cars to drinking fountains. The men and women, black and white, who launched the NAACP fully intended to challenge the legality of segregation even though the U.S. Supreme Court had already ruled segregation constitutional. In the 1896 case *Plessy v. Ferguson,* the Supreme Court declared that public facilities could be separate as long as they were equal. Such endorsement from the federal government was a reminder that white supremacy was not confined to the South. Northern states had not passed formal segregation laws, but informal customs presumed black inferiority, making it difficult for blacks to find housing or professional work in integrated settings, uncomfortable for them to shop or take recreation in white areas, and unpleasant, if not dangerous, for them to challenge racial barriers.

In 1910, racial prejudice permeated every region of the United States. National culture was suffused with religious and scientific claims that all nonwhite people were by nature inferior to all white people. Some racists said nonwhites were cursed by God; others said blacks were retarded in their biological evolution. Either way, the justification for formal and informal segregation was that black people were less intelligent than white people—and less moral.

The assumption of blacks' intellectual inferiority justified race segregation of schools and low investment in black schools. It also justified racists' dismissal of black political arguments, black scholarship, and black artistic endeavors as the flawed products of underevolved minds. Of equal importance in this racist campaign was the charge of blacks' moral inferiority. By defining all African Americans as childlike creatures with weak moral fiber, racists could blame poverty among blacks on their supposedly inherent laziness and dissipation. At the same time, the charge of moral inferiority allowed racists to depict all African American men and women as sexual beasts who posed a direct threat to respectable, civilized white society. So while white men in these years were never charged when they raped black women, the cry that a black man had raped a white woman often ignited white riots against black communities as well as white lynchings of black citizens. Even in the absence of such violence, the widely accepted image of the black American as a stupid, lazy, sexual predator worked powerfully well to deny African Americans their claims to equality.

It was in this racialized context that African Americans at the turn of the century tried to build respectable homes and stable communities. For guidance in this risky endeavor, they could draw from two very different racial strategies. One approach, articulated by Booker T. Washington, counseled blacks to accept the fact that they had to begin "at the bottom" and earn their way up. Washington, the principal of Tuskegee Industrial Institute, discouraged blacks from seeking college degrees or pursuing professions, arguing instead for vocational training and employment as domestic servants, farmers, artisans, shopkeepers, and industrial laborers. Washington believed that if blacks made a solid contribution in the marketplace, working hard and earning a steady living, buying homes and starting small businesses, then they would eventually be granted legal equality. Washington favored this economic strategy over black agitation for voting rights or challenges to segregation.

An alternative racial strategy available to African Americans at the turn of the century was articulated by Dr. W. E. B. Du Bois, who claimed that blacks would never make economic progress without the vote, access to all public facilities, collegiate as well as vocational education, and blunt denunciation by black leaders of all racist theories. Du Bois did not oppose vocational training or dismiss the value of hard, daily labor, but he held that all such efforts were futile if not coupled with political agitation for the rights the Constitution promised to all its citizens. He also insisted that black progress required leadership by a "talented tenth" of educated race leaders who could guide the masses out of the lowly status to which racism had consigned them.

In the 1890s, many blacks optimistically embraced Washington's economic emphasis on its practical merits. His "accommodationist" approach had, after all, garnered substantial funding from liberal whites for both educational and entrepreneurial efforts. But doubts about Washington's approach rose in the early 1900s along with mounting evidence that black progress in the marketplace did not earn blacks the respect promised. On the contrary, black economic success increased racists' hatred because it fundamentally challenged their belief in black laziness and stupidity. Well-dressed blacks were more vulnerable to verbal and physical abuse than those in humble clothing; blacks who owned their own businesses were often the targets of lynch mobs; and white rioters typically attacked black stores and rampaged through neighborhoods where blacks were homeowners.

The formation of the NAACP was, in fact, a response to a bloody riot in 1908 in Springfield, Illinois, in which the false cry of rape sent an angry white mob into the city's black neighborhood, leaving eight dead and dozens injured and causing thousands of dollars' worth of damage to black homes and businesses. The eruption of such racial violence in a northern city galvanized progressive whites and blacks, including W. E. B. Du Bois, into establishing an assertive, interracial organization that would challenge Washington's policy of accommodation. Du Bois resigned his professorship at Atlanta University in order to become the NAACP's director of publicity and research, even though the fledgling organization could not guarantee his salary. It was from his new post that Du Bois launched the monthly magazine *The Crisis: A Record of the Darker Races*, which was to serve as the official organ of the NAACP.

The Crisis was a hard-hitting political journal that ran sharp editorial critiques of racist policies and detailed reports on specific cases of racial discrimination alongside proud stories of African Americans' triumphs in defiance of racism. The magazine thus reflected Du Bois's rejection of any sort of accommodation to white supremacy and defined the NAACP in contrast to Booker T. Washington. But *The Crisis* also reflected attitudes that Du Bois shared with many followers of Washington, in particular the belief that black citizens must counter negative stereotypes by being especially ambitious, hard-working, moral, upright, well-read, well-groomed, and well-spoken—in short, respectable.

This set of prescriptions for black respectability can be viewed in several ways: as a daring resistance to racist images of bestial blacks, as blind obedience to the notion that blacks must earn their rights through good behavior, as a realistic strategy for making political and economic progress, and as a way for upwardly mobile blacks to set themselves above their more impoverished brothers and sisters. In fact, historians have employed every one of those interpretations when analyzing the attitudes evident in *The Crisis*. Such an array of arguments about blacks' values and motives is not a reflection of historians' confusion. It is a testament to the complicated mix of resistance and accommodation that African Americans needed to survive in the early decades of the twentieth century.

Using Advertisements as a Source

There are several possible strategies for investigating the values and aspirations of African Americans who subscribed to *The Crisis* magazine in the years between 1910 and 1912. The research could focus on the editorial content in the magazine, analyzing how Du Bois—who wrote most of the articles—presented his uncompromising stance on racial equality to his readers. Alternatively, the research could focus on the photographs used to illustrate the articles, examining how the very attractive, very respectable images of African American men, women, and children throughout the magazine appealed to readers' racial pride. Finally, the research could concentrate on the advertisements in the magazine, attending to both the needs and the desires that are inevitably reflected in these direct appeals to the magazine's readers.

From the first issue of *The Crisis* magazine in November 1910, advertising was included in its pages. "It is our purpose," explained Du Bois, "to make the advertising a means of real service to our readers as well as a source of income to us." The matter of income was not inconsequential. The NAACP had no reserve of funds for subsidizing the magazine. Du Bois had to make this controversial political publication a financial success in its own right, and he had to do it despite the opposition of Booker T. Washington, who had the power to tell many black businesses not to advertise in the defiant new journal. So when *The Crisis* began, a business owner's decision to take out an ad in the new magazine was as much a political statement as a commercial one. The advertiser both endorsed the NAACP's policies and calculated that there was a healthy market among readers of *The Crisis* magazine.

Confidence among the magazine's first advertisers was well rewarded. *The Crisis* was an immediate—and, to Du Bois, "phenomenal"—success. He had cautiously printed only one thousand copies of the first issue, and it sold out at ten cents per copy. In January 1911, *The Crisis* sold three thousand copies; in

February, four thousand; in March, six thousand. By 1913, the magazine had a circulation of thirty thousand while membership in the NAACP was only three thousand. With those kinds of figures, Du Bois gained an independence within the organization that made it impossible for NAACP officers to rein in his rhetoric even when they feared he might offend potential white supporters.

The circulation figures also meant that *The Crisis* was an attractive place to advertise if your target audience was Americans who agreed with Du Bois's editorial stance on race. Analysis of the magazine's advertisements can help to answer the historical question, who was the first audience for *The Crisis*? It seems logical to expect that Du Bois's readers were the elite—the "talented tenth"— that Du Bois saw as having the education, self-esteem, ambition, and professional status to demand racial equality. But in 1913, there were only a few thousand African Americans with college degrees, fewer than three thousand black physicians, and not even one thousand black lawyers, nowhere near the thirty thousand purchasers of *The Crisis*. The audience must have extended beyond Du Bois's favored elite, but in what direction? The magazine's advertisements offer clues to understanding the makeup of the audience.

Advantages and Disadvantages of Working with Advertisements

When trying to determine a community's values and aspirations—what it is that a group of people care about and who they hope to become—historians often turn to advertisements because the whole purpose of advertising is to appeal to the needs and values of its target audience. Historians can read ads to determine what products were available to consumers seeking to feed, clothe, and house themselves and to learn how advertisers defined those basic needs. Advertising also tells us what luxury products were on the market and what hopes and dreams advertisers appealed to when persuading consumers to spend on luxuries.

There are particular advantages to using advertisements from a narrowly targeted publication like *The Crisis*. Correspondence and records from the NAACP tell us that Du Bois exercised a strong editorial hand in accepting ads for the magazine, which makes it more valid for a historian to argue that the attitudes conveyed in the advertising are consistent with the political position of *The Crisis*. The magazine certainly ran no ads for Cream of Wheat cereal or Aunt Jemima pancake mix, products whose trademark images were African American figures in smiling, servile roles. But it is unlikely that those companies even tried to advertise in *The Crisis*. None of the day's popular, widely advertised products like Ivory Soap, Gold Medal Flour, Pabst's Blue Ribbon Beer, or Coca-Cola ever appeared in *The Crisis*. Those national, white-owned companies could reach black consumers, including the readers of *The Crisis*, through the pages of white-owned publications. They did not contribute advertising revenue to black daily newspapers and certainly not to a journal as outspoken as *The Crisis*.

From the historian's point of view, the absence of such national advertising— and its revenue—in black publications like *The Crisis* is itself valuable evidence of the extent of economic segregation in the United States early in the twentieth century. Advertising in *The Crisis* reveals the dimensions of the separate black economy, and those ads can be analyzed for evidence of the strengths and the weaknesses in that economy. Du Bois agreed with Washington that blacks must pursue economic independence and prosperity. The ads in *The Crisis* provide information on how African Americans were pursuing that goal. They offer us a taste of the variety of black economic pursuits and remind us that blacks could be found all along the class spectrum, from poor to working class to middle class to wealthy. Analysis of *The Crisis* advertisements can also aid in exploring the subtle ways in which black Americans asserted their economic and moral respectability in their segregated country.

Because we live in an advertising-drenched society and, as consumers, we "analyze" ads every day, it is often easier for us to examine ads from the past than other sorts of historical documents. However, that familiarity can be a disadvantage in using this kind of source because it may lead us into exaggerating just how much ads can tell us. We can correct for this by remembering that we don't buy every product we see advertised; we don't even "buy" all the advertisers' claims made about the products we do purchase. Therefore, we do not want to jump to the conclusion that *The Crisis* readers literally or figuratively bought everything in the magazine's ads. Advertising, in fact, cannot tell us what people actually did buy; for that, we would need every company's sales figures. The virtual impossibility of ever finding such figures, especially for small, black businesses, forces us to rely on ads as indirect evidence of economic activity, but we must remember that it is indirect.

The biggest mistake we can make in using ads as historical evidence is to pull one or two particularly funny or startling ads out of context and use them to represent the attitudes of an entire population of consumers. If all advertising is an indirect measure of a community's beliefs and behavior, then certainly no single ad can be used to represent an entire community's values. To guard against overgeneralization, historians analyze whole sets of ads over a defined period of time, looking at the ordinary alongside the unique, before making any claims about the audience to whom the ads were directed. As an illustration of the need for caution when analyzing a single ad, consider this example from the November 1911 issue of *The Crisis*. In most respects, it is typical of the magazine's ads, but in one respect it is very unusual:

Social class of soap users?

Who is taking the risk in this deal?

Do You Want to Make Money?

CANVASSERS TO SELL SPHINX HANSOPE

Used in garage, machine shop, factory and home. Twenty-five boxes for $1.25; you sell for $2.50. Whitens the skin, softens the hands, prevents chapping, heals cracks and sores. The first aid in burns. Strictly antiseptic.

SPHINX LABOR-SAVING SOAP CO., Inc.
117 West Street, New York City

What is being sold here?

Significance of this claim?

This ad, like many in *The Crisis*, was not selling a product; it was selling a job, an opportunity to make money. In the straightforward fashion that was typical of *Crisis* ads, it listed the ostensible virtues of the product, gave the price and profit, and described the potential market. In the sample of advertisements included in this chapter, you will find several ads similar to this one and can use them to theorize about the magazine's audience. What you will seldom find in other ads from the early years of *The Crisis* are references to skin whitening. Other press outlets for black advertisers carried many skin whitening (and hair straightening) products, but *The Crisis* did not. This reminds us that Du Bois's political views shaped the magazine's advertising. It also reminds us that it would be a mistake to use this one, atypical ad to argue that *Crisis* readers aspired to whiter skin, just as it would be a mistake to base any generalization on one single ad.

The sample of ads included in this chapter are representative of the types of ads carried in *The Crisis* between 1910 and 1913. In the magazine itself, most ads were crowded together at the back, in a six-page section called "The Advertiser." Because the ads were not dispersed among the magazine's articles, readers not seeking certain products and services could simply skip the advertisements. You will want to consider that fact in your analysis. More generally, however, you will want to explore how this sample of advertisements can be used to understand African Americans' needs and values at a time when white racists sought to deny to blacks any measure of independence or respectability.

Working with the Source

To aid your work with these advertisements, they have been arranged by descriptive categories: housing, economic opportunities, education and race pride, beauty and fashion. On page 101 you will find alternative ways of categorizing the ads for the purposes of historical analysis. As you peruse these ads, keep track of examples that illustrate these analytical categories, which move us beyond static description and toward detection of social patterns.

Analytical Categories	Examples in the Ads
The separate black economy resulting from segregation	
The Crisis readers' access to economic opportunity and upward mobility	
The use of religion, education, and gender to affirm black equality and respectability	

The Source: Advertisements from *The Crisis*, November 1910–March 1913

HOUSING

Philip A. Payton, Jr., Company
The Crisis, Volume 1, January 1911, p. 35

How to Elevate the Moral and Civic Tone of the Negro Community

Negroes—good, bad and indifferent—as long as they have lived in tenements, have had to live shamefully intermingled. Formerly they were forced to live in ramshackle tenements that had been abandoned by the whites, at exorbitant rents for wretched accommodations. But now, thanks to the thrift and enterprise of certain progressive Negro real estate agents, they may live in houses having the same conveniences and accommodations as the whites. While, happily, the physical surroundings of the Negro tenant have been radically altered, unhappily his moral surroundings remain unchanged. How, then, can we improve his moral surroundings? Co-operation is a *sine qua non* in the solution of this problem. Tenants MUST co-operate with their agents and agents MUST co-operate with one another in ameliorating the moral and civic condition of Negro communities.

Let the agent compel a prospective tenant to furnish references satisfying fair and reasonable requirements as imposed by, agreed upon and accepted *in toto* by all agents. The respectable tenant will be glad to do it. Any tenant not furnishing such references should be "jim-crowed," as it were, from decent neighborhoods.

This matter of bettering the moral and civic condition of Negro communities is a case of a wheel within a wheel. As has been emphasized before, the agent can do absolutely nothing without co-operation. Ministers wielding great influence over large congregations can lend a powerfully helping hand, if they will. We must all pull together. We cannot work resultfully in factions. It is unquestionably within our power to do it, if all others do their respective parts and the colored real estate agent does his.

Desirable Apartments for Desirable Tenants
Also Homes for Sale on Easy Terms

Philip A. Payton, Jr., Company

New York's Pioneer Negro Real Estate Agents
B R O K E R S ══════ A P P R A I S E R S

TELEPHONES
917 - 918 HARLEM   **67 West 134th St., New York City**

2   *White Rose Working Girls' Home*
The Crisis, Volume 1, March 1911, p. 4

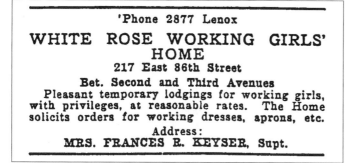

'Phone 2877 Lenox
WHITE ROSE WORKING GIRLS'
HOME
217 East 86th Street
Bet. Second and Third Avenues
Pleasant temporary lodgings for working girls,
with privileges, at reasonable rates.   The Home
solicits orders for working dresses, aprons, etc.
Address:
MRS. FRANCES R. KEYSER, Supt.

3   *Hotel Dale*
The Crisis, Volume 2, July 1911, p. 127

NEW JERSEY

HOTEL DALE
CAPE MAY, NEW JERSEY

This magnificent four-story structure, with every modern convenience, has just been completed at a cost of $50,000.

It is, without exception, the finest and most complete hostelry in the United States for the accommodation of our race.

The view from the hotel is magnificent: on the front, overlooking the celebrated golf links, the vista stretches away to take in the beautiful driveways and farms of the inland section of the Cape.   The rear commands an extensive view of the harbor and sea.   The invigorating ocean breezes reach every section of the hotel.

The Hotel Dale contains one hundred light, airy and luxuriously furnished rooms with every modern convenience.   Electric lights throughout the entire house.   Suites with bath and long distance telephone connections.

The open-air amusements available to the guests are numerous.   The lawn of the hotel contains both croquet and tennis courts.

The sea bathing at Cape May is unsurpassed on the Atlantic Ocean.   It is remarkable for its fine surf and is perfectly safe at all times for women and children.   The hotel has its own private bath houses.

The sailing and fishing in the harbor and adjacent sounds are always attractive and boats may be had at all times.

The hotel is under the personal management of the owner, E. W. Dale, one of the most progressive and successful business men of our race.   His experience as a hotel man has enabled him to use his very thorough knowledge of details in bringing the equipment of his hotel to perfection.

E. W. DALE, Owner and Proprietor

Mention THE CRISIS.

ECONOMIC OPPORTUNITIES

Bussing-Wheaton Kitchen Supplies
The Crisis, Volume 4, April 1912, p. 266

Agents—Big Money

Selling our seven-piece combination kitchen set, made up of articles absolutely needed in every household. They sell on sight. Mr. Jarvis sold fifty sets in one day. Send $1 for sample. Sent prepaid to any address in United States or Canada. Also our improved Slidewell Casters for chairs, which sell to everybody everywhere. Set of four sent postpaid for 15 cents.

BUSSING-WHEATON CO.
23 PARK ROW   DEPT. A   NEW YORK

Jackson Specialty Company
The Crisis, Volume 5, November 1912, p. 46

Don't Slave for Wages

Be your own boss. We show you how.
Particulars free.

JACKSON SPECIALTY CO.
Box 22A   East Lynn, Mass.

 **6**

N.Y. & N.J. Industrial Exchange

The Crisis, Volume 1,
November 1910, p. 19

7

International Realty Corporation

The Crisis, Volume 2,
October 1911, p. 262

Cottman & Cottman Shipping
The Crisis, Volume 1, December 1910, p. 32

The Firm for the Negro Farmers and Shippers to Deal With
Try Us Before Shipping Elsewhere.

FRUITS AND VEGETABLES   OYSTERS AND GAME   POULTRY AND EGGS

COTTMAN & COTTMAN

WHOLESALE COMMISSION MERCHANTS.   107 Pine Street, Philadelphia, Pa.
Reference: The People's Savings Bank   Bell 'Phone Connection: Lombard 4035

Nyanza Drug Co. & Pharmacy
The Crisis, Volume 1, December 1910, p. 32

NYANZA DRUG CO.
(Incorporated.)

35 W. 135th ST.,   NEW YORK CITY

CAPITAL STOCK, $15,000

Shares $5.00

Write for information. The best paying investment ever offered our people.

NYANZA PHARMACY

is the only colored Drug Store in New York City, and the purpose of the Corporation is to establish chains of stores, carrying Drugs and everything incidental to the Drug business. It is really the indisputable duty of every self-respecting member of the race to give it his support.

AGENTS WANTED EVERYWHERE

Blackdom, New Mexico
The Crisis, Volume 3,
February 1912, p. 170

WANTED

500 Negro families (farmers preferred) to settle on FREE Government Lands in Chaves County, New Mexico. Blackdom is a Negro colony. Fertile soil, ideal climate. No "Jim Crow" Laws. For information write

JAS. HAROLD COLEMAN

Blackdom - - - - - New Mexico

EDUCATION AND RACE PRIDE

11   *Wilberforce University,* The Crisis, Volume 2, May 1911, p. 43

FORWARD!

March Your Son Off to Wilberforce.

The only school for Negro Youth which has a Military Department equipped by the National Government and commanded by a detailed United States Army Officer.

DEPARTMENTS:

MILITARY   CLASSICAL   THEOLOGICAL
NORMAL   SCIENTIFIC   MUSICAL
BUSINESS   TECHNICAL   PREPARATORY

Banking taught by the actual operations in the Students' Savings Bank.   Twelve Industries, 180 acres of beautiful campus, Ten Buildings.   Healthful surroundings, exceptional community.   Maintained in part by the State of Ohio.

W. S. SCARBOROUGH, President.
WM. A. JOINER, Superintendent, C. N. & I.

12   *Daytona Educational and Industrial School for Negro Girls*
The Crisis, Volume 4, September 1912, p. 213

The Daytona School became Bethune Cookman College in 1923. Mary Mc-Leod Bethune founded the National Council of Negro Women in the 1930s and was a close advisor to First Lady Eleanor Roosevelt.

Daytona Educational and Industrial School for Negro Girls

Daytona, Florida

It reaches, by reason of its location, a large territory of Negro children deprived of educational privileges.

Its comfortable home life and Christian influences insure a certain individual attention and superior training impossible in larger institutions of its kind.

Mrs. Frances R. Keyser, formerly in charge of the White Rose Home for Working Girls, in New York City, has been elected Principal of the Academic Department.   Write for catalog and detailed information.

MARY McLEOD BETHUNE
Founder and Principal

13

Knoxville College
The Crisis, Volume 2,
June 1911, p. 85

Knoxville College

Beautiful Situation, Healthful Location
The Best Moral and Spiritual Environment
A Splendid Intellectual Atmosphere
Noted for Honest and Thorough Work
Offers full courses in the following de-
partments: College, Normal, High School,
Grammar School and Industrial.
Good water, steam heat, electric lights,
good drainage. Expenses very reasonable.
Opportunity for Self-help.
Fall Term Opened Sept. 27, 1911.
For information address
President R. W. McGranahan
KNOXVILLE, TENN.

14

Provident
Hospital and
Training
School for
Colored Nurses
The Crisis, Volume
5, March 1913,
p. 260

Provident Hospital and Training School for Colored Nurses

Aim: To keep its technic equal to the best

Founded 1891

The first training school for colored
nurses in this country, Freedman's
excepted.

Comprises a training school for
nurses, hospital, dispensary, and
thoroughly equipped children's department; when funds are ample, post-
graduate work may be undertaken.

The hospital is open to all. The
races co-operate in the board of
trustees, in the medical staff and in
administration; the institution is the
only one of its kind in which a colored
man may act as interne.

Cost of buildings and equipment,
$100,000; free from debt. Endowment,
$50,000, contributed mostly by wills
made by colored men. Additional
endowment needed, $50,000.

The nurses' course covers three
years; training and instruction given
by both races, according to the highest
modern standards.

15 *Self-Published Books on the Race Question*
The Crisis, Volume 2,
March 1911, p. 32

RACE ADJUSTMENT
By KELLY MILLER, Howard University, Washington, D. C.   A Standard Book on the Race Question.

PRICE $2.00

Social Equality ....5 cents
An Appeal to Reason, open letter
    to John Temple Graves.......10 cents
Roosevelt and the Negro.......10 cents
Forty Years of Negro Education.10 cents
Ultimate Race Problem........10 cents
The Political Capacity of the
    Negro ....10 cents
The Talented Tenth............10 cents

ADDRESS AUTHOR

The Curse of Race Prejudice

JAMES F. MORTON, JR., A.M., *Author and Publisher*
    Forceful, rational, comprehensive. An arsenal of facts and unanswerable arguments. Invaluable for propaganda. Read the chapter on "The Bugbear of Social Equality," which is a veritable eye-opener. Thousands already sold. Agents wanted everywhere.

PRICE 25 CENTS
Address the Author at 244 West 143d Street,
New York. N. Y.

16 *Mary White Ovington on the Race Question*
The Crisis, Volume 2, July 1911, p. 132

Mary White Ovington was one of the white founders of the NAACP and was the organization's executive secretary for more than thirty years.

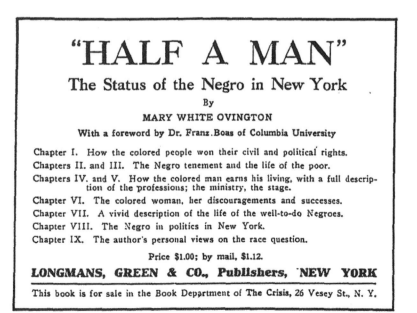

"HALF A MAN"
The Status of the Negro in New York
By
MARY WHITE OVINGTON
With a foreword by Dr. Franz Boas of Columbia University

Chapter I.   How the colored people won their civil and political rights.
Chapters II. and III.   The Negro tenement and the life of the poor.
Chapters IV. and V.   How the colored man earns his living, with a full description of the professions; the ministry, the stage.
Chapter VI.   The colored woman, her discouragements and successes.
Chapter VII.   A vivid description of the life of the well-to-do Negroes.
Chapter VIII.   The Negro in politics in New York.
Chapter IX.   The author's personal views on the race question.

Price $1.00; by mail, $1.12.

LONGMANS, GREEN & CO., Publishers, NEW YORK

This book is for sale in the Book Department of The Crisis, 26 Vesey St., N. Y.

17 *National Negro Doll Company*
The Crisis, Volume 2, July 1911, p. 131

Give the Child a Doll

The Most Beautiful of All the Toys on the Market Are the
NEGRO DOLLS

¶ YOUR child would be happy if it had a Negro doll such as are sent out by the National Negro Doll Company, Nashville, Tennessee. Every race is trying to teach their children an object lesson by giving them toys that will lead to higher intellectual heights. The Negro doll is calculated to help in the Christian development of our race. All dolls are sent by express, charges paid.

DOLLS FOR THE SEASON 1911-1912 NOW READY

Prices from 50c. up to $8.50

For Illustrated Booklets, Prices and Other Information, Send Five Cents to the
National Negro Doll Company
519 Second Avenue N., Nashville, Tenn.

R. H. BOYD, President   H. A. BOYD, Manager

BEAUTY AND FASHION

18 *Solomon Garrett, Tonsorial Artist*
The Crisis, Volume 1, December 1910, p. 33

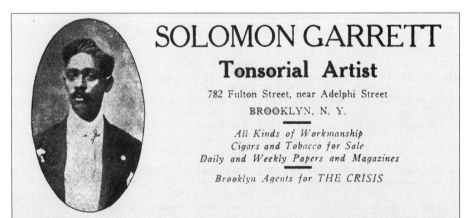

SOLOMON GARRETT
Tonsorial Artist

782 Fulton Street, near Adelphi Street
BROOKLYN, N. Y.

All Kinds of Workmanship
Cigars and Tobacco for Sale
Daily and Weekly Papers and Magazines

Brooklyn Agents for THE CRISIS

19 ## *Madame C. J. Walker Manufacturing Company*
The Crisis, Volume 4, January 1912, p. 130

Madame C. J. Walker was an enormously successful black entrepreneur who developed treatments for women's hair. She did not market those treatments as hair straighteners. She donated large sums of money to the NAACP's antilynching campaign and to Mary McLeod Bethune's school (see **Source 12** on p. 107).

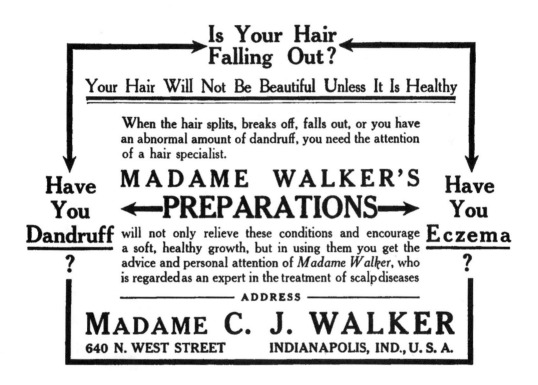

20   *The Dunbar Company: Face Powder*
The Crisis, Volume 5, December 1912, p. 104

It Has Come at Last

It had to come and it was for us to introduce it.

A Face Powder for Colored Women

CRISIS-MAID
Perfect Face Powder

Whether the complexion is cream, olive or brown, we have a tint to match it.

It is *scientifically perfect,* embodying certain ingredients soothing to the most sensitive skin, while a soft breath of Oriental perfume enhances its cosmetic value.

It is the final touch to milady's toilette; adding a certain inexpressible charm to her appearance, which evokes words of admiration from friends and passersby.

Its quality is unsurpassed.

Miss Clough says:

"Its quality equals that of the most expensive imported powders."

Price 50c. postpaid
Send 2c. stamp for sample

Address:
The Dunbar Company
EXCLUSIVE DISTRIBUTORS
26 Vesey Street New York

MISS INEZ H. CLOUGH
Formerly of the Williams and Walker Company;
now playing the "Big Circuit" in vaudeville.

Mention THE CRISIS.

Analyzing the Source

REFLECTING ON THE SOURCE

1. Now that you have examined a set of ads from *The Crisis*, what do you feel you can legitimately conclude about the magazine's readership? What do the ads *suggest* to you about this audience's needs and values?

2. Judging from the results of your categorization of the ads (see p. 101), what sort of economic opportunities could the segregated black economy offer to ambitious African Americans?

3. If you were using these primary sources to make a historical argument, would you say that *The Crisis* advertisements endorsed conservative notions of morality, gender roles, and personal success or that they radically challenged racist stereotypes—or that they did both?

MAKING CONNECTIONS

4. What other types of sources would you want to consult to test, confirm, or correct the impressions these ads created in your mind about *The Crisis* readers?

5. Historians typically focus on the philosophical gap between Booker T. Washington and W. E. B. Du Bois when writing about the years between 1900 and 1915. How might the evidence from these ads be used to argue that readers of *The Crisis* bridged that gap in their own political thinking and economic striving?

6. In the face of racist segregation, African Americans simultaneously advocated integration and created separate institutions, services, and businesses. Now that you have perused these advertisements, imagine the terms of the debate within the twentieth-century black community over whether integration or separatism was best for African Americans.

Beyond the Source

W. E. B. Du Bois served continuously as editor of *The Crisis* from 1910 until 1934, when he resigned in a heated—and somewhat ironic—disagreement with the NAACP board of directors over the issue of segregation. Du Bois had begun his political career in direct opposition to any black acquiescence to white-imposed, legally coded race segregation. During the 1920s, however, Du Bois became persuaded that black nationalism, rooted in strong, separate black communities, was the key to black advancement. He came to regard the NAACP's legal campaigns for racial integration as futile and threatening to black autonomy, and he increasingly looked for socialist solutions to America's economic inequalities.

Du Bois's belief in socialistic black nationalism foreshadowed the radical black politics of the late 1960s and early 1970s, but for young African

Americans in the 1920s, Du Bois seemed hopelessly out of date. Despite his enthusiasm for black pride and autonomy, Du Bois was too intellectual and too traditional in his gender attitudes to fully embrace the cultural experiments of the Harlem Renaissance, and he was too elitist to approve of Marcus Garvey's mass movement to rally working-class blacks in support of black nationalism. In fact, the advertising in *The Crisis* during the 1920s and early 1930s became more elitist as early promotions for get-rich-quick sales opportunities disappeared, along with many of the ads for small businesses, and were replaced by more ads for schools and colleges, beauty products, and books about famous African Americans. The combination of Du Bois's independent stance and the Great Depression caused the circulation of *The Crisis* to decline considerably by 1934. At that point, the NAACP board asserted its authority, insisting that the magazine's editorial policy conform to the organization's integrationist goals, and Du Bois quit — at age sixty-six.

For the next twenty-nine years, until his death at age ninety-five, Du Bois continued to evolve intellectually and politically; he produced several major scholarly works that are still read and admired today. During the anticommunist era of the 1950s, Du Bois was arrested and tried as a foreign agent but was acquitted. Nonetheless, the federal government deprived him of his passport and freedom to travel for several years. In 1960, when he was finally allowed to leave the United States, Du Bois moved to Ghana, in west Africa, and began work on the *Encyclopedia Africana.* He died in Ghana on August 27, 1963. News of Du Bois's death that day was announced from the speaker's platform at the March on Washington, D.C., where Martin Luther King Jr. delivered his "I Have a Dream" speech.

Throughout the twentieth century, the NAACP persisted in challenging the "separate-but-equal" principle that was put into American law in 1896. The organization funded lawsuit after lawsuit and was finally victorious when the Supreme Court ruled against racial segregation in the 1954 *Brown v. Board of Education* case. In the decades since, the NAACP has continued to work against race discrimination in legal, political, cultural, and educational arenas. *The Crisis* magazine continues to be the official publication of the National Association for the Advancement of Colored People and today has a circulation of 250,000. The magazine's Web site, **thecrisismagazine.com,** includes a "statement of purpose" announcing that *The Crisis* is "dedicated to the indefatigable pursuit of racial equality." In this regard, it is still operating very much as a legacy of W. E. B. Du Bois.

Finding and Supplementing the Source

All of the advertisements for this chapter were taken from issues of *The Crisis* magazine published between November 1910 and March 1913. Bound volumes containing past issues of *The Crisis* are available in many libraries and through interlibrary loan. Some aspiring historian needs to write a modern, complete history of the NAACP. For a chronicle of the organization's early history, see Charles F. Kellogg, *NAACP: A History of the National Association for the Advancement of Colored People* (Baltimore, Md.: Johns Hopkins University Press, 1967). For current information on the NAACP and *The Crisis*, see the Web sites **naacp.org** and **thecrisismagazine.com**. Additional background on black activism in the early twentieth century can be found in John Hope Franklin and August Meier, *Black Leaders of the Twentieth Century* (Urbana: University of Illinois Press, 1982); Kevin K. Gaines, *Uplifting the Race: Black Leadership, Politics, and Culture in the Twentieth Century* (Chapel Hill: University of North Carolina Press, 1996); and Deborah Gray White, *Too Heavy a Load: Black Women in Defense of Themselves* (New York: Norton, 1999).

For histories of American advertising, see James D. Norris, *Advertising and the Transformation of American Society, 1865–1920* (New York: Greenwood, 1990); Roland Marchand, *Advertising the American Dream: Make Way for Modernity, 1920–1940* (Berkeley: University of California Press, 1985); and Marilyn Kern-Foxworth, *Aunt Jemima, Uncle Ben, and Rastus: Blacks in Advertising, Yesterday, Today, and Tomorrow* (Westport, Conn.: Praeger, 1994).

CHAPTER 6

Measuring Mental Fitness

Government IQ Tests during World War I

When the U.S. Congress declared war on Germany on April 6, 1917, the president of the American Psychological Association (APA), Robert Yerkes, moved quickly to ensure that psychologists would be given a role to play in the war effort. "In the present perilous situation," Yerkes wrote in an urgent message to the APA council, "it is our duty to cooperate to the fullest extent and immediately toward the increased efficiency of our Army and Navy." During his intense lobbying effort in the month of May, Yerkes convinced the top brass in the U.S. Army (though not in the navy) that psychologists could be of service in sorting and categorizing the millions of raw recruits that the government was rapidly drafting into the military. Yerkes promised the army that experts in the new field of intelligence testing could develop and administer exams precise enough to match each recruit's mental abilities to the right military job.

Wartime often presents opportunities for scientific and technological experts to try out new methods in the name of improved military performance. The beneficiaries of such experiments vary. In the case of intelligence testing in World War I, it was not the army or the soldiers who particularly benefited from the program. Instead, the two groups that profited from the army tests were professional psychologists, who gained new legitimacy from their high profile in wartime, and those political activists who used the psychologists' interpretations of the tests to claim that the racial superiority of white people from northern and western Europe was now a proven scientific fact. So while army officials at U.S. military training camps in 1917 and 1918 doubted that written tests administered by a bunch of "mental meddlers" from university psychology departments could tell who would make a good soldier or officer, plenty of civilians during and after the war embraced the results of the army's mental tests in order to advance their own professional and political interests.

The military draft instituted at the start of America's participation in World War I put over four million men in uniform. Thirteen percent of those soldiers were African American, and 20 percent were foreign-born who represented at least forty-nine different foreign languages. The vast majority of draftees were under the age of thirty, and 70 percent worked as either farmhands or manual laborers. Among white native-born recruits, the median number of years in school was 6.9; among immigrants, it was 4.7; and among Southern blacks, half had less than 2.6 years of schooling. One sample of white native-born soldiers found that only 18 percent had attended high school and most had not graduated. Given this profile, it is not surprising that close to a quarter of those drafted into the U.S. Army were classified as illiterate in English.

Two different sets of tests were administered to the recruits: "alpha" tests for those literate in English and "beta" tests for those not literate in English. Robert Yerkes and his colleagues in the psychological testing movement were insistent that the test questions they asked of this diverse and minimally educated population of recruits were free of cultural and educational bias and would measure only "native intellectual ability." While admitting that school experience had some influence, Yerkes insisted that "in the main the soldier's inborn intelligence and not the accidents of the environment determined his mental rating or grade."

These references to "native intellectual ability" and "inborn intelligence" are cues that Yerkes, like his colleagues Lewis Terman and Carl Brigham, subscribed to a "hereditarian" view of mental ability. According to this view, intelligence was a unified, universal human characteristic that was passed genetically from parents to children. Like height or weight, intelligence could be measured by a standardized instrument, like a yardstick or a scale, and that instrument—the mental test—could be reliably administered, regardless of the cultures or life experiences of the test takers. Indeed, it was Lewis Terman who invented the notion of the "intelligence quotient," or IQ, which was derived by dividing a person's test score, expressed in terms of "mental age," by the person's actual chronological age. According to hereditarians, an individual's IQ revealed the mental capacity transmitted in the family genes.

Not all psychologists in these years were hereditarians. Some took the "environmental" position that the defining fact of life is the unique capacity of human beings to be influenced, for better or for worse, by their environment. Environmentalists therefore argued that an individual's performance on a mental test reflected that individual's life experience and education as much, if not more, than it did the individual's genetic inheritance. This position did not mean that environmentalists opposed the use of mental tests. In fact, Alfred Binet, the French researcher who first developed a standardized intelligence test, was a staunch environmentalist. But Binet took the position that tests of mental abilities could describe only a single individual's intellectual ability; tests could not reveal the genetic or environmental causes of that ability but could be useful for diagnosing and treating an individual's learning problems.

Binet opposed the administration of mental tests to large groupings of people or the use of such tests to generalize about the mental abilities of whole categories of people.

World War I gave those U.S. psychologists devoted to intelligence testing a chance to convince the American public that testing was a valid and useful social practice. Given that opportunity, psychologists temporarily tabled their debates over heredity and environment and stifled their differences over individualized versus group tests. Only after the war did the environmentalists realize that the hereditarians had taken control of the national discussion about mental testing and intended to use the results of the wartime tests to support the political view that certain categories of people were inherently more intelligent than other groups and, thus, more worthy of admittance to the United States as immigrants or more worthy of receiving tax dollars for their segregated, all-white schools.

Hereditarian psychologists like Yerkes, Terman, and Brigham drew directly from the aggregate results of wartime tests when making their postwar arguments for inherited, categorical differences in human intellectual abilities. By the time the war ended in November 1918, psychologists based at twenty-four training camps around the United States were administering two hundred thousand tests per month. All told, close to half of all soldiers drafted into the wartime army, about 1.75 million, were tested before shipping out. Both the alpha and the beta tests were scored on a point scale that was converted into letter grades ranging from A to E. An A signified that the individual was "a high officer type"; a B suggested "splendid sergeant material"; a C indicated that the subject was a "good private type, with some fair to good NCO (noncommissioned officer) material"; those who scored a D were "usually fair soldiers, but often slow in learning"; and those who scored a half-grade lower than D were thought to be marginally fit for regular service. If a recruit scored a grade of E, he was declared unfit for regular army service.

When reporting to the American public about the army's wartime mental testing program, Yerkes and his colleagues did not emphasize the weak correlation between test scores and army officers' independent assessment of their soldiers' intelligence. Nor did they discuss the fact that army officials often ignored the testers' recommendations when placing soldiers in jobs. Instead, they pointed to the broader social implications of the tests, alerting the public to the fact that only 12 percent of the recruits tested scored in the A or B range and that the translation of recruits' intelligence scores into "mental age" indicated an average of just over thirteen years. The mental age for "normal" intelligence was set at sixteen years, while a "moron" was defined as an adult performing intellectually at a mental age below twelve years. So the hereditarians' first claim was that the tests revealed an alarming number of morons in the young, male adult population of the United States in 1918.

Environmentalists interpreted this test result as evidence that the United States had a serious educational problem, noting that 86 percent of native-born white recruits were literate enough to qualify for the alpha test, but only 44 percent of foreign-born recruits, 67 percent of Northern blacks, and 35 percent of Southern blacks qualified. The hereditarians said the pattern of intelligence scores was the same for both alpha and beta tests, so literacy due to schooling was irrelevant. In their published discussions of the tests, both Yerkes and Brigham presented charts showing that 13 percent of all native-born white test takers ranked in the A or B range, but only 4.6 percent of foreign-born whites scored that high and just 1.4 percent of African Americans placed in those ranks. They then noted that only 24 percent of native-born whites scored in the D to E ranks while 44.6 percent of foreign-born whites sank to that level and fully 67.5 percent of African Americans were in those low ranks. Yerkes and Brigham denied that practice with test taking in school accounted for these differences in scores, arguing instead that "native intelligence" was the original factor determining "continuance in school." They similarly denied that a health factor like hookworm disease, common among Southern blacks, could explain these low test scores; on the contrary, they said, it was innately low intelligence that caused the poverty that produced such health problems.

In presenting the test results to the public, the hereditarians also had to explain the fact that immigrants scored higher the longer they had been residents in the United States. Hereditarian psychologists denied that this meant individual experience influenced the test results. Instead, they produced more charts, matching foreign countries to test scores, in order to argue that it was not actually length of stay in the United States but country of origin that determined test performance. This was a politically significant argument because anti-immigrant activists at the time were claiming that "old immigrants"—those from northern and western Europe—were intellectually superior to the "new immigrants" from southern and eastern Europe, who had been arriving in much greater numbers since 1900. According to Brigham, the immigrant "group coming to this country in the years 1903 to 1907 had a higher average intelligence than the 1908 to 1912 group, and a lower average intelligence than immigrants coming to this country 1898 to 1902." Thus, the hereditarian psychologists interpreted the army mental test scores in a way that supported those political activists, known as "nativists," who wanted to restrict the number of new immigrants coming from southern and eastern Europe on the grounds that they were, quite literally, morons.

When the U.S. Army originally agreed to bring Robert Yerkes and his colleagues into military training camps to administer mental tests, it had no intention of providing hereditarian psychologists with a huge tax-supported laboratory in which to test their nascent theories of innate intelligence. Rather, the army hoped to increase its efficiency in processing and placing millions of raw recruits in suitable military jobs. In the end, no one claimed that the army's goals had been achieved, but many agreed with James Cattell, Columbia University's premier psychologist, when he said that "the army intelligence tests have put psychology on the map of the United States, extending in some cases beyond these limits into fairyland."

Using Intelligence Tests as a Source

There are at least four research questions that would prompt a historian to take a close look at the tests administered to army recruits during World War I. A historian of science studying the ways in which cultural attitudes shape scientists' assumptions would want to examine these questions for evidence of what the biologist Stephen J. Gould termed "the tenacity of unconscious bias." So, too, a historian of science, particularly of the field of psychology, would need to be well acquainted with the types of questions used in the army tests in order to make comparisons with intelligence tests used before and after the war and to discuss the evolution of test design, the scientific and cultural assumptions influencing design, and the methodological errors and corrections made in test design over the years.

A social historian interested in showing the ways in which cultural prejudices about race and ethnicity were expressed in actual practice might very well examine the interpretations of the test results in the postwar writings of Yerkes and Brigham and others. Although the social historian's focus would likely be on the use of the test results to advocate for specific laws and policies, a familiarity with the tests themselves would greatly strengthen the historian's discussion of the cultural climate that fostered mental tests, race segregation, and immigration restriction. Finally, a historian trying to capture the lived experience of the young men drafted into the U.S. Army during World War I would undoubtedly read through the tests and probably try to take a few of them, if only to attempt bridging the gap that separates those raw recruits from the historian writing about them.

A historian would want to peruse tests like the "digit and symbol" test for illiterate recruits such as the one shown below from Robert M. Yerkes, *Psychological Examining in the United States Army,* Volume 15, *Memoirs of the National Academy of Sciences*. In the actual test, the men were presented with six double rows of fifteen boxes and given the "key" for filling in the empty rows. Each recruit was allotted three minutes to fill in all ninety boxes. To better understand how a recruit might have felt when taking the digit and symbol test, give yourself thirty seconds to fill in these fifteen boxes, using the key provided.

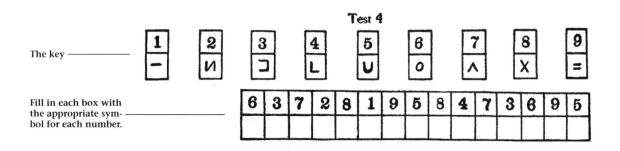

Advantages and Disadvantages of Working with Intelligence Tests

For anyone writing a history of intelligence testing in the United States, the army tests are an invaluable primary source because they show what the test designers regarded as an unbiased tool for measuring "innate" intelligence. The tests are, therefore, a tool for measuring the cultural blinders worn by many psychologists early in the twentieth century, helping the historian to illustrate the assumptions shared by prominent researchers at the time.

There are, however, disadvantages to working with intelligence tests, and historians must exercise caution when studying these tests in isolation from other types of sources. For the historian of science, the tests do not entirely speak for themselves; additional knowledge and information would be needed in order to fully analyze these tests or tell a complete story about their creation. All historians of science must be trained to understand the research methods and research reports of the scientists they are studying, so any historian of psychology who wanted to analyze the army tests as one step in the evolution of the profession's approach to testing would need independent knowledge of the assumptions, strategies, methods, and fallacies that govern intelligence testing, as well as access to tests that preceded and followed the army tests.

A historian of psychology who wanted to narrate the story behind the army tests would need a different set of supplementary material. The tests themselves, for example, cannot reveal that before the war, Robert Yerkes actually criticized Lewis Terman for designing group tests that did not adequately separate school skills from what Yerkes called "innate" intelligence. Letters and memos from the early months of the war are needed to show that Yerkes chose to put aside his scientific disagreements with Terman because Terman had created the only fully operational, easily scored group test available—and Yerkes was late in delivering the tests he had promised to the army. The tests themselves are valuable for seeing what the available testing method was in 1917, but the tests do not reveal Yerkes' professional and political motivations for adopting an instrument he knew to be flawed. Nor can the tests reveal errors in the scoring methods used by Yerkes and his team. For example, as a scientist, Yerkes knew that scores of zero indicated the test was invalid in some way, either because the test taker had not understood instructions, or had not known how to use a pencil, or was too flustered to address the assigned task in the few minutes allotted. Looking at the tests can help the historian understand how zero scores might occur, but, again, reading the memos between Yerkes and the psychologists at the camps is necessary for an understanding of how the pressure of time, the lack of adequate funding, and the desire to keep the program operating caused Yerkes to include zero scores in the final results and thus compromise basic principles of scientific methodology.

The historian interested in tracing the ways that cultural prejudices get translated into tangible social policy would find in the tests a gold mine of evidence. Like the historian of science, the social historian could analyze the class and ethnic biases that produced a series of tests the designers regarded as bias-free and could use that analysis to discuss the cultural gap between the intellectual elite in U.S. society and those they intended to study and serve.

But the tests alone would not suffice for the historian writing about the various interest groups in the United States who later used the test results to argue for immigration restriction or to blame the low intelligence of nonwhites for their lack of education. Here, again, the tests would provide vital illustrative data, but the historian would need the psychologists' written analyses of the test results to get the full spectrum of attitudes that informed the testing process. For example, the tests themselves make clear that army recruits had very little time in which to complete each section; speed was of the essence, which critics said was a factor confounding the results. By reading Carl Brigham's 1922 report on the tests, however, the historian learns that the tests' defenders were untroubled by the charge that the "hurry up" aspect of the test might skew an immigrant's performance. Brigham argued that such a "hurry up" quality was "typically American" and therefore a "fortunate" feature of the testing situation. According to Brigham, "ability to adjust to test conditions" was part of "our definition of intelligence," so if the immigrant army recruit was unable to adjust to a "typically American," "hurry up" situation, then that recruit lacked the sort of innate intelligence desirable in the army—and in the United States in general. A historian would need familiarity with the tests in order to appreciate the "hurry up" quality Brigham was defending and also would need to read psychologists like Brigham in order to know how those empowered to interpret the tests viewed the testing situation.

Finally, of course, the historian seeking to recapture the young army recruits' experience would want to take some of the tests to get a taste of that aspect of their training. This exercise is risky if the historian leaps to believing that taking an old test eliminates the gulf that separates us from those who once lived in that other country we call "the past." But just as risky for a historian is the failure to practice the imaginative skill of human empathy. Historians not only analyze historical data through the long lens of time but also try to imagine what the past felt like, looked like, smelled like; they are always balancing their analysis of how multiple factors shaped past events with their empathy for the human beings whose lives were altered by those factors and events.

As you work through the army tests provided here, try to place yourself in an army training camp in Nebraska in 1918. Imagine that you are an Italian immigrant whose family moved to Tampa, Florida, in 1905, when you were five years old. Now you're away from home, living among strangers, learning how to march in formation, how to carry and shoot a rifle, how to pack and repack your duffel bag, how to stay out of your sergeant's way. You're trying to keep up your patriotic spirit about going out and killing some "Huns" while trying not to be scared. In the midst of all that, an officer shows up at your barracks and announces that it is your turn to take the "mental tests." You've probably already met with a doctor and answered a few questions to prove that you are not crazy. Now you have to prove that you are not, in the parlance of the day, "feebleminded." Maybe the officer who escorts you to the test indicates his view that the tests are stupid and should not be taken seriously; maybe the officer respects the tests and warns you that you had better do well on them if you hope to amount to anything in the army.

Once you get to the camp's testing site—a spare storage room with poor lighting, poor acoustics, and no fresh air—you are given a literacy test to determine if you should take the alpha tests for those literate in English or the beta tests for those not literate in English. Sometimes, when a high number of illiterates crowd into the camp's beta test, the harried examiners arbitrarily lower the literacy score needed to qualify to take the alpha test. As a boy, you attended an American school and learned how to read and write English, but most of your reading in the last eight years has been of Italian-language newspapers. Will your English be good enough to qualify for the alpha test? Do you want it to be?

Once inside the test room, the instructions you receive, in writing or orally, are given very quickly, and you cannot ask questions if you do not understand the instructions. For you and the other ninety men crammed into the too-small testing space with too few desks (see Figure 6.1), the tests take less than an hour, and the examiner is constantly barking at you to hurry up. It is hard to hear everything the examiner says, but you don't recall him saying that it is impossible to complete any one of the tests. And no one pauses to show the guy next to you how to hold the pencil that is needed for both the alpha and beta tests. Indeed, one examiner later recalls how "touching" it was "to see the intense effort . . . put into answering questions, often by men who never before had held a pencil in their hands." Touching or not, try to imagine this sort of scenario as you take the following tests.

Figure 6.1 Group examination in a Hospital Ward, Camp Lee, October 1917

Working with the Source

Test yourself as you work through the following sources. According to Yerkes' report, if you scored under 55 percent on the beta test or below 21 percent on the alpha test, you qualified as a "moron" but still could potentially be a good private in the army. Use this table to record your scores.

	Completed in allotted time?	Score
1. The Maze		_____ of 3 correct
2. Cube Analysis		_____ of 8 correct
3. Picture Completion		_____ of 9 correct
4. Disarranged Sentences		_____ of 20 correct
5. Arithmetical Problems		_____ of 10 correct
6. Information		_____ of 20 correct

The Source: Beta Tests for Illiterate Soldiers and Alpha Tests for Literate Soldiers

BETA TESTS FOR ILLITERATE SOLDIERS

Soldiers deemed illiterate in English were given eight different types of tests. These beta tests were administered to 14 percent of the native-born white recruits, 56 percent of the foreign-born whites, 33 percent of the Northern blacks, and 65 percent of the Southern blacks. You have already seen one type of beta test, the "digit and symbol" test. Below are three more, along with the exact instructions that the soldiers received before each test. Test administrators read these precise instructions from a standardized script.

 ## Beta Test #1: The Maze

The soldiers were given two minutes to complete five mazes. Give yourself one minute, twenty seconds to complete three.

Instructions: "Now turn your papers over. This is test 1 *here* (pointing to page of record blank). Look." After all have found the page, examiner continues, "Don't make any marks till I say, 'Go ahead.' Now *watch.*" After touching both arrows, examiner traces through the first maze with pointer and then motions the demonstrator to go ahead. Demonstrator traces path through first maze *with crayon*, slowly and hesitatingly. Examiner then traces second maze and motions to demonstrator to go ahead. Demonstrator makes one mistake by going into a blind alley. . . . Examiner shakes his head vigorously, says "No—no," takes the demonstrator's hand and traces back to the place where he may start again. Demonstrator traces rest of maze so as to indicate an attempt to make haste. . . . Examiner says "Good." Then holding up blank, "Look here," and draws an imaginary line across the page from left to right for every maze on the page. Then "All right. Go ahead. Do it (pointing to men and then to books). Hurry up." The idea of working fast must be impressed on the men during the maze test. Examiner and orderlies walk around the room, motioning to men who are not working, and saying, "Do it, do it, hurry up, quick." At the end of 2 minutes examiner says, "Stop! Turn over the page to test 2."

Source: All of the IQ tests in this chapter are reprinted from Robert M. Yerkes, *Psychological Examining in the United States Army*, Volume XV, *Memoirs of the National Academy of Sciences.* Submitted to the Surgeon General of the Army as the Official Report of the Division of Psychology of the Surgeon General, and published with the approval of the Department of War (Washington, D.C.: Government Printing Office, 1921), 204, 205, 206, 251, 252, 254, 256.

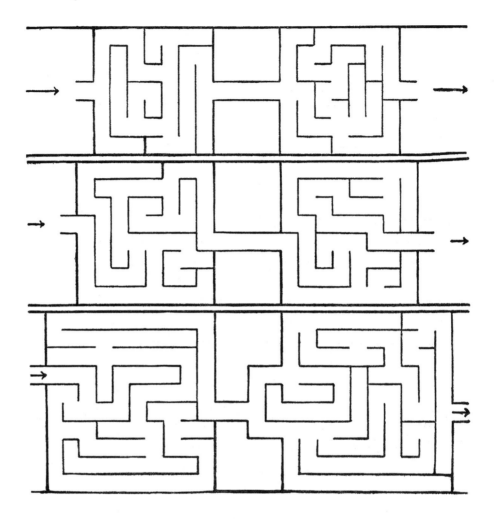

 Beta Test #2: Cube Analysis

The soldiers were given two and one-half minutes to calculate the number of cubes in sixteen drawings. Give yourself one minute, fifteen seconds to make the calculation for eight drawings. (Test answers are provided at the bottom of p. 127.)

Instructions: "This is the test 2 *here*. Look." After everyone has found the page — "Now watch." The order of procedure is as follows:

(1) Examiner points to the three-cube model on the blackboard, making a rotary movement of the point to embrace the entire picture.

(2) With similar notion he points to the three-cube model on the shelf.

(3) Examiner points next to picture on blackboard and asks, "How much?"

(4) Examiner turns to cube model and counts aloud, putting up his fingers while so doing, and encouraging the men to count with him.

(5) Examiner taps each cube on the motions to demonstrator, asking him "How much?"

(6) Demonstrator (pointing) counts cubes on blackboard silently and writes the figure 3 in proper place.

Throughout the demonstration the counting is done deliberately, not more rapidly than one cube per second. At end of demonstration examiner points to page and says, "All right. Go ahead." At the end of 2½ minutes he says, "Stop! Look at me and don't turn the page."

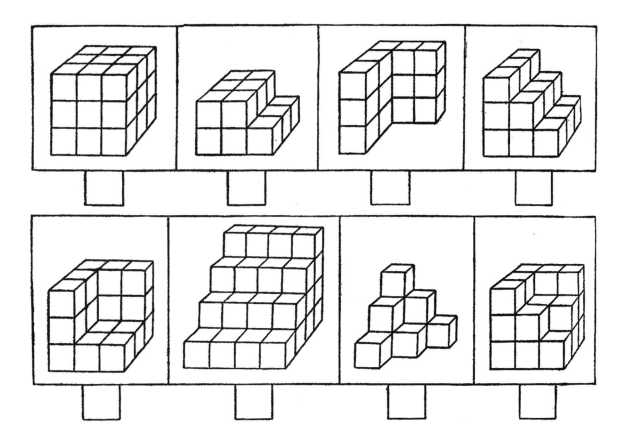

3   *Beta Test #6: Picture Completion*

The soldiers were given three minutes to "fix" twenty pictures. Give yourself ninety seconds to fix nine pictures. (Test answers are provided at the bottom of this page.)

Instructions: "This is test 6 *here*. Look. A lot of pictures." After everyone has found the place, "Now watch." Examiner points to hand and says to demonstrator, "Fix it." Demonstrator does nothing, but looks puzzled. Examiner points to the picture of the hand, and then to the place where the finger is missing and says to demonstrator, "Fix it; fix it." Demonstrator then draws in finger. Examiner says, "That's right." Examiner then points to fish and place for eye and says, "Fix it." After demonstrator has drawn missing eye, examiner points to each of the four remaining drawings and says, "Fix them all." Demonstrator works samples out slowly and with apparent effort. When the samples are finished examiner says, "All right. Go ahead. Hurry up!" During the course of this test the orderlies walk around the room and locate individuals who are doing nothing, point to their pages and say, "Fix it. Fix them," trying to set everyone working. At the end of 3 minutes examiner says, "Stop! But don't turn over the page."

ALPHA TESTS FOR LITERATE SOLDIERS

Soldiers who tested as "literate" in English were also given eight different types of tests. The alpha tests were administered to 86 percent of the native-born white recruits, 44 percent of the foreign-born recruits, 67 percent of the Northern blacks, and 35 percent of the Southern blacks. Included here are three of the alpha tests along with the exact written instructions that accompanied them. The army examiners rotated different versions of each test so soldiers could not predict the exact questions they would receive on any given day.

4 | *Alpha Test #3: Disarranged Sentences*

The soldiers were given two minutes, ten seconds to complete this test. (Test answers are provided at the end of the test on p. 130.)

Instructions: "The words MORNING THE RISES EVERY SUN in that order don't make a sentence; but they would make a sentence if put in the right order: THE SUN RISES EVERY MORNING and the statement is true. Again, the words ANIMAL A IS THE RARE DOG would make a sentence if put in the right order: THE DOG IS A RARE ANIMAL but the statement is false. Below are twenty mixed-up sentences. Some of them are true and some are false. When I say go, take these sentences one at a time. Decide what each sentence would say if the words were straightened out, but don't write them yourself. Then, if what it would say is true, draw a line under the word true; if what it would say is false, then draw a line under the word false. If you cannot be sure, guess. Begin with No. 1 and work right down the page until time is called."

1. wood guns of made are . . . . .true   false

2. people are many candy of fond . . . . true   false

3. war in are useful airplanes the . . . . true   false

4. must die men all . . . . .true   false

5. property floods life and destroy . . . . true   false

6. grow a climate oranges cold in . . . . true   false

7. days there in are week eight a . . . . .true   false

8. months warmest are summer the. . . . . true   false

9. are and apples long thin. . . . . .true   false

10. clothing valuable are for and wool cotton. . . . . .true   false

11. health necessary camp a is to clean. . . . . .true   false

12. Germany of Wilson king is England and . . . . true   false

13. work like all men . . . . .true   false

14. water cork on float will not . . . . true   false

15. iron paper made of is filings . . . . true   false

16. tropics is in the produced rubber . . . . true   false

17. fish hunt and like boys to never . . . . .true   false

18. size now of guns use are great in . . . . true   false

19. bushes trees roots have and their air the in . . . . true   false

20. not bees lazy and are ants called . . . . .true   false

---

Answers: 1: guns are made of wood/true; 2: many people are fond of candy/true; 3: airplanes are useful in the war/true; 4: all men must die/true; 5: floods destroy life and property/true; 6: oranges grow in a cold climate/false; 7: there are eight days in a week/false; 8: the summer months are warmest/true; 9: apples are long and thin/false; 10: wool and cotton are valuable for clothing/true; 11: a clean camp is necessary to health/true; 12: Wilson is king of England and Germany/false; 13:all men like work/false; 14: cork will not float on water/false; 15: paper is made of iron filings/false; 16: rubber is produced in the tropics/true; 17: boys never like to fish and hunt/false; 18: guns now in use are of great size/true; 19: trees and bushes have their roots in the air/false; 20: ants and bees are not called lazy/true.

5   *Alpha Test #2: Arithmetical Problems*

Soldiers were given five minutes to solve twenty of these word problems. Give yourself two minutes and thirty seconds to solve ten of them. (Test answers are provided at the end of the test on p. 131.)

Instructions: "Attention! Look at the directions at the top of the page while I read them. Get the answers to these examples as quickly as you can. Use the side of this page to figure on if you need to. I will say stop at the end of five minutes. You may not be able to finish all of them, but do as many as you can in the time allowed.—Ready—GO!"

1. If 24 men are divided into squads of 8, how many
   squads will there be?   Answer: _____

2. A company advanced 5 miles from their trenches
   and retreated three miles. How far were they from
   their trenches then?   Answer: _____

3. A regiment marched 40 miles in five days. The first day they marched 9 miles, the second day 6 miles, the third 10 miles, the fourth 8 miles. How many miles did they march the last day?   Answer: _____

4. If it takes 6 men 3 days to dig a 60-foot trench, how many men are needed to dig it in half a day?   Answer: _____

5. A rectangular bin holds 400 cubic feet of lime. If the bin is 10 feet long and 5 feet wide, how deep is it?   Answer: _____

6. A recruit spent one-eighth of his spare change for post cards and four times as much for a box of letter paper, and then had 90 cents left. How much money did he have at first?   Answer: _____

7. If a man runs a hundred yards in 10 seconds, how many feet does he run in a fifth of a second?   Answer: _____

8. A U-boat makes 8 miles an hour under water and 15 miles on the surface. How long will it take to cross a 100-mile channel, if it has to go two-fifths of the way under water?   Answer: _____

9. A ship has provisions to last her crew of 500 men 6 months. How long would it last 1200 men?   Answer: _____

10. A certain division contains 3,000 artillery, 15,000 infantry and 1,000 cavalry. If each branch is expanded proportionately until there are in all 20,900 men, how many will be added to the artillery?   Answer: _____

Answers: 1: 3; 2: 2; 3: 7; 4: 36; 5: 8; 6: $2.40; 7: 6; 8: 9; 9: 2.5; 10: 300.

6 *Alpha Test #8: Information*

Soldiers were given four minutes to complete forty of these sentences. Give yourself two minutes to complete twenty of them. (Test answers are provided at the end of the test on p. 133.)

Instructions: In each of the sentences below, you have four choices for the last word. Only one of them is correct. In each sentence draw a line under the one of the four words which makes the truest sentence. If you cannot be sure, guess.

1. Seven-up is played with   rackets   cards   pins   dice

2. Denver is in   Ohio   Georgia   Colorado   Michigan

3. The Leghorn is a kind of   horse   chicken   fish   cattle

4. The main factory of the Ford automobile is in   Bridgeport   Cleveland   Detroit   Youngstown

5. Silk comes from a kind of   crab   worm   beetle   plant

6. The Declaration of Independence was signed in   Detroit   Boston   Philadelphia   Concord

7. The artichoke is a   fish   lizard   vegetable   snake

8. The forward pass is used in   tennis   hand-ball   chess   foot ball

9. Jess Willard is a   fortune-teller   labor-leader   pugilist   singer

10. Revolvers are made by   Smith & Wesson   Armour & Co.   Ingersoll   Anheuser-Busch

11. The currant grows on a   tree   vine   sheep   bush

12. General Lee surrendered at Appomatox in   1812   1886   1865   1832

13. A first-class batter now averages around   .300   .900   .600   .100

14. The Pittsburgh team is called   Giants   Cubs   Pirates   Tigers

15. The Union Commander at Mobile Bay was   Dewey   Sampson   Schley   Farragut

16. Among the allies of Germany is   Norway   Rumania   Bulgaria   Portugal

17. To set fire to a house is called   larceny   incest   mayhem   arson

18. The spark-plug of a gas engine belongs in the   crank case   manifold
    cylinder   carburetor

19. The author of the "Scarlet Letter" is   Poe   Hawthorne   Cooper
    Holmes

20. John Sargent is a well-known   author   scientist   politician
    painter

Answers: 1/cards; 2/Colorado; 3/chicken; 4/Detroit; 5/worm; 6/Philadelphia; 7/vegetable; 8/foot ball; 9/pugilist; 10/Smith & Wesson; 11/bush; 12/1865; 13/.300; 14/Pirates; 15/Farragut; 16/Bulgaria; 17/arson; 18/cylinder; 19/Hawthorne; 20/painter.

Analyzing the Source

REFLECTING ON THE SOURCE

1. If you were writing about the experience of a young soldier in a training camp in 1918, how might your own experience taking the tests influence your story?

2. If you were either a historian of science or a social historian writing about the effect of cultural attitudes on the army's intelligence tests, what four examples would you select from the six tests you just studied to illustrate your argument? What point would you want to make with those four examples?

3. In addition to using these tests to explore the ethnic and racial prejudices of the psychologists who designed and analyzed these tests, how might the test questions here also be used to illustrate a gap between the economic classes in America in 1918? In your judgment, which test questions best illuminate that gap?

MAKING CONNECTIONS

4. In the decade preceding World War I, many African Americans in the southern United States migrated northward to cities such as Chicago, Cleveland, New York, and Detroit. How could a historian use the army's statistical profile of who took beta tests and who took alpha tests to explain the reasons blacks migrated north? How could a historian of science use those same statistics to show the fallacy in hereditarians' claim that all African Americans, as a single category, are innately less intelligent than all white Americans?

5. Between 1900 and 1930, enrollment in American public high schools increased by 747 percent (from 519,251 to 4,399,422 students), even though state laws allowed students to leave school at age fourteen. How might environmental psychologists and educators in the 1920s have used the results of the army intelligence tests to argue for increased funding for public high schools and increased attention to night schools for adolescents in the workforce?

6. Our society continues to test individuals' intellectual performance in order to place them in jobs, schools, and treatment programs. Psychologists today state that these current tests measure experience, not innate abilities, but critics argue that the tests are still culturally biased and, thus, poor measures of experience. What, for you, is the strongest argument in favor of using tests for placement purposes? What is the strongest argument against using such tests?

Beyond the Source

The most direct result of the army's mental testing program was to popularize psychological testing. As one historian has put it, "if psychology had not in fact contributed significantly to the war, the war had contributed significantly to psychology." One study of popular magazines published between 1900 and 1930 found very few articles on intelligence testing before the war, but after the war there were more popular articles on intelligence testing than on any other topic in the sciences. During the 1920s, a groundswell of enthusiasm for intelligence testing was a great boon to the producers of such tests. Lewis Terman's call for "a mental test for every child" became a popular slogan in the 1920s; by 1923, 125 cities were regularly using such tests to sort students into the correct "track" in school, and hundreds of businesses were using them to screen job candidates. By 1930, there were 130 different types of mental tests on the market. Psychology was no longer an obscure, rarefied field of study. Through the vehicle of intelligence tests, psychology established itself as a practical discipline whose claim to measuring and quantifying human mentality gave it the scientific status of physics or chemistry. This was precisely the outcome Robert Yerkes had hoped for at the start of World War I.

The popularity of intelligence testing gave the army's experiment two additional, indirect avenues of social influence in the 1920s: one avenue led in the direction of the environmentalists, the other in the direction of the hereditarians. Environmentalists used the results of the army's tests (and subsequent batteries of school tests) to argue that the United States was failing to "Americanize" its immigrants. The problem, said the environmentalists, was not that immigrants were innately less intelligent but that they were uneducated in the language, the culture, the values, and the politics of American society. Historians of Americanization programs can point to numerous examples of the arrogance, intrusiveness, and insensitivity of such educational campaigns, but they are quick to point out that advocates of Americanization were at least optimistic about immigrants' abilities to contribute to U.S. society. By definition, people who mounted educational campaigns believed in their clients' capacity to learn.

By contrast, the hereditarians drew on the army's intelligence tests and subsequent mental tests to argue that nonwhites and southern and eastern Europeans were innately, irrevocably inferior in intellectual capacity to whites from northern and western Europe. In 1921 and 1924 the United States established, for the first time in its history, quotas on the number of Europeans who could emigrate to the United States, and those quotas were consciously designed to let in more northern and western Europeans than southern and eastern Europeans. Historians who study the immigration exclusion movement do not find that the army testing program directly caused passage of the quota laws; momentum for those laws was building in certain quarters before World War I. But racism and nativism became particularly ferocious in the United States after the war, and the test data provided by hereditarian psychologists endowed rising prejudice with scientific legitimacy.

In sharp contrast to the optimism of the environmentalists, the psychologist Carl Brigham concluded his 1923 report on the army tests, *Study of American Intelligence*, with the dire warning that American intelligence was declining and would continue to decline unless "really important steps" were taken to prevent the "continued propagation of defective strains in the present population." For Brigham, immigration restriction was only a start in the right direction; native white Americans' willingness to control the reproduction of others would, he predicted, "determine the future course of our national life"(p. 210).

Twenties-style immigration quotas remained in place in the United States until 1965, but the American people proved unwilling to systematically limit the reproduction of citizens or immigrants in the country. Over the decades, hereditarian claims were disproved by the flood of psychological testing programs the hereditarians themselves had unleashed. Gradually, the environmentalist position came to dominate the field of psychological testing, and assumptions about "innate" intelligence were replaced with questions about the ways in which the environment shapes what we know and how we know it. Today, those who design and administer tests do not call them "intelligence" tests; they call them "achievement" tests, and they insist that the tests measure only the information and skills a person has acquired, not any inborn intellectual ability. Still, the debate rages about whether it is possible, in a diverse society, to design national, standardized tests, such at the SAT or the ACT, that accurately assess an individual's facility with recalling and using information if the content of the questions is utterly foreign to the individual's life experience. So while modern society has rejected hereditarian beliefs in innate intelligence, it has not resolved the debate over cultural bias in standardized tests.

Finding and Supplementing the Source

All of the army tests and the examiners' directions to test takers can be found in Robert M. Yerkes, *Psychological Examining in the United States Army*, Volume XV, *Memoirs of the National Academy of Sciences*. Yerkes' 890-page report was submitted as the Official Report of the Division of Psychology of the Surgeon General and published with the approval of the Department of War (Washington, D.C.: Government Printing Office, 1921). A 300-page presentation of the tests and their results was made available to the public in the book *Army Mental*

Tests, compiled and edited by Clarence S. Yoakum and Robert M. Yerkes and published "with the authorization of the War Department" by Henry Holt and Company, New York, 1920. Carl Brigham's very political presentation of the test results, *Study of American Intelligence* (Princeton, N.J.: Princeton University Press, 1923), opened with a foreword by Robert Yerkes.

Among the excellent studies of the history of intelligence testing in the United States are *Psychological Testing and American Society, 1890–1930,* a collection of articles edited by Michael M. Sokal (New Brunswick: Rutgers University Press, 1987); Raymond E. Fancher, *The Intelligence Men: Makers of the IQ Controversy* (New York: W. W. Norton and Company, 1985); Paul Davis Chapman, *Schools as Sorters* (New York: New York University Press, 1988); Franz Samelson, "Putting Psychology on the Map: Ideology and Intelligence Testing," in *Psychology and Social Context,* edited by Allan R. Buss (New York: Irvington Publishers, 1979); and Daniel J. Kevles, "Testing the Army's Intelligence: Psychologists and the Military in World War I," *Journal of American History* 55 (December 1968): 565–81. In addition, the evolutionary biologist Stephen Jay Gould included an insightful critique of the army tests and Yerkes' interpretation of them in *The Mismeasure of Man* (New York: W. W. Norton and Company, 1981).

Several historians of World War I also include some analysis of the mental testing program in their discussions of the training of the American Expeditionary Force in 1918. See David M. Kennedy, *Over Here: The First World War and American Society* (New York: Oxford University Press, 1980); Ronald Schaffer, *America in the Great War: The Rise of the War Welfare State* (New York: Oxford University Press, 1991); Edward M. Coffman, *The War to End All Wars: The American Military Experience in World War I* (New York: Oxford University Press, 1968); and Gary Mead, *The Doughboys: America and the First World War* (Woodstock, N.Y.: The Overlook Press, 2000).

The contemporary debate about the testing of students has generated a huge literature. Two popular studies that consider both the history and modern impact of the SAT are David Owen and Marilyn Doerr, *None of the Above: The Truth Behind the SATs* (Lanham, Md.: Rowman and Littlefield, 1985, 1999), and Nicholas Lemann, *The Big Test: The Secret History of the American Meritocracy* (New York: Farrar, Straus and Giroux, 1999). Critiques of all sorts of student testing can be found at **fairtest.org.**

CHAPTER 7

Flappers in the Barrio

A Chapter from a Historian's Book

The 1920s are one of the most notoriously misrepresented eras in American popular culture. Our image of the "roaring" decade is dominated by "the flapper," a young woman in a knee-high chemise, smoking a cigarette, dancing the Charleston, and swinging her long beads. That image embodies our collective sense that the Twenties were a time of bold change; the war was over, the Victorian era was past, and modern life had begun. In fact, the era was a time of serious struggle between modernizing forces for change, conservative forces that wanted to maintain Victorian social customs, and reactionary forces that wanted to turn the clock back on the democratic gains of the Progressive era. Rather than a decade of unbridled experimentation, the Twenties were a time of intense negotiations between a world we view as "traditional" and a world we recognize as "modern." Two cultures that made their mark on the 1920s, the youth culture and the Mexican American culture, offer insight into the subtleties of these negotiations.

The mere existence of an identifiable, self-conscious youth culture was evidence of change. Adolescence in American society had, historically, been a time of apprenticeship in adult culture, either in paid jobs where youth were surrounded by and supervised by adults, or in family roles on the farm, in the shop, or in the kitchen. Between 1920 and 1930, however, the share of adolescents spending their days clustered together in high schools increased from 23 percent to 38 percent, and the privileged slice of youth who could attend colleges for four years increased sharply from 8 percent in 1920 to 12 percent in 1930. This concentration of young people served as a critical mass of trendsetters and consumers who defined a separate youth culture. The females among these students, and their wage-earning cohort, announced their generational identity by discarding corsets in favor of looser, shorter dresses, bobbing their hair short, wearing makeup, smoking cigarettes, drinking prohibited liquor, and dancing to jazz music.

Advocates for these trends used such superficial behaviors as proof that the passage of woman suffrage in 1920 had ushered in a new day of sexual equality. Reactionaries were appalled that their just-enacted prohibition on alcohol was being scorned by youth who, though apolitical in every other way, seemed to define themselves in joyful opposition to this particular law. Traditionalists, especially women who had fought for woman suffrage, worried that young women were trading in a cultural legacy of female moral authority, women's sole claim to power in American society, in exchange for the freedom to play with men by men's rules.

In all of the anxious commentary about wanton youth, few noticed how little had actually changed. Across class, race, and ethnicity, young people in the 1920s still assumed that men were destined to be income-earning husbands and fathers and that women were still meant to be at home as wives and mothers. The number of women who chose to live independent of marriage actually decreased in the 1920s; 90 percent of women workers continued to be segregated into just ten occupational categories (including clerical work, domestic service, sales, schoolteaching, and nursing); and women's wages continued to be two-thirds that of men's. The overall number of wives working for pay increased in this decade, but this was a response to inadequate pay for working-class men rather than a sign of female liberation. Despite appearances to the contrary, the fundamentals of family structure and gender roles were unchanged in the "Roaring Twenties."

The styles introduced by 1920s youth culture mostly affected people's experiences before marriage. Traditional "courtship" with the person you intended to marry was replaced with "dating" a variety of people before committing to marriage, and the very private sexual overtures of betrothed Victorian couples gave way to more casual "necking" and "petting" with a series of partners. This modern form of sexual expression sometimes occurred in that new and dangerous dating machine, the chaperone-free automobile. But necking just as often took place in party settings, which guaranteed that free expression would not go far enough to turn into scandal. After all, contraception was still technically illegal and largely inaccessible for single women, and unwed mothers were still stigmatized and economically stranded. Elders' fears for young women's sexual safety were not, therefore, baseless; when playing by men's rules, unprotected women always took a bigger risk for higher stakes. The evidence from the 1920s suggests, however, that most young people understood this. So while they drank, danced, kissed, and caressed with greater abandon than their parents, they also established their own customs that preserved the traditional family system they would inherit.

Just as discussions of youth culture in the 1920s have typically exaggerated change, so have popular portrayals of Mexican American culture in this era often overstated the homogenizing threat of mass media. The assumption has been too easily made that Mexican ethnic identity survived only in rigid isolation from modernity, and that movies, magazines, radios, phonographs, and advertising spelled the loss of that identity. But here again, as with youth culture, the evidence suggests negotiation and accommodation between the old and the new.

Exclusionary laws passed in the 1920s put quotas on the number of southern and eastern European immigrants allowed into the United States, but powerful western farmers in need of field labor insisted that there be no limit on immigrants from Mexico or Latin America. The demand for Mexican labor combined with the disruptions to village life caused by the 1910 Mexican revolution and expanded rail service between Mexico and the United States meant that the Mexican population in California increased from 90,000 to nearly 360,000 in the 1920s, more than four times the overall growth rate for the state.

The largely working-class population of Mexican Americans in the United States in the 1920s contended with poverty and racism. Very few from Mexico enjoyed a comfortable place among that 40 percent of Americans who earned over half of the nation's total income in the twenties; none were included in the elite 5 percent of Americans who took in about 30 percent of the nation's income. Mexicans Americans, like most U.S. workers, were in that bottom 55 percent that lived on 20 percent of the nation's income, typically earning below the $2,000 poverty line for a family of four. Racial prejudices compounded Mexican Americans' economic problems. Those nativists who viewed Mexicans as a "menace" to U.S. civilization and wanted them barred from immigrating drew on existing attitudes toward blacks and Native Americans to bolster their arguments. Mexicans, they said, were as intellectually "low-powered as the Negro" and as morally corrupt as the average "Amerind." One writer claimed that Mexican fathers commonly earned money by prostituting their daughters, concluding that the Mexican man's attitude toward women was like "that of an Indian buck toward his squaw."

In the face of these hostile elements, Mexican American parents struggled to sustain a strong, moral family life and to create a Mexican American culture that combined Mexican traditions with U.S. opportunities. The expansion of national consumer brands, mass marketing, and chain stores in the 1920s did not immediately eliminate local ethnic businesses in cities like Los Angeles. Nor did the rise of a mass media in film, radio, and the recording industry dictate Anglo cultural homogeneity. During the 1920s, one-third of Mexican families owned radios, which were tuned to local, Spanish-language radio broadcasts. When U.S. law forbade the import of Mexican-made records, a Mexican American recording business emerged in Los Angeles marketing urban *corridos*, a genre of storytelling folk song that proved eminently adaptable for singing about modern city life. Ninety percent of Mexican families went to local movie houses in the 1920s, spending as much as $22 a year for shows that combined Mexican American vaudeville acts with silent pictures that posed no language barrier. To take advantage of this burgeoning market, Hollywood made some movies explicitly for Mexican American audiences with stars like Ramon Navarro and Delores del Rio.

To a Mexican traditionalist, such embrace of modern media products looked like corruption of an old and dignified culture. To the U.S. nativist, Mexican participation in the creation of modern media looked like degradation of Anglo-American culture. But for those immigrant parents from Mexico working to raise children who could make the most of U.S. opportunities while retaining a Mexican identity, the cultural process was a fluid, daily mix of ethnic traditions and new circumstances. Like Anglo-American parents, Mexican American parents had a clear goal: family formation and family cohesion within a culture that fit the modern marketplace. Whatever their ethnicity, parents in the 1920s sought to protect that goal against the new demands that work, school, and a consumer culture made on their children, especially their daughters. Modern forces tended to emphasize individual achievement, individual identity, and individual choice, all of which could disrupt family cohesion. Parents' success in the 1920s at containing modern impulses within the traditional family system is a study in cultural accommodation.

Using Secondary Sources as a Source

In every other chapter of this book, you are examining different sorts of "primary" sources. These are the original documents that historians examine and interpret in order to create the books and articles which we often think of as "history" but which are technically called "secondary sources." In this chapter, you have the opportunity to observe how a practicing historian, Dr. Vicki L. Ruiz, integrates primary sources from the 1920s and oral interviews with Mexican American women to create a new perspective on both the era's youth culture and ethnic family life. By examining an excerpt from Ruiz's book, *From Out of the Shadows: Mexican Women in Twentieth-Century America,* you can consider the different parts and processes that go into the construction of a secondary source out of primary sources.

There are two basic types of secondary sources in history: books and articles. Ideally, the writers of both books and articles do the same things: they tell a story about the past, they provide an interpretation of that story, and they relate their story and their interpretation to other historians' stories and interpretations. When readers of history become alert to these three operations they increase their command of both books and articles. In this sense, reading secondary works of history is rather like using computers: we can more fully exploit their potential if we are acquainted with all of their operating features and we grasp the logic driving the basic system.

In the opening pages of "The Flapper and the Chaperone," chapter three of her book, Ruiz performs the operations that are central to any secondary work of history. She conveys the story by opening with a scene in a barrio hall and immediately identifying tension between young women and their chaperones. In the second paragraph, Ruiz makes three arguments about the evidence she is going to present on generational conflict in the 1920s and 1930s, or "between the wars." Next, she describes the oral histories she will be drawing upon because they are the primary source that make her study special. And, along the way, she introduces you to other historians—immigration historians, consumer culture historians, Chicano historians, 1920s historians—who she will be drawing into her discussion. By the end of the first two and one-half pages, Ruiz has acquainted you with her story, her arguments, some of her primary sources, and the other types of historians she has learned from. If you are aware that these are standard features in a secondary history, and that they typically appear early in the text, you will be alert to them as you read.

The key feature to identify in any secondary source is the historian's main argument. This means figuring out what the historian, not the reader, would say is the most important conclusion to be drawn from the evidence. One trick to identifying a historian's thesis lies in remembering that a thesis must be an argument, so a thesis statement must be arguable; it must be open to debate. Consider Ruiz's second paragraph from "The Flapper and the Chaperone":

Ruiz is asserting a pattern in the data	An examination of events like this one reveals the ways in which young Mexican women in the United States between the wars rationalized, resisted, and evaded parental supervision. It offers a glimpse into generational conflict that goes beyond the more general differences in acculturation between immigrants and their children. Chaperonage existed for centuries on both sides of the political border separating Mexico and the United States. While conjuring images of patriarchal domination, chaperonage is best understood as a manifestation of familial oligarchy whereby elders attempted to dictate the activities of youth for the sake of family honor. A family's standing in the community depended, in part, on women's purity. Loss of virginity not only tainted the reputation of an individual, but of her kin as well. For Mexicano immigrants living in a new, bewildering environment filled with temptations, the enforcement of chaperonage assumed a particular urgency.[2]	**Is this debatable?**
Ruiz is using the language of argument here		
Ruiz is making a claim for larger meaning of her evidence		

2. For colonial New Mexico, Ramón Gutiérrez convincingly demonstrates how family honor was tied, in part, to women's *vergüenza* (literally, shame or virginity). See Ramón Gutiérrez, "Honor, Ideology, and Class Gender Domination in New Mexico, 1690–1846," *Latin American Perspectives* 12 (Winter 1985): pp. 81–104. . . . I contend that since mothers and elder female relatives played major roles in enforcing chaperonage, strict supervision of daughters related more to what I term "familial oligarchy" than to patriarchal control.

What more can be learned from her note?

This paragraph, coming very early in the chapter, alerts the reader to three positions Ruiz is going to take: first, that young Mexican women in the United States "rationalized, resisted, and evaded parental supervision"; second, that parental supervision was an expression of "family oligarchy," not patriarchy; third, that chaperonage took on new significance in the United States. We can figure that these are arguments, in contrast to a factual statement like "chaperonage existed for centuries," because they are open to debate. Ruiz's description of the young women's three types of reactions to parental supervision represents her own characterization of their behavior; another historian might describe the behavior differently. Her claim that chaperonage "assumed particular urgency" challenges a popular assumption that immigrants are forced to drop their cultural traditions in the United States. And her assertion that "chaperonage is best understood" as a function of "familial oligarchy" even "while conjuring images" of patriarchy conveys, through language choice, that Ruiz is taking an argumentative stance. When a historian tells a reader that a behavior is "best understood" a certain way, that historian is arguing against other ways of interpreting that behavior. When a historian uses words with strong connotations, such as "conjuring" and "images," that historian is saying that other interpreters have been misled by appearances. By noticing such language, readers can sense that Ruiz is carving out a particular position on a scholarly argument about oligarchy, which means government by a few, and patriarchy, which means government by elder males. Notice that note 2 confirms that suspicion. When Ruiz writes "I contend," she is making clear that this is her own position.

So what is the central thesis of Ruiz's chapter on "The Flapper and the Chaperone"? Is it that young women adopted one of three reactions to parental supervision? Is it that chaperonage was an expression of "familial oligarchy"? Or is it that chaperonage had a particular "urgency" in the U.S. context? Ruiz's second paragraph alerts us to these related arguments but does not tell us which one represents the main point she plans to draw from the evidence. By noting these opening arguments, we can keep track of which arguments the historian discusses the most fully, supports with the most evidence, or gives the most emphasis in the conclusion.

Advantages and Disadvantages of Working with Secondary Sources

For students of history, the distinct advantage of a secondary source is that it pulls together a massive amount of materials that may be scattered in archives and libraries around the world. The historians who examine and interpret such mounds of primary sources are doing a lot of work for the reader. Historians add even more value to their work by explaining how the interpretive story they are telling with their sources compares to the interpretations other historians have made about similar sources and related stories. When historians inform their readers about the broader literature, known as the "historiography," they are giving readers a perspective on a whole set of historical narratives and arguments, not just their own.

The disadvantage of secondary sources is directly connected to their advantage: readers do not have immediate access to all of the primary and secondary sources that the historian used to construct the story and the argument. It can be difficult, therefore, for readers to check a historian's work. A reader's gratitude to a historian for collecting, organizing, and interpreting an array of materials rests squarely upon the reader's trust that the historian has been accurate and honest in presenting the documents and arguments. Trusting that a historian has not falsified or manipulated the data is not the same as assuming that the historian's interpretation is the "right" one. Trust in this case simply means the reader has confidence that the historian has not hidden or manufactured evidence. The historical profession relies on two practical methods to guard against violation of readers' trust: documentation in endnotes and peer review of books and articles.

Nonhistorians often laugh (or sigh) over historians' extensive documentation in endnotes. Why, you might ask, are the few pages of Ruiz's book included here accompanied by thirty-eight endnotes? The answer is that those notes tell the reader where to find the primary and secondary sources that the historian used to support the story and the argument. In Ruiz's note 2, for example, she supports her claim about the importance of unmarried daughters' virginity by referring to the work of Ramón Gutiérrez. It is not Ruiz's purpose to prove this claim; her aim is to build upon it. A reader who doubts this claim or wants to know more about it is invited to consult Gutiérrez. In this way, endnotes serve as a gathering place where readers can see how one historian has drawn from the work of other historians and can locate the work of those other historians. Equally important are endnotes that guide the reader to the precise location of the primary documents or, as you will see in Ruiz's notes, provide information on the people she interviewed. Historical works that provide this sort of documentation offer readers greater assurance that evidence was not fabricated, just as explicit reference to other historians' work offers some guarantee that the work you are reading was not plagiarized or stolen from others.

The custom of review is, along with endnotes, the historical profession's way of preventing or at least identifying fraudulent work. Reviewers often disagree with a historian's argument, but they do not often charge fraud; evidence, after all, can be used honestly and accurately and still be subject to different interpretations. Reviewers raise alarms of fraud only if they find that primary sources cited do not exist or do not contain the evidence the endnotes say they contain, or if whole sentences and paragraphs in one work appear to have been lifted, without quotation marks or citation, from another historian's writing. Recently, serious scandals have erupted over popular works of history in which primary sources were fabricated or in which the work of other historians was not properly credited. In some but not all of these cases, the books were published by nonacademic presses and had not been reviewed before publication by professional historians.

Dismaying as it is to find out that some individuals who write secondary works of history are dishonest, or at least very sloppy, it is also reassuring to know that inaccuracies and acts of plagiarism are discovered, exposed, and taken very seriously. Those who commit such frauds are publicly embarrassed, their careers are tainted if not ruined, grants and prizes are taken away, books are withdrawn from stores, new book contracts are torn up, lawsuits are pursued, television appearances and public speaking engagements are cancelled. As cumbersome, therefore, as peer reviews and endnotes may appear, it is useful to view them as the profession's way of making sure that historians are honest with one another and with the reading public.

Working with the Source

In her second paragraph, Ruiz articulates three arguments. A reader can track those three arguments as a way of determining her central thesis or the point she most wishes to make with the evidence. In reading through the chapter, use this table to follow Ruiz's development of those three arguments.

	Evidence Provided, by Page Number
Argument #1: Young women responded to parental supervision in three ways.	
Argument #2: Parental supervision was an expression of "family oligarchy," not patriarchy.	
Argument #3: Chaperonage "assumed a particular urgency" in the U.S. context.	

The Source: *From Out of the Shadows: Mexican Women in Twentieth-Century America* by Vicki L. Ruiz

 ## Chapter Three, "The Flapper and the Chaperone"

Imagine a gathering in a barrio hall, a group of young people dressed "to the nines" trying their best to replicate the dance steps of Fred Astaire and Ginger Rogers. This convivial heterosocial scene was a typical one in the lives of teenagers during the interwar period. But along the walls, a sharp difference was apparent in the barrios. Mothers, fathers, and older relatives chatted with one another as they kept one eye trained on the dance floor. They were the chaperones—the ubiquitous companions of unmarried Mexican-American women. Chaperonage was a traditional instrument of social control. Indeed, the presence of *la dueña* was the prerequisite for attendance at a dance, a movie, or even church-related events. "When we would go to town, I would want to say something to a guy. I couldn't because my mother was always there," remembered María Ybarra. "She would always stick to us girls like glue. . . . She never let us out of her sight."[1]

An examination of events like this one reveals the ways in which young Mexican women in the United States between the wars rationalized, resisted, and evaded parental supervision. It offers a glimpse into generational conflict that goes beyond the more general differences in acculturation between immigrants and their children. Chaperonage existed for centuries on both sides of the political border separating Mexico and the United States. While conjuring images of patriarchal domination, chaperonage is best understood as a manifestation of familial oligarchy whereby elders attempted to dictate the activities of youth for the sake of family honor. A family's standing in the community depended, in part, on women's purity. Loss of virginity not only tainted the reputation of an individual, but of her kin as well. For Mexicano immigrants living in a new, bewildering environment filled with temptations, the enforcement of chaperonage assumed a particular urgency.[2]

Historians Donna Gabaccia and Sydney Stahl Weinberg have urged immigration historians to notice the subtle ways women shaped and reshaped their environments, especially within the family. In addition, pathbreaking works by Elizabeth Ewen, Andrew Heinze, and Susan Glenn examine the impact of U.S. consumer culture on European immigrants.[3] Indeed, while some Mexican-American youth negotiated missionary idealizations of American life, other

Source: Vicki L. Ruiz, *From Out of the Shadows: Mexican Women in Twentieth-Century America* (New York: Oxford University Press, 1998), 12–26.

teenagers sought the American dream as promised in magazines, movies, and radio programs. . . .

For Mexican Americans, second-generation women as teenagers have received scant scholarly attention. Among Chicano historians and writers, there appears a fascination with the sons of immigrants, especially as *pachucos*.[4] Young women, however, may have experienced deeper generational tensions as they blended elements of Americanization with Mexican expectations and values. This chapter focuses on the shifting interplay of gender, cultures, class, ethnicity, and youth and the ways in which women negotiate across specific cultural contexts blending elements as diverse as celebrating Cinco de Mayo and applying Max Factor cosmetics.

In grappling with Mexican-American women's consciousness and agency, oral history offers a venue for exploring teenage expectations and preserving a historical memory of attitudes and feelings. In addition to archival research, the recollections of seventeen women serve as the basis for my reconstruction of adolescent aspirations and experiences (or dreams and routines).[5] The women themselves are fairly homogeneous in terms of nativity, class, residence, and family structure. With two exceptions, they are U.S. citizens by birth and attended southwestern schools. All the interviewees were born between 1908 and 1926.[6] Although three came from families once considered middle class in Mexico, most can be considered working class in the United States. Their fathers' typical occupations included farm worker, miner, day laborer, and railroad hand. These women usually characterized their mothers as homemakers, although several remembered that their mothers took seasonal jobs in area factories and fields. . . .

Chicano social scientists have generally portrayed women as "the 'glue' that keeps the Chicano family together" as well as the guardians of traditional culture.[7] Whether one accepts this premise or not, within families, young women, perhaps more than their brothers, were expected to uphold certain standards. Parents, therefore, often assumed what they perceived as their unquestionable prerogative to regulate the actions and attitudes of their adolescent daughters. Teenagers, on the other hand, did not always acquiesce in the boundaries set down for them by their elders. Intergenerational tension flared along several fronts.

Like U.S. teenagers, in general, the first area of disagreement between an adolescent and her family would be over her personal appearance. As reflected in F. Scott Fitzgerald's "Bernice Bobs Her Hair," the length of a young woman's tresses was a hot issue spanning class, region, and ethnic lines. During the 1920s, a woman's decision "to bob or not bob" her hair assumed classic proportions within Mexican families. After considerable pleading, Belen Martínez Mason was permitted to cut her hair, though she soon regretted the decision. "Oh, I cried for a month."[8] Differing opinions over fashions often caused ill feelings. One Mexican American woman recalled that as a young girl, her mother dressed her "like a nun" and she could wear "no make-up, no cream, no nothing" on her face. Swimwear, bloomers, and short skirts also became sources of controversy. Some teenagers left home in one outfit and changed into another at school. Once María Fierro arrived home in her bloomers. Her father inquired, "Where have you been dressed like that, like a clown?" "I told him the truth," Fierro explained. "He whipped me anyway. . . . So from then on whenever I went to the track meet, I used to change my bloomers so that he wouldn't see that I had gone again."[9] . . .

The use of cosmetics cannot be blamed entirely on Madison Avenue ad campaigns. The innumerable barrio beauty pageants, sponsored by *mutualistas*,[10] patriotic societies, churches, the Mexican Chamber of Commerce, newspapers, and even progressive labor unions, encouraged young women to accentuate their physical attributes. Carefully chaperoned, many teenagers did participate in community contests from La Reina de Cinco de Mayo to Orange Queen. They modeled evening gowns, rode on parade floats, and sold raffle tickets.[11] Carmen Bernal Escobar remembered one incident where, as a contestant, she had to sell raffle tickets. Every ticket she sold counted as a vote for her in the pageant. Naturally the winner would be the woman who had accumulated the most votes. When her brother offered to buy $25 worth of votes [her mother would not think of letting her peddle the tickets at work or in the neighborhood], Escobar, on a pragmatic note, asked him to give her the money so that she could buy a coat she had spotted while window-shopping.[12]

The commercialization of personal grooming made additional inroads into the Mexican community with the appearance of barrio beauty parlors. Working as a beautician conferred a certain degree of status—"a nice, clean job"—in comparison to factory or domestic work. As one woman related:

> I always wanted to be a beauty operator. I loved makeup; I loved to dress up and fix up. I used to set my sisters' hair. So I had that in the back of my mind for a long time, and my mom pushed the fact that she wanted me to have a profession—seeing that I wasn't thinking of getting married.[13]

While further research is needed, one can speculate that neighborhood beauty shops reinforced women's networks and became places where they could relax, exchange *chimse* (gossip), and enjoy the company of other women.

During the 1920s, the ethic of consumption became inextricably linked to making it in America.[14] The message of affluence attainable through hard work and a bit of luck was reinforced in English and Spanish-language publications. Mexican barrios were not immune from the burgeoning consumer culture. The society pages of the influential Los Angeles–based *La Opinion*, for example, featured advice columns, horoscopes, and celebrity gossip. Advertisements for makeup, clothing, even feminine hygiene products reminded teenagers of an awaiting world of consumption.[15] One week after its inaugural issue in 1926, *La Opinion* featured a Spanish translation of Louella Parsons' nationally syndicated gossip column. Advertisements not only hawked products but offered instructions for behavior. As historian Roberto Treviño related in his recent study of Tejano newspapers, "The point remains that the Spanish-language press conveyed symbolic American norms and models to a potentially assimilable readership."[16]

Advertisements aimed at women promised status and affection if the proper bleaching cream, hair coloring, and cosmetics were purchased. Or, as one company boldly claimed, "Those with lighter, more healthy skin tones will become much more successful in business, love, and society."[17] A print ad [in English] for Camay Soap carried by *Hispano America* in 1932 reminded women readers that "Life Is a Beauty Contest."[18] Flapper fashions and celebrity testimonials further fused the connections between gendered identity and consumer culture. Another promotion encouraged readers to "SIGA LAS ESTRELLAS" (FOLLOW THE STARS) and use Max Factor cosmetics.[19] . . .

In her essay "City Lights: Immigrant Women and the Rise of the Movies," Elizabeth Ewen has argued that during the early decades of the twentieth century, "The social authority of the media of mass culture replaced older forms of family authority and behavior." Ewen further explained that the "authority of this new culture organized itself around the premise of freedom from customary bonds as a way of turning people's attention to the consumer market place as a source of self-definition."[20] Yet Mexican women had choices (though certainly circumscribed by economic considerations) about what elements to embrace and which to ignore. . . . Mexican-American women teenagers positioned themselves within the cultural messages they gleaned from English and Spanish-language publications, afternoon matinees, and popular radio programs. Their shifting conceptions of acceptable heterosocial behavior, including their desire "to date," heightened existing generational tensions between parents and daughters.

Obviously, the most serious point of contention between an adolescent daughter and her Mexican parents regarded her behavior toward young men. In both cities and rural towns, close chaperonage was a way of life. Recalling the supervisory role played by her "old maid" aunt, María Fierro laughingly explained, "She'd check up on us all the time. I used to get so mad at her." Ruby Estrada recalled that in her small southern Arizona community, "all the mothers" escorted their daughters to the local dances. Estrada's mother was no exception when it came to chaperoning her daughters. "She went especially for us. She'd just sit there and take care of our coats and watch us."[21] . . .

Faced with this type of situation, young women had three options: they could accept the rules set down for them; they could rebel; or they could find ways to compromise or circumvent traditional standards. "I was *never* allowed to go out by myself in the evening; it just was not done," related Carmen Bernal Escobar. In rural communities, where restrictions were perhaps even more stringent, "nice" teenagers could not even swim with male peers. According to Ruby Estrada, "We were ladies and wouldn't go swimming out there with a bunch of boys." Yet many seemed to accept these limits with equanimity. Remembering her mother as her chaperone, Lucy Acosta insisted, "I could care less as long I danced." "It wasn't devastating at all," echoed Ruby Estrada. "We took it in stride. We never thought of it as cruel or mean. . . . It was taken for granted that that's the way it was."[22] In Sonora, Arizona, like other small towns, relatives and neighbors kept close watch over adolescent women and quickly reported any suspected indiscretions. "They were always spying on you," Estrada remarked. Women in cities had a distinct advantage over their rural peers in that they could venture miles from their neighborhood into the anonymity of dance halls, amusement parks, and other forms of commercialized leisure. With carnival rides and the Cinderella Ballroom, the Nu-Pike amusement park of Long Beach proved a popular hangout for Mexican youth in Los Angeles.[23] It was more difficult to abide by traditional norms when excitement loomed just on the other side of the streetcar line.

Some women openly rebelled. They moved out of their family homes and into apartments. Considering themselves freewheeling single women, they could go out with men unsupervised as was the practice among their Anglo peers. Others challenged parental and cultural standards even further by living with their boyfriends. In his field notes, University of California economist Paul Taylor recorded an incident in which a young woman had moved in with her Anglo boyfriend after he had convinced her that such arrangements were common among Americans. "This terrible freedom in the United States," one Mexicana lamented. "I do not have to worry because I have no daughters, but the poor *señoras* with many girls, they worry."[24]

Those teenagers who did not wish to defy their parents openly would "sneak out" of the house to meet their dates or attend dances with female friends. Whether meeting someone at a drugstore, roller rink, or theater, this practice involved the invention of elaborate stories to mask traditionally inappropriate behavior.[25] In other words, they lied. In his study of Tucson's Mexican community, Thomas Sheridan related the following saga of Jacinta Pérez de Valdez:

> As she and her sisters grew older, they used to sneak out of the house to go to the Riverside Ball Room. One time a friend of their father saw them there and said, "Listen, Felipe, don't you know your daughters are hanging around the Riverside?" Furious, their father threw a coat over his longjohns and stormed into the dance hall, not even stopping to tie his shoes. . . . Doña Jacinta recalled. "He entered by one door and we left by another. We had to walk back home along the railroad tracks in our high heels. I think we left those heels on the rails." She added that when their father returned, "We were all lying in bed like little angels."[26] . . .

The third alternative sometimes involved quite a bit of creativity on the part of young women as they sought to circumvent traditional chaperonage. Alicia Mendeola Shelit recalled that one of her older brothers would accompany her to dances ostensibly as a chaperone. "But then my oldest brother would always have a blind date for me." Carmen Bernal Escobar was permitted to entertain her boyfriends at home, but only under the supervision of her brother or mother. The practice of "going out with the girls," though not accepted until the 1940s, was fairly common. Several Mexican-American women, often related, would escort one another to an event (such as a dance), socialize with the men in attendance, and then walk home together. In the sample of seventeen interviews, daughters negotiated their activities with their parents. Older siblings and extended kin appeared in the background as either chaperones or accomplices.[27] . . .

Of course, some young women did lead more adventurous lives. A male interviewer employed by Mexican anthropologist Manuel Gamio recalled his "relations" with a woman met at a Los Angeles dance hall. . . . Elisa "Elsie" Morales . . . helped support her family by dancing with strangers. Even though she lived at home and her mother and brother attempted to monitor her actions, she managed to meet the interviewer at a "hot pillow" hotel. To prevent pregnancy, she relied on contraceptive douches provided by "an American doctor." Although Morales realized her mother would not approve of her behavior, she noted that "she [her mother] is from Mexico . . . I am from there also but I was brought up in the United States, we think about things differently." Just as Morales rationalized her actions as "American," the interviewer perceived her within a similar, though certainly less favorable, definition of Americanization. "She seemed very coarse to me. That is, she dealt with one in the American way." Popular corridos, such as "El Enganchado" and "Las Pelonas," also touched on the theme of the corrupting influence of U.S. ways on Mexican women.[28] If there were rewards for women who escaped parental boundaries, there were also sanctions for those who crossed established lines.

Women who had children out of wedlock seemed to be treated by their parents in one of two ways—as pariahs or prodigal daughters. Erminia Ruiz recalled the experiences of two girlhood friends:

> It was a disgrace to the whole family. The whole family suffered and . . . her mother said she didn't want her home. She could not bring the baby home and she was not welcome at home. . . . She had no place to go. . . . And then I had another friend. She was also pregnant and the mother actually went to court to try to get him to marry her. . . . He hurried and married someone else but then he had to give child support.[29] . . .

Autonomy on the part of young women was hard to win in a world where pregnant, unmarried teenagers served as community "examples" of what might happen to you or your daughter if appropriate measures were not taken. As an elderly Mexicana remarked, "Your reputation was everything."[30] In this sense, the chaperone not only protected the young woman's position in the community, but that of the entire family.

Chaperonage thus exacerbated conflict not only between generations but within individuals as well. In gaily recounting tales of ditching the *dueña* or sneaking down the stairwell, the laughter of the interviewees fails to hide the painful memories of breaking away from familial expectations. Their words resonate with the dilemma of reconciling their search for autonomy with their desire for parental affirmation. It is important to note that every informant who challenged or circumvented chaperonage held a full-time job, as either a factory or service worker. In contrast, most woman who accepted constant supervision did not work for wages. Perhaps because they labored for long hours, for little pay, and frequently under hazardous conditions, factory and service workers were determined to exercise some control over their leisure time. Indeed, Douglas Monroy has argued that outside employment "facilitated greater freedom of activity and more assertiveness in the family for Mexicanas."[31]

It may also be significant that none of the employed teenagers had attended high school. They entered the labor market directly after or even before
the completion of the eighth grade. Like many female factory workers in the
United States, most Mexican operatives were young, unmarried daughters
whose wage labor was essential to the economic survival of their families. As
members of a "family wage economy," they relinquished all or part of their
wages to their elders. According to a 1933 University of California study, of the
Mexican families surveyed with working children, the children's monetary
contributions constituted 35 percent of total household income.[32] Cognizant
of their earning power, they resented the lack of personal autonomy.

Delicate negotiations ensued as both parents and daughters struggled over
questions of leisure activities and discretionary income. Could a young woman
retain a portion of her wages for her own use? If elders demanded every penny,
daughters might be more inclined to splurge on a new outfit or other personal
item on their way home from work or, even more extreme, they might choose
to move out, taking their paychecks with them. Recognizing their dependence
on their children's income, some parents compromised. Their concessions,
however, generally took the form of allocating spending money rather than re-
laxing traditional supervision.[33] . . .

Chaperonage triggered deep-seated tensions over autonomy and self-
determination. "Whose life is it anyway?" was a recurring question with no satisfactory answer. Many women wanted their parents to consider them dutiful
daughters, but they also desired degrees of freedom. While ethnographies provide scintillating tales of teenage rebellion, the voices of the interviewees do
not. Their stories reflect the experiences of those adolescents who struggled
with boundaries. How can one retain one's "good name" while experiencing
the joys of youth? How can one be both a good daughter and an independent
woman?

To complete the picture, we also have to consider the perspective of Mexican immigrant parents who encountered a youth culture very different from
that of their generation. For them, courtship had occurred in the plaza; young
women and men promenaded under the watchful eyes of town elders, an atmosphere in which an exchange of meaningful glances could well portend en-
gagement. One can understand their consternation as they watched their
daughters apply cosmetics and adopt the apparel advertised in fashion magazines. In other words, "If she dresses like a flapper, will she then act like one?"
Seeds of suspicion reaffirmed the penchant for traditional supervision.

Parents could not completely cloister their children from the temptations
of "modern" society, but chaperonage provided a way of monitoring their activities. It was an attempt to mold young women into sheltered young ma-
trons. But one cannot regard the presence of *la dueña* as simply an old world
tradition on a collision course with twentieth-century life. The regulation of
daughters involved more than a conflict between peasant ways and modern
ideas. Chaperonage was both an actual and symbolic assertion of familial
oligarchy. A family's reputation was linked to the purity of women. As reiter-
ated in a Catholic catechism, if a young woman became a "faded lily," she and

her family would suffer dire consequences.[34] Since family honor rested, to some degree, on the preservation of female chastity (or *vergüenza*), women were to be controlled for the collective good, with older relatives assuming unquestioned responsibility in this regard. Mexican women coming of age during the 1920s and 1930s were not the first to challenge the authority of elders. Ramón Gutiérrez in his pathbreaking scholarship on colonial New Mexico uncovered numerous instances of women who tried to exercise some autonomy over their sexuality.[35] The Mexican-American generation, however, had a potent ally unavailable to their foremothers — consumer culture. . . .

Even the Spanish-language press fanned youthful passions. On May 9, 1927, *La Opinion* ran an article entitled, "How do you kiss?" Informing readers that "el beso no es un arte sino una ciencia" [kissing is not an art but rather a science], this short piece outlined the three components of a kiss: quality, quantity, and topography. The modern kiss, furthermore, should last three minutes.[36] Though certainly shocking older Mexicanos, such titillating fare catered to a youth market. *La Opinion,* in many respects, reflected the coalescence of Mexican and American cultures. While promoting pride in Latino theater and music, its society pages also celebrated the icons of Americanization and mass consumption. . . .

United States consumerism did not bring about the disintegration of familial oligarchy, but it did serve as a catalyst for change. The ideology of control was shaken by consumer culture and the heterosocial world of urban youth. . . .

Mexican-American women were not caught between two worlds. They navigated across multiple terrains at home, at work, and at play. They engaged in cultural coalescence. The Mexican-American generation selected, retained, borrowed, and created their own cultural forms. Or as one woman informed anthropologist Ruth Tuck, "Fusion is what we want — the best of both ways."[37] These children of immigrants may have been captivated by consumerism, but few would attain its promises of affluence. Race and gender prejudice as well as socioeconomic segmentation constrained the possibilities of choice. . . .

In 1959, Margaret Clark asserted that the second-generation residents of Sal si Puedes [a northern California barrio] "dream and work toward the day when Mexican Americans will become fully integrated into American society at large."[38] Perhaps, as part of that faith, they rebelled against chaperonage.

Mexican-American adolescents felt the lure of Hollywood and the threat of deportation, the barbs of discrimination, and the reins of constant supervision. In dealing with all the contradictions in their lives, many young women focused their attention on chaperonage, an area where they could make decisions. The inner conflicts expressed in the oral histories reveal that such decisions were not made impetuously.

Notes

1. Interview with María Ybarra, December 1, 1990, conducted by David Pérez.
2. For colonial New Mexico, Ramón Gutiérrez convincingly demonstrates how family honor was tied, in part, to women's *vergüenza* (literally, shame or vir-

ginity). See Ramón Gutiérrez, "Honor, Ideology, and Class Gender Domination in New Mexico, 1690–1846," *Latin American Perspectives* 12 (Winter 1985): 81–104, and Ramón Gutiérrez, *When Jesus Came, the Corn Mothers Went Away: Power and Sexuality in New Mexico, 1500–1846* (Stanford: Stanford University Press, 1990). I contend that since mothers and elder female relatives played major roles in enforcing chaperonage, strict supervision of daughters related more to what I term "familial oligarchy" than to patriarchal control.

3. Donna R. Gabaccia, *From Sicily to Elizabeth Street* (Albany: SUNY Press, 1984); Sydney Stahl Weinberg, "The Treatment of Women in Immigration History: A Call for Change," in *Seeking Common Ground: Multidisciplinary Studies of Immigrant Women in the United States,* ed. Donna Gabaccia (Westport, Conn.: Greenwood Press, 1992), pp. 3–22; Stuart and Elizabeth Ewen, *Channels of Desire* (New York: McGraw-Hill, 1982); Elizabeth Ewen, *Immigrant Women in the Land of Dollars* (New York: Monthly Review Press, 1985); Andrew Heinze, *Adapting to Abundance* (New York: Columbia University Press, 1990); Susan A. Glenn, *Daughters of the Shtetl* (Ithaca: Cornell University Press, 1990).

4. Mauricio Mazón's *The Zoot Suit Riots* (Austin: University of Texas Press, 1984) and the Luis Valdez play and feature film *Zoot Suit* provide examples of the literature on *pachucos*. A doctoral student at Princeton University, Eduardo Pagán is completing a dissertation on pachucos and the politics of race during World War II.

[*Pachucos* were groups of young Mexican American men in the southwestern United States in the 1920s, 1930s, and 1940s who adopted a unique style of dress, including a long suit coat, and defied the efforts of American schools and police to force them to abandon their ethnic identity. — Ed.]

5. I would like to introduce these women by grouping them geographically. María Fierro, Rose Escheverria Mulligan, Adele Hernández Milligan, Beatrice Morales Clifton, Mary Luna, Alicia Mendeola Shelit, Carmen Bernal Escobar, Belen Martínez Mason, and Julia Luna Mount grew up in Los Angeles. Lucy Acosta and Alma Araiza García came of age in El Paso and Erminia Ruiz in Denver. Representing the rural experience are María Arredondo, and Jesusita Torres (California), María Ybarra (Texas), and Ruby Estrada (Arizona). As a teenager, Eusebia Buriel moved with her family from Silvis, Illinois, to Riverside, California. *Note:* Of the seventeen full-blown life histories, nine are housed in university archives, seven as part of the *Rosie the Riveter* collection at California State University, Long Beach. I appreciate the generosity and longstanding support of Sherna Gluck who has given me permission to use excerpts from the *Rosie* interviews. This sample also does not include oral interviews found in published sources.

6. The age breakdowns for the seventeen interviewees are as follows: nine were born between 1908 and 1919 and eight between 1920 and 1926. This sample includes some who were chaperoned during the 1920s and others who were chaperoned during the thirties and forties. As a result, the sample does not represent a precise generational grouping, but instead gives a sense of the pervasiveness and persistence of unremitting supervision.

7. George J. Sánchez, "'Go After the Women': Americanization and the Mexican Immigrant Woman 1915–1929," in *Unequal Sisters: A Multicultural Reader in U.S. Women's History,* 2nd ed., eds. Vicki L. Ruiz and Ellen Carol DuBois (New York: Routledge, 1994), p. 285.

8. F. Scott Fitzgerald, *Flappers and Philosophers* (London: W. Collins Sons and Co., Ltd., 1922), pp. 209–46; Emory S. Bogardus, *The Mexican in the United States* (Los Angeles: University of Southern California Press, 1934), p. 741; Martínez

Mason interview, p. 44. During the 1920s, Mexican parents were not atypical in voicing their concerns over the attitudes and appearance of their "flapper adolescents." A general atmosphere of tension between youth and their elders existed— a generation gap that cut across class, race, ethnicity, and region. See Paula Fass, *The Damned and the Beautiful: American Youth in the 1920's* (New York: Oxford University Press, 1977).

9. Interview with Alicia Mendeola Shelit, Volume 37 of *Rosie the Riveter,* p. 18; Paul S. Taylor, *Mexican Labor in the United States, Volume II* (Berkeley: University of California Press, 1932), pp. 199–200; Interview with María Fierro, Volume 12 of *Rosie the Riveter,* p. 10.

10. [*Mutualistas* were mutual aid societies, similar to those formed by other immigrant groups. These precursors to insurance companies in ethnic communities made it possible for members to pool their resources to pay for medical expenses, funerals, or other economic emergencies.—Ed.]

11. Rodolfo F. Acuña, *Community Under Siege: A Chronicle of Chicanos East of the Los Angeles River, 1945–1975* (Los Angeles: UCLA Chicano Studies Publications, 1984), pp. 278, 407–408, 413–14, 418, 422; *FTA News,* May 1, 1945; interview with Carmen Bernal Escobar, June 15, 1986, conducted by the author. For an example of the promotion of a beauty pageant, see issues of *La Opinion,* June–July 1927.

12. Escobar interview, 1986.

13. Sherna B. Gluck, *Rosie the Riveter Revisited: Women, The War and Social Change* (Boston: Twayne Publishers, 1987), pp. 81, 85.

14. The best elaboration of this phenomenon can be found in Roland Marchand, *Advertising the American Dream: Making Way for Modernity, 1920–1940* (Berkeley: University of California Press, 1985).

15. For examples, see *La Opinion,* September 26, 1926; May 14, 1927; June 5, 1927; September 9, 1929; January 15, 1933; January 29, 1938. Lorena Chambers is currently writing a dissertation focusing on the gendered representations of the body in Chicano cultural narratives. I thank her for our wonderful discussions.

16. Vicki L. Ruiz, "'Star Struck': Acculturation, Adolescence, and Mexican American Women, 1920–1940" in *Small Worlds: Children and Adolescents in America,* eds. Elliot West and Paula Petrik (Lawrence: University of Kansas Press, 1992): 61–80; Roberto R. Treviño, "*Prensa Y Patria:* The Spanish-Language Press and the Biculturation of the Tejano Middle Class, 1920–1940," *The Western Historical Quarterly,* Vol. 22 (November 1991): 460.

17. *La Opinion,* September 29, 1929.

18. *Hispano-America,* July 2, 1932. Gracias a Gabriela Arredondo for sharing this advertisement with me, one she included in her seminar paper, "'Equality' for All: Americanization of Mexican Immigrant Women in Los Angeles and San Francisco Through Newspaper Advertising, 1927–1935 (M.A. seminar paper, San Francisco State University, 1991).

19. *La Opinion,* June 5, 1927.

20. Stuart Ewen and Elizabeth Ewen, *Channels of Desire* (New York: McGraw-Hill, 1982), pp. 95–96.

21. Fierro interview; Estrada interview.

22. Escobar interview, 1986; Estrada interview, pp. 11, 13; interview no. 653 with Lucy Acosta conducted by Mario T. García, October 28, 1982 (on file at the Institute of Oral History, University of Texas, El Paso), p. 17. I wish to thank Rebecca Craver, coordinator of the Institute of Oral History, for permission to use excerpts from the Acosta interview.

23. Estrada interview, p. 12; Shelit interview, p. 9; Antonio Ríos-Bustamante

and Pedro Castillo, *An Illustrated History of Mexican Los Angeles, 1781–1985* (Los Angeles: Chicano Studies Research Center, UCLA, 1986), p. 153.

24. Paul S. Taylor, "Women in Industry," field notes for his book, *Mexican Labor in the United States, 1927–1930,* Bancroft Library, University of California, 1 box; Richard G. Thurston, "Urbanization and Sociocultural Change in a Mexican-American Enclave" (Ph.D. dissertation, University of California, Los Angeles, 1957; rpt. R and E Research Associates, 1974), p. 118; Bogardus, *The Mexican,* pp. 28–29, 57–58. *Note:* Paul S. Taylor's two-volume study, *Mexican Labor in the United States,* is considered the classic ethnography on Mexican Americans during the interwar period. A synthesis of his field notes, "Women in Industry," has been published. See Taylor, "Mexican Women in Los Angeles Industry in 1928," *Aztlán,* 11 (Spring 1980): 99–131.

25. Interview with Belen Martinez Mason, Volume 23 of *Rosie the Riveter,* p. 30; interviews with Erminia Ruiz, July 30, 1990, and February 18, 1993, conducted by the author; Thomas Sheridan, *Los Tucsonenses* (Tucson: University of Arizona Press, 1986), pp. 131–32.

26. Sheridan, *Los Tucsonenses, loc. cit.*

27. Shelit interview, pp. 9, 24, 30; Ruiz interviews (1990, 1993); Escobar interview; García interview; Martínez Mason interview p. 30; Hernández Milligan interview, pp. 27–28; interview with María Arredondo, March 19, 1986, conducted by Carolyn Arredondo; Taylor notes.

28. "Elisa Morales," interview by Luis Recinos, April 16, 1927, Biographies and Case Histories II folder, Manuel Gamio Field Notes, Bancroft Library, University of California; Taylor, *Mexican Labor,* Vol. II, pp. vi–vii; Gamio, *Mexican Immigration,* p. 89. The corrido "El Enganchado" in Volume two of *Mexican Labor* offers an intriguing glimpse into attitudes toward women and Americanization.

29. Ruiz interview (1993).

30. Discussion following my presentation, of "The Flapper and the Chaperone," May 28, 1995. Comment provided by B. V. Meyer.

31. Douglas Monroy, "An Essay on Understanding the Work Experiences of Mexicans in Southern California, 1900–1939, *Aztlán,* 12 (Spring 1981): 70. *Note:* Feminist historians have also documented this push for autonomy among the daughters of European immigrants. In particular, see Peiss, *Cheap Amusements,* Glenn, *Daughters of the Shtetl,* E. Ewen, *Immigrant Women;* and Alexander, "The Only Thing I Wanted Was Freedom." See also Meyerowitz, *Women Adrift.*

32. Heller Committee for Research in Social Economics of the University of California and Constantine Panuzio, *How Mexicans Earn and Live,* University of California Publications in Economics, XIII, No. 1, Cost of Living Studies V (Berkeley: University of California, 1933), pp. 11, 14, 17; Taylor notes; Luna Mount interview; Ruiz interviews (1990, 1993); Shelit interview, p. 9. For further delineation of the family wage economy, see Louise A. Tilly and Joan W. Scott, *Women, Work, and Family* (New York: Holt, Rinehart, and Winston, 1978).

33. These observations are drawn from my reading of the seventeen oral interviews and the literature on European immigrant women.

34. Rev. F. X. Lasance, *The Catholic Girl's Guide and Sunday Missal* (New York: Benziger Brothers, 1905), Esther Pérez Papers, Cassiano-Pérez Collection, Daughters of the Republic of Texas Library at the Alamo, San Antonio, Texas, pp. 279–80. I have a 1946 reprint edition passed down to me by my older sister who had received it from our mother.

35. Gutiérrez, "Honor, Ideology," pp. 88–93, 95–98.

36. *La Opinion,* May 9, 1927.

37. Ruth Tuck, *Not With the Fist: Mexican Americans in a Southwest City* (New York: Harcourt Brace, 1946), p. 134.

38. Margaret Clark, *Health in the Mexican American Culture* (Berkeley: University of California Press, 1959), p. 20.

Analyzing the Source

REFLECTING ON THE SOURCE

1. Now that you have read "The Flapper and the Chaperone," which of the arguments set forth in the second paragraph do you think Ruiz most wants to convey to you in this chapter? Do you base your decision on the amount of space she devotes to each argument, on the amount of evidence she provides, or on her emphasis in the conclusion?

2. Endnotes tell a reader about the primary sources a historian examined in the course of reaching the conclusions presented in the book or article, and they identify the other historians consulted. Read through the first ten endnotes on pages 152–54. What is the balance of primary sources to secondary sources in those endnotes? Are those two types of sources separated and noted differently in the endnotes? How can you distinguish between primary and secondary sources in the notes?

MAKING CONNECTIONS

3. A modern argument, shared by both U.S. immigration historians and U.S. popular culture historians, is that human beings tend to exercise some sort of creative agency in their lives, even when they lack the power of wealth, age, or gender, or when they face prejudice and discrimination. How does Vicki Ruiz's chapter on "The Flapper and the Chaperone" reflect this theoretical trend in the historiography (historical literature)? Why do you think historians are paying more attention to human agency, after a period in the 1970s when the focus was on how people are made victims? What are the potential risks and gains from this focus on agency?

4. Present-day historians, more than historians in earlier eras, go to great effort to tell their stories using the "voices" of the people involved. Ruiz achieved this by using oral histories, including interviews conducted with her mother, Erminia Ruiz. Do you, as a reader, have as much confidence in oral histories as other types of sources? Are they similar to memoirs, and if so, how? Do the benefits of oral histories outweigh, for you, the potential problems with them?

Beyond the Source

The stories of American youth culture and Mexican American culture in the 1920s offer similar echoes of the old notion that "the more things change, the more they stay the same." Despite all the worry over the sexual mores of youth or the assimilation of Mexicans teens into American popular culture, the fact remained that young men and women intended to follow the family traditions they had inherited, and Mexican American kids were not rejecting Mexican culture, they were integrating it with American culture. As Ruiz observes in another section of her book, "in challenging chaperonage, Mexican-American teenagers did not attack the foundation of familial oligarchy—only its more obvious manifestation."

When abrupt and severe change arrived in the form of the Great Depression of the 1930s, white, middle-class couples who had been teens in the 1920s were ill-prepared for the notion that the wife might need to work for pay outside the home. Young Mexican Americans, who had fashioned their own acculturation to the United States, were similarly ill-prepared when the U.S. government moved to remedy the unemployment of whites by forcing the repatriation of thousands of Mexicans. This meant that some young people, raised on American popular culture, found themselves exiled to their families' villages in remote parts of Mexico, where there were more chaperones than radios.

The population of Mexicans who remained in the United States in the wake of repatriation were largely American-born. Many of them demonstrated their commitment to building a Mexican American culture in the 1930s by utilizing New Deal opportunities to create strong labor unions that benefited from ethnic loyalty. The seventeen women that Ruiz interviewed for her chapter on "Flappers" all stayed in the United States. Seven of the women married Euro-American men, and all combined their household responsibilities as wives and mothers with wage work outside the home, in jobs ranging from airplane manufacture to retail sales. In most cases, their supervision of their daughters in the 1950s reflected a mixture of old and new: they did not require chaperones or harp as much on "family honor," but they made very clear the daughter's need to preserve her reputation by preserving her virginity.

In sketching these patterns, Vicki Ruiz herself engaged in the mixing of old and new that is expected of secondary works in history. She dug around in library shelves and research archives and unearthed the sorts of photographs, newspaper articles, advertisements, and social science research from the 1920s that typically comprise a historian's primary sources. She then expanded the available Mexican American women's "memoirs" by adding new oral histories to those that already existed. Ruiz read and interpreted these primary sources in the light of recent interpretations that have emerged from other studies of immigrant women's lives, youth culture and consumer culture in the 1920s, and Mexican American history. The result is a story of Mexican American women that adds much new information to our existing knowledge while affirming a collective, contemporary view among American historians that immigrants, youth, workers, consumers—in short, most women and men—are not passive in the face of traditional family controls or modern advertising. They actively and creatively combine the competing elements in their lives in ways that make economic, family, and cultural survival possible.

Ruiz's work is the first, not the last, book on Mexican American women's lives in the twentieth century. Like all who write works of secondary history, she consciously pointed to places where more research is needed and provided documentation that would allow future researchers to build on her work. Ruiz thereby entered into the ongoing collaboration among historians to build on one another's work in the creation of a richer story of the past.

Finding and Supplementing the Source

The secondary source excerpt for this chapter was taken from chapter three, "The Flapper and the Chaperone," of *From Out of the Shadows: Mexican Women in Twentieth-Century America* by Vicki L. Ruiz (New York: Oxford University Press, 1998). This book is readily available in libraries and bookstores. As in most professional history books, Ruiz includes an acknowledgments section where she lists the names of a dozen professional historians who read and commented on all or part of her manuscript before it was published. By reading a book's acknowledgments, preface, and introduction, you can often determine if the work has been reviewed by other historians, either as anonymous judges or as helpful colleagues. In the case of history articles published in professional journals, you know that they have been prescreened, judged, and probably revised because they cannot achieve publication without that vetting process.

Useful companions to Vicki Ruiz's study are Douglas Monroy, *Rebirth: Mexican Los Angeles from the Great Migration to the Great Depression* (Berkeley: University of California Press, 1999); George J. Sanchez, *Becoming Mexican American: Ethnicity, Culture, and Identity in Chicano Los Angeles, 1900–1945* (New York: Oxford University Press, 1993); and Frances Esquibel Tywoniak and Mario T. Garcia, *Migrant Daughter: Coming of Age as a Mexican American Woman* (Berkeley: University of California Press, 2002).

For the interaction of modern consumer culture in the 1920s with youth, ethnic groups, and women, see Paula S. Fass, *The Damned and the Beautiful: American Youth in the 1920's* (New York: Oxford University Press, 1979); Lizabeth Cohen, *Making a New Deal: Industrial Workers in Chicago, 1919–1939* (New York: Cambridge University Press, 1990); and Kathy Peiss, *Hope in a Jar: The Making of America's Beauty Culture* (New York: Metropolitan Books, 1999).

CHAPTER 8

Painting a New Deal

U.S. Post Office Murals from the Great Depression

In the spring of 1941, Gustaf Dalstrom was hard at work painting a mural on the wall of the post office in St. Joseph, Missouri. On the eve of World War II, the federal government's New Deal was in its ninth year of struggle against economic depression, but recovery was elusive and unemployment still too common. Gustaf Dalstrom had a job thanks to the New Deal's public arts program, and citizens of St. Joseph came to watch him work, equipped with lists of questions prepared by the local schools' art director. Dalstrom willingly paused in his labors to give brief talks about art in general and mural painting in particular.

The scene of *Negro River Music* that Dalstrom was painting on the wall of the city's main post office had sparked controversy when the design sketches were first printed in the local newspaper. Inspired by the music of Stephen Foster, a white American songwriter who idealized African American life, the mural depicted a group of blacks happily gathered for song and dance. A local delegation from St. Joseph's African American community met with the committee of civic leaders who had approved the design to complain that the imagery portrayed blacks as "lazy people with no other thoughts but singing, dancing, and clowning." This protest by African Americans against their depiction in a government-sponsored mural was not successful; the local leaders and federal officials who approved the design argued that the mural celebrated the important role of Negro music in American life. Other protests by local groups against New Deal post office mural designs did succeed, especially when backed by political clout. Unionized mine workers in Kellogg, Idaho, for example, had the support of local mine owners when the workers protested against *Mine Rescue,* a mural depicting an injured mine worker being carried out of the mine on a stretcher. Kellogg citizens of all classes agreed that this image was far too depressing for mine workers and their families to gaze upon as they stood in line at the city's post office. In countless other communities, the complaints registered by citizens were less sweeping but of great local significance: the tobacco leaves in the design for Whiteville, North Carolina, were the wrong shape; the texture of the sand in the Fort Pierce, Florida, mural was too fine; the Cheyenne depicted in the design for Watonga, Oklahoma, were dressed like Navajo.

Whether local citizens applauded or disdained the artwork that civic leaders and federal officials installed in local post offices in the 1930s, and whether or not their ideas for revision were incorporated into the artists' plans, the fact remains that this New Deal program inspired unprecedented public discussion of public art and marked a new era in public funding of the arts in America. Before the 1930s, the federal government played no role in sponsoring the visual arts in America. Those with the wealth to be art patrons enjoyed the control they exercised over the art world and the status that control signified; they had no desire to encourage public investment in the arts. On the other hand, those without the wealth to purchase art regarded it as an elite luxury and did not demand that their taxes go to public support of the visual arts. Artists, meanwhile, debated whether public funding for the arts would enliven American art or invite government control over artistic expression.

The New Deal instituted dramatic changes in the government's relationship to the arts, giving artists and the public an opportunity to consider the value of publicly funded arts programs. Under the leadership of President Franklin Delano Roosevelt, the government created arts programs for two purposes: as "work relief" for artists who could not sell their art in depression-ridden America and as a visual boost to uplift the nation's sagging spirits. The best-known New Deal arts program was operated by the Works Progress Administration (WPA). Known as the Federal Arts Program (FAP), it was created to provide artists with a steady income. Some in Congress viewed artists more as subversives than as workers and did not want to subsidize them. But New Deal lobbyists argued that it was better to pay artists $1,200 a year to continue creating art, and then put that art in government buildings, than to hand out welfare checks and get nothing in return. Between 1935 and 1943, ten thousand artists were subsidized by the FAP, and they produced tens of thousands of works of art that were displayed in federal, state, county, and municipal buildings for decades to come. These FAP artists were not told what to paint or sculpt or photograph; their monthly checks were not tied to government approval of what they were creating. Some FAP art was not approved for display in public buildings, but artists were not denied funding because the government disliked their art.

When it came to commissioning art meant to uplift the nation, however, the New Deal took a different approach, one that involved much more control over the actual content of the art produced with government funds. It was here that the Treasury Department's program to sponsor post office murals played a vital role. This program was separate from the WPA's Federal Arts Program; it was also less well known and longer lasting. Through this program, artists submitted competing sketches to local committees of citizens who then worked with Treasury Department officials to select the winning design for the town's post office wall. While the artists commissioned to create the post office artwork were paid by the government for their labor, the purpose of the Treasury's post office program was not to provide relief to starving artists. The purpose was to create public art that would inspire Americans to believe in their own capacity to overcome the fiercely hard times of the 1930s.

President Roosevelt and those who worked in his New Deal administration saw the Depression as a crisis of national spirit as much as a financial crash. They believed that public art that conveyed a message of faith and confidence in the working people of America would energize the government's recovery efforts. Those government efforts were controversial, however; some in the United States did not approve of the government's New Deal activism. While the post office murals were intended to inspire and uplift the citizenry, they were also politically useful for generating goodwill toward the federal government—and the Roosevelt administration. An upbeat, colorful, mural-sized reminder of the best in American life, painted on the wall of the local post office, could restore local confidence while at the same time reminding voters that a strong, activist federal government provided valuable goods, including postal service and public art.

The New Deal's post office murals were funded under an already existing federal law that set aside 1 percent of the cost of all new federal buildings for "embellishments." Under the New Deal, the Treasury Department was in charge of the many new federal building projects the government undertook to revitalize the nation's construction industry, and the "Section for Fine Arts" within the Treasury Department was in charge of providing wall art for the eleven hundred new U.S. post offices that local labor constructed in every congressional district in the union. It was the Fine Arts Section of the Treasury Department that sponsored all of the competitions and commissions for the post office murals, and the visual product of this particular government program came to be called "Section art."

The distinguishing feature of Section art was its patriotic loyalty to a particular movement in the artistic world known as "American Scene" painting. Artists who joined this movement defined themselves in opposition to abstract European modernism and saw themselves as the creators of a uniquely American vision. Like so many other aspects of the New Deal, Section art's emphasis on American Scene painting fostered a coalition between rural conservatives, represented by "Regionalists" in the art world, and urban radicals, who were the "Social Realists" among artists. Both Regionalists and Social Realists rejected abstract modernism, with its fractured forms and destabilized shapes, as a foreign indulgence that was unrelated to the real lives of real Americans, whom these antimodernists sought to represent. Regionalists, however, tended toward paintings that idealized traditional rural life, while Social Realists sought to protest the social injustices of the urban, industrial world.

Because of its steady devotion to the American Scene style, Section art garnered both popularity and criticism. As an approach to visual expression, it was generally applauded by local committees charged with approving a mural design. Before World War II, most Americans shared the American Scene school's dislike of modern art; they much preferred art that not only depicted but also celebrated everyday people engaged in familiar activities. The local committees of "leading" citizens—the town's businessmen, club women, teachers, clergy, librarian, postmaster—resonated to the Treasury section's emphasis on art that captured local images and distinct regional histories. These committees tended to align with the New Deal desire to represent citizens' experience in a style that was both recognizable and inspirational.

As we have seen, however, American Scene mural designs could evoke local criticism if citizens saw a bit too much realism in the image of a miner on a stretcher or too much Regionalist sentimentalism in the image of "clowning" African Americans. By declaring the local mural to be a realistic representation of the community, Section art invited scrutiny over who in the community was being represented and how realistically.

At the same time, modern artists criticized the Treasury's unwritten requirement that murals adhere to the American Scene style, calling it government control of artistic expression. Several emerging modern artists of the day, including Jackson Pollock, refused even to submit sketches to the Treasury's Fine Arts Section in protest against such control.

In the end, like so many other aspects of the New Deal, the Treasury Department's public art program in U.S. post offices was a mix of political radicalism, cultural conservatism, and smart politics. It was politically radical in making the state a very active agent in the American arts but culturally conservative (and politically smart) in offering a style of art capable of winning the widest popular support from the American citizenry.

Using Paintings as a Source

Historians study visual art for at least three reasons. Art historians are interested in the development over time of different styles of artistic expression; they might, for example, trace the evolution from representational paintings to impressionist renderings to abstract works. Art historians might also trace the artistic evolution of a particular artist—for example, Jackson Pollock or Georgia O'Keeffe—in order to see the influence of new ideas, new styles, and new techniques on the artist's work. Social historians, on the other hand, study paintings for insight into the society in which the art was produced. In examining Section art, social historians can trace the visible lines of conflict and cooperation between those in the 1930s who were nostalgic for an imagined, simpler past and those who wanted to fight for an imagined, better future. Those two impulses, so evident in American politics during the Depression years, were also evident in the Regionalist and Social Realist schools of the American Scene art movement.

Paintings, like written texts, are best understood when we have a sense of the specific context in which the artist or author was working. When studying Section art, for example, it is useful to remember that both the Treasury Department officials and the local post office artistic committees strongly favored American Scene paintings. Artists who wished to win a Section art commission quickly learned to "paint Section," which meant toning down tendencies toward modern, abstract imagery and emphasizing the positive qualities of common Americans. It is also useful to know that while the Treasury Department never stated its preference for the American Scene style, it did very explicitly state that the content of all post office art had to fit into one of three categories: the history of the U.S. postal service itself, the history of the local community, or a scene from the community's everyday life. In the case of Detroit, Michigan, for example, everyday life in the 1930s meant the auto industry. William Gropper—who would go on to become a major figure in Social Realist art after World War II—won the commission for Detroit's Northwestern Branch Postal Station with his design for *Automobile Industry:*

Is labor individual or collective?

A strictly realistic rendering of an auto plant?

Significance of out-sized bodies?

Scale of the men to their machines?

Gropper's blending of realism, romanticism, and abstraction in this 1941 mural can help a historian grasp the ways in which Americans in the 1930s, and especially supporters of the New Deal, believed that workers were dwarfed by industrial capitalism but at the same time were the real engine that kept society going. It also provides a visual representation of the ways in which modernism, in the slight abstractions we see in this painting, crept into the mainstream of 1930s art and life.

Advantages and Disadvantages of Working with Paintings

There are art historians today who dismiss the Treasury's post office "embell-ishments" as not really being art at all because the original vision of every artist commissioned to do a mural was so altered, corrected, and revised by Treasury officials and local committees that the final product does not qualify, in their view, as artistic. Ironically, it is precisely this feature of Section art—the fact that it conformed to the aesthetic tastes of a broad swath of Americans—that makes it particularly useful for historians who want to grasp the mood of the 1930s.

Historians who use paintings for insight into social attitudes do not have to assess whether the art they are examining is "good" art or not. For histori-ans, popular art, even if it is "bad" art, has value by revealing what styles had wide appeal at a particular time (and what styles did not). An artistic style's popularity contributes to our understanding of those creating and viewing art in a certain era. Section art is an excellent illustration of the value of paintings in historical analysis. When we know that Social Realist and Regionalist painters rejected modern art on the grounds that it was a European expression ill-suited to capturing authentic American culture, we enrich our sense of America's proud isolation from the world in the years preceding World War II. When we see how often and how delicately Section art balanced the Social Re-alists' defense of industrial workers with the Regionalists' idealizing of rural life, we get a visual distillation of the conflicts and resolutions Americans faced when their modern economy collapsed under them. And when we remember that Section art was consciously intended to inspire citizens to believe in their productive capacities, and that community members did influence the art's content, we can treat post office paintings as the common ground that artists, citizens, and government officials shared when defining American aspirations.

Because paintings can be such a satisfying source of social evidence, histo-rians must be doubly cautious not to overstate their significance. In many soci-eties, including American society, paintings have often been the province of the rich; the popularity of a particular artistic style in the 1880s, for example, tells the historian only what was popular among an elite group of art patrons, not what was visually meaningful to the majority of citizens. Moreover, in all societies, painters are among those with a unique vision; by definition, they see the world differently than nonartists do—and differently from many other artists. For that reason, historians must be careful not to rely on the work of one artist or even one school of art to make generalizations about the society in which the art was produced. To guard against that sort of methodological error, historians study not only paintings themselves but also the art world and the political world surrounding those paintings. Context allows the historian to understand that Social Realists from the 1930s may appear conservative today because Social Realism rejected abstract modernism, but at the time it was the Social Realists who looked radical for criticizing social and economic injustice while modernists seemed smugly unconcerned with the world's problems. So, too, it is research into historical background, not the paintings themselves, that helps the historian to explain why the government wanted to combine senti-mental Regionalism and defiant Social Realism under the patriotic tent of American Scene painting. Visual art makes social and political trends come to life, and that is of inestimable value to the historian. But without the contextual background, we cannot make optimal use of paintings as historical documents.

The ten post office murals included here all evoke the theme of "work." This sample was drawn from different regions of the United States and from all three of the Treasury Section's categories: postal history, local history, and everyday life. By focusing on the theme of work, this array of paintings gives you an opportunity to consider the kinds of depictions of industrial and agri-cultural workers that local citizens and the federal government found unifying and uplifting. Consider the role of race and gender in these murals. How often and in what settings do nonwhite men or women of any race appear as workers? Why did American culture in the Depression place so much emphasis on the powerful, productive labor of the nation's white men?

As you analyze these works of art, consider both the content and the style used to convey that content. Once you have examined each mural individually, sit back and think about what conclusions you can draw from this set of murals as a whole. If you had visited these ten post offices over the course of three weeks in 1942, how would you have felt about America's past—and future?

Working with the Source

There are a number of social trends that you can discern as you examine these post office murals. On page 166 is a table you can use to keep track of the artis-tic styles, work styles, gender roles, and racial roles that you discern in the paintings.

In considering each painting's artistic style, you may want to also ask your-self if any sort of modern "abstraction" is used in any of these American Scene paintings. If so, what is the artist's purpose in distorting shapes and sizes? Re-garding work values, you can assume that the images here are a representative sample of both individual and group work. Which is more emphasized in the murals?

When noting patterns in gender and race, you should recognize that spe-cial efforts were made to include depictions of white women and nonwhite men and women in this sample. Even so, ask yourself if you would know from this selection of murals that American women comprised 22 percent of the labor force in 1930, nonwhite women were twice as likely to be employed for pay as white women, and nonwhites comprised over 10 percent of the labor force.

	Artistic Style: Social Realism or Regionalism?	Work Style: Individualistic or Collective?	Gender: Men's Jobs? Women's Jobs?	Race: White Jobs? Nonwhite Jobs?
1. *The Riveter*				
2. *Development of the Land*				
3. *Assorting the Mail*				
4. *Postman in a Storm*				
5. *Legend of James Edward Hamilton*				
6. *Tennessee Valley Authority*				
7. *Plowshare Manufacturing*				
8. *Orange Picking*				
9. *Tobacco Industry*				
10. *Mining*				

The Source: Post Office Murals Depicting "Work" in Local Communities, 1936–1942

1 The Riveter *by Ben Shahn*
Bronx, New York, 1938

Shahn, a Lithuanian immigrant, was one of the best known and most politically active artists to paint Section art. *The Riveter* was one of several panels that made up the mural *Resources of America,* which Shahn and his wife, Bernarda Bryson, painted for the Bronx post office.

Development of the Land *by Elsa Jemne*, Ladysmith, Wisconsin, 1938

Jemne was a native of St. Paul, Minnesota, who had studied in Europe before World War I. She was criticized by both Treasury officials and the citizens of Ladysmith for inaccurately rendering the size and scale of the farmer and his corn in conveying her celebratory message.

3 Assorting the Mail *by Reginald Marsh*, Washington, D.C., 1936

There is no record of citizen complaints in Washington, D.C., about Marsh's nonliteral depiction of mailroom labor.

4 Postman in a Storm *by Robert Tabor*
Independence, Iowa, 1938

Tabor was born in Independence, Iowa, and lived most of his life there. When he lost his traveling sales job during the Depression, he began to paint. He was funded by the WPA's Federal Arts Program before winning a Treasury Section commission for this mural.

5 Legend of James Edward Hamilton — Barefoot Mailman
by Stevan Dohanos, West Palm Beach, Florida, 1940

Dohanos painted six scenes evoking the life of this Florida mailman, who died in 1887 "in the line of duty." Dohanos said in an interview in 1982 that "there is a difference of opinion as to whether sharks or alligators" caused Hamilton's demise.

6 Tennessee Valley Authority *by Xavier Gonzalez*
Huntsville, Alabama, 1937

President Roosevelt regarded creation of the Tennessee Valley Authority (TVA) in 1933 as one of the great achievements of the New Deal. Through the TVA, which covers over forty thousand square miles, the federal government built dams that brought electricity to the rural southeast, and it became actively involved in planning the region's resource conservation, agricultural, and industrial policies.

7 | ## Plowshare Manufacturing *by Edward Millman*
Moline, Illinois, 1937

John Deere started building steel plows for prairie farming in Moline, Illinois, in 1837. Despite the Depression, the Deere Company celebrated its centennial as the leading employer in Moline with a record $100 million in gross sales.

174

8 ### Orange Picking *by Paul Hull Julian*
Fullerton, California, 1942

The "second Gold Rush" to California occurred in the early 1900s, when families from the midwest moved westward in hope of making it rich in citrus farming. By 1942, family farming had largely been replaced by agribusiness, which hired migrant labor from Mexico.

9 ### Tobacco Industry *by Lee Gatch*
Mullins, South Carolina, 1940

For murals in southern post offices, the Treasury Section and its artists sought a balance between deference to the local power structure and a desire to depict African American life. So while supervisors were seldom depicted in industrial or agricultural murals outside the south, they were included in southern murals about work. At the same time, local southern committees asked that murals not show the poor whites who actually worked alongside blacks in the cotton and tobacco fields.

Mining *by Michael Lensen*, Mount Hope, West Virginia, 1942

The United Mine Workers of America was a union founded in 1890, but it struggled for legitimacy until the passage of the National Labor Relations Act of 1935 during the New Deal. The act established federal mechanisms for union formation and bargaining with employers. Mine workers in 1942 were led by John L. Lewis, the charismatic UMW president who gave his union a high profile on the national labor scene in the New Deal years.

Analyzing the Source

REFLECTING ON THE SOURCE

1. Now that you have "toured" these murals from all over the country, how would you summarize the New Deal's message to the people about how their economy works and who, exactly, makes it work? What two murals would you select from this group as the clearest expressions of the government's message?

2. Did you find any difference in artistic style, work style, or composition of the workforce between the industrial murals and the agricultural murals? Was there some other factor, such as prominence of technology, that seemed to distinguish one group of murals from another?

MAKING CONNECTIONS

3. There are politicians and historians who argue that by using such positive images of the American economy the New Deal actually saved the reputation of capitalists in their darkest hour. Others argue that the New Deal's government activism undermined capitalism and created a workers' state. Could you use the murals to support or challenge either of those positions? Do the murals suggest a third position?

4. The Treasury Section on Fine Arts sought to "stimulate the development of American art in general." Is that an appropriate goal for the government? How does a program like the Treasury Section achieve such a goal? How might it hinder that goal?

Beyond the Source

Many of the Treasury-sponsored murals painted for the New Deal still survive in post offices all over the United States or in buildings that used to be post offices. Some survive only in photographs because their buildings were torn down. Still others have not survived at all. What has most definitely endured is the national debate about public funding for the arts that was ignited by the New Deal of the 1930s.

Public funding for the arts had dried up by 1942, when the U.S. government turned all of its resources toward fighting World War II. But in the years following the war, political debates over artistic styles resumed. Many artists from the Social Realist school, such as William Gropper, became targets of the anticommunist McCarthy investigations because of the artists' critical view of capitalism. At the same time, anticommunists also expressed hostility to the modern, abstract art movement, which seemed to have subversive qualities of its own. One New York editorial claimed, "Modern art is communistic because it is distorted and ugly. . . . Art which does not glorify our beautiful country in plain, simple terms that everyone can understand breeds dissatisfaction . . . those who create and promote it are our enemies."

World War II had changed America's place in the world, however, and many Americans embraced the modern art movement as a sign of this nation's closer ties to Europe and its more sophisticated status as a global power. President John F. Kennedy argued that America's modern, innovative art was a global advertisement for the authenticity of American freedom and predicted government support of artists' unshackled experimentation would prove that the United States, unlike the Soviet Union, was a truly free and civilized society. Like Franklin Delano Roosevelt, Kennedy combined genuine idealism about the uplifting power of art with a belief that government support of the arts was in the nation's self-interest.

In late 1965, two years after Kennedy's assassination, President Lyndon B. Johnson was able to turn Kennedy's dream into reality by incorporating the National Endowment for the Arts (NEA) into his Great Society program. In doing so, Johnson endorsed Kennedy's view (and Roosevelt's) that a truly great nation demonstrated its respect for freedom and civilization by generously funding artists' unpredictable search for self-expression. In their enthusiasm for this ideal, NEA supporters did not address the possibility that artists might use their public arts funding to create art that expressed unpopular criticisms of American life. No one set up any mechanisms for resolving conflicts between government-funded artists and taxpayers who disagreed with those artists' views.

The NEA program to provide grants on the order of $5,000 to individual artists was only one of a variety of NEA programs operating between 1967 and 1995. Over the course of those twenty-eight years, thousands of young, experimental artists were given financial aid when they were selected by a "peer panel" of artists who reviewed applications for NEA grants. At the same time, the NEA gave more substantial grants to local arts organizations, museums, and art schools. Coincident with, and likely related to, the creation of the NEA, the arts flourished in the United States in these years, and artists found many more opportunities for creating, displaying, and selling their art than ever before in this country.

The success of the arts in the United States intersected with the end of the cold war in a volatile way. The political debate shifted away from freedom and communism toward sexuality and race. In that context, many conservative activists combined their concerns over large government with their fears of artistic expression by homosexuals and nonwhites who seemed to challenge traditional values. In 1989, when these activists learned that the NEA had given a $30,000 grant to the Institute of Contemporary Art in Philadelphia which had, in turn, organized an exhibit of Robert Mapplethorpe's nude photos showing multiracial sex acts in a sadomasochistic gay subculture, they were enraged at this use of taxpayer dollars. Mapplethorpe's death from AIDS that year only confirmed his status as a dangerous outsider whose work threatened, as one opponent put it, to "pollute" the body politic.

The ironic result of this incident was that Congress voted, in 1995, to abolish all NEA grants to individual artists, even though funding for the Mapplethorpe exhibit had come through a grant to an organization. Today, the NEA funnels all of its now-reduced funds through local arts organizations, which are on notice not to support individual artists who might threaten the organization's future funding. The debate over whether taxpayer support for artistic freedom should require citizens to fund images they find repugnant has not ceased. But, as with the New Deal, the government's support for the NEA has stimulated lively public debate over the place of the arts in a democratic society.

Finding and Supplementing the Source

The most complete study of post office murals is Marlene Park and Gerald E. Markowitz, *Democratic Vistas: Post Office and Public Art in the New Deal* (Philadelphia: Temple University Press, 1984). It recounts the history of the Treasury Section project in lively detail and provides images of 162 murals along with a complete listing, by state, of most Section murals and sculptures. Barbara Melosh includes many examples of post office murals in *Engendering Culture: Manhood and Womanhood in New Deal Public Art and Theater* (Washington, D.C.: Smithsonian Institution Press, 1991), her larger study of the ways gender and race were depicted in New Deal art. In *Wall-to-Wall America: A Cultural History of Post Office Murals in the Great Depression* (Minneapolis: University of Minnesota Press, 1982), Karal Ann Marling uses one Section-sponsored competition to explore larger themes related to art and the Depression and to make some provocative arguments about the effect of the Depression on people's artistic tastes. Additional examples of mural art and discussions of that art can be found in Richard D. McKinzie, *The New Deal for Artists* (Princeton, N.J.: Princeton University Press, 1973); Belisario R. Contreras, *Tradition and Innovation in New Deal Art* (London: Associated University Presses, 1983); and chapter 14 of Edward Lucie-Smith, *Art of the 1930's* (London: Weidenfeld and Nicholson, 1985).

For discussions of the history of federal government involvement in the arts in America, see Alan Howard Levy, *Government and the Arts: Debates over Federal Support of the Arts in America from George Washington to Jesse Helms* (Lanham, Md.: University Press of America, 1997), and Michael Brenson, *Visionaries and Outcasts: The NEA, Congress, and the Place of the Visual Artist in America* (New York: The New Press, 2001). Current grants from the National Endowment for the Arts are listed on its Web site at **arts.endow.gov.**

CHAPTER 9

Challenging Wartime Internment

Supreme Court Records from
Korematsu v. United States

On Friday afternoon, May 30, 1942—almost six months after the Japanese bombing of Pearl Harbor—Fred Korematsu was arrested as he was standing outside a drugstore in San Leandro, California, smoking a cigarette and waiting for his girlfriend, Ida Boitano. The police charged Korematsu with violating a military order directed at residents of California, Oregon, and Washington who were "enemy aliens" born in Japan or U.S. citizens of Japanese descent. All were to report to an "assembly center," with just one suitcase in hand, prepared for evacuation from their homes and wartime "detention" in one of ten "relocation centers," or internment camps, that the government had constructed in isolated areas of eastern California, Idaho, Utah, Arizona, Wyoming, Colorado, and Arkansas. Fred Korematsu's Japanese-born parents and American-born brothers had reported, as ordered, to the Tanforan assembly center south of San Francisco by May 9. Indeed, virtually all who fell under the military order obeyed it. But Fred chose to disobey the order, and from that individual act arose one of the most famous Supreme Court cases in American history.

Fred Korematsu did not set out, at age twenty-two, to place his name at the center of the U.S. debate over civil liberties in wartime. He was a working-class Californian, a trained welder, a graduate of Castlemont High School in Oakland, and a registered voter, but he was not at all a political activist. He had tried to enlist in the army six months before Pearl Harbor. If gastric ulcers had not made Korematsu ineligible, he would have joined five thousand other Americans of Japanese descent already serving in the U.S. armed forces. Once war broke out in December 1941, Korematsu's personal goal was to move to the midwest with his white girlfriend and stay out of all the anti-Japanese trouble

180

brewing on the west coast in the wake of Japan's attack on Pearl Harbor. Nativists who had long opposed Japanese settlement in the United States used the occasion of war with Japan to stir up fears and hostilities. Since the bombing in Hawaii had left west coast residents feeling vulnerable, and since 88 percent of the U.S. residents of Japanese descent lived on the west coast, the anti-Japanese campaign was concentrated in that region.

For Japanese living in the United States, trouble began immediately after Pearl Harbor with implementation of a U.S. war plan to arrest all suspicious "enemy aliens" who might be involved in espionage. The Japanese attack had thrust America into a world war with European allies against Japan, Germany, and Italy. But German and Italian "enemy aliens" living throughout the United States were questioned only if they were affiliated with profascist organizations, and only half of the ten thousand questioned were interned during the war for their political beliefs. Government policy toward Japanese on the Pacific Coast was entirely different. There, the U.S. government moved to evacuate all forty thousand immigrants born in Japan. None of those immigrants, known as issei, were American citizens because the U.S. naturalization law in force since 1790 stipulated that an immigrant had to be "white" to be eligible for citizenship. Nativists convinced their allies in the military and in Congress that resentment over this race-based rule, and the 1924 law excluding all future Japanese immigrants, would cause the issei to be loyal to Japan during war.

In the two months following the attack on Pearl Harbor, key members of the army's command staff in San Francisco and of the California congressional delegation expanded the evacuation plan to include all U.S.-born children of Japanese immigrants. The plan to evacuate the 72,000 American citizens, known as nisei, was based on the belief that they, too, posed a security threat to the United States. Advocates of the plan argued, without proof, that Japanese espionage in Hawaii had facilitated the Pearl Harbor attack. Interestingly, no one ever proposed evacuating Hawaii's residents of Japanese descent, who constituted one-third of the Hawaiian population and were a vital part of the Hawaiian workforce. Evacuation of all west-coast Japanese, who made up only 1 percent of the region's population, did not hurt the general economy but helped those associations of California growers who had for decades sought to eliminate direct competition from successful Japanese American farmers. Those with economic interests thus joined forces with anti-Japanese nativists during wartime to support exclusion of all Japanese without regard for citizenship status and without individual questioning about political loyalties.

The debate within the government over treatment of Japanese Americans reflected a conflict between military necessity and constitutional rights. Advocates of military necessity won the debate by making three assertions: first, that Japanese Americans on the west coast constituted an espionage threat because of their strategic location, their racial loyalty to Japan, and their bitterness over U.S. racism; second, that because "the Occidental[1] eye cannot readily distinguish one Japanese resident from another," effective surveillance of suspicious

---

[1] The "Occident" means Europe and America, as opposed to the "Orient" or Asia.

individuals would be impossible; and, third, that "their racial characteristics are such that we cannot understand or trust even the citizen Japanese." In other words, the fact of American racism was used to predict Japanese disloyalty and to explain why government officials could not distinguish the loyal from the disloyal through the same process of individual questioning used with European American fascists.

On February 4, 1942, an 8:00 P.M. curfew was imposed on all Japanese Americans living in the Pacific states. On February 19, President Franklin D. Roosevelt issued Executive Order 9066, which gave the U.S. military independent authority to designate sensitive areas during wartime, including the authority to determine which persons were to be excluded from those areas, and to provide transportation, food, and shelter for anyone evacuated. A month later, the U.S. Congress endorsed FDR's action with Public Law 503. The very broad wording of both the executive order and the new law allowed Lieutenant General John DeWitt, U.S. commander of the western region of the United States, maximum latitude in taking whatever protective measures he thought necessary in wartime. Aware of the bitter claims that lax security was to blame for Pearl Harbor, and politically sympathetic to the anti-Japanese activists, DeWitt was determined that no sabotage or espionage would take place on the west coast under his command.

Like all Japanese Americans, Fred Korematsu paid close attention to the public debate over evacuation in the winter and spring of 1942. By the time FDR issued Executive Order 9066, Fred had already been expelled from his local labor union for his Japanese heritage, and he was planning to take advantage of the government suggestion that Japanese Americans voluntary relocate inland before any official evacuation proceedings began. But Fred, like many others, waited too long to relocate. On March 27, 1942, just four days after General DeWitt issued the first formal evacuation order, the government issued a "freeze" order, which meant that Japanese Americans could no longer voluntarily move inland. As a Japanese American, Fred could not leave the west coast with his girlfriend. But when General DeWitt announced on March 30 that an evacuation "was in prospect for practically all Japanese," Fred knew he would be evacuated to a camp if he stayed on the west coast. So he quickly underwent plastic surgery to disguise his ethnicity, and he acquired a fake I.D., thinking he could evade the authorities and escape with his girlfriend The ruse did not work; at the end of May, Fred was still identifiable as a Japanese American and the San Leandro police picked him up—probably on a tip from his girlfriend.

The American Civil Liberties Union (ACLU), which was established during World War I to challenge government violations of the Bill of Rights during wartime, faced a real dilemma during World War II. Members of the national board were closely aligned with President Roosevelt and hesitated to criticize his wartime policies, but ACLU activists on the west coast were anxious to challenge the constitutionality of Japanese internment. Despite opposition from the ACLU leadership in Washington, D.C., ACLU lawyers in San Francisco and Seattle sought out Japanese American citizens who had been arrested for violating military orders and tried to convince them to become a "test case." Fred Korematsu was one of only four Japanese Americans among the relatively few who violated orders in the first place to agree to challenge the order instead of paying the fine and quietly entering an internment camp. All four cases were complicated along the way by legalistic machinations, judicial technicalities, divisions within the ACLU and among the lawyers for the Japanese Americans, and serious disagreement between the War Department and the Justice Department over how to defend the government's internment policy.

It took two and one-half years for Fred Korematsu's case to reach the Supreme Court. In those years, Fred was interned at a relocation camp in Topaz, Utah, where he experienced the dry, dusty, and desolate conditions under which tens of thousands of Japanese Americans lived for years, and where he met with some hostility from those Japanese Americans who believed he was unwise to challenge the government's policies. Fred, like many other nisei, was allowed out of the camp on a work furlough, since his loyalty was never in question, and he worked in Salt Lake City and later in Detroit. Indeed, by the time Korematsu's case reached the Supreme Court in October 1944, tens of thousands of nisei were living in the midwest and on the east coast, away from the anti-Japanese hysteria in the Pacific states. They had been released from camps on work furloughs or to enroll in U.S. universities and colleges. Others were distinguishing themselves in wartime battle. The 442nd Regimental Combat Team, composed entirely of nisei from the internment camps, was the most decorated unit in the U.S. Army.

In the months before the *Korematsu* decision was handed down, members of FDR's administration were arguing for the end of Japanese American internment, and the general who had replaced DeWitt on the west coast had declared evacuation no longer a military necessity. Organized protests by some Japanese Americans in the internment camps had raised the hackles of anti-Asian activists, so FDR postponed the end of the detention policy until after the November 1944 election. On December 17, 1944, the U.S. government announced that those Japanese Americans certified as loyal would not be detained or excluded from the west coast after January 2, 1945. The next day, the Supreme Court announced its decision in Fred Korematsu's case: his conviction for violating the evacuation order was upheld; the military order itself was judged to be constitutional.

Using Supreme Court Records as a Source

The U.S. Constitution provides for a system of federal courts with a Supreme Court as the final arbiter of the constitutionality of all lower court rulings. The Supreme Court is empowered to rule in any case it chooses, but the Court rules in relatively few of the nation's legal disputes. Every year, close to five thousand petitions are filed asking the Supreme Court to consider a case that has already been heard in a lower federal court or a lower state court, but the Court chooses to hear only seventy to eighty cases each year. Often, the nine justices who sit on the Supreme Court select those cases that raise significant constitutional questions about the rights of the individual and the powers of the government. As the "supreme" arbiters of the law in the United States, the justices deliberate on those issues where they see the need for a "precedent," an authoritative rule or principle governing future cases in all lower courts. Historians examine lawyers' arguments and justices' decisions in Supreme Court cases to determine which legal issues were most pressing in a particular era and to see which arguments put forth at the time persuaded justices to render a precedent-setting decision. Both the arguments and decisions offer a window into a moment in history.

At first glance, the Supreme Court's ruling in *Korematsu v. United States* appears to establish the principle that the federal government has the constitutional authority to select a group of citizens based on their race and evacuate them from their homes for the purpose of indefinite detention. However, when we read the actual records from the case, including the Supreme Court justices' opinions in the case, we find that the rule defined the government's authority in very narrow terms. We also find that the most precedent-setting statement in the Court's ruling turned out to be the claim that "all legal restrictions which curtail the civil rights of a single racial group are immediately suspect. . . . courts must subject them to the most rigid scrutiny." Even as it was allowing wartime violation of one group's civil rights in 1944, the Court was setting a broad, new legal rule that later courts could choose, and did choose, to follow. Henceforth, all cases of racial discrimination would be judged according to a new principle, which came to be called "strict scrutiny."

Historians must read the lawyers' arguments and the justices' decisions in the *Korematsu* case if they want to understand exactly how the Supreme Court managed to craft a ruling that was both narrow and broad. It is from the clues in those records that the historian can then track down explanations for why the Court ruled as it did in *Korematsu v. United States.*

Advantages and Disadvantages of Working with Supreme Court Records

The Supreme Court consists of nine individuals who are appointed by the president and approved by the Senate and who sit on the high court for life. It takes only five justices to render a precedent-setting decision; in the *Korematsu* case, the decision was rendered by six justices. The other three justices "dissented" from the majority's opinion and wrote, as dissenting justices often do, their own opinions on why the majority was wrong. All of these written opinions are useful additions to the historical record; dissenting opinions are sometimes an unofficial signal to what a future court will decide when the majority shifts.

On the one hand, then, a great advantage to Supreme Court records is that they offer the historian concise, generally well-written summaries of a legal debate that was sufficiently urgent and heated to capture the Court's attention. Indeed, the written arguments that the lawyers on both sides of the case present to the justices are called "briefs" because they are supposed to be concise summaries of core issues and legal precedents in the case. As well, justices' opinions can give historians an efficient overview of legal history and contemporary reasoning relevant to the case. On the other hand, these records are full of legal terminology and references to previous, precedent-setting cases that the lawyers or justices want to cite as support for their positions. Any historian working with court records must be prepared to learn the terms and study the precedents.

Despite the advantages of working with court records, as a source, historians must be careful to remember that the writings of nine Supreme Court justices and a handful of lawyers are not a valid measure of popular opinion: they are not a poll; they are not a democratic election. Historians cannot be seduced into mistaking these well-articulated arguments for all Americans' views—maybe they are, maybe they are not. The records themselves cannot tell us that. Nor can the records fully reveal all the background factors shaping the arguments and decisions in the case. A careful reading of the records, however, can tell a historian where to dig into the background.

Consider these excerpts from an "amicus curiae" brief, meaning a "friend of the court" brief, filed by the attorneys general of the states of California, Oregon, and Washington in the *Korematsu* case. These particular friends were speaking on the side of the government, offering the Court their views on why the military evacuation of Japanese Americans was justified in wartime. This brief, like most, offered claims of fact, constitutional principle, and legal precedent to support its position:

Factual claim to military necessity

Korematsu

Both the time required to examine this large group and the lack of an adequate test of loyalty and trained personnel, made treatment upon an individual basis impossible in the face of the emergency which required prompt action. The appellant, however, claims that the evacuation was the result of pressure brought by exclusion agitation groups and

Reference to legal precedent set in another wartime case the year before

Japanese baiters . . . This charge was partly dissipated when this court held in *Hirabayashi v. United States* (320 U.S. 81 [1943]), that the curfew order . . . was issued for reasons of military necessity. . . . The exclusion of persons from critical areas in time of war, when required by military necessity, is within the scope of the joint war powers of the Congress and the President. . . . Of course, such an exercise of the war power must be reasonable under the circumstances that satisfy the "due process" requirements of the Fifth Amendment.

Use of constitutional principles

Hence, . . . the only substantial question here is whether or not . . . there existed a rational basis for the decisions of the military commander to evacuate and exclude all persons of Japanese ancestry from the Pacific coastal areas. . . . In holding

Did the facts justify placing military need over the Fifth Amendment?

Factual claims *and* legal precedent

that there was a reasonable basis for the application of curfew to all persons of Japanese ancestry, citizens and aliens alike . . . within the Western Defense Command, this court, in the *Hirabayashi* case, found that the following factors provided a reasonable basis.

So factual claims accepted by Supreme Court in prior case should be accepted in *Korematsu* case

The amicus curiae brief then listed thirteen factors that made evacuation of Japanese Americans reasonable under the circumstances. Among the reasons: the attack on Pearl Harbor put the Pacific Coast in danger; war production facilities on the Pacific Coast were in danger; the majority of Japanese Americans lived on the Pacific Coast; white hostility had increased Japanese solidarity; Japanese American children attended Japanese language schools; in 1927, the vast majority of U.S.-born children of Japanese descent held dual citizenship; the Japanese consulate was influential with Japanese community elders in United States.

In the lawyers' briefs and justices' opinions that follow, you will see repeated the issues raised in this one amicus curiae brief. Like any historian studying the case, you will need to keep track of the factual claims, constitutional principles, and legal precedents cited on both sides and in the justices' ruling decision and their dissenting opinions. Ultimately, the justices of the Supreme Court had to rule on these questions: Would they accept (or, to use court language, "take judicial notice" of) the factual claims made in General DeWitt's *Final Report* about the security threat posed by Japanese Americans after Pearl Harbor? Were those factual claims strong enough to pass the "rigid" or "strict" scrutiny required for the government to ignore the Fifth Amendment to the Constitution, which states that every individual is to be granted "due process of law"? Did the circumstances on the west coast justify denying individual Japanese Americans a hearing and trial before being detained in an internment camp and thus "deprived of life, liberty, or property"? Could the just-decided *Hirabayashi* case (where the Supreme Court unanimously ruled that pre-internment conditions justified an 8:00 P.M. curfew on all west coast residents of Japanese descent) be used as the legal precedent for the much more intrusive order to leave one's home and enter a detention camp? And could the order to evacuate—which was the only order Korematsu was charged with disobeying—properly be called an order for indefinite detention in an internment camp? Could it not be more narrowly defined as simply an order to report to an assembly center with no implication of future detention? These are the questions the Supreme Court had to answer in coming to a decision. By reading some of the court records, you can see how those questions were debated and decided. You can also watch for clues that alert a historian to dig deeper into the background for an explanation of why the Court chose to announce a bold, broad principle like "strict scrutiny" in its ruling and then rely on the narrow *Hirabayashi* precedent for an equally narrow ruling that the *Korematsu* case was only about evacuation. Why did the Court avoid the really big question of indefinite detention? Do the records help you build an explanation for such a curiously mixed ruling?

Working with the Source

You may use the table on page 187 to keep track of the different sorts of arguments put forth in the lawyers' briefs and justices' opinions included in this chapter's source documents.

	Argument made by:	Argument for:	Argument against:
Factual claims about military necessity			
Constitutional issues of due process and war powers			
Legal claims to precedents in prior cases			

The Source: Briefs and Supreme Court Opinions in *Korematsu v. United States,* October Term, 1944

Part Three of the Brief Submitted by the Solicitor General of the United States and the Department of Justice Supporting Korematsu's Conviction

In this section of its three-part brief, the Justice Department spoke directly to the question of "whether the evacuation from the local region of persons of Japanese ancestry . . . was a valid exercise of the war power under the circumstances." The footnotes in this section were part of the Justice Department's brief and constituted an important part of its claim to factual evidence.

The situation leading to the determination to exclude all persons of Japanese ancestry from Military Area No. 1 and the California portion of Military Area No. 2 was stated in detail in the Government's brief in this Court in *Hirabayashi v. United States.* . . . That statement need not be repeated here.[1] In brief, the facts which were generally known in the early months of 1942 or have since been disclosed indicate that there was ample ground to believe that imminent danger then existed of an attack by Japan upon the West Coast. This area contained a large concentration of war production and war facilities. Of the 126,947 persons of Japanese descent in the United States, 111,938 lived in Military Areas No. 1 and No. 2, of whom approximately two-thirds were United States citizens. Social, economic, and political conditions . . . were such that the assimilation of many of them by the white community had been prevented. There was evidence indicating the existence of media through which Japan could have attempted, and had attempted, to secure the attachment of many of these persons to the Japanese Government and to arouse their sympathy and enthusiasm for war aims. There was a basis for concluding that some persons of Japanese ancestry, although American citizens, had formed an

[1] The *Final Report* of General DeWitt (which is dated June 5, 1943, but which was not made public until January, 1944) . . . is relied on in this brief for statistics and other details concerning the actual evacuation. . . . We have specifically recited in this brief the facts relating to the justification for the evacuation, of which we ask the Court to take judicial notice, and we rely upon the *Final Report* only to the extent that it relates to such facts.

Source: *Landmark Briefs and Arguments of the Supreme Court of the United States: Constitutional Law,* Volume 42, edited by Philip B. Kurland and Gerhard Casper (Washington, D.C.: University Publications of America, 1976), 213–15.

attachment to, and sympathy and enthusiasm for, Japan.[2] It was also evident that it would be impossible quickly and accurately to distinguish these persons from other citizens of Japanese ancestry. The presence in the Military Areas Nos. 1 and 2 of persons who might aid Japan was peculiarly and particularly dangerous. . . . The persons affected were at first encouraged and assisted to migrate under their own arrangements, but this method of securing their re-moval . . . was terminated by Public Proclamation No. 4. . . . it was necessary to restrict and regulate the migration from the Area in order to insure the orderly evacuation and resettlement of the persons affected. . . . The rate of self-arranged migration was inadequate, partly because of growing indications that persons of Japanese ancestry were likely to meet with hostility and even violence.

[2] In addition to the authorities cited in the Hirabayashi brief, see Anonymous (An Intelli-gence Officer), "The Japanese in America, the Problem and the Solution," *Harper's Magazine,* October, 1942 . . . See also "Issei, Nisei, Kibei," *Fortune Magazine,* April, 1944.

2   *Brief Submitted by Wayne M. Collins, Counsel for Appellant*

Mr. Collins's impassioned, ninety-eight-page (not-so) brief made a variety of arguments against the military necessity for and constitutionality of evac-uation and internment. The excerpts below, including the footnote, in-dicate the tone of Collins's brief and his arguments regarding General DeWitt's motives in interpreting Executive Order 9066 as an evacuation and internment order.

If [General DeWitt] really believed these people to be spies and saboteurs . . . why did he delay from December 7, 1941, to March 30, 1942, before removing the first contingent to assembly centers? . . . Was General DeWitt so blind that he didn't realize that in the interval between December 7, 1941, and the date of his unprecedented orders . . . boards of investigation could have examined the loyalty of each of the prospective deportees . . . They could have been exam-ined in less time than it took to build the shacks that were to house them.[1] The inconvenience and cost of examining would have been trifling. The cost of

[1] The General issued several hundred individual civilian exclusion orders against "white" naturalized citizens of prior German and Italian allegiance whom he deemed dangerous. These were given individual hearings on the question of their loyalty. . . . If the General had time to provide examinations for these individuals can he be heard to deny he had time to examine Japanese descended citizens before evacuating them? His special treatment of these whites proves his bias against the native-born yellow citizen.

Source: Landmark Briefs and Arguments of the Supreme Court of the United States, 119, 152, 161, 163, 165, 196.

housing, evacuation and administration of his program has cost this country many millions. . . . Why did he keep secret the reasons he insisted upon this frenzied evacuation? How could this nation abide the secret reasons he carried in his head when we had neither evidence nor ground to believe him to have been the wisest man in the nation? What are the facts upon which he would justify the outrage he perpetrated? . . .

What one day will be celebrated as a masterpiece of illogic . . . appears in General DeWitt's letter of February 14, 1942, one month before the evacuation commenced. (*Final Report,* p. 34). He characterizes all our Japanese as subversive. . . . He states . . . that "the Japanese race is an enemy race" and the native-born citizens are "Americanized" but their "racial strains are undiluted" and being "barred from assimilation by convention" may "turn against this nation" upon which he concludes . . . "112,000 potential enemies, of Japanese extraction, are at large today. There are indications that these are organized and ready for concerted action. . . . The very fact that no sabotage has taken place to date is a disturbing and confirming indication that such action will be taken."

He tells us on page 18 of his [*Final Report*] that there "were many evidences of this successful communication of information to the enemy, information regarding positive knowledge on his part of our installations." He doesn't tell us who communicated this information, however, or when it was communicated. . . . In a footnote on page 8 of his report he informs us that after evacuation "interceptions of suspicious or unidentified radio signals and shore-to-ship signal lights were virtually eliminated and attacks on outbound shipping from West Coast portions appreciably reduced." He doesn't charge any alien or citizen of Japanese pedigree with signalling the enemy however. Had there been any signalling to the enemy by any person neither he nor the F.B.I. would have hesitated to arrest the guilty. . . . No arrests were made. . . . No charges filed against anyone. . . .

Who is this DeWitt to say who is and who is not an American and who shall and who shall not enjoy the rights of citizenship? . . . General DeWitt let Terror out to plague these citizens but closed the lid on the Pandora's box and left Hope to smother. It is your duty to raise the lid and revive Hope for these, our people, who have suffered at the hands of one of our servants.

3   *Amicus Curiae Briefs Submitted by the American Civil Liberties Union*

Due to conflict within the ACLU, that organization was not Korematsu's attorney-of-record, but it did submit a "friend of the court" brief to persuade the Supreme Court to hear the *Korematsu* case and submitted another at the time of the hearing. These excerpts are taken from both briefs as is footnote 2.

October 1943 Brief Asking the Supreme Court to Review the Judgement of the Ninth Circuit Court of Appeals

We believe that this case presents the question of the power of the military to detain citizens against whom no charges have been preferred. We contend that no such power has been granted by Congress, or could be constitutionally granted.

The issue is presented because the evacuation orders . . . made it quite plain that not evacuation only was required, but indefinite detention as well. . . . That the evacuation and detention were part of a single integrated program is made clear in a recently published report by the War Department. . . .

We submit that the Congress gave neither to the President nor to military authorities any power so far reaching, and that in the absence of legislation the President has no such power even in time of war. . . . It is only when martial law has been declared that executive authority may be exercised over citizens. . . . Finally, we submit that even the President and the Congress, acting together, may not detain citizens of the United States against whom no charges have been preferred. . . . the framers [of the Constitution] permitted the suspension of the writ of habeas corpus,[1] by which unlawful detention was normally challenged, but permitted such suspension only in time of invasion or insurrection. . . . only at a time of direst immediate emergency, not at all as a precautionary measure.

October 1944 Brief Asking the Supreme Court to Overturn Fred Korematsu's Conviction

General DeWitt does try to show military necessity by reference to reported illegal radio signals which could not be located, lights on the shore, and the like . . . The Government's brief . . . contains no reference . . . to illicit radio signals, signal lights . . . or to . . . hidden caches of contraband. . . . Moreover, in several respects the recital in the DeWitt Report is wholly inconsistent with the

---

[1] [A writ of habeas corpus is an order that a prison official bring a prisoner before a court to show that the prisoner has been arrested and detained for actual legal cause. — Ed.]
Source: Landmark Briefs and Arguments of the Supreme Court of the United States, 81–83, 302–4.

facts of public knowledge. It is well known, of course, that radio detection equipment is unbelievably accurate. . . . Secondly, the fact that no person of Japanese ancestry has been arraigned for any sabotage or espionage since December 7, 1941, certainly suggests, in view of the unquestionable efficiency of the F.B.I., that no such acts were committed. . . . Nowhere in [DeWitt's *Final Report*] is there a line, a word, about the reports of other security officers. General DeWitt does not tell us whether he consulted either the Director of the Federal Bureau of Investigation or the Director of the Office of Naval Intelligence. . . . Since no recommendation from either the Office of Naval Intelligence or the F.B.I. are referred to, one can only assume either that they were not sought or that they were opposed to mass evacuation.[2]

[2] There is a fair indication that, whether or not its recommendations were asked, the Office of Naval Intelligence would have stated that mass evacuation was wholly unnecessary. In *Harper's Magazine* for October, 1942, there is an article by an anonymous officer . . . [which] is almost certainly from the Office of Naval Intelligence, which has always been understood as primarily concerned with Japanese intelligence work. The concluding paragraph states: "To sum up: the entire 'Japanese Problem' has been magnified out of its true proportion, largely because of the physical characteristics of the people. It should be handled on the basis of the *individual*, regardless of citizenship, and *not* on a racial basis."

 ## *Amicus Curiae Brief Submitted by the Japanese American Citizens' League on Behalf of Fred Korematsu*

The JACL submitted a two-hundred-page "friend of the court" brief that emphasized Japanese American assimilation and loyalty to the U.S. government. In response to the charge that Japanese American loyalty was in doubt because many held dual citizenship, the JACL brief explained that, prior to 1924, Japanese law automatically conferred Japanese citizenship on any child born of Japanese parents anywhere in the world. After Japanese Americans persuaded the Japanese government to change that law, the percentage of U.S.-born children of Japanese descent holding dual citizenship plummeted by 85 percent.

It has been necessary to present the evidence concerning the assimilation, loyalty and contributions of Americans of Japanese ancestry because. . . . [in] all the loose talk about "lack of assimilation" and "close-knit racial groups" there is no hint that the trained investigators who have pursued the subject for years were even consulted. . . . Dr. Robert E. Park, chairman of the Department of Sociology of the University of Chicago, directed a large-scale study of resident

Source: Landmark Briefs and Arguments of the Supreme Court of the United States, 504–6, 527–28.

Orientals. . . . [and] determined that the American of Japanese ancestry "born in America and educated in our western schools is culturally an Occidental, even though he be racially an Oriental.". . .

The civilians who, because they were influenced by Pearl Harbor sabotage rumors, became panic-stricken and requested evacuation . . . did not know the facts. Perhaps the politicians . . . too, were ignorant. But General DeWitt, who ordered the evacuation, certainly must have been aware of the truth and must have been cognizant of the grounds on which his fellow officer, General Delos C. Emmons, refused to order mass internment of the persons of Japanese descent in Hawaii.

Why then did General DeWitt, in spite of what he knew or could easily have learned, act upon the advice of racists and mean-spirited economic rivals? We contend that General DeWitt accepted the views of racists instead of the principles of democracy because he is himself a confessed racist. . . . On April 13, 1943, in testifying before the House Naval Affairs Committee in San Francisco, General DeWitt . . . said:

> A Jap's a Jap. . . . I don't want any of them. We got them out. . . . They are a dangerous element, whether loyal or not. It makes no difference whether he is an American citizen. Theoretically, he is still a Japanese and you can't change him.

5 ▌ ## *The Opinion of the Supreme Court,*
Issued December 18, 1944

Justice Hugo L. Black issued the eight-page majority opinion of six of the Court's nine judges. Chief Justice Harlan Stone and Justices Stanley Reed, Felix Frankfurter, Wiley Rutledge, and William O. Douglas concurred. All of those justices, except for Chief Justice Stone, were appointed to the Supreme Court by President Franklin Delano Roosevelt.

It should be noted, to begin with, that all legal restrictions which curtail the civil rights of a single racial group are immediately suspect. That is not to say that all such restrictions are unconstitutional. It is to say that courts must subject them to the most rigid scrutiny. Pressing public necessity may sometime justify the existence of such restrictions; racial antagonism never can. . . . Executive Order 9066 . . . declared that "the successful prosecution of the war requires every possible protection against espionage and against sabotage. . . . In *Hirabayashi v. United States* . . . we sustained a conviction obtained for violation of the curfew order. . . . It was because we could not reject the finding of the

Source: United States Reports, Vol. 323: Cases Adjudged in the Supreme Court at October Term, 1944, 214–24.

military authorities that it was impossible to bring about an immediate segregation of the disloyal from the loyal that we sustained the validity of the curfew order as applying to the whole group. In the instant case, temporary exclusion of the entire group was rested by the military on the same ground. . . .

We uphold the exclusion order as of the time it was made and when the petitioner violated it. In doing so, we are not unmindful of the hardships imposed by it upon a large group of American citizens. But hardships are part of war, and war is an aggregation of hardships. . . . Citizenship has its responsibilities as well as its privileges, and in time of war the burden is always heavier. . . . The contention is that we must treat these separate orders [for exclusion and for detention] as one and inseparable; that, for this reason, if detention in an assembly or relocation center would have illegally deprived the petitioner of his liberty, the exclusion order and his conviction under it cannot stand. . . . We cannot say . . . that his presence in that [assembly] center would have resulted in his detention in a relocation center. . . . It is sufficient here to pass upon the [exclusion] order which petitioner violated. To do more would be to go beyond the issues raised, and to decide momentous questions not contained within the framework of the pleadings or the evidence in this case. . . . To cast this case in the outlines of racial prejudice, without reference to real military dangers which were presented, merely confuses the issue.

 ## *Justice Owen J. Roberts, Dissenting from the Majority*

Justice Roberts was one of only two justices on the Supreme Court in 1944 who had not been appointed by President Roosevelt. In his five-page dissent, Justice Roberts criticized the majority's reliance on the *Hirabayashi* precedent and its claim that it was valid to rule narrowly on evacuation and not address the question of detention without trial.

The predicament in which the petitioner thus found himself was this: he was forbidden, by Military Order, to leave the zone in which he lived; he was forbidden, by Military Order, after a date fixed, to be found within that zone unless he were in an Assembly Center located in that zone. General DeWitt's report to the Secretary of War concerning the program of evacuation and relocation of Japanese makes it entirely clear . . . that an Assembly Center was a euphemism for a prison. No person within such a center was permitted to leave except by Military Order. . . . The civil authorities must often resort to the expedient of excluding citizens temporarily from a locality. . . . If the exclusion . . . were of that

Source: United States Reports, Vol. 323: Cases Adjudged in the Supreme Court at October Term, 1944, 225–30.

nature the *Hirabayashi* case would be an authority for sustaining it. But the facts above recited . . . show that the exclusion was part of an overall plan for forcible detention. . . . The two conflicting orders, one which commanded him to stay and the other which commanded him to go, were nothing but a cleverly devised trap to accomplish the real purpose of the military authority, which was to lock him up in a concentration camp. . . . We know that is the fact. Why should we set up a figmentary and artificial situation instead of addressing ourselves to the actualities of the case?

7   *Justice Frank Murphy, Dissenting from the Majority*

> Justice Murphy had voted with all the other justices in the 1943 *Hirabayashi* case, upholding a curfew for west coast residents of Japanese descent. But his written opinion in the case stated that such a curfew for one ethnic group bore "a melancholy resemblance to the treatment accorded to members of the Jewish race in Germany" and "goes to the very brink of constitutional power." In his ten-page dissent from the majority's decision in the *Korematsu* case, Justice Murphy focused on balancing military necessity and citizens' constitutional rights.

In dealing with matters relating to the prosecution and progress of a war, we must accord great respect and consideration to the judgements of the military authorities . . . their judgements ought not to be overruled lightly by those whose training and duties ill-equip them to deal intelligently with matters so vital to the security of the nation. At the same time, however, it is essential that there be definite limits to military discretion, especially where martial law has not been declared. Individuals must not be impoverished of their constitutional rights on a plea of military necessity that has neither substance nor support. . . . the military claim must subject itself to the judicial process of having its reasonableness determined. . . . the action [must] have some reasonable relation to the removal of dangers of invasion, sabotage, and espionage. But the exclusion of all persons with Japanese blood in their veins has no such reasonable relation . . . because [it] must necessarily rely for its reasonableness on the assumption that *all* persons of Japanese ancestry may have a dangerous tendency to commit sabotage and espionage. . . . It is difficult to believe that reason, logic or experience could be marshalled in support of . . . this erroneous assumption of racial guilt. In [General DeWitt's] *Final Report* . . . he refers to all individuals of Japanese descent as "subversive," as belonging to an "enemy race" whose "racial strains are undiluted." . . . Justification for the exclusion is

Source: United States Reports, Vol. 323: Cases Adjudged in the Supreme Court at October Term, 1944, 233–42.

sought . . . mainly upon questionable racial and sociological grounds not ordinarily within the realm of expert military judgement. . . . A military judgement based upon such racial and sociological considerations is not entitled to the great weight ordinarily given the judgements based upon strict military considerations. . . . I dissent, therefore, from this legalization of racism.

   ## *Justice Robert Jackson, Dissenting from the Majority*

In his six-page dissent, Justice Jackson challenged the relevance of *Hirabayashi* as a precedent and distinguished between the immediate decisions of the military and the precedent-setting decisions of the Supreme Court.

It is said that if the military commander had reasonable military grounds for promulgating the orders, they are constitutional and become law and the Court is required to enforce them. There are several reasons why I cannot subscribe to this doctrine.

It would be impracticable and dangerous idealism to expect or insist that each specific military command in an area of probable operations will conform to conventional tests of constitutionality. . . . But if we cannot confine military expedients by the Constitution, neither would I distort the Constitution to approve all that the military may deem expedient. That is what the Court appears to be doing, whether consciously or not. I cannot say, from any evidence before me, that the orders of General DeWitt were not reasonably expedient military precautions, nor could I say that they were. But even if they were permissible military procedures, I deny that it follows that they were constitutional. . . .

Much is made of the danger to liberty from the Army program of deporting and detaining these citizens of Japanese extraction. But a judicial construction of the due process clause that will sustain this order is a far more subtle blow to liberty than the promulgation of the order itself. A military order, however constitutional, is not apt to last longer than the military emergency. . . . But once a judicial opinion rationalizes such an order to show that it conforms to the Constitution . . . the Court for all time has validated the principle of racial discrimination. . . . The principle then lies about like a loaded weapon ready for the hand of any authority that can bring forward a plausible claim of an urgent need. Every repetition imbeds that principle more deeply in our law and thinking and expands it to new purposes. . . . A military commander may overstep the bounds of constitutionality, and it is an incident. But if we review and

Source: United States Reports, Vol. 323: Cases Adjudged in the Supreme Court at October Term, 1944, 242–48.

approve, that passing incident becomes the doctrine of the Constitution. There it has a generative power of its own. . . . Nothing better illustrates this danger than does the Court's opinion in this case. It argues that we are bound to uphold the conviction of Korematsu because we upheld one in *Hirabayashi v. United States,* when we sustained these orders in so far as they applied a curfew requirement to a citizen of Japanese ancestry. . . . Now the principle of racial discrimination is pushed from support of mild measures to very harsh ones, from temporary deprivations to indeterminate ones. And the precedent which it is said requires us to do so is *Hirabayashi.* . . . Because we said that these citizens could be made to stay in their homes during the hours of dark, it is said we must require them to leave home entirely; and if that, we are told they may also be taken into custody for deportation; and if that, it is argued they may also be held for some undetermined time in detention camps. How far the principle of this case would be extended before plausible reasons would play out, I do not know.

Analyzing the Source

REFLECTING ON THE SOURCE

1. What factual claims about the military necessity of Japanese American evacuation were in dispute in this case? Did any of the justices question the military's claims?

2. Reviewing your notes on factual claims, constitutional principles, and legal precedent (p. 187), which arguments do you think most influenced the majority's narrow ruling on the legitimacy of evacuation? Which arguments shaped their broad ruling on "strict scrutiny"?

3. Why do you think the majority rendered both a narrow and a broad ruling? Based on the background material provided here and comments in the court records, what additional research would you conduct to test your theory?

MAKING CONNECTIONS

4. In the previous chapter, "Painting a New Deal," about New Deal murals, President Franklin D. Roosevelt is described as a proponent of an activist government that could uplift the average working people of the United States. In what ways did FDR's wartime Executive Order 9066 contradict his New Deal presidency and in what ways was it consistent with his conduct during the New Deal years?

5. Since the terrorist attacks of September 11, 2001, and the passage of the U.S. Patriot Act, legal scholars have debated whether the Supreme Court's opinion in *Korematsu v. United States* might be used as a precedent for categorical incarceration of Arabs as a military necessity in the war on terrorism. As you will see in

"Beyond the Source," Korematsu's conviction was later overturned by a lower court, but the Supreme Court's 1944 ruling in the case still stands. Could you imagine the Supreme Court today citing the *Korematsu* opinion as a precedent justifying evacuation or detention of Arabs in the name of national security?

Beyond the Source

In April 1984, forty years after the Supreme Court declared Fred Korematsu guilty of disobeying a military order, his case was reconsidered in the U.S. District Court for Northern California, and his conviction was overturned. This was an extraordinary turn of events, unprecedented in U.S. legal history, and it occurred because a lawyer and legal historian, Peter Irons, conducted thorough historical research and found evidence he never even dreamed existed.

Irons set out in 1981 simply to write a book about the Japanese American cases on curfew, evacuation, and internment. In digging through the unexamined records of the Justice Department, however, Irons happened upon written evidence that the Justice Department and the War Department were aware of falsification of data in General DeWitt's *Final Report*. Edward Ennis, the lawyer in the Justice Department charged with preparing the government's defense in the *Korematsu* case, had not received DeWitt's report until after the Supreme Court had read it and relied on it for the *Hirabayashi* decision. Ennis read the report skeptically, especially those sections that claimed that Japanese Americans had used signaling equipment and radio transmissions to engage in acts of espionage. Ennis investigated and learned that the FBI, the Office of Naval Intelligence, and the Federal Communications Commission had all reported to DeWitt that every rumor of such espionage had been thoroughly investigated and found false; all signals from the coast and all radio transmissions had been accounted for. In including the rumors but excluding the agencies' findings in his *Final Report,* DeWitt had knowingly falsified the only existing claims to a "military necessity" for evacuation of all Japanese Americans.

Ennis alerted Solicitor General Charles Fahy and Assistant Secretary of War John McCloy that the Justice Department would be engaged in a suppression of evidence if it did not report these findings to the Supreme Court. Fahy and McCloy refused to inform the Supreme Court that the *Final Report* was falsified, but did refrain from using that false evidence in the written brief and did agree to include the footnote, which you read in the Justice Department's brief, subtly indicating limited confidence in DeWitt's report. A surviving outline of Fahy's oral argument indicates he planned to quote from the *Final Report*'s espionage rumors in addressing the Supreme Court, but since the Justice Department has lost the transcript of Fahy's presentation, there is no proof that Fahy knowingly misled the Court on the matter of Japanese American espionage. In retrospect, Ennis regretted not resigning from his Justice Department position over this issue, but he thought he could do more good on the inside. Indeed, he slipped his information to the lawyers for the ACLU, and you can see in their amicus brief an effort to alert the Supreme Court to flaws in the *Final Report.*

When Peter Irons told sixty-two-year-old Fred Korematsu that the "military necessity" evidence used in his case had been falsified and that he had legal grounds to seek a reversal, Korematsu told Irons to go ahead with the case. Irons worked with a team of Japanese American lawyers, all children of citizens who had been interned during the war. The Justice Department offered to "pardon" Korematsu rather than face exposure of falsified evidence in open court. Korematsu replied that the Justice Department should, instead, seek a pardon from him.

In 1984, after reviewing the evidence, U.S. District Court Judge Marilyn Hall Patel overturned Korematsu's conviction on the grounds that a "fundamental error" had occurred in the original trial. With Fred Korematsu sitting before her in court, Judge Patel said:

> *Korematsu* remains on the pages of our legal and political history. As a legal precedent it is now recognized as having very limited application. As a historical precedent it stands as a constant caution that in times of war or declared military necessity our institutions must be vigilant in protecting constitutional guarantees. It stands as a caution that in times of distress the shield of military necessity and national security must not be used to protect governmental actions from close scrutiny and accountability. It stands as a caution that in times of international hostility and antagonisms our institutions, legislative, executive, and judicial, must be prepared to protect all citizens from the petty fears and prejudices that are so easily aroused. (*Korematsu v. United States* 584 F. Supp. 1406 [N.D. Cal. 1984]).

Between 1949 and 1980, very slow progress was made in the effort to compensate Japanese Americans for their financial losses as a result of relocation and detention. In 1980, because of pressure from the Japanese American Citizens' League and Japanese American elected officials, the Congress established the Commission on Wartime Relocation and Internment of Civilians to review the facts surrounding implementation of Executive Order 9066 and "recommend appropriate remedies." Peter Irons's research findings were among the facts available to this government commission. Still, progress was slow, but in 1988, four years after Fred Korematsu was exonerated, President Ronald Reagan signed the Civil Liberties Act, which provided for a $20,000 redress payment to each of the sixty thousand surviving internees, including Fred Korematsu.

Before his conviction was overturned, Korematsu had not even told his children that he was a convicted criminal. After it was overturned, Korematsu welcomed opportunities to speak about his case. In an interview for the film *Of Civil Wrongs and Rights: The Fred Korematsu Story,* he said: "In order for things like this to never happen, we have to protest. Protest but not with violence, otherwise they won't listen to you, but you have to let them know, otherwise they're not going to hear you. So, don't be afraid to speak up."

Finding and Supplementing the Source

The unabridged texts of the Supreme Court justices' majority opinion and the three dissenting opinions in *Korematsu v. United States* are included in a series published by the federal government: *United States Reports*, Volume 323: Cases Adjudged in the Supreme Court at October Term, 1944 (Washington, D.C.: Government Printing Office, 1945), pp. 214–248. This publication is available in any law library, and if you know the date of any Supreme Court decision you wish to read, you can find it in the appropriate volume of this series. It is also quite easy to get all of the justices' opinions in the *Korematsu* case, and in other major Supreme Court cases, by using a basic Web search engine to search the name of the case. The Web sites FindLaw (**caselaw.lp.findlaw.com***)* and the Touro Law Center (**tourolaw.edu**), for example, will provide the full text of the *Korematsu* opinions.

To read the full text of the lawyers' briefs and the amicus briefs submitted to the Supreme Court in *Korematsu v. United States,* see *Landmark Briefs and Arguments of the Supreme Court of the United States: Constitutional Law,* Volume 42, edited by Philip B. Kurland and Gerhard Casper (Washington, D.C.: University Publications of America, 1976), 3–563. There are no transcripts of the lawyers' oral arguments in the *Korematsu* case before the Supreme Court. The Court itself did not provide for the recording and transcription of oral arguments until 1955. Solicitor General Charles Fahy, who argued the government's case, reputedly hired a private stenographer to record his arguments, but the Justice Department now claims that those transcriptions have been lost.

Historians have studied Japanese American internment from various angles, including the personal experiences of those interned, the political conflicts outside and inside the camps, and the government's administration of the camps. An excellent bibliographical guide to the rich written and film literature on general Japanese American history and the internment in particular is included in *Japanese American Internment during World War II: A History and Reference Guide* by Wendy Ng (Westport, Conn.: Greenwood Press, 2002). Among the best works on the subject are Roger Daniels, *Prisoners without Trial: Japanese Americans in World War II* (New York: Hill and Wang, 1993); Leslie T. Hatamiya, *Righting a Wrong: Japanese Americans and the Passage of the Civil Liberties Act of 1988* (Palo Alto: Stanford University Press, 1993); John Tateishi, *And Justice for All: An Oral History of the Japanese American Detention Camps* (New York: Random House, 1984); Charles Kikuchi, *The Kikuchi Diary: Chronicles of an American Concentration Camp* (Urbana: University of Illinois Press, 1973); and Akemi Kikumura, *Through Harsh Winters: The Life of a Japanese Immigrant Woman* (Novato, Calif.: Chandler and Sharp, 1981).

Two books by Peter Irons trace the Supreme Court cases and the subsequent efforts to overturn them: *Justice at War* (New York: Oxford University Press, 1983) and *Justice Delayed: The Record of the Japanese American Internment Cases* (Middletown, Conn.: Wesleyan University Press, 1989). *Personal Justice Denied* is the very informative report of the Commission on Wartime Relocation and Internment of Civilians. A one-volume edition, with a foreword by Tetsuden Kashima (Washington, D.C.: The Civil Liberties Education Fund, and Seattle: University of Washington Press, 1997) is widely available.

Among the Web sites that offer information about Japanese American internment, see the National Archives' collection of photographs and documents at **archives.gov** and the Japanese American National Museum at **janm.org**. Among the excellent films available on internment are *The Rabbit in the Moon,* Emiko Omori's beautiful and controversial examination of various ways in which Japanese Americans resisted internment, and *Of Civil Wrongs and Rights: The Fred Korematsu Story,* in which producer Eric Paul Fournier traces Korematsu's original case and the efforts by Peter Irons and a team of Japanese American lawyers to get the conviction overturned.

CHAPTER 10

The Cold War in the Middle East

Diplomatic Communications from the Suez Crisis

On election day, November 6, 1956, Americans awoke to the news that twenty-two thousand British and French soldiers had invaded Egypt to take control of the Suez Canal and that Soviet tanks were rolling into Budapest, Hungary, to crush the Hungarians' bid for independence. So much for the myth that the 1950s were tranquil or that President Dwight D. Eisenhower governed in easy times. The cold war between the United States and the Soviet Union was at its hottest in these years, and as the American people went to the polls to reelect Eisenhower, they faced the potential for world war on two fronts.

In the view of the U.S. State Department, there was not much to be done in the case of Hungary. America had ceded that ground to Soviet influence at the end of World War II and was not prepared to start a war for liberation in eastern Europe. Of course, the United States would have welcomed the opportunity to denounce the Soviet invasion of Budapest as proof of communist oppression of satellite nations. But any chance to turn the Hungarian situation to Western advantage in the global contest for the allegiance of small nations was shattered once Britain and France launched their assault on Egypt. In the world court of public opinion, it was difficult to argue that a Soviet attack on Hungary was any more menacing than an attack by former Western colonial powers on a sovereign Arab state.

President Eisenhower (known as "Ike") was famously cool in a crisis, but on this occasion he was furious. His closest European allies had deceived him, secretly colluded with Israel to attack Egypt, and—in his view—thereby improved the Soviets' position in the Middle East. At the height of the crisis, Ike exploded in disbelief that the British and the French could be so "stupid" as to invite the hatred of the entire Arab world and "dare us" to intervene to restore peace and order in that volatile region.

Historians and political scientists agree that the Suez crisis of November 1956 marked a turning point in Western relations with the Middle East. From that moment forward, the United States replaced Britain and France as the key Western player in military, economic, and diplomatic relations in the region. The ill-conceived attempt by the British and French to capture control of the Suez Canal confirmed the Arab view that their former colonial rulers could not be trusted and that Israel was in league with Western imperialists. Since America's historical hands were the cleanest and its economic capacity the strongest, it became the main competitor against the Soviets for the loyalty of both the Arab states and Israel in the cold war.

At the outset of any review of the series of events that culminated in the Suez crisis, it is important to recognize the different perspectives of the nations involved. For the Arab states, especially for Egypt, the crisis of 1956 was one of national sovereignty and dignity; it was about Egypt's right to control its own borders and the commerce passing within those borders through the Suez Canal. For France and Britain, it was a crisis of influence and control. Accustomed to asserting their will in the Mideast since the nineteenth century, these two war-weakened powers could not adjust to the post–World War II reality of Arab autonomy and Egyptian defiance. For Israel, it was a crisis of security. Fearful of a Soviet-armed Egyptian government leading a hostile Arab coalition, the Israelis believed that a preemptive strike was vital for their survival. For the United States, however, the Suez crisis was all about global positioning in the cold war and maintaining a global balance of power with the Soviets. Because it was so focused on its own global agenda, the United States often overlooked the local, nationalistic passions at play in the region; the Americans were surprised when Britain, France, Israel, and Egypt all acted on national agendas that threatened to disrupt the cold war global order with a hot war in the Suez.

As a one-hundred-mile commercial waterway linking the Mediterranean Sea and the Gulf of Suez (see Map 10.1 on p. 204), the Suez Canal was one of the engineering triumphs of the nineteenth century. It was also a commercial triumph because it meant goods could be shipped between Europe, the Middle East, and Asia without having to sail all the way around Africa. Built by the French between 1866 and 1869, the Suez Canal was initially operated by a private French stock company. But Britain took control of the canal and its stock at the same time that it took control of the Egyptian state in 1882. From that moment until after World War II, Britain and Egypt were in an uneasy colonial relationship; every halting step toward Egyptian independence was followed by British reassertions of authority in the name of military and economic security.

In the years following the end of World War II, Egypt's moves to establish independence from Britain were clouded by this history of distrust on both sides. Negotiations to bring about British military evacuation from the canal zone dragged on into the early 1950s. Dealings were complicated by Britain's imperial desire for a level of influence it could no longer afford and its cold war

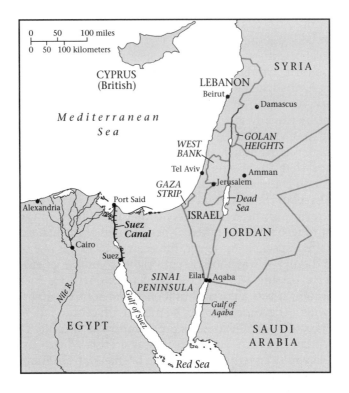

Map 10.1 The Suez Crisis of 1956

desire for Egyptian cooperation in a Mideast defense pact against the Soviets. The Egyptians, meanwhile, drew on the history of the Suez Canal to confirm their suspicions of any defense pact that might compromise their independence from the West. Along with their Arab allies, the Egyptians were also enraged at Britain and the United States for supporting the United Nations' creation of the state of Israel.

From the Western standpoint, creation of a homeland state for the Jewish people, who had suffered the horrors of the Holocaust, was a humanitarian act that also ensured a pro-Western presence in the Middle East. From the Arab standpoint, however, Israel was a foreign invader, displacing Palestinian people from their land. Israel's successful resistance against the attack by its Arab neighbors in 1948 only increased the tensions. As a result of that war, Israel increased its territorial size by 40 percent, and the refugee Palestinian population rose to almost a million. In addition, Israel encouraged massive immigration from Jews around the world, and Egypt denied Israel access to the Suez Canal.

President Eisenhower and his secretary of state, John Foster Dulles, viewed these regional and nationalistic conflicts through the lens of cold war strategy. Both Ike and Dulles disdained European colonialism, but neither grasped that their offers of economic and military aid in exchange for alignment against the Soviets looked a lot like colonialism to emerging nations. Countries like Egypt wanted the autonomy to make economic and diplomatic deals beneficial to their own interests, irrespective of cold war alignments. For Eisenhower and Dulles, however, the cold war was the top priority. They would not, for example, provide arms to any country involved in the conflict over Palestinian territory. The United States wanted the Palestinian conflict settled, not escalated, because it wanted to enlist both Arabs and Israelis in the battle against the Soviet Union.

Regrettably, the United States made a move toward violating its no-arms policy in 1954, when it offered Egypt's dynamic, young leader, Gamal Abdel Nasser, $27 million in arms as a reward for settling the protracted negotiations over British evacuation from the Suez Canal. The following year, the United States withdrew that offer out of concern that it would fuel the tensions it wanted to quell. Insulted by this U.S. reversal and believing he needed arms for the unending border war with the Israelis, Nasser turned to the Soviets for help. In the fall of 1955, one year before the Suez crisis, Nasser announced that he had negotiated to buy weapons from Czechoslovakia, a Soviet satellite that had also supplied the Israelis with arms in the 1948 war. In response, the Israelis purchased arms from the French, who hated Egypt for supporting the Algerians' war of independence against France.

Eisenhower and Dulles were angered by the Egyptian-Czech arms deal because it upset their effort to keep the Soviets out of the Mideast. But the United States hoped to draw Nasser away from future Soviet ties and enlist Egypt in Western regional defense pacts by financing Nasser's great dream: the construction of the Aswan Dam across the Nile, which would harness the irrigation and energy potential of the river. Pro-Israeli lobbyists in the United States opposed the Aswan Dam project (as did American cotton growers, since Egypt proposed to pay back the aid with sales of Egyptian cotton). Still, Ike and Dulles pursued the Aswan Dam deal because it fit their cold war strategy to link Egypt with the West.

Nasser did not share the U.S. interest in cold war alliances; he was operating first and foremost as an independent nationalist. Though he wanted U.S. aid for the Aswan Dam, he also wanted to maintain a flow of arms from the Soviet bloc for the fight with Israel, and he needed to demonstrate his autonomy from the West in order to stand tall as an Arab leader. In February of 1956, therefore, Nasser asserted Egypt's "neutrality" in the cold war by recognizing Communist China as a nation separate from Taiwan.

Nasser's defiance of Western cold war interests scuttled both State Department and congressional support for the Aswan Dam project. In July of 1956, the United States claimed that an unstable Egyptian economy made investment in the project unwise. Nasser was furious that the United States had insulted his nation's dignity by not admitting that the cold war was the reason for withdrawing support for the Aswan Dam. In a two-and-one-half hour speech to a quarter million people in Cairo on July 26, Nasser announced that Egypt had the resources to pay for the project another way: it would nationalize the Suez Canal, and all tolls paid by commercial traffic would go into the nation's treasury, not to the Canal company. Indeed, at the very moment that Nasser was delivering the speech, Egyptian officials were peacefully taking command of the canal operations.

The United States was disturbed by this action, but the British and French were enraged. Beyond their postcolonial shock at the sheer effrontery of Nasser's move, there was the fact that Europeans, not Americans, held most of the Suez Canal company stock that Nasser was proposing to buy up. Moreover, in the 1950s, it was Europeans, not Americans, whose economies depended on oil coming from Arab countries through the Suez Canal. Neither the British nor the French, however, were militarily prepared to retaliate immediately against Egypt. So between the time of Nasser's nationalization of the canal in late July and the British-French-Israeli attack on Egypt in early November, the Eisenhower administration attempted to negotiate a settlement before the crisis erupted into war. Once the invasion occurred, the United States took action to bring about an immediate ceasefire and sought to remind people around the globe that while the Soviet Union posed as the protector of Egyptian sovereignty, it was invading Hungary and taking control of the government in Budapest.

Using Diplomatic Communications as a Source

The Suez Crisis, like most diplomatic crises in the twentieth century, was managed by individual diplomats presenting their countries' positions in closed-door, face-to-face meetings, in telephone conversations, and through written messages sent over the telegraph wires. Diplomats in 1956 did not have access to e-mail or fax machines, but their methods of communication were much more rapid than in earlier eras, when diplomats and their written dispatches could travel no faster than a horse or a ship. Governments communicate their public positions to other governments through avenues other than direct contact between individuals, of course. Leaders hold press conferences and give formal speeches, governments issue formal declarations of policy, government officials give interviews to the press—and leak information to the press—all in hope of persuading other nations to settle a dispute such as the 1956 Suez crisis in a way favorable to their country's interests. But the nitty-gritty work necessary for resolving any international crisis is done by daily communications between diplomats working for the same country or different countries. These messages are seldom quoted in our newspapers, but the agreements that emerge (or fail to emerge) from such dialogues are the stuff of headlines.

In the United States, the State Department compiles the government's public foreign policy papers along with diplomatic letters and telegrams, notes taken in private meetings, and even notes from phone conversations. These documents are then published in a series of bound volumes titled *Foreign Relations of the United States* or "FRUS." All of the diplomats' communications included in this chapter's "Source" section were taken from volume 16 of the 1955–1957 set of FRUS documents, and each tells where the original document can be found. Volume 16 is subtitled "Suez Canal Crisis, July 26–December 31, 1956," and it is 1,344 pages long, which gives you some idea of the number of documents included in each FRUS volume for every topic and time period.

You will be reading just a small selection of diplomatic communications, which will introduce you to the ways in which government officials express their positions to each other. A historian working on any aspect of the Suez crisis would read through all 1,344 pages, watching for patterns, relationships, and points of view that may have previously gone unanalyzed. It is by taking the time to listen to what all the documents have to say, by not picking through the documents for confirmation of preconceived arguments, that historians arrive at new insights and improve upon existing narratives.

Historians studying the Suez crisis would bring considerable background to their examination of FRUS, volume 16, but each document would raise new questions to ponder. No single document answers all of a historian's questions, but each can alert a historian to watch for potential patterns or trends. Consider the possibility that a historian was researching the Suez crisis as a chapter on the U.S.-Soviet relationship in the 1950s, a relationship often described as a diplomatic chess game in which both players used guile and bluster to check their opponent. Below you will find a memorandum of a conversation between Secretary of State John Foster Dulles and Soviet Foreign Minister Dmitri Shepilov that took place four weeks after Nasser nationalized the Suez Canal. While reading this document, a historian would be noting both familiar and curious features of this chess match between experienced diplomats of similar rank representing nations that have been locked in a cold war for more than ten years.

AUGUST 20, 1956, 12:15 P.M. AT THE U.S. EMBASSY, LONDON

We don't know who specifically took notes	From Department of State, Conference Files; Lot 62 D 181, CF 746. Secret. Prepared by the U.S. Delegation.

From Department of State, Conference Files; Lot 62 D 181, CF 746. Secret. Prepared by the U.S. Delegation.

We don't know who specifically took notes

This conversation occurred at an international conference on the Suez crisis, at which the U.S. proposed creation of an international board for managing the Suez Canal

Mr. Shepilov expressed his appreciation for Mr. Dulles' kindness in sending him a preliminary draft of his proposed resolution. . . . The Secretary said he hoped that this draft would obtain Soviet agreement. Mr. Shepilov replied no, he could not say that. The Secretary said speaking seriously he did not think the differences should be too great. Mr. Shepilov replied that unfortunately the differences were serious. . . . After their conversation on Saturday he had thought it might be possible to find an acceptable compromise and that instead of the more rigid and one-sided formula of international operation with Egyptian participation, there might be substituted the formula of Egyptian operation with foreign participation. . . . The Secretary said that . . . many private people throughout the world would be affected in their

Familiar diplomatic civilities

Dulles was known for being suspicious of the Soviets. Did he really not think their differences in this case would be too great? Or was he trying to avoid a cold war confrontation?

Asserting capitalist operating principles to underscore differences with the communists?

Positions the Soviet Union as the champions of Egyptian sovereignty

willingness to invest money [in] an operation which gave the Egyptian Government control in perpetuity over the Canal. . . . Mr. Shepilov said [they should] avoid any appearance of inequality or laying down in advance, as did this draft, a formula which envisaged international control in the form of a concession, which could only be regarded as inimical to Egyptian sovereignty. The Secretary pointed out that the U.S. had a number of arrangements with other countries . . . but did not feel that reflected on our sovereignty or dignity. Mr. Shepilov said it was impossible to reflect on U.S. dignity since it was a great power. Egypt on the other hand had only recently thrown off colonial rule.

Did Dulles really not see any power difference between the U.S. and Egypt?

Mixing diplomatic flattery with sharp advice

Advantages and Disadvantages of Working with Diplomatic Communications

This memorandum of an off-the-record conversation has the great advantage of showing historians how two very powerful diplomats from opposing nations interacted with each other, at least when their staff members were in the room. We can detect here the "performance" of honest exchange, a sort of stylized candor that befits two seasoned chess players who want to stay in the game without giving it away. Access to such direct communications allows us to compare the style of exchange between opponents with that used by U.S. officials in communication with one another, or by U.S. officials in communication with their ostensible allies. FRUS records allow us to trace not only the different countries' diplomatic positions but also the varying tones of voice they used to express those positions.

The disadvantage of such documents is that they can make us feel as if we were in the room and can mask the fact that someone took these notes and chose how to phrase what each man said. In this case, we don't know who wrote the document but we do know that person worked for Secretary Dulles and may have had his or her own career motives or political reasons for preserving certain aspects of the conversation and deleting others. A disadvantage with all FRUS documents is that they provide only the records created by or received by the United States. A historian seeking a complete picture of the Suez crisis would want to examine documents from the former Soviet Union (which are available now to a degree they were not during the cold war), as well as documents from the British, French, Egyptians, and Israelis. This can pose daunting language problems and explains why diplomatic histories are often limited to discussions of just one or two nations or are written as a collaboration between historians who know different languages.

Even if a historian designed a study that focused solely on the U.S. experience in the Suez crisis, reliance on volume 16 would not guarantee complete access to all relevant documents for two reasons: government logistics and government secrecy. Logistically, the Office of the Historian in the U.S. State Department, which is charged with compiling and publishing FRUS, cannot always locate every document relevant to a diplomatic incident. Moreover, publication of FRUS volumes is often delayed. The research and recovery task has grown enormously since it first began in 1861. So while FRUS policy is to publish a volume on a particular event or era within thirty years, the public historians who work at the State Department cannot always meet that target. Volume 16 on the 1956 Suez crisis, for example, was not published until 1990.

Beyond the logistical problems, the public historians who create each FRUS volume often come into conflict with government officials from the State Department or the CIA who wish to conceal information about diplomatic relations. The preface to every FRUS volume includes a statement of guidelines first adopted in 1925:

> The editing of the record is guided by the principles of historical objectivity. There may be no alteration of the text, no deletions without indicating the place in the text where the deletion is made, and no omission of facts which were of major importance in reaching a decision. Nothing may be omitted for the purpose of concealing or glossing over what might be regarded by some as a defect of policy.

These guidelines were not backed up with the power of congressional legislation until 1991. There had been a firestorm of controversy in 1990 when a diplomatic historian on the FRUS Advisory Committee publicly resigned to protest CIA suppression of documents on U.S. involvement in a 1953 Iranian coup. In the wake of that censorship scandal, Congress passed a law requiring that FRUS be a "thorough, accurate, and reliable record."

It is the job of historians—and citizens—to make sure the government obeys the law in these matters. The passage of the Freedom of Information Act (FOIA) in 1966 helps that effort by ensuring the rights of citizens to petition the government to release information on the citizen's timetable, not the government's. Historians can, for example, petition for release of diplomatic communications before they are published in FRUS. But, first, their request has to be processed along with requests from thousands of other citizens and researchers. And, second, the documents they seek must be "declassified." As you will see in the following examples of diplomatic communications, the State Department can classify a document as "top secret," "secret," or "confidential." The government labels a document "top secret" if it expects that unauthorized disclosure of the information in that document would cause "exceptionally grave damage" to national security. A document is deemed "secret" if its unauthorized disclosure could be expected to cause "serious damage" to national security, while a "confidential" document's disclosure would cause only "damage." Documents are automatically declassified after twenty-five years, which is one reason FRUS volumes are not expected to be published in less than thirty years. As you read through this selection of diplomatic communications from the 1956 Suez crisis, imagine trying to write a history of the event in 1968 when some of these documents were still classified "top secret" or "secret," and even the Freedom of Information Act could not force the government to declassify the documents you needed for your research.

Working with the Source

You can use the documents included here to perform three kinds of analysis. First, you can use them to investigate the claim that the U.S. position in the Suez crisis was shaped more by cold war politics than concern for the national sovereignty of Egypt. You can use them as well to find out whether FRUS documents, which were created by or received by U.S. officials, can shed light on other nations' bargaining positions. And finally, you can use them to consider the problem of reliability: Do you find communications between U.S. diplomats more trustworthy than communications between U.S. diplomats and representatives of other countries? Do you find direct texts of messages more reliable than a third party's report on what was said? What cues do you use to judge a document's reliability?

The twelve sources in the following section are arranged chronologically from the start to the end of the Suez crisis. The table on page 211 groups the documents according to whether they are "internal," between officials of the U.S. government, or "external," between U.S. officials and representatives of either Britain, France, or the Soviet Union. As you read through them, use this table for recording evidence on all three issues: the U.S. position, other nations' positions, and your sense of the document's reliability.

	Evidence of U.S. Focus on Cold War	Evidence of Other Nations' Positions	Evidence of the Document's Reliability
Internal Documents			
1. Eisenhower and Dulles			
3. Byroade to State Department			
5. Dillon to State Department			
9. Dulles to Eisenhower			
11. Eisenhower to Hazlett			
External Documents			
2. Eisenhower to Eden			
4. Eisenhower to Eden			
6. Eden to Eisenhower			
7. Eisenhower to Eden			
8. Dulles, Lloyd, and Pineau			
10. Eisenhower to Eden and Mollet			
12. Eisenhower to Bulganin			

The Source: Conversation Memoranda, Messages, Letters, and Telegrams from the Suez Crisis, July 30, 1956–November 11, 1956

---

1   *Memorandum of a Telephone Conversation between President Dwight D. Eisenhower and Secretary of State John Foster Dulles,* **Washington, D.C., July 30, 1956, 11:44 A.M.**

Within hours of Nasser's nationalization announcement, representatives of the U.S., British, and French governments began conferring in London. In the phone conversation reported below, Dulles told the President that their two closest allies were "taking a stronger line" than the United States on the Suez situation. In response, the president reaffirmed what he called "our stand."

We should not be indifferent to the rights of people who are invested in this. Egypt should operate the Canal efficiently and carry out its promise to those affected—show we are not indifferent but are not going to war over it. Say we are moderate but firm but not going to be hysterical and rush into it.

The Sec. said the British and French want to use force not really because of the Canal situation primarily but because they feel this act should be knocked down or have grave repercussions in North Africa and the British position in other countries. The Sec. said if we called a special session of Congress [to authorize use of force] with nothing to go on except what we have now it would be picked up as an effort to back French colonialism in North Africa, etc. and the Democrats would make a political issue of it and it would be a mess. The Pres. said . . . we have to find a way of using the Canal and efficiently. . . . insist on proper operation of the Canal and we must get a broader base for operating in the future—now we are in the position of just protecting someone's private property.

Source: Eisenhower Library, Dulles Papers, White House telephone conversation. Transcribed by Phyllis Bernau, Special Assistant to Secretary of State Dulles.

2   *Letter from President Dwight D. Eisenhower to British Prime Minister Anthony Eden,* July 31, 1956

Dear Anthony:

From the moment Nasser announced nationalization of the Suez Canal Company, my thoughts have been constantly with you. . . . Until this morning, I was happy to feel that we were approaching decisions as to applicable procedures somewhat along parallel lines. . . . But early this morning I received the messages . . . of your decision to employ force without delay or attempting any intermediate and less drastic steps. . . . I cannot over-emphasize the strength of my conviction that some [intermediate] method must be attempted before action such as you contemplate should be undertaken. If unfortunately the situation can finally be resolved only by drastic means, there should be no grounds for belief anywhere that corrective measures were undertaken merely to protect national or individual investors, or the legal rights of a sovereign nation were ruthlessly flouted. . . . initial military successes might be easy, but the eventual price might become far too heavy. Should these means fail, and I think it is erroneous to assume in advance that they needs must fail, then world opinion would understand . . . that we simply could not accept a situation that would in the long run prove disastrous to the prosperity and living standards of every nation whose economy depends directly or indirectly on East-West shipping.

As ever,

D.E.

Source: Eisenhower Library, Whitman File, International File. Top Secret. The text bears the typewritten notion: "1 copy only retained. This."

3   *Telegram from the U.S. Ambassador to Egypt, Henry Byroade, to U.S. State Department,* August 4, 1956, 4 A.M.

Because they did not have sufficient military equipment or personnel stationed in the Mediterranean to take immediate action against Egypt, Britain and France agreed to participate in a "Suez Conference" in London in mid-August. Twenty-two of the forty-five nations using the Suez Canal were invited to the conference. Most of those invited were Western European, but an invitation was extended to President Nasser as well. It was

Source: Department of State Central Files, 974.7301/8–456. Secret.

Ambassador Byroade's job to represent the United States in Egypt and to maintain communication with Nasser.

Am aware that Department would wish me to take no initiative with Nasser at present time in absence of instructions. . . . However Nasser asked me to come see him even August 3 and there seemed no alternative but to comply. Nasser was relaxed and friendly. As a sidelight on the nature of this man he had spent the day in Alexandria with his children on the beach. . . . He made the following points:

1. He could not accept international control [of the Suez Canal]. This would mean that by formal agreement he was accepting not merely return of the form of colonialism exemplified by a "French company" but a permanent subordination to "nearly everybody." Everything he stood for and for which he had pledged himself to the people of Egypt was against this.

2. He did not see how he could accept participation in the proposed conference. He had been placed in the position of attending under threat of invasion. . . . and he could not help wondering whether British were not deliberately making it impossible for him to be represented. . . . Egypt would stand alone or perhaps with only Russia. . . . great propaganda against Egypt would be made if this turned out to be the case.

4. He was still groping as to what to do but felt his best recourse was to go to the United Nations without delay. In the U.N., Egypt would not be "so alone" as regards friends and choice of participating nations. . . .

5. He was ready to sign new international agreement "with anyone" guaranteeing freedom of passage and uninterrupted use of Suez Canal facilities. . . .

He stated that if case was taken to the UN, he felt that Egypt should take the position that all waterways of international importance should be discussed. He could then take the position he would accept any form of international control that was accepted by others. He mentioned most of the principal canal arteries in world including Panama Canal. I told him I thought he was treading on dangerous ground indeed.

4 *Letter from President Dwight D. Eisenhower to British Prime Minister Anthony Eden,* September 2, 1956

The Suez Conference was held in London between August 16 and August 23, 1956, without Egypt in attendance. While the conference was underway, Nasser announced that, since nationalization, 766 ships had safely navigated the canal, proving that Egypt was capable of peaceful and efficient operation of the waterway. Still, eighteen of the twenty-two nations at the conference voted for creation of an international board for operating, maintaining, and developing the Suez Canal. As the annotated example on pages 207–8 indicates, the Soviet Union did not approve of the plan for international control of the canal. The U.S. government devoted the month following the London conference to persuading Nasser to accept international control of the Suez and to persuading their ally Britain to refrain from taking preemptive military action.

Dear Anthony:

Now that the London Conference is over, our efforts must be concentrated on the successful outcome of the conversations with Nasser. . . . of course there should be no thought of military action before the influences of the UN are fully explored. . . . I regard it as indispensable that if we are to proceed solidly together to the solution of this problem, public opinion in our several countries must be overwhelmingly in its support. I must tell you frankly that American public opinion flatly rejects the thought of using force, particularly when it does not seem that every possible peaceful means of protecting our vital interests has been exhausted. . . . We have two problems, the first of which is the assurance of a permanent and efficient operation of the Suez Canal with justice to all concerned. The second is to see that Nasser shall not grow as a menace to the peace and vital interests of the West. In my view, these two problems need not and possibly cannot be solved simultaneously and by the same methods. . . . The first is the most important for the moment and must be solved in such a way as not to make the second more difficult. Above all, there must be no grounds for our several peoples to believe that anyone is using the Canal difficulty as an excuse to proceed forcibly against Nasser.

With warm regard,
As ever,

D.E.

Source: Eisenhower Library, Whitman File, International File. Top Secret.

Telegram from the U.S. Ambassador to France, Douglas Dillon, to U.S. State Department, September 3, 1956, 2 P.M.

Dillon reported here on his conversation with two top officials from the French Foreign Ministry. Neither he nor anyone in the U.S. or British government knew that two days earlier the French had enlisted the Israelis in a joint plan to attack Egypt.

Concerning the basic issue, Joxe and Daridan reaffirmed (1) French wish to facilitate and in no way jeopardize the work of the committee of five [which was negotiating with Nasser about international control]; (2) French desire to avoid military action; (3) French determination that Nasser shall accept international administration of canal and shall not even appear to emerge triumphant from the present crisis.

Source: Department of State, Central Files, 974.7301/9-356. Top Secret; Priority.

Message from British Prime Minister Anthony Eden to President Dwight D. Eisenhower, September 6, 1956

Dear Friend:

Thank you for your message [of September 2] and for writing thus frankly. There is no doubt as to where we are agreed. . . . namely that we should do everything we can to get a peaceful settlement. . . . [Our] divergence springs from a difference in our assessment of Nasser's plans and intentions. May I set out our view of the position. In the 1930's Hitler established his position by a series of carefully planned movements. These began with the occupation of the Rhineland and were followed by successive acts of aggression. . . . His actions were tolerated and excused by the majority of the population of Western Europe. It was argued either that Hitler had committed no act of aggression against anyone or that it was impossible to prove that he had any ulterior designs. . . . I think the dangers [now] are clear. If Nasser says [to the other Arab nations], "I have nationalised the Suez Canal. I have successfully defied eighteen powerful nations . . . I have expropriated all Western property. Trust me and withhold oil from Western Europe. Within six months or a year the continent of Europe will be on its knees before you." Will the Arabs not be prepared to follow his lead?

Source: Eisenhower Library, Whitman File, International File. Secret.

You may feel that even if we are right it would be better to wait until Nasser has unmistakably unveiled his intentions. But this is the argument that prevailed in 1936. . . . if our assessment is correct and if the only alternative is to allow Nasser's plans quietly to develop until this country and all Western Europe are held to ransom by Egypt acting at Russia's behest it seems to us that our duty is plain. We have many times led Europe in the fight for freedom. It would be an ignoble end to our long history if we tamely accepted to perish by degrees.

With kindest regards,
Yours ever,

ANTHONY

7 *Message from President Dwight D. Eisenhower to British Prime Minister Anthony Eden,* September 8, 1956

Dear Anthony . . .
You are making of Nasser a much more important figure than he is. . . . I shall try to give you a somewhat different appraisal of the situation. . . . we can expect the Arabs to rally firmly to Nasser's support in either of two eventualities.

The first of these is that there should be a resort to force without thoroughly exploring and exhausting every possible peaceful means of settling the issue, regardless of the time consumed, and when there is no evidence before the world that Nasser intends to do more than to nationalize the Canal Company . . . The second would be . . . a capitulation to Nasser and complete acceptance of his rule of the Canal traffic. . . . the result that you and I both want can best be assured by slower and less dramatic processes than military force. There are many areas of endeavor which are not yet fully explored because exploration takes time. . . . a semi-permanent organization of user governments . . . which would give the users the rights which we want. . . . economic pressures which, if continued, will cause distress in Egypt. . . . Arab rivalries to be exploited and which can be exploited if we do not make Nasser an Arab hero. . . . alternatives to the present dependence upon the Canal and pipelines. . . .

Nasser thrives on drama. If we let some of the drama go out of the situation and concentrate upon the task of deflating him through slower but surer processes, I believe the desired results can more probably be obtained. . . .

With warmest regard,
As ever your friend,

D.D.E.

Source: Eisenhower Library, Dulles Papers, Misc. Papers—U.K. Suez Crisis. Secret.

Memorandum of a Conversation between U.S. Secretary of State John Foster Dulles, Foreign Minister of Britain Selwyn Lloyd, and Foreign Minister of France Christian Pineau, Secretary Dulles's Hotel Room, New York City, October 5, 1956, 10:15 A.M.

Britain and France asked the United Nations Security Council to take up the Suez Canal question in early October, over two months after Nasser nationalized the canal. By then, the gap between the United States and its allies, France and Britain, was glaringly evident.

Dulles: I thought it was a good idea to have an intimate meeting to discuss questions of substance. . . . We feel somewhat out of touch with your thinking. . . . as to your real purpose [in turning to the U.N.] Was it to be an attempt to find a peaceful settlement? Or was it to be an attempt to get the U.N. behind you to clear the way for greater freedom of action and stronger measures? . . . Now, there must be real understanding as to what is planned. None of us can take for granted that the other will go along blindly. The issues are too momentous for that.

It is the military estimate of President Eisenhower, who assuredly is well qualified to have an opinion, that military measures would start a war which would be extremely difficult to bring to an end and that before it was ended the sympathies of all the Middle East, Asia and African peoples would be irrevocably lost to the West—and lost to such an extent as to pose a very grave problem for the next generation. . . . Elections in this country are not a factor. . . . There are indeed some who think the re-election of President Eisenhower would be assured if there was a war. . . . You can be assured our policies are not swayed by political considerations.

Lloyd: We don't think the United States realizes the importance that France and the UK attach to the Suez. It is not merely the Canal, but all of the Middle East, Algeria, Morocco, and Tunisia. . . . We are risking all of our influence in that part of the world. We are willing to do all in our power not to use force, but Nasser surely will go farther and farther. . . . Russia is back of him. The chief of all navigation in the Canal Zone now is a Russian. We risk Russian domination of the whole area. The temporizing tactics of the U.S. alarm us. We will play the game in the Security Council but we will not get bogged down in procedure . . . let us try to negotiate on the basis of the 18-power policies [developed at the London Conference in August], and, if not, then give us our liberty of action. . . . But we cannot get drawn into a long-term negotiation. I

Source: Department of State, Central Files, 974.7301/10-556. Top Secret; Eyes Only. Drafted by U.S. Representative to the United Nations, Henry Cabot Lodge.

think that after the general exposition is finished there should be a private meeting, beginning Tuesday, then we could adjourn for two or three days, resume Friday, and if anything can come out of negotiation that should be enough time.

Dulles: If you have ever argued in an Egyptian bazaar in Cairo you will know that they don't work that fast.

9 Message from Secretary of State John Foster Dulles to President Dwight D. Eisenhower, New York City, October 5, 1956

Dulles reported on the events that occurred on the first day of the United Nations Security Council meeting to discuss the Suez Canal question.

[Before the meeting, Soviet Foreign Minister] Shepilov came to see me. He talked pleasantly about [the Soviets'] desire to seek a settlement. I reminded him that when he had talked the same way in London, Soviet propaganda was doing its best to sabotage our effort by violent anti-Western propaganda. I said that while the United States was using its full influence to moderate the British and the French, the Soviet Union was merely trying to egg on the Egyptians to greater excesses. I said the measure of our respective efforts was to be found in the fact that I was today the most unpopular man in France and Britain and he was the most popular man in Egypt. Shepilov was obviously disconcerted but reaffirmed his real desire this time to try to accomplish a settlement. He talked about a negotiating group. . . . indicated that [the Soviets] might go along with my procedure.

After [the Security Council] meeting, Fawzi, the Egyptian Foreign Minister, came to see me. He indicated a desire for settlement and emphasized particularly the importance of getting more money to develop the Canal and suggested this might be the cover for some form of foreign participation in the Canal operations. . . . He also indicated that they would like to negotiate directly with us. . . . Phleger [legal advisor to the State Department] is planning to meet with the Egyptian lawyer tomorrow.

Faithfully yours,

FOSTER

Source: Department of State, Central Files, 974.7301/10-656. Top Secret.

Message from President Dwight D. Eisenhower to British Prime Minister Anthony Eden and French Prime Minister Guy Mollet, October 30, 1956

By the middle of October, the meetings at the United Nations had produced progress toward an agreement in which Egypt and the Suez Canal users would cooperate in operating the canal, free transit would be guaranteed to all (though Israel was not confident of its inclusion in this guarantee), and Egypt's sovereignty would be respected. But on October 22, the British were secretly briefed on the French-Israeli plan to attack Egypt. Ironically, the scheme rested on the Tripartite Declaration, issued in 1950, which stipulated that if any Arab nation were attacked, the United States, Britain, and France were pledged to intervene. Once Israel attacked Egypt, therefore, Britain and France could claim the right to step in to the region with their forces.

On the night of October 29, Israeli paratroopers staged a surprise attack on Egyptian troops stationed in the Sinai desert, east of the Suez Canal. The next morning, the United States and the Soviet Union submitted separate resolutions to the U.N. Security Council calling for Israel to withdraw. Britain and France vetoed those resolutions. U.S. communication with these allies was now so broken that the president of the United States was dependent on press reports to learn of Britain's and France's actions.

Dear Mr. Prime Minister:

I have just learned through the press of the 12-hour ultimatum which you and the French (UK) Government have delivered to the Government of Egypt requiring, under threat of forceful intervention, the temporary occupation by Anglo-French forces of key positions at Port Said, Ismailla and Suez in the Suez Canal Zone. I feel[1] I must urgently express to you my deep concern at the prospect of this drastic action. . . . It is my sincere belief that peaceful processes can and should prevail to secure a solution which will restore the armistice condition as between Israel and Egypt and also justly settle the controversy with Egypt about the Suez Canal.

Sincerely,

Dwight D. Eisenhower

---

[1] In a lengthy endnote in FRUS, the editors explain that drafts of this message indicate the president first wrote "It is my urgent plea that you should not take this drastic action," but following a phone conversation with Secretary of State Dulles, the wording became "I feel I must urge upon you what seems to me the greatest unwisdom in taking this drastic action." The FRUS editors could not determine who made the final change to the sentence.

Source: Eisenhower Library, Dulles Papers, Misc. Papers—U.K. (Suez Crisis). A note on the source indicates that at 3:30 P.M., "Identical messages delivered by phone to Paris and London Embassies for Immediate telephonic delivery to Eden and Mollet."

11 *Letter from President Dwight D. Eisenhower to Swede Hazlett, Retired Naval Officer and Ike's Boyhood Friend,* November 2, 1956

On November 5, British and French planes began to bomb Egyptian airfields near the canal and their ships proceeded through the Mediterranean toward the Suez Canal zone. In an effort to thwart the invaders' stated goal of keeping the Suez Canal open, Nasser blocked the canal by sinking fifty international commercial vessels that were at the time traveling through the canal.

The Mid East thing is a terrible mess. . . . It does not seem to me that there is present in the case anything that justifies the action that Britain, France and Israel apparently concerted among themselves and have initiated. The 1888 Treaty[1] says nothing at all as to how the Canal is to be operated . . . I think, therefore, that no one could question the legal right of Egypt to nationalize the Canal Company. And what really became the apparent or legal bone of contention was "Shall the world's users of the Canal, which is guaranteed as an international waterway in perpetuity, be privileged to use the Canal only on the sufferance of a single nation?" Even this, in my opinion, is not the real heart of the matter. The real point is that Britain, France and Israel have come to believe—probably correctly—that Nasser was their worst enemy in the Mid East and that until he is removed or deflated, they would have no peace. I do not quarrel with the idea that there is justification for such fears, but I have insisted long and earnestly that you cannot resort to force in international relationships because of your fear of what might happen in the future. . . .

Give my love to Ibby and the family.
As ever, . . .

---

[1] The "1888 treaty" refers to the Constantinople Convention in which Great Britain, France, Russia, Germany, Austria-Hungary, Spain, the Netherlands, Italy, and Turkey pledged themselves to the "free navigation" of the Suez Canal "without distinction of flag."

Source: Eisenhower Library, Whitman File, Eisenhower Diaries. Personal.

12 *Message from President Dwight D. Eisenhower to Soviet Premier Nikolai Bulganin,* November 11, 1956

> The British and French launched their land invasion of Egypt at Port Said on November 5, 1956. The United Nations instantly condemned the invasion as aggression and the Soviet Union — welcoming an international diversion from its invasion of Hungary on November 4 — threatened to get involved militarily. Meanwhile, the United States quietly withdrew financial support from the troubled British economy and the value of the British pound plunged overnight. Over thirty thousand Londoners demonstrated in protest of the invasion, and a majority of the British public began to call for Prime Minister Anthony Eden's resignation. The French and Israelis remained steadfast, but Eden quickly agreed to a ceasefire. France and Israel were forced to withdraw, and a European invasion that had been planned for three months collapsed within eighteen hours. President Eisenhower had waited throughout the invasion before replying to a message from his Soviet counterpart, Premier Bulganin.

I refer to your message to me of November 5. The fighting in the Near East has now been brought to an end through the efforts of the United Nations, the body properly responsible for accomplishing this. It is essential that peace be totally restored to the area and that no action be taken which would in any way exacerbate the situation there.

With respect to your suggestion that the United States join with the Soviet Union in a bipartite employment of their military forces to stop the fighting in Egypt, it is our view that neither Soviet nor any other military forces should now enter the Middle East area except under United Nations mandate. . . . The introduction of new forces under these circumstances would violate the United Nations Charter, and it would be the duty of all United Nations members, including the United States, to oppose any such effort.

It is difficult to reconcile your expressed concern for the principles of morality and the objectives of the United Nations with the action taken by Soviet military units against the people of Hungary. Your letter to me of November 7 concerning this tragic situation was deeply disappointing. Were the Soviet Government now able to comply with the Resolutions of the U.N. on the subject of Hungary, it would be a great and notable contribution to the cause of peace.

DWIGHT D. EISENHOWER

Source: Department of State, Central Files, 674.84A/11-1156. Secret. Transmitted to Moscow in Priority telegram . . . with the instruction: "Please deliver soonest following message from President to Marshal Bulganin. Confirm date and time delivery."

Analyzing the Source

REFLECTING ON THE SOURCE

1. Drawing on the FRUS communications you read, how would you summarize the key differences between the U.S. position, the British position, and the Egyptian position during the Suez crisis?

2. If you could gain access to other nations' internal communications for only one week of the Suez crisis, which nations' records would you want to see and which week's communications would you ask to examine? Why those nations and that particular week?

3. In reading through the selection of diplomatic communications in the previous section, what cues did you find yourself using to determine your level of trust in the reliability of a document?

MAKING CONNECTIONS

4. President George W. Bush announced his Bush Doctrine of "preemptive war" in the months prior to the invasion of Iraq in March 2003. Compare President Bush's stance on preemptive war to President Eisenhower's. Compare, too, the U.S., British, and French positions on preemptive war in 1956 with their positions in the Iraq war of 2003.

5. The Internet has made possible electronic distribution of government documents such as FRUS. Some in Congress have proposed that the government cease all printing of bound volumes of such documents for distribution to libraries around the United States and rely entirely on the Web. In a debate on such a proposal, what arguments would you put forth to support reliance on the Web? What arguments would you make for continuing printing and distribution of hard copies of government documents?

Beyond the Source

The cold war ended with the dissolution of the Soviet Union in late 1991. Our twenty-first century focus on Islamic fundamentalism, Mideast terrorism, the Israeli-Palestinian conflict, Afghanistan, Iraq, and Iran makes the cold war seem long ago and far away. But today's international disputes are rooted in Mideast contests between the United States and the Soviet Union, and the Suez crisis was the key event that positioned these two opponents to play their high-stakes chess game on Mideast soil.

As a result of their failed invasion of Egypt, Britain and France lost their century-long positions of leadership in the Mideast; the governments from both countries fell as a result of the Suez defeat, Britain suffered serious economic reversals, and the Algerian campaign to win independence from France ultimately succeeded in 1962. Meanwhile, Nasser became a great Arab hero for standing up against an imperialistic European invasion. Until his death from a heart attack in 1970, Nasser was such a compelling representative of Arab nationalism that even Egyptian critics of his socialism did not speak out. In the aftermath of the Suez crisis, the Soviet Union basked in the glow of Nasser's popularity by providing Egypt with $2 billion in arms and full financing of the Aswan Dam, which became a Soviet-sponsored showpiece in the Mideast.

There was a brief moment following the Suez crisis when the United States enjoyed a new level of trust in the Mideast. Nations struggling to achieve autonomy in a polarized, cold war world saw President Eisenhower's firm stand against the invasion as evidence that the United States respected national sovereignty and was willing to risk cold war alliances for that principle. Just two months after the crisis was resolved, however, in January 1957, Ike altered this perception of the United States as a neutral force for freedom in the Mideast when he announced his "Eisenhower Doctrine." Like the Truman Doctrine enunciated by his predecessor a decade earlier, Eisenhower's doctrine established that anticommunism was the guiding principle around which all U.S. foreign policy pivoted. In his speech setting forth the Eisenhower Doctrine, the president said relatively little about Arab nationalism, Arab control of its oil resources, or the need to settle the Israeli-Arab dispute over borders and Palestinian refugees. Ike's focus was on the threat of "International Communism" in the region, and the Democratic Congress supported that focus by granting military and economic aid for any Mideast nation that opposed the Soviet Union and aided Western interests in the region, including oil interests.

The United States became the major Western power in the Mideast because of its stance in the Suez crisis, but that stance was unusual for the United States in the decades following World War II. Typically, the United States sided with its European allies and opposed Arab leaders who sought too much independence from cold war alignments. Recall, for example, the scandal that broke in 1991 when a FRUS advisor revealed that the CIA was trying to suppress documents about U.S. involvement in an Iranian coup. That coup occurred in 1953, three years before the Suez crisis, because Britain and the United States wanted to replace an independent Iranian premier (who nationalized British-held oil fields) with the anti-Soviet, pro-Western Shah. The United States was repaid for that coup in 1979 when an Islamic revolution against the repressive shah took fifty-four American hostages and held them for 444 days. In the face of Iran's nationalist hatred of America, the U.S. government sought a new ally in the region and found one in Iraq's Saddam Hussein, who received massive economic and military aid in the 1980s in return for his support of Western cold war and oil interests and his opposition to Iran. In this case, as in so many others in the Mideast, cold war alliances shaped initial policies and continued to dictate alignments even as the cold war itself was waning.

Many today argue that the Soviet Union was fatally weakened by its ten-year military occupation of Afghanistan. The United States ensured that this would be a costly venture for the Soviets by supplying arms to local Islamic insurgents who later took power as the Taliban and who were brutally oppressive rulers of Afghanistan. In hindsight, especially since the September 11, 2001, terrorist attacks in the United States, some have challenged the wisdom of a cold war policy that brought the Taliban to power. But when President Jimmy Carter's national security advisor, Zbigniew Brzezinski, was questioned on the subject in a 1998 interview, he replied, "What is most important to the history of the world? The Taliban or the collapse of the Soviet empire? Some stirred-up Moslems or the liberation of Central Europe and the end of the Cold War?"[1]

For many who lived through the cold war, nothing seemed more important than the defeat of the Soviet Union. President Eisenhower's conduct during the Suez crisis showed his capacity to exercise restraint in achieving that goal, but restraint was not always the U.S. policy in the cold war Mideast. As the United States struggles in the twenty-first century to build trust and peace with the people of that region, students of history will be reminded that one generation's focus on a single international contest can spawn an array of conflicts for the next generation.

Finding and Supplementing the Source

Foreign Relations of the United States (FRUS), like other official government documents, can be found in bound volumes in any one of the 1,300 U.S. libraries designated as "federal depository" libraries. These are libraries that automatically receive the federal documents printed and published by the U.S. Government Printing Office. If you want to find the federal depository library nearest you, consult "GPO Access" at **access.gpo.gov**. If you want to find out if there is a FRUS volume for a time period and issue you are researching, you can go to the State Department's Web site for a complete listing of all FRUS volumes: **state.gov/r/pa/ho/frus/c4035.htm**. This same site lists all FRUS volumes available online.

In the vast literature on the Suez crisis, two lively and accessible books are *Warriors at Suez* by the journalist Donald Neff (New York: Simon and Schuster, 1981) and *No End of a Lesson: The Story of Suez* by Anthony Nutting (London: Constable & Company Ltd., 1967); Nutting resigned his post as British minister of state for foreign affairs during the crisis. The crisis is examined from the Egyptian point of view in *Cutting the Lion's Tale: Suez through Egyptian Eyes* by Mohamed H. Heikal (Westminster, Md.: Arbor House Publishing Co., 1987). *One Day in the World's News* by Wilbur Schramm (Stanford, Calif.: Stanford University Press, 1959) is a straightforward reproduction in English of fourteen newspapers from around the world for November 2, 1956. It offers the most direct access to a global overview of the Suez and Hungarian crises. *Parting the*

---

[1] Interview with Zbigniew Brzezinski appeared in *Le Nouvel Observateur*, January 15–21, 1998, p. 76. The English version of this French publication did not include this interview. It was translated by William Blum at **members.aol.com/bblum6/brz.htm**.

Desert: The Creation of the Suez Canal (New York: Knopf, 2003) by Zachary Kara-bell is a modern examination of this nineteenth-century engineering feat.

The British government opened its files on the Suez crisis in 1987 and the U.S. State Department published its FRUS volume on the crisis in 1990. Among the newer books that reflect increased access to British and U.S. documents are *Divided We Stand: Britain, the U.S. and the Suez Crisis* (London: Hodder & Stoughton, 1991) by W. Scott Lucas and *Dawn Over Suez: The Rise of American Power in the Middle East, 1953–1957* (Chicago: Ivan R. Dee, 1992) by Steven Z. Freiberger. The release of the FRUS documents coincided with an ongoing re-assessment of Eisenhower's style of leadership as president. Two collections of articles about Eisenhower include studies of his conduct of the Suez crisis: *Re-examining the Eisenhower Presidency*, edited by Shirley Anne Warshaw (Westport, Conn.: Greenwood Press, 1993) and *Reevaluating Eisenhower: American Foreign Policy in the 1950's,* edited by Richard A. Melanson and David Mayers (Urbana: University of Illinois Press, 1987). You can explore the holdings of the Eisenhower Presidential Library at **eisenhower.archives.gov**. The most cursory surf through the Eisenhower site, or any of the presidential library sites, will reveal why Congress funds these repositories of presidential papers and why historians find them so valuable.

The Web is a vital source of information on government documents and government secrecy. You can explore government holdings by visiting the National Archives at **archives.gov**. George Washington University maintains a National Security Archive that collects and publishes declassified documents acquired through the Freedom of Information Act (FOIA), and it provides information on how to use FOIA; see **gwu.edu/~nsarchiv/nsa/foia.html**. The Federation of American Scientists maintains one of the most active and most respected Web sites on government secrecy, where it publishes *Secrecy News* and provides links to other Web sites that expose government secrecy; see **fas.org**.

CHAPTER 11

Speaking of Equality

The Senate Debate on the Civil Rights Act of 1964

Abraham Lincoln emancipated the slaves," declared President John F. Kennedy in 1962, on the hundredth anniversary of the Emancipation Proclamation, "but in this century, our Negro citizens have emancipated themselves." It was this sort of celebratory rhetoric that convinced civil rights activists across America that their dynamic, young, articulate president was on their side and that he supported their grassroots uprising against segregation, discrimination, and racial prejudice. In truth, Kennedy wanted an end to all the street demonstrations, sit-ins, and freedom rides that disrupted the political order of his administration. Shocking photos of Southern sheriffs turning dogs and hoses on peaceful black marchers created the sort of cold war propaganda for the Soviet Union in Africa and Asia that Kennedy sought to avoid. And public demands from leaders like Martin Luther King Jr. that the federal government take strong action on civil rights threatened Kennedy's plan to keep racial politics out of his legislative deal-making with Southern Democrats in Congress.

As much as he wanted to, though, President Kennedy could not control or curtail the civil rights movement. His administration's record between 1961 and 1963 reveals a reluctance to take political risks for the cause of racial justice, but Kennedy's public image as a supporter of civil rights encouraged activists to believe that this was the moment when black history in America could be turned around. It was the people's confidence that they could create change, not Kennedy's initiatives, that ultimately forced the president to catch up with the civil rights movement. On June 11, 1963, two and one-half years after making his inaugural pledge to fight for human rights "at home," Kennedy went on national television to declare that "the time has come for this nation to fulfill its promise" of equal rights for all, and to announce that he was sending a new civil rights bill to Congress. This speech culminated a week in which the U.S. Justice Department deployed the national guard so that two black citizens of Alabama could exercise their right to enroll at the state's public university, and black and white citizens throughout the segregated south staged 160 separate pro–civil rights demonstrations. The civil rights bill that Kennedy submitted to Congress following his televised speech included, along with voting rights and educational access, a highly controversial "public accommodations" provision that outlawed racial discrimination in restaurants, hotels, and theaters.

No black leaders had been involved in drafting this civil rights bill. In segregated America in 1963, there were no black citizens in the U.S. Senate, only four blacks in the House of Representatives, just one African American adviser to the president, and a handful of blacks in the executive branch. The thousands of citizens who lobbied and demonstrated for civil rights in the early 1960s pressed their suit right up against the halls of power, but they did not have a seat in those halls. However encouraging Kennedy's rhetoric about blacks emancipating themselves, the reality of power was different. If the racial system was going to change, if African Americans were going to peacefully gain rights in the United States, then the whites in the U.S. Congress had to vote to make that happen. In the summer of 1963, Kennedy was not optimistic about the votes in Congress and warned a gathering of civil rights leaders at the White House that "we may all go down the drain" with a doomed civil rights bill. A. Philip Randolph, the seventy-four-year-old black leader and veteran lobbyist, told Kennedy, "It's going to be a crusade, then. And I think that nobody can lead that crusade but you, Mr. President."

Three months later, John F. Kennedy was dead, and his assassination meant that Lyndon Baines Johnson, from the thoroughly segregated state of Texas, was now president. Those who feared that Johnson's ascendancy meant the end of the civil rights bill did not consider that before he became Kennedy's vice president, Johnson (popularly known as LBJ) had been the most canny and persuasive Senate majority leader in U.S. history. LBJ had led the Senate in passing the 1957 and 1960 civil rights bills, which created the Civil Rights Commission and the civil rights division of the Department of Justice. Those who doubted LBJ's civil rights credentials were unaware that he had advised President Kennedy to take the high ground by declaring racial justice a moral imperative. He had also advised the Kennedy Democrats to give up negotiating with the Senate's Southern segregationists, who were all Democrats, and instead build alliances with Northern, moderate Republicans who supported civil rights legislation.

As a Southerner, LBJ knew about racism and segregation in a way that Kennedy never could. He also knew from experience, as Kennedy did not, that America's blacks could wait no longer; they were, Johnson told a Kennedy aide, "tired of this patient stuff and tired of this piecemeal stuff"; it was time to "pull out the cannon." Johnson believed that almost any problem could be solved by legislation, and he was typically prepared to use any tool at his disposal to achieve a legislative goal. When Kennedy's assassination thrust Johnson into the presidency, he waited only five days to announce that "no memorial oration or eulogy could more eloquently honor President Kennedy's memory than the earliest possible passage of the Civil Rights bill for which he fought so long." Though Kennedy had actually fought less than six months for the bill, LBJ appealed to Americas' grief for its martyred president in expressing his hope "that the tragedy and torment of these terrible days will bind us together in a new fellowship, making us one people in our hour of sorrow."

When the second session of the Eighty-eighth Congress opened in January 1964, everyone—including the Southern segregationists in the House and Senate—knew that the political ground had shifted irrevocably. Now, polls showed that 62 percent of Americans supported civil rights legislation, the Johnson White House was choreographing what the *Congressional Quarterly* called "some of the most intensive and effective behind-the-scenes lobbying in modern legislative history," dozens of organizations—from the NAACP and the AFL-CIO to the National Council of Churches of Christ and the National Council of Jewish Women—were lobbying for the bill, and both Democrats and Republicans in Congress were stepping over party lines to deliver the legislation. In this new political atmosphere, Southern Democrats lost their traditional control over Northern Democrats. Since the start of the New Deal in 1933, Southern Democrats had supported a strong federal role in programs like Social Security and agricultural subsidies. In exchange, Northerners did not use federal power to challenge the prerogative of Southern states to limit black voting rights and black access to public accommodations. Northern Democrats' obedience to this thirty-year political arrangement ceased in 1963 when the Kennedy and Johnson administrations advocated a new coalition with pro–civil rights, Northern Republicans.

The Kennedy administration, on LBJ's advice, had urged the House of Representatives to take up the civil rights bill before the Senate considered it. The bill had a better chance in the House for two reasons: first, the House Judiciary Committee, which had to approve the bill before the whole House voted on it, was chaired by Emmanuel Celler, a Jewish liberal from New York who supported civil rights. Second, the House had rules limiting the length of debate on any bill to prevent consideration of legislation from dragging on and on. Mindful of these advantages, the bill that the House of Representatives sent to the Senate on February 10, 1964—less than three months after Kennedy's assassination—was actually stronger than the original bill. The tougher bill now included a prohibition against racial discrimination in employment in any workplace with over twenty-five employees. In an attempt to defeat this "nefarious" legislation, Congressman Howard W. Smith, an eighty-year-old segregationist from Virginia, introduced an amendment to include "sex" alongside race, creed, color, and national origin as categories protected against discrimination in employment or public life. Smith thought his colleagues in the House of Representatives would defeat the entire bill rather than give women equal rights, but he misjudged the historical moment. Smith's "sex" amendment was accepted, and the bill became an even more sweeping piece of legislation. With 152 Democrats and 138 Republicans in favor (and 96 Democrats and 34 Republicans against), the civil rights bill was passed by the House of Representatives and sent to the Senate for approval, amendment, or defeat.

The Senate presented a much more difficult situation than the House. There, the Judiciary Committee was chaired by James O. Eastland of Mississippi, whose belief in racial segregation was matched by his talent for killing civil rights bills in committee before they reached a full Senate vote. Moreover, the Senate had no rule limiting debate on a single bill. If a bill reached the full Senate for a vote, a handful of senators could choose to continue debating it as long as they had strength to stand and draw breath. In that situation (known as a "filibuster"), debate continued until the other senators simply gave up and agreed to set aside the vexing bill so they could turn to other Senate business— or until sixty-seven of the Senate's one hundred members voted cloture, which meant debate was terminated and a vote would be taken. Between 1917, when the Senate first allowed for cloture and 1964, there had been only twenty-eight attempts to end a debate and force a vote on a bill; only five of those attempts had succeeded. Since 1937, Southern senators had defeated all eleven attempts to end their filibusters of civil rights bills, which meant those eleven bills had died without ever coming to a vote.

In 1964, pro–civil rights senators, under President Johnson's leadership, dodged segregationist obstructions by using an obscure Senate rule to bypass Eastland's Judiciary Committee and move the civil rights bill directly to the floor of the Senate. There, Democrats and Republicans worked as a team to keep the bill alive and craft compromise language. To strengthen their hand, President Johnson announced that he was not afraid of a filibuster. "I don't care how long it takes," he declared. "I don't care if the Senate doesn't do one other piece of business this year. . . . We are not going to have anything else hit the Senate floor until this bill is passed." The greatest threat of filibuster was always that no other Senate business would be conducted. To that threat the president (and one-time "master" of the Senate) said, in effect, "so what?"

As it turned out, the Eighty-eighth Congress did very little business between March 9 and March 26, when senators debated bypassing the Judiciary Committee, and virtually no other business between March 30 and June 19, when the members of the U.S. Senate held a continual debate about the merits of the civil rights bill, formally known as "H.R." (for "House Resolution") 7152. The high point of that debate came on June 10, when, for the first time in American history, the U.S. Senate was able to muster a two-thirds vote in favor of cloture on a civil rights bill, thereby ending the fifty-seven-day filibuster and forcing a vote. Senators then spent a few days considering various amendments, but the bill the Senate passed by a vote of seventy-three to twenty-seven was so similar to the House bill that it was quickly reapproved by the House and went immediately to the White House for President Johnson's signature on July 2, 1964. Before signing the bill, LBJ announced that the historic denial of "inalienable rights" to American citizens could no longer continue; "the law I sign tonight," he said, "forbids it."

Using Senate Speeches as a Source

The Civil Rights Act of 1964 was an aggressive, explicit, and detailed commitment to federal enforcement of the legal equality of all U.S. citizens. The eleven sections of this twenty-two-page law added up to the most assertive civil rights legislation to win approval in Congress in the twentieth century. If you were to look at just the bill's vote tallies—in the House, 290 for and 130 against; in the Senate, 73 for and 27 against—you might conclude that this powerful law won easy passage in the Congress, but nothing could be farther from the truth. Behind those votes lay a century's worth of civil rights activism in local communities culminating in a historic set of events on the floor of the U.S. Senate in Washington, D.C.

The one hundred white senators who debated H.R. 7152 for fifty-seven days from the end of March, through April and May, and into June of 1964 were engaged in a dramatic, national discussion of the U.S. Constitution and American race relations. On one level, they were debating just how far the federal government could legally go in prohibiting race discrimination; on another level, they were debating whether racial discrimination was morally compatible with democracy. The strategic maneuver by the bill's supporters to bypass the Senate Judiciary Committee meant that there was no testimony about the bill from constitutional lawyers, civil rights activists, African American citizens, or prosegregation citizens; any argument that a senator wanted to make for or against the legislation had to be introduced by that senator himself in the filibuster on the Senate floor.

A filibuster is the legislative equivalent of a military siege: it is physically as well as intellectually taxing. The opponents of H.R. 7152 hoped to wear down the bill's supporters just by keeping the debate going. LBJ had already announced that he did not care if Senate business was stalled by the filibuster, but there was still the exhaustion factor to contend with. Opponents of the bill were organized into three six-member teams; when the six members of one team were on the floor, the other two teams' members were resting. By contrast, the pro–civil rights forces had to have fifty-one senators, a majority, on the floor of the Senate at all times in order to survive a "quorum call." According to the rules of the filibuster game, if the number of senators on the floor falls short of a majority when anyone calls for a quorum, then the filibuster succeeds and the bill dies without coming to a vote. Disciplined cooperation between Republican and Democratic supporters of civil rights maintained a quorum and kept H.R. 7152 alive for twelve weeks while the Senate leadership collected the requisite sixty-seven votes to approve a cloture motion, end the filibuster, and bring the bill to a vote.

The selection of speeches included in "The Source" section of this chapter were delivered on the floor of the Senate either during the filibuster or right before the filibuster, when senators were debating the proposal to bypass the Judiciary Committee. Some selections are taken from speeches that lasted two or three hours; most of the selections focus on the "public accommodations" aspect of H.R. 7152 (often referred to as "Title II"), which prohibited race discrimination in privately owned businesses such as restaurants and hotels.

Advantages and Disadvantages of Working with Senate Speeches

Historians can analyze Senate speeches the way they would analyze any political speech but can also analyze them as unique expressions of Senate procedures. Like all political speeches, Senate speeches are designed to persuade. Rhetoric is the art of verbal persuasion; the goal is always to convince the listener to cast a vote or take an action or write a check on behalf of a particular partisan purpose. The great advantage of all political speeches is that no matter how many lies or distortions are uttered, a speech always reveals what that speaker truly believes to be the most persuasive approach to winning support from a particular audience. In the case of Senate speeches, every senator has two audiences to consider: voters back home and colleagues in the Senate.

Senators design their remarks first to please or persuade their constituents, so historians may use Senate speeches as an indirect guide to the voter attitudes that senators were addressing. A particular advantage to using Senate speeches from the 1964 civil rights debate is that every senator knew his words were being quoted in home state newspapers and could affect his reelection. A speech in this debate, therefore, had to appeal to popular opinion back home and had to be one the senator could defend on the stump. On this bill, no senator could casually trade a vote in exchange for a new bridge or highway; the stakes were too high. Congressional politics-as-usual was momentarily interrupted by the political idealism driving the civil rights movement from the street and onto the Senate floor. In some filibusters in the past, senators had dragged out debate by reading from the newspaper or the phone book, but that did not occur in this instance. Supporters of the bill chose to actively debate the opponents staging the filibuster. So for fifty-seven days all senators spoke directly to the racial and constitutional questions raised by H.R. 7152. The advantageous result is that the speeches in this debate provide historians with an unusually reliable record of the public positions senators were willing to take on these questions in 1964.

At the same time, historians know that senators in a floor debate speak to one another in rather veiled ways. Consider, for example, this excerpt from a speech by Senator Sam Ervin, a prosegregation Democrat from North Carolina who opposed H.R. 7152. Senator Ervin's comments were made on March 18, 1964, during the debate over whether to bypass the Judiciary Committee. At this point, opponents of the bill such as Ervin were trying to convince their colleagues that this bill needed a full committee investigation.

Raises the issue of states' loss of power under this federal legislation

This reference to a jurist from the early twentieth century highlights Ervin's expertise as a constitutional lawyer

This argument was meant to appeal to senators sympathetic to racial justice but worried about overextending federal powers

Predicts that H.R. 7152 would endow agencies of the executive branch with powers that belong to Congress

Refers to the president of the Senate, who is the vice president of the United States; during this debate, however, "Mr. President" refers to the president pro tem of the Senate, the senator presiding "at the time" (pro tempore)

If Congress enacts the bill it will say that a part of the legislative power is to be vested in the Department of Health, Education, and Welfare, that a part of the legislative power is to be vested in the Housing Administration, and that a part of the legislative power is to be vested in the Department of Commerce. . . . Is that what we wish to do with the legislative power of the United States? . . . Suffice it to say, Mr. President, that the bill undertakes to centralize in the Federal Government powers over the lives of the people, which the Constitution vests in the States or reserves to the people themselves. . . . As Chief Justice White declared, in substance, in *McCray v. United States,* 195 U.S. 27, 55, the safety of our institutions depends upon its strict observance by all those who hold offices created by the Constitution. That statement by Chief Justice White is something which Senators should take to heart.

Senator Ervin's focus on the bill's threat to congressional power and its threat to states' powers does not provide historians with dramatic prosegregationist rhetoric. In that sense, a disadvantage of Senate speeches is that they can appear legalistic and indirect. Background research is required to see that Ervin's constitutional emphasis was part of a strategy to shift senators' attention from the issue of race relations and toward the legislative specifics of H.R. 7152. Once that sort of background is established, however, Senate speeches reveal much about the techniques senators use to influence their colleagues into voting their way.

Historians turn to Senate speeches, as they do to all sorts of political speeches, for evidence of what true or false arguments were appealing to particular audiences, and they turn to Senate speeches for signs of that institution's unique operations. No historian, however, could turn to the Senate debate on the civil rights bill of 1964 for evidence of the African American perspective on racism in the United States. It was precisely because of racism that no African Americans sat in the U.S. Senate when the Civil Rights Act was under debate. But the advantage, as well as the disadvantage, of these particular speeches is that they reveal how elite, white men were grappling with the issue of American racism. Since elite, white men were the ones passing the laws in the United States at that time, we can learn much about the political attitudes of the day by listening to the words they chose and the points they emphasized to advance their positions for or against H.R. 7152, the civil rights bill of 1964.

Working with the Source

Ten Senate speeches are excerpted in the following section; most of the excerpts focus on Title II of H.R. 7152, the section prohibiting racial discrimination in public accommodations. Each senator who delivered a speech believed that his argument would win voters' support for his stance on H.R. 7152 and would convince Senate colleagues to either kill the bill or bring it to a vote. Supporters and opponents of the bill knew that fifty-one votes were needed in the Senate to pass H.R. 7152—if the bill came to a vote. But that was a big "if." Could the bill's supporters garner the sixty-seven votes needed to end the filibuster? Would the bill's twenty-seven opponents convince twenty-four colleagues to join with them in killing the bill by simply not showing up for a quorum call? As you read these speeches, keep in mind that opponents of the bill did not need to convince twenty-four colleagues that racial discrimination was a good thing. They just needed to convince twenty-four colleagues that H.R. 7152 was a bad piece of legislation, so it would be best to give up, go home, and let the filibuster succeed. Watch for arguments that appealed to voters' opinions on broad questions of racial equality and civil rights and for arguments that appealed to other senators' constitutional concerns over this particular bill. Use the table on page 235 to record the various positions that each senator took regarding H.R. 7152.

	Position on H.R. 7152	Arguments Regarding Race Discrimination	Arguments Regarding this Particular Bill
1. Senator Mike Mansfield			
2. Senator Richard Russell			
3. Senator John Stennis			
4. Senator Hubert Humphrey			
5. Senator Thomas Kuchel			
6. Senator Sam Ervin			
7. Senator Strom Thurmond			
8. Senator James O. Eastland			
9. Senator Everett Dirksen			
10. Senator Barry Goldwater			

The Source: Speeches from the Senate Debating the Civil Rights Act of 1964

 Majority Leader Mike Mansfield (D-Montana), February 17, 1964

> Senator Mansfield was the elected leader of the Democratic majority in the Senate. It was his job to shepherd the civil rights bill through the Senate to victory. In his opening address to the Senate on H.R. 7152, he named Senator Hubert Humphrey (D-Minnesota) and Senator Thomas Kuchel (R-California) as the senators with "direct responsibility" for handling the bill, and he defended his decision to procedurally bypass Senator Eastland's Judiciary Committee.

The civil rights bill has now arrived from the House. In the near future, the leadership will propose to the Senate that this measure be placed on the calendar, without referral to committee, and that, subsequently, the Senate as a body proceed to its consideration.

The procedures which the leadership will follow are not usual, but neither are they unprecedented. And the reasons for unusual procedures are too well known to require elaboration.

The substance of the bill has been discussed and debated, not for a week or a month, but for years. President Johnson has prescribed for civil rights legislation an urgency second to none. . . . Whatever any Senator may lack in understanding of the substance of the bill will, I am sure, be made up in extensive discussion on the floor of the Senate. . . . This approach is to be preferred in connection with a bill of such wide ramifications, for, in fact, the substance of the civil rights legislation falls with almost equal validity within the purview of several committees. . . .

Mr. President, speaking for myself, let me say at the outset that I should have preferred it had the civil rights issue been resolved before my time as a Senator or had it not come to the floor until afterward. The Senator from Montana has no lust for conflict in connection with this matter. . . . But, Mr. President, great public issues are not subject to our personal timetables; they do not accommodate themselves to our individual preference or convenience. They emerge in their own way in their own time. . . . We hope in vain if we hope that this issue can be put over safely to another tomorrow, to be dealt with by another generation of Senators.

The time is now. The crossroads is here in the Senate. . . . If the Senate were to choose the course of evasion and denial, we would leave this body a less significant and less respected factor in the Government of the United States than it was when we entered it. I implore the Senate, therefore, to consider deeply the consequences of such a course. . . . The Senate's role [ought to be that of] a

Source: Senator Mike Mansfield, opening address to the Senate, on February 17, 1964, HR 7152, 88th Cong., 2nd sess., *Congressional Record* 110, pt. 3 (1964), 2882–2884.

leading participant, an essential and active participant, in shaping the continuing process of equalizing opportunities, that all Americans may share fully in the promise of the Constitution. . . . Senators would be well advised to search, not in the Senate rules book, but in the Golden Rule for the semblance of an adequate answer on this issue.

2 *Senator Richard Russell (D-Georgia),*
February 25, 1964

> Here Senator Russell argued against Senator Mansfield's motion to move H.R. 7152 past the Judiciary Committee. President Kennedy's regard for Senator Russell as a friend and mentor had been one factor stalling his initiative on civil rights legislation.

I can understand the concern with the anticipated legislative situation on the so-called civil rights bill; but I hope, in this time of great pressure, that the Senators will not lose completely their sense of perspective. I hope Senators will look into the parliamentary question that would be involved, as to whether one member of the Senate . . . has the right by a single objection to bypass the committees of the Senate and bring a bill to the calendar. That is the issue that will be before the Senate from a parliamentary standpoint. . . . I hope Senators will not consider this a dilatory action on my part. It is not part of a filibuster. I am seeking only to remind the Senate of its responsibilities and of the desirability of not throwing its rules out the window when a certain type of legislation comes along. We should apply the same rule whether we are enthusiastically in favor of a piece of legislation or whether we are against it.

Source: Senator Richard Russell, February 25, 1964, HR 7152, 88th Cong., 2nd sess., *Congressional Record* 110, pt. 3 (1964), 3498.

3 *Senator John Stennis (D-Mississippi),*
March 10, 1964

> The Senate did not vote to bypass hearings in the Judiciary Committee until March 26, over a month after Senator Mansfield's opening remarks. But even before that procedural matter was settled, senators began debating the merits of the bill itself. In this speech, Senator Stennis was arguing against Title II of H.R. 7152, which prohibited racial segregation in public accommodations.

Source: Senator John Stennis, March 10, 1964, HR 7152, 88th Cong., 2nd sess., *Congressional Record* 110, pt. 4 (1964), 4818.

I recognize that Congress has great power in many fields but it should not—and I trust the Senate will not—attempt to use this power to wipe out and eradicate inherent and basic individual rights which are clearly beyond the reach of governmental control. Included in this is the right to acquire and own property and to use, or to restrict the use of it, as one sees fit; the right of an independent proprietor to operate his business as he sees fit; and the right of an individual to choose his own associates and customers.

I submit, Mr. President, that the basic constitutional issues involved in Title II of H.R. 7152 are of much greater significance and importance than our personal feelings and convictions about racial matters and the merits of integration.

Let us look at what Title II proposes to do. . . . Under the terms of the bill, the heavy hand of Federal control will extend to private business establishments. . . . The owners and operators of [these] establishments . . . will be divested of their long-recognized right to enjoy and utilize their property as they see fit. . . . These rights are fundamental and they cannot be impaired by the Federal Government under the guise of protecting the real or fancied rights of other individuals.

. . . I believe that the designation of the businesses covered in H.R. 7152 as public accommodations is itself a misnomer and is, therefore, calculated to deceive. The enterprises enumerated in the bill are in no sense public accommodations . . . [they] are private enterprises and are privately owned and operated. No person has any vested right in them except the individual or individuals who own them. . . . All of this means that in considering H.R. 7152 . . . we must never forget that it is our own Constitution with which we are tinkering.

 ### *Senator Hubert Humphrey (D-Minnesota),* **March 30, 1964**

> Senator Humphrey presented, as Democratic floor leader for H.R. 7152, a sixty-eight-page overview of the entire bill. Humphrey spoke for over three hours in his opening remarks on the legislation he had been advocating for fifteen years.

I have been privileged to initiate this debate, and I would like my colleagues to know that it is my intention to address myself to all eleven titles of the bill. At the conclusion of my remarks, I shall be more than happy to attempt to answer questions or to engage in debate . . . but during my presentation I shall not yield. . . . I sincerely hope that Senators opposed to this legislation will be equally willing to permit the Senate to work its will, after an opportunity for searching examination and analysis of every provision. We issue this friendly challenge: we will join

Source: Senator Hubert Humphrey, March 30, 1964, HR 7152, 88th Cong., 2nd sess., *Congressional Record* 110, pt. 5 (1964), 6528, 6531–6532.

with you in debating the bill; will you join with us in voting on H.R. 7152 after the debate has been concluded? Will you permit the Senate and, in a sense, the Nation, to come to grips with these issues and decide them, one way or another? This is our respectful challenge. I devoutly hope it will be accepted. . . .

Mr. President, I turn now to Title II, one of the most important, significant, and necessary parts of the bill. This title deals with discrimination in places of public accommodation, a practice which vexes and torments our Negro citizens perhaps more than any other of the injustices they encounter. . . . It is difficult for most of us to fully comprehend the monstrous humiliations and inconveniences that racial discrimination imposes on our Negro fellow citizens. . . . He can never count on using a restroom, on getting a decent place to stay, on buying a good meal. These are trivial matters in the life of a white person, but for some 20 million American Negroes, they . . . must draw up travel plans much as a general advancing across hostile territory. . . . The Committee on Commerce has heard testimony from travel experts that if a Negro family wants to drive from Washington, D.C., to Miami, the average distance between places where it could expect to find sleeping accommodations is 141 miles. . . . What does such a family do if a child gets sick midway between towns where they will be accepted? What if there is no vacancy? . . .

Ironically, the very people who complain most bitterly at the prospect of Federal action are the ones who have made it inevitable. . . . This proposed legislation is here only because too many Americans have refused to permit the American Negro to enjoy all the privileges, duties, responsibilities and guarantees of the Constitution of the United States.

5 *Senator Thomas Kuchel (R-California),* March 30, 1964

In this speech, Senator Kuchel presented, as Republican floor leader for H.R. 7152, his overview of the entire bill.

Discrimination has been demonstrated and documented in a long and sordid series of illegal and unconstitutional denials of equal treatment under law in almost every activity of many of our fellow men. Thus, such legislation as we now have before us cannot be ignored, nor can the issue be avoided, no matter from which State a Senator might come. . . .

Every American is aware that discrimination in public accommodations has motivated most of the 2,100 demonstrations which occurred in the last half of 1963. Public accommodations legislation is certainly nothing new. . . . Thirty of the fifty States and the District of Columbia have laws of this

Source: Senator Thomas Kuchel, March 30, 1964, HR 7152, 88th Cong., 2nd sess., *Congressional Record* 110, pt. 5 (1964), 6556–6558.

kind. . . . There can be no question but that segregation in public accommodations obstructs and restricts interstate travel and the sale of related goods and services. The market for national entertainment such as community concerts, athletic competitions and motion pictures is surely restricted by such a situation. National industries seeking new sources of manpower and availability to growing urban markets are inhibited from locating their offices and plants in areas where racial strife is likely to occur.

But discrimination in public accommodations is not simply a matter of economics, it is a matter of morality and of constitutional right. . . . Mr. President, some citizens . . . have written me expressing the fear that Title II invades the right of a businessman to control his private property. Logically and unquestionably, any businessman should have the right to refuse to serve the drunk, the disorderly, the disreputable. He still will be free to refuse to serve the drunk, the disorderly and the disreputable. He will still be free to set standards for dress and conduct for persons in his establishment. But, under the mandate of the Constitution, he would have to apply these same standards to all customers and thus could not deny service to anyone solely because of his race, religion, or national origin. What is wrong with that?

 ### *Senator Sam Ervin (D-North Carolina),* April 11, 1964

> Here Senator Ervin argued against Title II of H.R. 7152, the prohibition on racial segregation in public accommodations. Ervin would gain new fame and popularity in 1973 when he chaired the special Senate committee investigating the Watergate burglary. Senate Leader Mike Mansfield appointed Ervin to the chair because he was so strict about the Constitution.

If the bill is passed in its present form, it will signal the destruction of constitutional government in the United States as we have known it. . . . There would be a complete end of the Federal system which divides the powers of government between the Federal government on the national level and the States on the local level. . . . This bill, and especially the public accommodations provision of the bill . . . does not attempt to regulate interstate commerce at all. It undertakes to regulate the use of privately owned property and the rendition of personal services within the borders of the States. It has been acknowledged from the very beginning of the establishment of the Republic to this date by every court that has dealt with the subject that the power to regulate the use of privately owned property and the rendition of personal services within the borders of the States is a power which belongs to the States, not to Congress. . . .

I wish to call the attention of the Senate to the Federal Food, Drug and Cosmetic Act of 1937. This act is based upon the power of Congress, under the

Source: Senator Sam Ervin, April 11, 1964, HR 7152, 88th Cong., 2nd sess., *Congressional Record* 110, pt. 6 (1964), 7700, 7703.

interstate commerce clause [of the Constitution], to prohibit commerce in adulterated or deleterious or misbranded drugs, food, and the like.... In that respect, that act of Congress is entirely different from the proposals of the pending bill, for the pending bill does not constitute an effort to regulate or exclude the transmission across State lines of anything. Instead, the pending bill constitutes a brazen effort to regulate the use of privately owned property and the rendition of personal services within the borders of a State.

7 *Senator Strom Thurmond (D-South Carolina),* April 14, 1964

In this speech, Senator Thurmond argued against Title VII of H.R. 7152, the prohibition against race or sex discrimination in employment. Thurmond had led a prosegregation defection from the Democratic Party in 1948 when Senator Humphrey introduced a civil rights plank into the party platform. That year, Thurmond ran for president on the "Dixiecrat" ticket and won 2 percent of the vote.

I agree that a man should be permitted to operate his own private business in the way he wishes. He should also be permitted to hire all white people, if he wishes to do that; or all Chinese, or all Filipinos, or people of any other race; or to hire some of each. He should be permitted to hire people in whatever proportion he wants to hire them. Our Government was founded on the theory of freedom.... When we deny a man the right to choose his own employees for his own business, we are denying him a very vital right of freedom. He knows better than anyone else what kind of people he wants to have work with him in his line of work....

I believe most Negroes are happier among their own people.... I believe people generally are happier among their own kind. Arabs are probably happier among other groups of Arabs. I think the Jews are happier among their own people. I believe that white people are happier among their own people. It does not mean they dislike anybody. It does not mean that they have prejudice against anybody. Nature made us like that. The white men inhabit Europe; the yellow men, Asia; the red men inhabited America; the black men, Africa. I do not know what God had in mind; but He must have had something in mind....

The southern people have warm affection for the Negro. They understand the Negroes and have tried to help them.... The Negroes are much better off as a result of their coming to this country. The progress they have made has not been the result of activities on the part of people who are seeking votes by defending the so-called civil rights legislation. The people who are primarily responsible for the progress of the Negroes are the southern people, because the South is where most of the Negroes have lived until recent years. The South has

Source: Senator Strom Thurmond, April 14, 1964, HR 7152, 88th Cong., 2nd sess., *Congressional Record* 110, pt. 6 (1964), 7903.

had this problem. It is familiar with it and has had to bear it. The people of the South have borne up bravely. They have done much for the Negroes.

Senator James O. Eastland (D-Mississippi), April 18, 1964

It was Senator Eastland's Judiciary Committee that Senator Mansfield navigated past in order to get the civil rights bill heard on the floor of the Senate. Here Eastland argued against H.R. 7152 in general and Title II in particular.

Mr. President, H.R. 7152 . . . is, in my judgement, the most monstrous and heinous piece of legislation that has ever been proposed in the entire history of the U.S. Congress. It is inconceivable that the great mass of American people would not repudiate this bill out of hand if they were advised and understood its exact character and nature. . . . It is my duty to resist enactment. . . . Government by force and intimidation either borders on or crosses the border into anarchy, and today in many areas of the United States we are witnessing . . . a concerted and deliberate effort by certain minority groups to frighten and intimidate elected and appointed representatives of the people into giving them advantages, privileges, jobs and preferment. . . . We are witnessing a character of conduct that is lawless in its nature and designed to teach the children of this country to be disrespectful of authority; to violate the law; to invade the private and personal property of others, and to take by force that which they do not own and have no right to acquire. We can say what we please, but the proposed Civil Rights Act is a direct result of this widespread unlawful agitation, and those who would give it their whole-hearted support are, in a very real sense, unwittingly supporting anarchy itself. Appeasement was the road that led to World War II.

Source: Senator James O. Eastland, April 18, 1964, HR 7152, 88th Cong., 2nd sess., *Congressional Record* 110, pt. 6 (1964), 8355–8356.

Senator Everett Dirksen (R-Illinois), June 10, 1964

Though Senator Kuchel was technically in charge of persuading Republicans to support H.R. 7152, Senator Dirksen proved to be the pivotal Republican figure in the debate. For weeks, he negotiated revisions in the bill's federal powers that made it more acceptable to rural Republican voters. In this speech, Senator Dirksen argued, after fifty-seven days of Senate filibuster, to end the debate on H.R. 7152 by voting for cloture.

Source: Senator Everett Dirksen, June 10, 1964, HR 7152, 88th Cong., 2nd sess., *Congressional Record* 110, pt. 10 (1964), 13319–13320.

When he spoke these words in his deep, melodious voice, every member of the Senate was present to hear him.

Mr. President, it is a year ago this month that the late President Kennedy sent his civil rights bill and message to the Congress. For two years, we had been chiding him about failure to act in this field. At long last, and after many conferences, it became a reality. . . . Today, the Senate is stalemated in its efforts to enact a civil rights bill. . . . To argue that cloture is unwarranted or unjustified is to assert that in 1917, the Senate adopted a rule which it did not intend to use. . . . It was adopted as an instrument for action when all other efforts failed. . . . There are many good reasons why cloture should be invoked and a good civil rights measure enacted. . . .

First. It is said that on the night he died, Victor Hugo wrote in his diary, substantially this sentiment: "Stronger than all the armies is an idea whose time has come." The time has come for equality of opportunity in sharing in government, in education, and in employment. It will not be stayed or denied. It is here. . . .

Second. Years ago, a professor who thought he had developed an incontrovertible scientific premise submitted it to his faculty associates. Quickly they picked it apart. In agony he cried out, "Is nothing eternal?" To this one of his associates replied, "Nothing is eternal except change." . . . America grows. America changes. And on the civil rights issue we must rise with the occasion. That calls for cloture and for enactment of a civil rights bill. . . .

Third. There is another reason—our covenant with the people. For many years, each political party has given major consideration to a civil rights plank in its platform. Go back and reexamine our pledges to the people as we sought a grant of authority to manage and direct their affairs. Were these pledges so much campaign stuff or did we mean it? Were these promises on civil rights but idle words for vote-getting purposes or were they a covenant meant to be kept? If all this was mere pretense, let us confess the sin of hypocrisy now and vow not to delude the people again. . . .

Fourth. . . . There is another reason why we dare not temporize with the issue which is before us. It is essentially moral in character. It must be resolved. It will not go away. Its time has come. Nor is it the first time in our history that an issue with moral connotations and implications has swept away the resistance, the fulminations, the legalistic speeches, the ardent but dubious arguments, the lamentations and the thought patterns of an earlier generation and pushed forward to fruition. . . .

Pending before us is another moral issue. Basically it deals with equality of opportunity in exercising the franchise, in securing an education, in making a livelihood, in enjoying the mantle of protection of the law. It has been a long, hard furrow and each generation must plow its share. . . . Today is the one-hundredth anniversary of the nomination of Abraham Lincoln for a second term for the presidency on the Republican ticket. . . . At Gettysburg 101 years ago he spoke of "a new nation, conceived in liberty and dedicated to the proposition that all men are created equal." . . .

That has been the living faith of our party. Do we forsake this article of faith, now that the time for our decision has come?

There is no substitute for a basic ideal. We have a firm duty to use the instrument at hand; namely, the cloture rule, to bring about the enactment of a good civil rights bill.

I appeal to all Senators. We are confronted with a moral issue. Today let us not be found wanting in whatever it takes by way of moral and spiritual substance to face up to the issue and to vote cloture.

10 *Senator Barry Goldwater (R-Arizona),* June 18, 1964

In this speech, Senator Goldwater explained his decision to vote against H.R. 7152 the day before the final vote was taken and the bill passed, 73 to 27. Senator Goldwater led a conservative resurgence within the Republican Party in 1964 and, just a few weeks after delivering this speech, was nominated to run as the Republican candidate for president against the Democrats' President Johnson. He won only 39 percent of the vote, doing best in the southern states.

Mr. President, there have been few, if any, occasions when the searching of my conscience and the reexamination of my views of our constitutional system have played a greater part in the determination of my vote than they have on this occasion.

I am unalterably opposed to discrimination or segregation on the basis of race, color, or creed, or on any other basis; not only my words, but more importantly my actions through the years have repeatedly demonstrated the sincerity of my feeling in this regard. . . .

I realize fully that the Federal Government has a responsibility in the field of civil rights. . . . My public utterances during the debates [on the 1957 and 1960 civil rights acts] reveal clearly the areas in which I feel that Federal responsibility lies and Federal legislation on this subject can be both effective and appropriate. Many of those areas are encompassed in this bill and to that extent, I favor it. . . . The two portions of this bill to which I have constantly and consistently voiced objections, and which are of such overriding significance that they are determinative of my vote on the entire measure, are those which would embark the Federal Government on a regulatory course of action with regard to private enterprise in the area of so-called public accommodations and in the area of employment—to be more specific, titles II and VII of the bill. I find no constitutional basis for the exercise of Federal regulatory authority in

Source: Senator Barry Goldwater, June 18, 1964, HR 7152, 88th Cong., 2nd sess., *Congressional Record* 110, pt. 11 (1964), 14318–14319.

either of these areas; and I believe the attempted usurpation of such power to be a grave threat to the very essence of our basic system of government; namely, that of a constitutional republic in which 50 sovereign States have reserved to themselves and to the people those powers not specifically granted to the Central or Federal Government. . . .

I repeat again: I am unalterably opposed to discrimination of any sort and I believe . . . some law can help—but not law that embodies features like these, provisions which fly in the face of the Constitution and which require for their effective execution the creation of a police state. . . . If my vote is misconstrued, let it be, and let me suffer its consequences. Just let me be judged by the real concern I have voiced here. . . . My concern is for the entire Nation, for the freedom of all who live in it and for all who will be born into it.

Analyzing the Source

REFLECTING ON THE SOURCE

1. What were the arguments of opponents of H.R. 7152 in favor of racial segregation? What were their constitutional arguments against the bill? How do you think the tactics of the filibuster shaped the opponents' arguments to their fellow senators?

2. What did you find to be the most convincing arguments put forth by the supporters of H.R. 7152 in response to the bill's opponents?

3. Do you have any reason to think that opponents of H.R. 7152 were emphasizing different points in their Senate speeches than they would emphasize in political speeches back home? Do you have any reason to think there was a difference between supporters' speeches in the Senate and back home? What other types of sources would you consult to test your hypotheses?

MAKING CONNECTIONS

4. How were the opponents' arguments against H.R. 7152 similar to the position adopted by George Pullman back in 1894? How were they similar to the position of Fred Korematsu's lawyers in 1944? What do these three chapters in modern American history suggest about the evolving relationship between the individual citizen and the federal government?

5. In the decades following the Senate debate on H.R. 7152, both Senator Sam Ervin and Senator Barry Goldwater enjoyed respect and stature as national political leaders. By contrast, Senator Strom Thurmond continued to be so controversial that, in the fall of 2002, Senator Trent Lott of Mississippi was forced to resign as the Senate Republicans' majority leader because he publicly praised Senator Thurmond's 1948 campaign for the presidency. Based on what you read in these speeches, why do you think Ervin and Goldwater fared better than Thurmond in post-1964 national politics?

Beyond the Source

The most immediate and dramatic effect of the 1964 Civil Rights Act was in the desegregation of public accommodations throughout the Southern states. Many had predicted violent resistance to the integration of restaurants, swimming pools, hotels, and movie theaters, but a survey of fifty-three Southern cities in the summer of 1964 found "widespread compliance" and only scattered cases in which whites assaulted blacks for integrating a public place. Resistence was quelled in December 1964 when the Supreme Court ruled unanimously in *Heart of Atlanta Motel v. United States* that the commerce clause of the U.S. Constitution empowered the Congress to proscribe racial integration in public accommodations throughout the nation.

The Civil Rights Act of 1964 proved, almost immediately, to be inadequate in achieving equal voting rights for all Americans in all regions of the nation. Title I of the Civil Rights Act aimed at ensuring voting rights, but enforcement of that provision was dependent upon federal district judges in the South who were typically hostile to black voting rights. Even before the ink was dry on President Johnson's signature on the Civil Rights Act, activists from various civil rights organizations fanned out across the south to wage a black voter registration drive known as "Freedom Summer." At the same time, Johnson ordered the exhausted staff at the Justice Department to write the "goddamnest, toughest voting rights act you can devise." Not only did Johnson agree with Martin Luther King Jr. that power at the ballot box was essential for racial progress, he also knew that the pro–civil rights Democratic Party had now lost many white Southern votes to the Republican Party and would need to compensate by increasing the number of black voters.

With the experience of the Civil Rights Act to build upon, the Justice Department, the Democratic leadership in Congress, and Republicans like Everett Dirksen were able to get the Voting Rights Act through Congress in less than half the time it had taken to pass the civil rights bill. The Senate once again voted cloture on a civil rights bill, and President Johnson signed it on August 6, 1965. The Voting Rights Act of 1965 drew on the Constitution's Fifteenth Amendment to assert federal authority over voting practices across the United States. The act effectively eliminated a state's right to set literacy tests, poll taxes, and other special hurdles to voting. Between 1960 and 1971, the percentage of blacks registered to vote increased from 5 percent to 59 percent in Mississippi, from 14 percent to 55 percent in Alabama, and from 16 percent to 46 percent in South Carolina.

The Civil Rights Act and the Voting Rights Act eliminated racial barriers to voting and public accommodations. The 1964 act also prohibited discrimination in hiring or school admissions and established the Equal Employment Opportunities Commission (EEOC), which enabled tens of thousands of men and women to file complaints against employers for racial or sexual discrimination. In addition to eliminating barriers, President Johnson went in pursuit of "affirmative action," a phrase he coined, to advance access to educational and employment opportunities. There is no federal law mandating affirmative action in the United States, but there are federal regulations requiring any employer or educational institution that accepts federal money to establish programs for recruitment, training, hiring, or admissions that aim for a demographic profile of the workforce or student body that reflects the demographic profile of the local community. Most states and many private institutions have, since the 1960s, adopted their own affirmative action plans to encourage employers and educational institutions to take initiatives to end discrimination against historically subordinated groups of people, especially African Americans and women.

Affirmative action has been far more controversial than the Civil Rights Act or the Voting Rights Act because it does more than eliminate barriers. As an operating policy, affirmative action says that if two applicants for a position are equally qualified by every other measure, but one applicant is from a group underrepresented in that workplace or that school, then the member of the underrepresented group should be chosen. Opponents of affirmative action argue that the policy repeats the segregationists' error of defining Americans by their race. Proponents have long argued that an affirmative correction is necessary to reverse historic patterns of discrimination and have more recently argued that race-conscious policies create a level of diversity in offices and classrooms that is beneficial to all Americans, across race.

This debate was tested in 2003 when the Supreme Court ruled on lawsuits from two citizens charging racial discrimination by the University of Michigan and the University of Michigan Law School. Both plaintiffs charged they were not admitted to the university because they were white. In its 5-to-4 decision upholding the law school's flexible affirmative action plan for admissions, the Court's majority said that diversity was such an educational benefit to all students that the state had a "compelling interest" in considering race and ethnicity as one part of admissions decisions. In a 6-to-3 decision, however, the Court declared Michigan's undergraduate admissions system as so rigid and formulaic in awarding "points" for race or ethnicity that it crossed the line into categorical race discrimination. These two Supreme Court decisions do not end the debate over whether affirmative action is a worthwhile corrective or unfortunate continuation of racial discrimination in the United States, but they do give those engaged in the debate more guidance in balancing a national commitment to diversity and justice with a national commitment to individual opportunity regardless of the color of one's skin.

Finding and Supplementing the Source

The *Congressional Record,* like the *Foreign Relations of the United States,* can be found in any federal depository library (see "Finding and Supplementing the Source" in Chapter 10 for more about federal depository libraries). The *Congressional Record* is published every day, and congressional rules dictate that every issue contains "a substantially verbatim account of remarks made during the proceedings" of that date. According to congressional rules, members can make technical or grammatical changes in the printed record if they are submitted by midnight of that day's session, and they can submit an "Extension of Remarks" within thirty days of a session. But "in no event," according to congressional rules, "would actually uttered remarks be removable" from the day's record.

The three thousand pages of Senate debate on H.R. 7152 are spread out over six different, dated volumes of the *Congressional Record,* from February 17, 1964, until June 19, 1964. The Congress publishes a detailed index to each session of the *Record,* so it is possible to look up specific terms like "public accommodations," or names like "Sam Ervin," and find all the pages on which the term or person appears in that congressional session. It is possible to read the *Congressional Record* since 1994 online and to consult the *Congressional Record* index since 1983 online—see **gpoaccess.gov/databases.html.**

In the last thirty years, American historians have produced an impressive body of literature on the civil rights movement of the 1950s and 1960s. Within that literature, there are two books that focus on the history of the Civil Rights Act of 1964. *The Longest Debate: A Legislative History of the 1964 Civil Rights Act* by Charles and Barbara Whalen (Washington, D.C.: Seven Locks Press, 1985) is an accessible narrative written in a journalistic style that pays close attention to the political maneuvering in both the House and Senate. *To End All Segregation: The Politics of the Passage of the Civil Rights Act of 1964* by Robert D. Loevy (Albany: State University of New York Press, 1990) presents much the same material but more from the analytical standpoint of a political scientist. Loevy has also edited *The Civil Rights Act of 1964: The Passage of the Law That Ended Racial Segregation* (Albany: State University of New York Press, 1997), which includes essays by key participants.

For readable books that place the story of the Civil Rights Act of 1964 in the context of the whole civil rights movement, see Richard Reeves, *President Kennedy: Profile of Power* (New York: Simon and Schuster, 1993); Robert Mann, *The Walls of Jericho: Lyndon Johnson, Hubert Humphrey, Richard Russell, and the Struggle for Civil Rights* (New York: Harcourt Brace & Company, 1996); Taylor Branch, *Pillar of Fire: America in the King Years, 1963–65* (New York: Simon and Schuster, 1998); and David Garrow, *Bearing the Cross: Martin Luther King, Jr., and the Southern Christian Leadership Conference* (New York: William Morrow and Company, 1986).

Web sites that provide more information on the Civil Rights Act of 1964 include **congresslink.org/civil/essay.html** and **congresslink.org/civil/cr10 .html.** The entire text of the law can be found at **usinfo.state.gov/usa/ infousa/laws/majorlaw/civilr19.htm.** An excellent source of information on weekly developments in Congress is *The Congressional Quarterly,* a weekly magazine that focuses on the Senate and House of Representatives and on legislation pending in Congress.

CHAPTER 12

A Son Writes Home

Letters from the Vietnam War

"The longer I'm over here, the more I think we should get out quickly, almost no matter how." Jeff Rogers announced that hopeless view in a letter to his parents on April 20, 1969, after five months as a naval officer on board a hospital ship anchored off the coast of Vietnam. Jeff's despair over the war was not unusual among those serving "in country" in 1969; nor was it unusual for men and women in the service to write home expressing their despair. Jeff Rogers's letters home are notable only because his father was William P. Rogers, the secretary of state in Richard Nixon's administration. In fact, Jeff Rogers was the only child of a high-ranking administration official to serve in Vietnam during the Nixon years. Over the course of Jeff's one-year tour of duty in Vietnam, from early November 1968 through October 1969, he provided his father with a more direct, candid view of the war than a secretary of state typically gets in military reports or intelligence briefings.

Jeff Rogers did not go to Vietnam enthusiastically, but he did go willingly. He enlisted in the navy in 1968 after a year at Harvard Medical School convinced him that he did not want to be a doctor. Up until that moment in his life, the twenty-four-year-old Rogers had enjoyed all the privileges his father's success could afford. When Jeff, his sister, and his two brothers were children in Washington, D.C., their father was serving as attorney general in President Dwight Eisenhower's administration. Later, when William Rogers was influencing public policy as a partner in a powerful Washington, D.C., law firm, Jeff attended Sidwell Friends' School with the Nixon daughters and then went to Dartmouth College, from which he graduated in 1966. That was the year after President Lyndon Johnson authorized the initial escalation in Vietnam and the year before an energetic antiwar movement coalesced on college campuses. Jeff

Figure 12.1 *Ensign Jeff Rogers with His Father, Secretary of State William P. Rogers*
This photograph was taken in May 1969, when the secretary of state made an official tour of Vietnam. Source: Courtesy of Jeff Rogers.

avoided the early disruptions of the war, gliding smoothly from Dartmouth to Harvard Medical School, but his decision to withdraw from Harvard put Jeff at unfamiliar risk.

In America in 1968, any young man who left school was likely to be drafted into the army, and William P. Rogers's son was no exception. Jeff had to immediately weigh all the options that his peers were weighing: get drafted, enlist, apply for conscientious objector status, or move to Canada. A physician had even offered to write Jeff a bogus medical excuse. In the end, he chose to enlist in the navy, as his father had done in World War II, and went to officer candidate school (OCS), where he trained to be a ship's navigator. Family privilege did not keep Jeff out of Vietnam; indeed, he was one of the few from his class in OCS to be assigned to the war zone. His parents greeted the assignment with a mix of pride and apprehension.

The same week Jeff arrived in Vietnam, Richard Nixon, a Republican, won the 1968 presidential election, defeating Lyndon Johnson's vice president, Hubert Humphrey. During the campaign, Nixon railed against U.S. policy in Vietnam, blaming Vice President Humphrey along with President Johnson for not bringing "peace with honor." Nixon began his presidency believing that he could, within a year, disentangle the United States from the war and withdraw the 540,000 troops fighting there but still, somehow, "win the peace." To achieve that ambitious goal, Nixon appointed three key advisers: Melvin Laird to head the Defense Department; Jeff's father, William P. Rogers, to lead the State Department; and Henry Kissinger to serve as chair of the National Security Council. Nixon did not care that his old friend Bill Rogers lacked foreign policy expertise. Nixon wanted a loyal ally taking care of global business in the State Department so that he and Kissinger were free to manage Vietnam strategy.

Nixon believed that the battle to establish a noncommunist South Vietnam was a vital part of the cold war with the Soviet Union. So while he wanted to extricate the United States from Vietnam, he also wanted to leave behind a secure, independent, democratic, pro-U.S. government in Saigon, the capital of South Vietnam. This was Nixon's meaning when he spoke of "peace with honor." The key problem with Nixon's concept was that the mass of southern Vietnamese people did not see the situation in his cold war terms. They had not been consulted in 1954 when the Western powers divided Vietnam into a communist "North" Vietnam and a pro-U.S. "South" Vietnam; their cultural and historical identity was as "Vietnamese" people who were always struggling against outside powers to achieve national sovereignty. (See Map 12.1.) From their standpoint, North Vietnam's capital, Hanoi, was the symbol of national independence while the U.S.-supported capital in the south, Saigon, was a symbol of foreign intervention. Regardless of their views on communism, many Vietnamese living in the south supported Hanoi's claim that the war was about national reunification. As a result, southern civilians often aided the

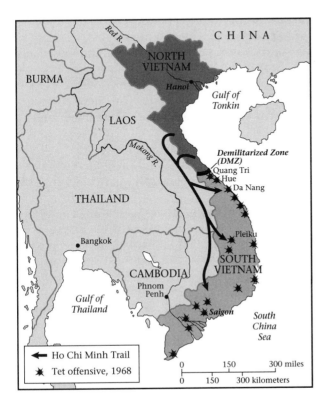

Map 12.1 The Vietnam War, 1954–1975

North Vietnamese army and their southern military allies, known as the Viet Cong.

Jeff Rogers was one of many Americans who wrote letters home from Vietnam expressing their shock, their anger, and even their shame at discovering that many Vietnamese people did not regard the United States as their champions and did not trust the U.S.-backed government in Saigon. The in-country experience of these Americans contradicted the claims of Presidents Johnson and Nixon that U.S. goals in Vietnam were within reach. By 1969, when Jeff Rogers was in Vietnam and his father was in the State Department, the majority of Americans doubted that an independent, democratic government in South Vietnam could emerge from the war, and they did not want to lose more American lives in a futile military effort. Already, thirty-two thousand Americans had died in Vietnam and over two million had done a tour of duty there. Nixon won the 1968 election largely because of his promise to end the war without sacrificing American honor, and 1969 was supposed to be the year that that promise was fulfilled.

As Ensign Jeff Rogers settled into his navigator's post on board the USS *Repose,* just off the coast of Vietnam, his father joined a debate within the Nixon administration about how to achieve peace with honor in Vietnam. The national security adviser, Henry Kissinger, focused on the "honor" aspect of Nixon's goal. He argued that the United States should escalate the war by increasing the bombing of North Vietnam. This act would pressure Hanoi into accepting peace terms that preserved a pro-U.S. government in Saigon and thus protected America's global dignity. Secretary of State Rogers and Secretary of Defense Laird focused on the "peace" aspect of Nixon's goal and opposed any bombing increases that would jeopardize ongoing peace talks in Paris or increase political divisions at home.

Though Nixon expected Rogers to defer to Kissinger on Vietnam policy, Rogers allied with Laird to advocate for withdrawal from Vietnam through a policy called "Vietnamization." In theory, this meant training and equipping the Army of the Republic of [South] Vietnam to wage its own war for an independent democracy against the Democratic Republic of [North] Vietnam. In reality, Vietnamization meant replacing American casualties with South Vietnamese casualties.

In the spring of 1969, Nixon publicly endorsed the Vietnamization policy and responded to America's war weariness by scheduling the withdrawal of 125,000 troops by April 1970. It was true that 434,000 Americans remained in country, and Americans suffered 60,000 casualties, including 11,000 deaths, in Vietnam in 1969. Still, Vietnamization and troop reductions pointed in the direction the majority of the American people desired: deescalation of the U.S. role in Vietnam. Unbeknownst to the American people, however, President Nixon simultaneously endorsed Kissinger's plan to escalate the war through increased bombing. Kissinger feared that a policy of Vietnamization would encourage Hanoi to simply wait out American withdrawal before taking over the south; he wanted to force a peace agreement that would prevent that outcome. Without the congressional authorization required by the Constitution, and against the advice of both Secretary Rogers and Secretary Laird, Nixon ordered the secret bombing of Hanoi's supply lines running north to south through Cambodia, Vietnam's neutral neighbor. Five years later, the House of Representatives debated whether this three-month, secret bombing campaign should be among the articles of impeachment against President Nixon for violating the Constitution. It was not included in the final articles of impeachment but continued to be a controversial course of action.

Jeff Rogers did not know about the secret bombing of Cambodia; William Rogers did not reveal government secrets to his son, nor did he dwell on his disagreements with Henry Kissinger. Jeff knew only what he read in the press, heard from others in the military, and saw for himself. His letters home gave the nation's secretary of state an intimate view of one young American's growing doubts about the American mission in Vietnam.

Using Letters as a Source

Jeff Rogers's letters home from Vietnam sat in a box in his Portland, Oregon, attic until the spring of 2001, when his son, Tyler, asked permission to use the letters as a primary source for a history paper in college. At that moment, Jeff's private writings were transformed into historical documents.

Letters have long served as a key source of eyewitness information for those engaged in all sorts of historical research and writing. Biographers rely on them for an intimate peek at how their subjects interacted with friends, relatives, and colleagues. Political and diplomatic historians turn to letters, such as those exchanged between President Eisenhower and British prime minister Anthony Eden during the Suez crisis of 1956, to see how political leaders privately discussed public matters. Historians of gender examine the language of letters between men and women to explore differences in power and self-expression; intellectual historians use them to trace the gradual, informal development of ideas among scholars in the past; historians of the family rely on letters to trace affection, authority, and animosity among relatives. Whether studying cold war debates over nuclear weapons, negotiations between employers and labor leaders, or the impact of slavery on marriage, historians turn to letters in order to "hear" how participants at the time felt, spoke, and communicated with one another on the most momentous and the most trivial aspects of their lives.

Advantages and Disadvantages of Working with Letters

The great advantage of letters is their immediacy. Unlike memoirs, the author's construction of a letter is not filtered through the leaky sieve of memory, nor have events and reactions been edited by subsequent experiences and reinterpreted through lessons the writer learned later. What is on the page in a letter constitutes some representation of what the author was thinking and feeling at the time the letter was written. Letters also give us the author's "voice," through the use of language, level of formality or informality, and general mode of self-presentation. But it is the overall immediacy that draws historians to letters. When they are lacking film footage, home movies, tape recordings, or face-to-face interviews with their subjects, historians crave the direct connection that letters seem to offer.

Letters can be misleading, however. Their immediacy suggests transparency, and historians can be seduced into believing that everything the letter writer wrote was exactly what that writer thought and felt at the time. Historians who draw on letters must keep in mind that the disadvantage of the source is that letters are a construction of words on the page, and those who write letters bring multiple, often unspoken, sometimes unconscious, motives to their correspondence. Those who want to use a letter as a historical source must first ask to whom was the letter directed — and how might that have shaped the letter's contents? In the case of Vietnam War letters, for example, did soldiers write differently to their mothers than to their girlfriends or to friends who had already done a tour of duty in country? Did soldiers who agreed with their parents about the war write more candidly than those who felt their parents did not understand the situation? Did soldiers employ one tone of voice or another in order to persuade particular readers of the sincerity and accuracy of their view of the war? Did they write to shock, to convince, to gain sympathy, or to vent anger?

Just as when reading memoirs or newspaper articles or Senate speeches, the historian reading letters must simultaneously keep track of the events reported, think about the writer's possible motives for presenting events one way and not another, and consider the effect of the writer's choice of words on the contemporary reader. On March 14, 1969, for example, Jeff Rogers complained to his parents about the inaccuracy of intelligence reports coming out of Vietnam. The historian reading this letter has to consider a variety of interpretations for Jeff's choices in constructing the letter as he did.

> **Even his father, the secretary of state?**
>
> **Did he change the subject to avoid offending?**

> **Was Jeff lecturing his father or warning him?**
>
> **Was Jeff trying to show that his opinions on the war were based on in-country experience?**

So if intelligence reports and press reports have such little relation to what really is happening, who does one believe? Worse, I really wonder if anyone knows what the true story is. The war is too fragmented, too spread out, and too multi-faceted to really be understood as far as who is accomplishing what.

About income tax. We don't have to file as long as we're in the Vietnam combat zone, so I'll wait until I get back to do that.

Yes, we occasionally have beach parties and I've gotten to swim once or twice. But we just got word that there had been a sniper incident at the beach we've been using so beach parties may be out.

It is possible to read a great deal into Rogers's particular construction of comments here. In fact, it is possible to read too much into them. A young man lying on his bunk on a humid Friday afternoon in the South China Sea is probably not plotting his letters precisely enough to warrant microscopic analysis. Historians who study letters must maintain a balance between underinterpreting and overinterpreting them. Without forgetting that multiple motives can shape a letter, it is often most useful to assume that the author of a letter wanted the recipient to read exactly what he said—for whatever reasons. Jeff's letter provides us with evidence that a sailor on board a ship off the coast of Vietnam heard enough press reports and eyewitness reports to conclude that the two seldom matched, and it tells us that his daily life was a disconcerting mix of beach parties and sniper attacks. We do not know from this one letter whether Jeff's arrangement of comments reflected a pattern of blending war commentary with mundane details of life, nor do we know if that pattern was motivated by the desire to telegraph some subtext to his parents. Indeed, Jeff himself now finds that "like any reader, I ponder what in the world I meant by some of what I wrote, and why I wrote as I did in those moments. As I read my own letters, I feel much like an historian doing research."

It is very risky to presume to interpret a single letter by an author whose situation and background is unknown. Historians can overcome this potential disadvantage by looking for patterns in a set of letters from one individual about whom they know something. We know a great deal about Ensign Jeff Rogers, who wrote the dozen letters included here to his father, Secretary of State William P. Rogers, his mother, Adele Langston Rogers, and his sister, Dale Rogers Marshall, between November 1968 and August 1969. We can provide context for these letters because of the public record on William P. Rogers and because Jeff Rogers himself is alive and able to supply background information. Historians analyzing letters found in an archive often lack such aids in decoding the correspondence before them.

As is often the case with collections of letters, we have only one side of the correspondence: Jeff's parents saved his letters, but Jeff did not save letters from his parents. This common disadvantage typically requires historians to infer what was being said by one correspondent based on the letters from another correspondent. In the case of Jeff Rogers's letters, the public record suggests (and Jeff confirms) that his father was quite circumspect in what he said to his son about Vietnam policymaking in the White House. It was only later, and largely through his mother, that Jeff learned of the ways in which the Nixon-Kissinger team excluded William Rogers from decisions, hid secrets from him, and ignored his advice in policymaking. Press reports at the time and later studies of the Nixon war policy have confirmed this pattern, but Secretary Rogers never publicly complained about his treatment. Adele Rogers, on the other hand, was willing to telegraph her own views on the role she wanted her husband to play in the war. In an interview for the *New York Times Magazine* on July 27, 1969, Mrs. Rogers told a reporter that Jeff's letters from Vietnam kept saying, "This is a very good war to end, Daddy, and you'd be a good man to end it."

Even though Jeff Rogers's letters from Vietnam typify the advantages and disadvantages that come with all correspondence as a historical source, Jeff Rogers himself was not typical of the Vietnam serviceman. At age twenty-five, he was five or six years older than the average soldier or sailor. As a white, college-educated volunteer who had been through officer candidate school, he was notably more educated than the tens of thousands of disproportionately nonwhite draftees coming out of high school to serve in country. Like those drafted for Vietnam duty, Jeff, an enlistee, served in Vietnam for just one year, but he was not with the mass of men (and women nurses) attached to infantry units and engaged in combat operations. Jeff's one year in Vietnam was spent as a navigator on the USS *Repose,* a 520-foot navy hospital ship anchored off the coast of southern Vietnam, between the city of Da Nang and the demilitarized zone that marked the border between the northern and southern halves of the country. Jeff's letters, unlike some from Vietnam, do not include reports of dangerous missions, ambushes in the jungle, or close calls. In contrast to those in battle units, Jeff did not have to hide fear and danger to protect the feelings of those at home. He wrote candidly about his boredom (a common theme in Vietnam letters), his worries about his own future, and his pride in his work. He wrote, too, about the strange contrasts between American luxuries, wartime horrors, military corruption, and Vietnamese survival.

Surely the most unusual thing about Jeff's letters is that they survived at all. Throughout history, letters have been destroyed because they brought back bad memories or said things the writer or recipient never wanted repeated; many more letters were simply lost or damaged or lay buried even now in a basement or attic somewhere in the world. Public figures often retain their professional letters and deposit them in library archives, and U.S. archives are rich with collections of letters. Though these collections often represent the most privileged and most literate members of society, there has been considerable effort in the last thirty years to find and place into archives the correspondence of average Americans. Jeff Rogers's letters survived because his mother was a letter writer and a letter saver. For years, she wrote a weekly "family letter" that went out to Jeff, his sister, and his two brothers, in order to share family news. Decades later, when Jeff's daughter Karin graduated from college, he presented her with a binder containing printed copies of all the e-mails she had written during four years away at school. This modern version of a letters collection is an important reminder of the changes that technology has created in future historians' access to that all-important source: letters. The telephone is the bane of the historian because it leaves no record of human exchanges which, in the past, would have been written down. E-mail, however, may be the historian's salvation. Once again, individuals are communicating in a form that can, if saved, provide a historical record.

"If saved." Those are the key words when thinking about written communication, old or new. Some letters in the past were saved, but most were not. Some combination of family habits, social class, race, gender, geography, and personal circumstances determined a letter's survival over time. What factors in the future will determine who saves which e-mails and why? Will you become someone whose experiences and relationships serve as a historian's source on life in the early part of the twenty-first century? You need not become famous to become a historical source; you need only to save your correspondence and make that correspondence available to historical researchers.

Working with the Source

A record of correspondence that stretches over a year offers the historian an opportunity to trace change in the attitudes of the letter writer and to link attitudinal change to the writer's experiences during that twelve-month period. To do this, every historian has to "track" the small print in each letter and watch its direction. As you read Jeff Rogers's letters home, use this table to keep notes on his attitudes toward the Vietnam War. Watch for experiences and observations that indicate a change in his view of the war, but note those comments indicating unchanged attitudes as well. Both are important for understanding how the war experience affected Jeff.

	Evidence of support for U.S. effort in Vietnam	Evidence of disillusionment with U.S. effort in Vietnam
1. November 10, 1968		
2. November 24, 1968		
3. December 7, 1968		
4. December 30, 1968		
5. February 18, 1969		
6. March 14, 1969		
7. April 20, 1969		
8. May 24, 1969		
9. May 31, 1969		
10. June 10, 1969		
11. June 23, 1969		
12. August 28, 1969		

The Source: Jeff Rogers's Letters from Vietnam, November 10, 1968–August 28, 1969

 ## *November 10, 1968*

> Jeff Rogers left Travis Air Force Base, northeast of San Francisco, California, on Friday, November 1, 1968, and after a series of airplane flights, he arrived in Vietnam on Tuesday, November 5, the day Richard Nixon was elected president. He devoted most of his first letter home to his parents to describing life aboard his hospital ship, the USS *Repose*.

Dear Mother and Dad,

. . . I'm quite impressed with and already proud of what this ship does. As they say, it's not about the traditional Navy—a lot of the stuff about secrecy, about protocol, about routine, and of course about weapons is irrelevant here. But it's obvious we do a vital job and a greatly appreciated one. Some statistics: in 1968 so far, 5,571 patients (2,624 battle casualties, 485 non-battle casualties, 2,590 disease) only 152 deaths and returned 2,834 to combat. We've had a total of 8,763 helicopter landings since we got on station in February, 1966 and not one accident.[1] . . . It's a little "heavy" at times directing down a helo [helicopter] that extends almost the full length of the landing pad onto a small area which is moving up and down ten feet or more, especially when you know that there may be someone close to dead already inside—minutes count. All kinds of patients are brought aboard—about 15-20 helos per day . . . [by boat] quite a few Vietnamese—some combat victims but many others for elective surgery or general care.

I feel good about doing something relatively positive in this war. But it's also a strange feeling of being almost farther from the war here. Standing on the bridge at night and watching flares, gunfire, and occasional ships firing in the distance while drinking coke or coffee, BS'ing with the men on watch, and thinking about going back to bed in an air conditioned room after eating a midnight breakfast if wanted—the two things contrast so much. And then supervising the carrying from the helos of bleeding, dying, sick patients. It's hard to know what my reaction to it all is yet. Mostly I've been too busy so far to have time to form a reaction. And we get so little news out here. Just occasional Armed Forces Radio and week or two old papers and magazines. Right now anyway somehow for me personally the war seemed worse when I was watching it on TV—maybe partly because of feeling frustrated to only be able to sit there. But for the guys brought aboard (and women civilians too), the war is <u>here</u> and a helluva lot worse than it is on TV. And for the doctors—they seem

---

[1] Later in the letter, Rogers noted that he just learned that these statistics, though available in news magazines, were supposed to be secret, so he added, "HUSH HUSH."

much more tired than the crew. . . . I was pleased with the outcome of the election. . . . I'm not surprised it was so close. Just like in '60. Another couple of weeks and it might have been reversed. Have you talked with Mr. Nixon, Dad? Must be kind of an awesome feeling for him now. . . .

Love, Jeff

2 *November 24, 1968*

Dear Dale and Don [Jeff's older sister and her husband],
. . . You speak of having trouble imagining me over here. Well, in a way, it's difficult to comprehend being over here. The American presence is so overwhelming here, it doesn't seem halfway around the world. . . . in the military, it's as if a portion of the U.S. had been transplanted over here and stuck in amongst little bits and pieces of a foreign, oriental country called Vietnam. Here I live with Americans, eat American food, drink fresh water (distilled aboard ship), watch occasional taped U.S. TV, listen to U.S. radio . . . and watch American military power fire at an invisible enemy. Never once in three weeks here have I even been aware of hearing Vietnamese talked. . . . The Vietnamese I have interacted with so far are either fluent in English or are too wounded or sick to talk. It's a strange war, but as attested to by the 34 guys we flew out yesterday by helicopter on stretchers on their way back home—a real one.

Love, Jeff

3 *December 7, 1968*

Jeff's job was to position the USS *Repose* at offshore locations as close as possible to battle areas so that helicopters carrying the wounded had quick access to the hospital. He also helped to direct the highly skilled helicopter pilots on to the ship's small landing pad and aided in the transfer of the wounded from the helicopters to the operating room.

Dear Dad,
. . . I was pleased to hear that Chief Justice Warren agreed to stay on. I assume that was your work—congratulations.[1] My major news is that I have taken over

---

[1] Chief Justice Earl Warren was appointed to the Supreme Court by President Eisenhower, when William Rogers was attorney general. Warren led the court in the *Brown v. Board of Education* decision, which desegregated public schools in 1954. Rogers approved this decision, but it was one that created enforcement problems for the Eisenhower administration, in which Richard Nixon served as vice president.

as navigator of the *Repose*. This won't change my job much because I've been doing the navigator work anyway. But . . . this gives me more leeway in making decisions. . . . So the *Repose* has definite advantages for a junior officer. It is one of the very few large ships on which an Ensign can become OOD ("officer of the deck") after only a month aboard (this is nothing great to my credit, as other Ensigns have made it in equal or less time, though some in much more). . . . Other advantages of the *Repose* for officers are the good living conditions, and the preferred treatment you get on next duty. I toured the crew's living quarters the other day, really for the first time—and they're pretty bad. Four small "bunks" in a stack, all very close together, and inadequate toilet and shower facilities. Compare to my two-room stateroom, bathroom shared by two people, and quiet. . . .

Disadvantages of the *Repose* are the full unbroken year over here and the unNavy-like nature of the ship—no weapons, unique organization, etc. . . . The biggest disadvantage of this ship is its monotonous and repetitious operating schedule. Pretty much the same times, same places, same operations. This simplifies navigation and much else but increases the tedium of a year over here. . . .

I really appreciate your letters too.

Love, Jeff

 ## *December 30, 1968*

Dear Mother and Dad,

. . . . The *Newsweeks* just started arriving; getting here when they are still current, which is great. . . . mail time both ways varies a lot. We've been spending three days in Da Nang harbor, where we get mail quickly; followed by three days off the DMZ,[1] where we get mail slowly or not at all. . . . We are scheduled to be off the DMZ on the 25th. We go to Subic [Bay Naval Base] in the Philippines on the 27th so at least we'll be in a little better shape for the New Year. On the way to Subic celestial navigation becomes important, so I should get some experience using a sextant with stars and the sun. We go to Subic four times a year for 5 or 6 days each time. But the ship hasn't gone anyplace else for 1½ years. . . . so unless the war changes, we stay <u>right</u> here. . . .

Since I stopped writing yesterday, the following things happened—all fairly typical of life on the *Repose*. I stood a 12 noon to 1600 OOD[2] watch during which we sent away various of the ship's boats to the Da Nang area for milk, mail, to take some of the crew to beach parties, to transport the Captain and other brass

---

[1] The "DMZ" was the demilitarized zone, which marked the border between the northern and southern halves of the country.

[2] According to the twenty-four-hour clock used in the military, "1600" is 4:00 P.M.; "OOD," as Jeff noted in a previous letter, means "officer of the deck."

to play tennis or amuse themselves. . . . Like a lot on the *Repose*, things often seem to be done haphazardly and the little things sometimes seem more important to the brass aboard (5 captains, 4 medical) than the big things, which is frustrating. The captain gets much madder if you are 5 minutes late with a boat for tennis than if a helicopter with 16 seriously wounded medevac (medical evacuation patients) is mistakenly sent one hour out of its way—both have happened.

[*Rogers then described his first trip ashore with thirty other officers to have dinner and drinks at the Officers Club at the Naval base in Da Nang.*] You feel a little foreign walking from the boat to the club. Mud streets, dodging motor scooters, being saluted by little Vietnamese military men, and almost being run over by little Vietnamese civilians. Then into the club and back to the pseudo-America where the Vietnamese waiters and waitresses seem to be the foreigners there to serve the big Americans. These parties are cherished by the Captain, Exec, and the doctors—but they turn off almost all of the junior officers in the ship's company—including me definitely. They take up time better used sleeping and the "regulars" become so obsessed with their little ventures that they become a real burden for those who have to prepare boats for them and see that everyone gets there and back. . . . quite a lot of trivia to take up the time we don't have between the important things. . . . this month promised to be very quiet—just administrative, with lookout for small craft and swimmers (patrol boats in the harbor, after dropping percussion grenades to keep away any Viet Cong swimmers who have a liking for sabotaging ships). . . .

Being on the periphery of a hospital here . . . I'm more convinced than ever that I was correct in leaving medicine. But I'm also less sure than ever of just what I want to do. One thing I've eliminated is a career in the Navy. . . .

Yes, we see some of the firing around Da Nang and near the DMZ. And we anchor close to the piers which have been shelled occasionally—but still we are relatively quite safe. . . .

Love, Jeff

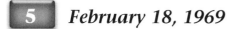

5   *February 18, 1969*

Dear Mother and Dad,
Though it's been quite a while since I wrote, not much new has happened in the interim. . . . Thirty days straight of floating with only a sandy, barren, low coastline in the distance. . . . There have been some kind of depressing times for me since Subic in that the initial excitement of the ship and activity of learning has worn off and now it's the prospect of 8½ more months of the same plus questions still about what I want to do in the future and about myself in general. But my spirits are pretty good now. I've been spending some time with the nurses, which is something of a diversion, though even there the conversation often revolves around the frustration of one year at sea, the frustration of this war, and the condition of the dead and dying patients. . . .

Everyone has been prepared for a large Tet offensive (Tet began yesterday, the 17th), though so far only minor increases in fighting seem to have occurred.[1] I've doubted all along that they would have a major offensive at this time. They are too smart to do so when we are all prepared for one. We'll see.

Seems like Nixon is doing a good job so far. I've heard only positive comments even from self-proclaimed "liberals." Seems to me the two basic elements are his air of calm, quiet efficiency and his open honesty with the press and public about his opinion. I think the latter is <u>very</u> important. The fact that no one in the administration seems disturbed by such trivial things as everyone knowing who the cabinet would be a day or two early is a hugely refreshing contrast to Johnson. As is his directness about his hopes and himself: i.e. "hope to win the respect and eventually the friendship of Negroes." If he can just keep speaking openly and honestly and acting on his own beliefs even when he starts to be criticized, as is inevitable, he should be a damn good president, I think.

I received and enjoyed the tapes you sent. It was reassuring to know you're still having ice cream with butterscotch sauce for dinner. . . . In your last letter, it annoyed me a little what you said about Dad not being able to ask about job suggestions for me. I'm not asking any special favors, in fact I've made it clear I don't want them. All I'm asking is that you keep your eyes open for possibilities. . . . I can't believe that any mention of the subject [of Jeff's search for a post after Vietnam] would be taken as an "order" as Mother suggests. . . . Which brings me to the whole subject of not using pull. I agree in general, but I think it's easy to be so sensitive to it (as I've been in the past) as to pass up opportunities and thus perhaps the chance to do something worthwhile for others. . . . Dad and I were talking once about families and Dad pointed out that an alternative to rejecting the parents, in effect, and starting on your own was to build on what the parents are and have done, and he used the Kennedys as an example. Well, one of the reasons the Kennedys have done so much is that they haven't been afraid to use their own and each other's influence. Though I, too, find the extremes they carry it to distasteful, there is definitely something to be said for not being afraid to use "pull" if one honestly believes it will be for the good of all. . . . So I repeat my original request made months ago: I'd appreciate it if Dad would let me know if he hears of any good Junior Naval Officer billets that exist in the D.C. area. . . . I don't think it's an unreasonable request to ask of my father, Secretary of State or not. Thanks. . . .

I found the following headline in the *Wall Street Journal* and it now is on my desk:

Cruise Ship Staves Off Ennui With Good Food and Endless Activities.

Love, Jeff

---

[1] Tet Nguyen Dan is the lunar New Year festival and marks the most important holiday in Vietnamese culture. This celebration of the beginning of spring is a time for family visiting, feasting, and gift giving. A year earlier, in 1968, the North Vietnamese and Viet Cong had staged a dramatic assault on the south during Tet. They inflicted so much damage that polls showed a majority of the American public doubted the United States was making progress in the war.

March 14, 1969

Jeff wrote this letter just three days before Nixon ordered secret bombing of Cambodia.

Dear Mother and Dad,

Nothing much new to report. Things stay the same here—which is one of the most discouraging aspects of this war. No apparent motion or progress, just a steady influx of dead and dying men. For the first time, yesterday, I felt a little sick to my stomach watching a helo land with six Marines straight off the battlefield—they looked pretty badly mangled when they took them off the helo. Soon found out I was right: 5 out of 6 were dead on arrival, the 6th died shortly after. Not that I'm not expecting to see death in a war, but all of it we see here seems harder to accept because we see or sense no progress towards any goal.

Another thing that bothers me about the war is the so-called "intelligence." First of all it seems to have little relation to what really happens. A case in point is the intelligence about the recent offensive. We were told a month before Tet they expected a big attack on Quang Tri during Tet, etc., etc. As far as I know there has still been no sizeable attack on Quang Tri, and the offensive began after Tet, is not the same type of offensive as was predicted, etc. Every few days we get classified intelligence messages saying that "tonite will be the big attack." Never happens.

And on the other side our press releases both exaggerate and underplay events. *Newsweek* described the attack on Da Nang as something like: "bombs raining in on the city, fires and secondary explosions throughout the city." We got there several hours after the attack and saw three fires, widely scattered, and little else. In general, things looked normal and only moderate damage was done to several military installations. Or another example was the explosion in the landing craft in Da Nang—an explosion we could see, hear, smell. Military press releases as reported on American Forces Vietnam radio network said one killed and 30 injured. In truth, over 30 were killed instantly and the whole landing area was a shambles.

So if intelligence reports and press reports have such little relation to what really is happening, who does one believe? Worse, I really wonder if <u>anyone</u> knows what the true story is. The war is too fragmented, too spread out, and too multi-faceted to really be understood as far as who is accomplishing what.

About income tax. We don't have to file as long as we're in the Vietnam combat zone, so I'll wait until I get back to do that.

Yes, we occasionally have beach parties and I've gotten to swim once or twice. But we just got word that there had been a sniper incident at the beach we've been using so beach parties may be out.

We have a change of command next month. Should be interesting to adjust to a new Captain. . . . This Captain now is quite lax and so we have things pretty easy, but I dislike him strongly, to be frank. His priority list is 1. His reputation and social status 2. Other niceties (but not necessities) like parties, uninterrupted church services, and short hair 3. the welfare and safety of patients. His attitude bothers me a lot. . . .

Love, Jeff

 ## *April 20, 1969*

Secretary of State Rogers and his wife were scheduled to make an inspection trip to Vietnam in the spring of 1969. Though Rogers was often frozen out of strategic planning for the war, his trip was intended to demonstrate the Nixon administration's continuing support for the war even as it laid plans to announce the Vietnamization policy.

Dear Mother and Dad,

Needless to say, when writing from Vietnam, things are the same. . . . I've been navigating without a Chief, but my men have been very efficient and we've been getting along pretty well. In fact I was real pleased with our navigating on the way back from Subic—our star sights coming out good. Also the Captain let me take the ship alongside an oiler the other day and that went well, the Captain of the oiler saying it was one of the best approaches he'd seen this deployment.

So there are a few high spots, but much just sitting around waiting and thinking, both of which can get pretty depressing. It's funny that many of the situations I've been in the past several years seem somehow prison-like or other-worldly. Even at college (though I hardly felt it there) a common expression was "When we get to the outside world." At med school the same: everyone looks forward to going out in the "real world." At OCS to extremes: "Only 28 days to freedom, back to the outside." And in Vietnam you hear everywhere, on the radio, etc.: "when you go back to the world—wonder how things are in the world." Or just civilian life in general referred to as the "outside." And then there's the added confinement, even with the material luxuries of being on a floating football field.

That confinement is one reason I've been wondering, Dad, if you plan to travel at all around Vietnam when you're here—if you still plan to come. It's a shame to be over here a year and see only the coastline and bits of Da Nang. I don't know if it's possible or ethical for me to travel around with you (or your entourage, that is) for a day or so, but it would be great if it would. If it's impossible, I certainly understand.

The longer I'm over here, the more I think we should get out quickly, almost no matter how. Even an initial small unilateral withdrawal might both demonstrate our ultimate peace goal and scare the South Vietnamese into doing a little more for themselves. As I've said before the thing that bothers me most about it all are the sickening sameness of each day, of the news reports, of the "battles," of the intelligence briefings, of the dead and dying people—there seems to be <u>no</u> progress or even change—just more dead and destroyed. The other aspect that makes me doubt that we should stay is the very strong impression that NO ONE REALLY KNOWS what's happening over here. . . . Our Captain says "the allies have really been winning a great victory in the A Shaw Valley" and Marines who have been wounded in the A Shaw Valley say we are getting wiped out there. . . . the government since '65 predicts changes that never occur, and doesn't predict the few that do, etc. It's not that there's a conspiracy to deceive, or a plan to keep the war going by the Vietnamese capitalists or the U.S. militarists or expansionist plans by the U.S.—as the radicals would have one believe. It's not that intentions are bad—it's just that knowledge of what's really happening is abysmal, and given the nature of the war and the country it's probably impossible to ever attain a complete, accurate picture. And if no one can really understand what's happening now, how can anyone decide what should happen or how to get there. Maybe I'm saying that the whole thing is beyond our control and we should stop trying to control it, because all we do meanwhile is waste men and money. The loss of men is obvious. The loss of money becomes clearer when you watch millions spent on the battleship *New Jersey*, then see it sit off the coast here, firing maybe 50 rounds a day far inland and read reports that it "destroyed 4 enemy bunkers and 2 tunnels, no known enemy killed." In fact, I think every U.S. Navy combatant ship over here could be pulled out without any noticeable effect on the war. (Supply ships and hospital ships are different.)

I like what the administration has been saying so far but, as you pointed out, it seems awfully important that results be "forthcoming," not just talk. Look forward to seeing maybe both of you next month.

Love, Jeff

P.S. If troops are pulled out of Vietnam, an excellent way to get them back would be on big white ships.

8 *May 24, 1969*

William and Adele Rogers made an official State Department visit to Vietnam between May 14 and May 19. On the first day of their visit, President Nixon went on national television to announce the new Vietnamization policy. Jeff Rogers was able to travel around the country with his parents for three or four days. Today, Jeff recalls visiting Hue with them and seeing some young recruits preparing to go out on their first mission, looking "petrified." He says his parents were deeply affected by the trip, including their visit on board the USS *Repose*.

Dear Dad,

I'm enclosing the death report on Forbes, the man with the blistered amputation you gave the purple heart to. They didn't think he would die, but he did.

The hospital people also wanted you to know so you could take it into account if you write letters to families.

Love, Jeff

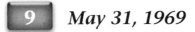

9   *May 31, 1969*

Dear Mother and Dad,
Hope the rest of your trip went well. As I wrote to Dad earlier, it was great to see both of you and a really good chance to see more of the country. . . . Am working on a collection of pictures of our trip to the *Repose*, some of which Mother would particularly like I suspect. . . . Don't know if you ever heard, also, that just before you went into the Intensive Care Unit to give purple hearts another patient died. Apparently they just covered him with a sheet while you were there and removed him later. But to most of the men over here and to their families that's what this war is about—not the pacification resettlement stuff you were shown on your trip.[1]

Love, Jeff

[1] "Pacification resettlement" was a wartime term for U.S. efforts to move South Vietnamese villagers away from areas controlled by the north or the Viet Cong and to persuade them that allegiance to the United States and Saigon promised greater political and economic freedom.

10   *June 10, 1969*

Dear Mother and Dad,
Generally things are the same. . . . Of course, people are standing by to see if there'll be any major changes in our operations with the beginning of withdrawal [crossed out] replacement, though it's probably doubtful I realize. If troops continue to be removed, it's going to be harder than ever for those who remain—and for the families of those wounded or killed. Also for those who are sent over here. Wonder if there's some way to stop sending any combat troops over here and use the natural end of men's tours to phase out our combat troops. Probably will be necessary to send replacement advisory and support military types for some time. But to send replacement frontline Marines, for example, who may have a 20% chance of getting killed or permanently maimed over here while troops are being withdrawn will be hard as hell on everyone. Anyway, I am pleased about the first move and hope that the process goes as quickly as possible or quicker. . . .

Mother, let me put in a correction. As long as you think it's a good story (I do too) and are going to be telling it, let me tell you how it really goes: This nurse did <u>not</u> say, as you said, "No it doesn't matter to me that your father is Secretary of ——— what is he secretary of?" This implies that she didn't know his position. She did. What really was said is as follows: Me: "Does my father's position make any difference to you one way or the other?" Her: "No, it doesn't matter to me that your father is Secretary of ——— (brief pause while her mind went blank for a second before she completed the sentence) Me (interrupting quickly during the pause): "Okay, okay, you've convinced me." The point is not that she didn't know what Dad is Secretary of, but that her mind went blank for a second just at the appropriate time. (Which perhaps indicated indeed that Dad's position was not in the forefront of her impression of me, which is what I was trying to ascertain.)

Love, Jeff

June 23, 1969

Dear Mother and Dad,
As always, things are the same. So there really is no news. There is very little talk about the replacement <———> withdrawal—obviously it doesn't affect at all the lives of most people over here. As a matter of fact, there is in general little talk about the general situation over here and what should be done. People just seem to have given up on the whole mess and only look forward to finishing their year (this is not a new development, having been that way since I arrived). . . .

Love, Jeff

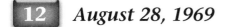

August 28, 1969

Dear Mother and Dad,
Got back from R&R a few days ago. It was great—especially the days of leave I took afterward to visit Pleiku. I was off the ship 13 days—somewhat longer than most R&R's to say the least. Six days in Tokyo . . . then back to Vietnam and up to the Pleiku area for three days. I was with an Army major I'd met in Saigon. He is really fine and was great to me—as were all his friends and associates, from the Commanding General on down (or "up" depending on what you think of Generals). I spent two days traveling in helicopters around the various Montagnard villages that the U.S. civic action people are working in. It is one of the most fascinating things I've seen. The people are truly primitive,

yet truly appreciative of the Americans—in both respects quite unlike Vietnamese. Again it confirmed my impression that one's attitude towards our involvement in Vietnam is conditioned <u>very</u> strongly by one's experience here, because there is a huge variety of possible types of experiences: from getting killed, which we see on the ship every day—to political involvement which I saw in Saigon—to the grateful smiles of some Montagnard chief—to obscene gestures towards and thievery from GI's that I see in Da Nang.

Watching the civic action work with the Montagnards raises again the moot question of whether we should be here at all—and the vital question of what to do now—abandoning some of these people too abruptly would be criminal now—but having Americans killed every day is equally criminal. . . . The chance to go into the villages and talk to the people leisurely and actually see what's going on was a good complement to my field trips with Dad in which we saw a great variety of places—but one felt it was all staged in the showplaces of Vietnam. This visit was the real places where the war is going on. . . .

I, for one, have been really pleased with all the major directions that you and the President have been steering policy, as well as pleased with the President's domestic plans. Do hope though that the next withdrawal from here isn't postponed too long. I worry that the administration will fall into the LBJ trap of trying too hard to save face for the U.S., i.e., not withdrawing in the face of enemy action. When in reality "face" is much less important than lives.

See you in two months.

Love, Jeff

Analyzing the Source

REFLECTING ON THE SOURCE

1. What did your notes on Jeff's letters reveal to you about the direction and timing of his changing attitudes toward the war? What personal experiences caused him to question U.S. involvement in Vietnam? Which six paragraphs from these twelve letters would you select to illustrate Jeff's evolution while in Vietnam?

2. Write a one-paragraph "interpretation" of the letters Jeff wrote on May 24 and May 31 (Sources 8 and 9), immediately after his parents' visit to Vietnam. How does your reading of all the other letters in this set influence your interpretation of these two short letters?

3. The sons of Secretary of State Dean Rusk and Secretary of Defense Robert McNamara, who served under President Johnson, developed stress-related illnesses while their fathers were presiding over the Vietnam War. Based on the letters excerpted here, how would you describe Jeff Rogers's reaction to his father's position in the Nixon administration? Do these letters provide you with enough evidence to characterize this father-son relationship?

MAKING CONNECTIONS

4. Jeff Rogers said that the United States should get out of Vietnam "quickly, almost no matter how." But shortly after the Vietnamization program began, Jeff complained that it made things "harder than ever for those who remain" (see Sources 7 and 10). What were Jeff's concerns about Vietnamization? How do his concerns amount to an argument for getting out of Vietnam? How do they amount to an argument for staying in country?

5. When the United States attacked Iraq in the spring of 2003, some Americans expressed concern that the experience there would replicate the Vietnam War. How does Jeff's August 28, 1969, letter (Source 12) call up similarities and differences between Vietnam and Iraq?

Beyond the Source

Jeff Rogers left Vietnam in late October 1969, a year after arriving there. He spent the second year of his navy service in Washington, D.C., in a naval division charged with training foreign naval officers. Because of his job in the navy, Jeff was able to accompany his father on a second State Department trip to Vietnam, where both father and son were investigating the progress of Vietnamization. The secretary of state approved his son's inclusion on the trip only because the navy had a legitimate job for him to do. In retrospect, Jeff regarded this trip as "another indication of Dad's integrity."

At the end of his tour of duty with the navy in 1970, Jeff Rogers enrolled at Yale Law School, where he was a classmate of Bill and Hillary Clinton. In 1973, he moved to Portland, Oregon, and began to practice law. That same year, President Nixon asked William P. Rogers for his resignation and named Henry Kissinger as the new secretary of state.

The war in Vietnam had officially ended in Paris in January 1973 when Secretary of State Rogers signed the formal "Agreement on Ending the War and Restoring Peace in Vietnam" along with the representatives of North and South Vietnam. The real end to the war came two years later, in April 1975, when troops from North Vietnam took over all of South Vietnam, including Saigon, forcing South Vietnamese and U.S. embassy officials and tens of thousands of civilians to escape by scurrying aboard helicopters and squeezing into airplanes and boats. This chaotic, undignified end to America's involvement in Vietnam was precisely the nightmare that Nixon had hoped to avoid when he dreamt of "peace with honor."

Between 1969, when Jeff Rogers was serving in Vietnam, and 1973, when his father signed the official peace agreement, the Nixon administration pursued Henry Kissinger's plan to use "brutal unpredictability" in aerial bombing to force Hanoi into a peace agreement that retained a separate government in the south and removed all North Vietnamese troops from the south. The bombing campaign of those years included an open renewal of bombing in

Cambodia and expanded bombing of the neighboring nation of Laos. In the spring of 1972, with only ninety-five thousand U.S. troops left in Vietnam, the government launched a massive bombing campaign over North Vietnam and placed mines in North Vietnamese harbors. Then, after winning reelection in November 1972 on the promise that peace was at hand, Nixon ordered the most massive bombing campaign yet against Hanoi, destroying factories, hospitals, and residential neighborhoods. These escalations of violence from the air did not elicit substantial concessions from Hanoi, but the intensified bombing significantly increased U.S. antiwar sentiment. With over 70 percent of Americans agreeing that it had been a mistake to send troops to Vietnam, Nixon and Kissinger finally acquiesced to a peace agreement that was strikingly similar to the terms Hanoi had offered back in 1969, before all the bombing. There was to be a coalition government in the south in which the Viet Cong would be legitimate participants, and the United States was to withdraw all of its troops without requiring a similar withdrawal of North Vietnamese troops. The humiliating debacle that occurred in April 1975 following an all-out military assault by North Vietnam marked the final triumph of these northern troops and the end to all hope for an independent coalition government in the south as the country was reunited under the Hanoi government.

In the four years between Hanoi's original proposal of peace terms in 1969 and U.S. acceptance of those terms in 1973, twenty-five thousand Americans and several hundred thousand Vietnamese died, making for a total of fifty-eight thousand American deaths and 1.7 million Vietnamese deaths between U.S. escalation of the war in 1965 and its end in 1973.

After resigning as secretary of state, William Rogers returned to his law practice in Washington, D.C., and only once returned to public life, to chair the commission investigating the explosion of the *Challenger* space shuttle in 1986. When William Rogers died in January of 2001, a journalist and former antiwar activist named Howard Fineman wrote an editorial in the *New York Times* in which he recalled being invited into the secretary of state's office for a conversation while an antiwar protest was underway outside the White House gates. According to Fineman, Secretary Rogers was the one man in the administration who treated peace protestors with respect, even though he feared that outspoken opposition prolonged the war. Other commentators at the time of his death noted that Rogers was never associated with any of the scandals that tainted the Nixon administration.

While in Vietnam, Jeff Rogers had predicted that Richard Nixon would be "a damn good president" if he "can just keep speaking openly and honestly and acting on his own beliefs even when he starts to be criticized." Over the years, however, the Nixon administration's paranoia over the antiwar movement and leaks to the press about war plans fostered increasing secrecy and illegal behavior. This pattern culminated in a desperate effort to control the election of 1972; since Nixon could not run as the president who had "won the peace" in Vietnam, he felt he had to manipulate the election in his favor. In retrospect, even Nixon's closest advisers have admitted that without Vietnam, there would have been no Watergate. It was his persistent failures in Vietnam and his inability to accept failure that led Nixon to authorize the illegal actions that eventually would have ended in his impeachment by the House of Representatives had he not resigned in August 1974.

Jeff Rogers has not left Portland, Oregon, since setting up his law practice there in 1973. He raised his two children, served as assistant U.S. attorney during the Clinton administration, and has been Portland's city attorney since 1985. Though he and his father had different political allegiances in the 1970s and 1980s, they continued to respect one another and to enjoy an active exchange of views through phone calls and, of course, letters.

Finding and Supplementing the Source

Jeff Rogers's letters are among the millions owned by private Americans. Jeff has not (yet) deposited them in a library archive and had never considered publishing them until his son's request to use them in a college paper led to their presentation here. The sheer chance involved with moving Jeff Rogers's letters from his attic to this book is not all that unusual in historical research. Sometimes, finding unpublished letters can be as easy as cleaning out a grandparent's basement and as difficult as placing ads in local newspapers and then traveling around the country to follow up on leads. In between those two poles, you will find that there are millions of unpublished letters dealing with every conceivable topic deposited in historical archives all across the United States. Imagination and the aid of a librarian and a Web browser can help you to discover if a person or topic of interest to you has relevant letters on file in any archive in the United States.

There are many published collections of letters, though surprisingly few are devoted to the letters of soldiers in Vietnam. The two collections of letters from Vietnam are *Dear America: Letters Home from Vietnam,* edited by Bernard Edelman (New York: New York Veterans Memorial Commission and Simon & Schuster, 1985), and *War Letters: Extraordinary Correspondence from American Wars,* edited by Andrew Carroll (New York: Washington Square Press, 2002). Only *Dear America* is devoted exclusively to Vietnam War letters. See, too, *Home before Morning: The Story of an Army Nurse in Vietnam* by Lynda Van Devanter (Amherst: University of Massachusetts Press, 2001), which uses letters to evoke a woman's experience in the war.

The historical literature on the Vietnam War is voluminous. *Nixon's Vietnam War* by Jeffrey Kimball (Lawrence: University Press of Kansas, 1988) examines the last five years of the war. Broader accounts can be found in George C. Herring, *America's Longest War: The United States and Vietnam, 1950–1975* (Philadelphia: Temple University Press, 1986); Marilyn Young, *The Vietnam Wars, 1945–1990* (New York: Harper Perennial, 1991); Stanley Karnow, *Vietnam: A History* (New York: The Viking Press, 1983); and Neil Sheehan, *A Bright Shining Lie: John Paul Vann and America in Vietnam* (New York: Vintage Books, 1989). See, too, Keith Beattie, *The Scar That Binds: American Culture and the*

Vietnam War (New York: New York University Press, 2000); Andrew E. Hunt, *The Turning: A History of Vietnam Veterans against the War* (New York: New York University Press, 1999); and Christian G. Appy, *Working-Class War: American Combat Soldiers and Vietnam* (Chapel Hill: University of North Carolina Press, 1993). Vietnam veterans have published a number of remarkable memoirs, including Philip Caputo, *Rumor of War* (New York: Holt, Rinehart, and Winston, 1977); Michael Herr, *Dispatches* (New York: Knopf, 1977); Tim O'Brien, *If I Die in a Combat Zone* (New York: Dell, 1973); and Ron Kovic, *Born on the Fourth of July* (New York: McGraw Hill, 1976).

CHAPTER 13

"Can This Marriage Be Saved?"

Marital Advice from Ladies' Home Journal, *1953–1988*

Readers of *Ladies' Home Journal*'s advice column "Can This Marriage Be Saved?" read about Amy and Joe in the May 1953 issue of the magazine. Married for fifteen years, the couple had no children but owned and ran a dry cleaning business together. Amy had thought the marriage was happy until she discovered that Joe was having an affair. Joe said the affair was only a symptom of his unhappiness with the fact that Amy "takes all the responsibility and makes all the decisions" in the shop, leaving Joe in the back, "at an ironing board." Joe longed to have a wife at home, rearing children. The column's marriage counselor reported that Amy and Joe resolved their problems when Amy agreed to work only in the mornings, leaving Joe in charge of the shop. Amy began "channeling her energies into making draperies and slip covers" and taking medical steps to increase her fertility. At the end of the article, the counselor assured her readers that Amy "has achieved more far more joy by working at being a wife than she ever achieved working in the shop!"

This resolution of marital problems strikes us as old-fashioned because gender roles in America have changed dramatically since the 1950s. As a result of the feminist movement of the early 1970s, notable changes have taken place in how women and men define their economic, domestic, and social responsibilities. Fundamental to these shifts in behavior have been changes in how Americans think about manhood and womanhood and in what they regard as ideal in marital relationships. Just the fact that we talk today about "gender" instead of "sex" reflects acceptance of the feminist notion that differences in male and female behavior are more often due to cultural learning than the dictates of nature.

These basic changes in American life, which we associate with the modern feminist movement, have their roots in gradual trends that started in the nineteenth century. Patriarchy was the dominant principle governing gender relations at that time, and it defined wives as economic dependents and husbands as economic providers. In reality, many women were important economic providers in their families, and women of the nineteenth century joined the paid workforce when the site for their productive labor shifted from the home to antebellum factories. Even married women steadily expanded their presence in paid jobs right up through the manufacturing frenzy of World War II, and though women lost their factory jobs after that war, they quickly reentered the workforce in clerical and other service jobs. By 1950, 24 percent of American wives were in the paid labor force, almost a 10 percent increase from 1940. As Amy and Joe's story indicates, however, the postwar period was marked by serious social tension over wives' role in the workforce.

Parallel to the long-term growth in wives' paid work, the number of children born by American women has steadily declined, from an average of seven children per adult female in 1800 to 3.5 children per adult female in 1900 to below two children per adult female in 2000. There was a reversal of this downward fertility trend with the post–World War II "baby boom," when all American women, including Amy, were urged to have children, and the fertility rate rose to 3.6 in 1960. But this growth in the U.S. fertility rate and family size proved temporary.

Long-term declines in women's childbearing and increases in wives' wage-earning culminated in the feminist movement in the late 1960s and early 1970s. This protest attracted wide support from American women because, in their experience, increased responsibilities in the workforce had not brought commensurate gains in income, promotions, or legal status. Nor had women's labor outside the home caused men to assume more housekeeping and child-care responsibilities within the home. By the end of the 1960s, many American women felt that they were shouldering great responsibilities, both at home and in their jobs, but were limited in pay and advancement opportunities and treated as childlike subordinates by male bosses, coworkers, and husbands.

A "first-wave" women's movement had, between 1848 and 1920, won women the right to vote but had not challenged the basic assumption that nature determined women's unpaid domestic role. The "second-wave" women's movement that erupted in the late 1960s directly addressed long-held beliefs about what was natural behavior for women and men. By documenting and demonstrating the fluidity of human behavior, the modern women's movement replaced the notion that a person's biological sex dictates his or her behavior with the idea that culture assigns gender behavior to males and females. The second-wave women's movement established the principle that gender is mutable; a changing culture can redefine appropriate conduct for women and men in the kitchen, the workplace, and the bedroom.

Ladies' Home Journal's marital advice column, "Can This Marriage Be Saved?," affords us a popular, practical window on the effect of the second-wave women's movement on Americans' definition of ideal husband-and-wife relations. Launched in 1953, the column recently celebrated its fiftieth anniversary and continues to be one of the most popular features of this enduring, mass-circulation magazine. *Ladies' Home Journal* was founded in 1883 and became the nation's first magazine with over a million subscribers in the early 1900s. By the time it introduced "Can This Marriage Be Saved?," the *Journal*'s circulation exceeded four million, and it has maintained that subscription level ever since. Throughout the twentieth century, the actual readership of the *Journal* far exceeded its subscription numbers because it was read in doctors' offices and beauty parlors and was circulated among friends.

In every facet of the magazine, from its recipes, beauty tips, and advertisements to its feature stories on celebrity women and its editorial advice on health, child rearing, and marriage, the *Journal* has maintained profits and popularity by combining old and new attitudes on gender. Even during times of tremendous change in female roles, the magazine has deftly blended the traditional with the modern. A study of this balancing act in "Can This Marriage Be Saved?" illuminates the ways in which a political movement like modern feminism gets mainstreamed into the popular culture.

One way to organize the marital advice offered in *Ladies' Home Journal* is by adopting the periodization typically used in U.S. women's history. For example, the years between 1953, when "Can This Marriage Be Saved?" began, and 1966, when the pro-feminist National Organization for Women (NOW) was founded, fits within the era often referred to as the "containment" years in American history. This term refers to the cold war policy of containing communism around the globe, but it also serves to remind us that cold war anxieties caused Americans to hold fast to traditional family arrangements. Even though a third of all wives were employed outside the home in this decade and over half of all college-educated wives were working by 1960, the popular culture defined all married women as "housewives" and presumed all were at home, living entirely on a husband's paycheck. This containment of women's image within a traditional role, despite real change in their behavior, was fueled by an old belief and a new one. The familiar notion that natural law dictated a dependent, private role for all women was combined with the cold war claim that American men's ability to support their families on one income proved U.S. capitalism's superiority over Soviet communism. In a climate of containment, women who protested such beliefs were labeled as either unpatriotic subversives or as unnatural neurotics suffering from what the psychologist Sigmund Freud had deemed a "masculinity complex."

The span of years between 1967 and 1978 are typically defined as the years of "uprising" in American women's history. During these years, coalitions of professional women, unionized women, African American women, ethnic women, lesbians, stay-at-home mothers, and political radicals worked to abolish women's economic, political, and sexual subordination. Even *Ladies' Home Journal* was a target of feminist protest. In March of 1970, over one hundred women occupied the *Journal*'s editorial offices in New York City, demanding that the magazine present a more varied and realistic picture of womanhood in its pages and provide more opportunities for women to rise in the magazine's editorial hierarchy. Those demands reflected the general grievances and specific goals of what was then called the "women's liberation movement." Feminists sought a more respectful public image, advances in their economic and political status, reform of laws related to reproduction and to violence against women, and a more equitable distribution of authority and domestic duties within marriage.

The years between 1979 and 1988 constitute, in current historical thinking, a time of "accommodation," when Americans carved out a middle ground between the ideals of the feminist movement and the backlash of conservatives who depicted feminists as the enemies of both men and the family. During the accommodation era, the dual-income family became the norm, for economic as well as social reasons. Men and women who were marrying and starting families in the 1980s often assumed a degree of gender flexibility and marital equality without being conscious of the role of feminism in shaping their attitudes. Historians debate whether feminism or traditionalism prevailed in the 1980s move to accommodation. In conducting that debate, they turn to sources like *Ladies' Home Journal*. Columns like "Can This Marriage Be Saved?" are useful primary documents for determining the direction of change and the amount of change in Americans' views on gender roles in marriage.

Using Advice Columns as a Source

Every edition of "Can This Marriage Be Saved?" ends optimistically because the *Ladies' Home Journal* intends to show that couples can take conscious action to rescue their marriages.[1] Historians bring a different agenda to their study of a mass-circulation advice column; their interest is in how marital happiness is defined and discussed in the popular culture and in how those definitions and discussions change over time. When studying advice columns, historians are not looking at the reality of marriage in the United States but at the popular culture's view of marriage. In fact, historians do not even need proof that the marriages profiled in the column actually existed in order to analyze how the *Journal*'s discussion of marriage evolved over time.

As it happens, the editors of *Ladies' Home Journal* have always emphasized that the cases and the advice in "Can This Marriage Be Saved?" derive from the actual files of accredited marriage counselors, though names and other identifiers are altered. From the 1950s through the 1970s, the *Journal* stated that the columns were "based on information from the files of the American Institute of Family Relations of Los Angeles, a nonprofit educational counseling and research organization with a staff of 70 counselors." Since the early 1980s, the marital cases profiled in the column have been drawn from the files of marriage

---

[1] *Ladies' Home Journal* has recently launched a new column called "Was This Marriage Saved?" in which the magazine's editors revisit couples profiled in an earlier column and update readers on how these once-troubled marriages have fared.

counseling centers all around the United States. The column's format has never changed; it starts with the wife's version of the marital situation, followed by the husband's version, and closes with the counselor's advice on what constructive steps each partner needs to take to save the relationship.

Advantages and Disadvantages of Working with Advice Columns

Historians can use popular culture sources, such as marital advice columns, as evidence of social values if the source is truly "popular," if it reflects a wide audience's dreams and fears and is so widely read that it actually contributes to public discussion of those dreams and fears. Because of its enduring popularity and consistent structure, a column like "Can This Marriage Be Saved?" can give historians a stable instrument for measuring shifts in the way Americans publicly discuss their marital expectations and disappointments. Historians can use the column to trace trends in the sorts of marital problems thought common enough to appeal to readers' interest and to detect changes in the marital ideals that advisers convey to couples.

The disadvantage in using marital advice published in a magazine is that the publication's editors are not trying to offer a scientifically representative sample of all marital problems in the United States at the time. The *Journal* editors' job is to calculate which marital problems are most relevant to their predominantly white, middle-class, female readers and which marital advice best suits their readers. The stories and the advice that appear in the column are consciously chosen to reflect the noncontroversial middle ground in American thinking on marriage. This limitation does not invalidate popular, published advice literature as a source of historical information, but it does mean that historians have to be very careful not to overstate what this literature demonstrates. Historians cannot claim that marital advice literature reveals the daily reality of all married people in the United States. The historian can say only that a long-running, popular column like "Can This Marriage Be Saved?" tells us which marital issues could be publicly discussed and which marital solutions were widely accepted among English-speaking, predominantly white, not impoverished and not politically radical elements of the U.S. female population. As long as historians are honest with their readers about what this sort of advice literature reveals, they can make valuable use of this surviving record to trace attitudes in mainstream popular culture.

Another potential disadvantage in analyzing this sort of popular culture material can arise from the sampling method historians use. Over 400 "Can This Marriage Be Saved?" columns appeared between 1953 and 1988, for example. The temptation, when consulting such a massive popular culture source, is to select only those examples, quotes, and illustrations that support our preexisting assumptions about an era. This flawed method can lead us to distort the record by making the sources say whatever we want them to say. Historians try to avoid this error by creating stable categories for analyzing and even quantifying what are often very unstable, slippery texts. No one pretends that this corrective makes such analysis purely objective because our assumptions still influence the categories we create and the decisions we make about how to categorize the comments in each column. Still, as you have seen in your own work with other sources in this book, when we are forced to sort our evidence into specific categories, we become more precise in our analysis.

Faced with 420 "Can This Marriage Be Saved?" columns published between 1953 and 1988, a historian would likely take two preliminary steps: first, read through several dozen columns representing the whole thirty-five year period in order to get a sense of the categories of problems discussed and the range of advice offered; second, decide on a sample size that yields sufficient data to be representative but does not entail coding all 420 columns. In the case of "Can This Marriage Be Saved?," an overview of the case studies published between 1953 and 1988 reveals a consistent focus on three big categories: (1) "division of labor"—who did what work to sustain the household; (2) "decision making"—who made the decisions in the family; and (3) "sexual dissatisfaction"—who was responsible for sexual happiness. As you can see from the table below, each category can be subdivided into a range of counseling advice.

DIVISION OF LABOR					
	Counselor's Advice				
Couple's Description of Marriage	Keep as is	Wife should start paid work	Wife should quit paid work	Husband should be more domestic	Husband should be less domestic
Wife domestic work; husband paid work					
Wife domestic work; husband paid & domestic work					
Wife paid & domestic work; husband paid work					
Wife paid & domestic work; husband paid & domestic work					

This coding instrument was developed by Jason Stohler for his undergraduate senior thesis. It allows the historian to systematically code the counselor's advice given in each column. The complete table appears on page 281 of "Working with the Source." In it, Stohler came up with additional categories to rank the counselor's advice for who controlled "decision making" in the family (for example, "husband sole decision maker") and which partner was responsible for any "sexual dissatisfaction" in the marriage (for example, "wife responsible for sexual happiness"). These detailed categories allowed Stohler to methodically analyze his sample of 4 columns per year over thirty-five years, or 140 total "Can This Marriage Be Saved?" columns.

This sort of coding instrument protects a historian from taking a biased sample of columns that deal with only certain problems or offer only one line of advice. But despite the benefits of using such a tool, no instrument can spare the historian from having to make difficult coding decisions. Consider, for example, this advice from "Can This Marriage Be Saved?" (*Ladies' Home Journal* 91 [April 1974], pp. 16, 20, 22) at the height of the second-wave feminist movement. The counselor quoted in this excerpt is commenting on a marriage in which the twenty-four-year-old wife, Julie, suffered from feelings of inferiority made worse by her shame that pregnancy had preceded her marriage to Rod, her difficulty managing a household with four children, and Rod's unwillingness to employ her in the lucrative family business:

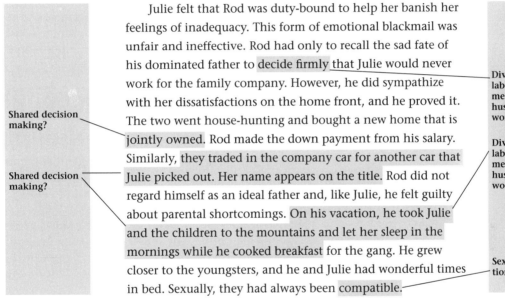

Shared decision making?

Shared decision making?

Julie felt that Rod was duty-bound to help her banish her feelings of inadequacy. This form of emotional blackmail was unfair and ineffective. Rod had only to recall the sad fate of his dominated father to decide firmly that Julie would never work for the family company. However, he did sympathize with her dissatisfactions on the home front, and he proved it. The two went house-hunting and bought a new home that is jointly owned. Rod made the down payment from his salary. Similarly, they traded in the company car for another car that Julie picked out. Her name appears on the title. Rod did not regard himself as an ideal father and, like Julie, he felt guilty about parental shortcomings. On his vacation, he took Julie and the children to the mountains and let her sleep in the mornings while he cooked breakfast for the gang. He grew closer to the youngsters, and he and Julie had wonderful times in bed. Sexually, they had always been compatible.

Division of labor: wife domestic work; husband paid work

Division of labor: wife domestic work; husband paid work

Sexual satisfaction not an issue

In order to code even one paragraph from one column, a historian would have to establish clear definitions of each category. "Division of labor," for example, seems clear enough but when faced with the counselor's approval of Rod cooking breakfast on vacation, should the historian code that as advice that Rod engage in *both* paid and domestic work? Since his culinary efforts seem to have been confined to vacation, and since nowhere else in the advice did the counselor suggest that Rod do more work at home, it seems more accurate to code "division of labor" as "Wife domestic work; husband paid work." The category for "Sexual Dissatisfaction" is easy to code in this case since neither the marriage partners nor the counselor treated this as a problem in the marriage. But what about "Decision Making"? Here, the distinction between "sole" decision maker, "primary" decision maker, and "shared" decision making has to be spelled out before any coding occurs. The historian may decide, for example, that a spouse is a "sole" decision maker if he or she unilaterally decides to purchase a new car and picks out that car without consulting the other spouse. A spouse is the "primary" decision maker if, after deciding to buy a new car, he or she then consults with the spouse about the brand or color. The term "shared decision making" applies when both the husband and wife discuss the need for a car, the financing of it, the brand, and the color. In coding the counselor's description of the changes Rod made to improve his marriage, the historian would have to decide whether the shared outcome—a jointly owned home and jointly owned car—means that the initial decisions to buy the new home and the new car were primarily Rod's or were shared with Julie. Because the answer to this question may not be clear from the source, the historian would need to keep notes on why and how such choices were made in order to create consistency where certitude is impossible.

Popular culture sources like advice columns are potentially rich veins of information about a society's beliefs and aspirations. Historians can mine those veins as long as they are careful with the tools they use and the claims they make about what their results reveal.

Working with the Source

In the source materials that follow, you will read excerpts from one containment-era column and one uprising-era column. You will also be able to examine the coding results reported by Jason Stohler, who sampled thirty containment-era columns and forty-eight uprising-era columns for his senior thesis, "How Was This Marriage Saved? Thirty-five Years of Advice from 'Can This Marriage Be Saved?'" (Grinnell College, 2000). Beginning with Source 5, you can engage in your own coding of six columns from the accommodation era to gauge the direction of change in marital advice in the 1980s. Use the coding tables on page 281 to keep track of your findings for Sources 5–10.

DIVISION OF LABOR					
	Counselor's Advice				
Couple's Description of Marriage	Keep as is	Wife should start paid work	Wife should quit paid work	Husband should be more domestic	Husband should be less domestic
Wife domestic work; husband paid work					
Wife domestic work; husband paid & domestic work					
Wife paid & domestic work; husband paid work					
Wife paid & domestic work; husband paid & domestic work					

DECISION MAKING			
	Counselor's Advice		
Couple's Description of Marriage	Husband sole decision maker	Husband primary decision maker	Shared decision making
Husband sole decision maker			
Husband primary decision maker			
Shared decision making			
Wife sole decision maker			
Wife primary decision maker			

SEXUAL DISSATISFACTION					
	Counselor's Advice				
Couple's Description of Marriage	Wife responsible for sexual happiness	Both responsible; wife more	Husband responsible for sexual happiness	Both responsible; husband more	Both should be responsible
Wife dissatisfied					
Husband dissatisfied					
Both dissatisfied; wife more dissatisfied					
Both dissatisfied; husband more dissatisfied					

The Source: "Can This Marriage Be Saved?" Advice Columns from *Ladies' Home Journal*, 1953–1988, with Analysis

This section includes eight "Can This Marriage Be Saved?" columns and two tables analyzing samples of this monthly feature of *Ladies' Home Journal*. Sources 1, 3, and 5–10 consist of excerpts from the counselor's advice portion of "Can This Marriage Be Saved?" The headnote preceding each source will give you background information on the difficulties experienced by the particular couple featured in that case study. Sources 2 and 4 represent a historian's analysis of a sampling of articles from *Ladies' Home Journal* for the containment (1953–1966) and uprising (1967–1978) eras. Using the tables on page 281, you can apply the same analysis to Sources 5–10, columns published during the accommodation era (1979–1988).

1   *"A Philandering Husband Is Worse Than None,"* September 1961

> Married in 1949, Gail and Guy already had one son when Guy was drafted into the cold war army and discovered "independence and fun" with the guys—and gals—in the service. After Guy's return to a sales position in Los Angeles, the couple had their second son, and Guy began a series of casual affairs with women he met at work. Gail perceived Guy as an indecisive procrastinator, so she chose the house they bought, planned and executed the landscaping, laid the brick patio, and painted the interior. When Guy's expenditures on his girlfriends put the family into debt, Gail "decided to take charge" of the family finances, but Guy did not always tell Gail about his raises, and commission work allowed him to lie to her about his income. For Guy, Gail's household management and her devotion to their sons meant that he felt extraneous. Gail had told the boys about their father's affairs and shortcomings, she had ceased taking care of her personal appearance, and she had cultivated the allegiance of Guy's mother and aunts, leaving him feeling that he was "the only male in a world of chattering, conniving females, just the way I used to feel as a boy."

Gail and Guy were two confused people. Gail instinctively wanted to be treated like a woman, but she behaved in a self-willed, assertive, highly independent manner. Her loving father had unwittingly done her a disservice by encouraging her tomboy ways, by laying undue stress on her skill in pursuits generally regarded as masculine. Already self-conscious because of her unusual height,

Source: Can This Marriage Be Saved?, *Ladies' Home Journal*, September 1961, pp. 24, 26, 28.

Gail became even more uneasy as she looked around and decided that everybody liked her cute little sisters but that only her father liked her. . . . She was unaware of her insensitive treatment of Guy. Nor was she aware that she was persistently presenting herself to her husband as a "good guy," a talented Mr. Fix-it-and-Do-it-All, the only way she knew to win approval. It was a hard lesson for Gail, but she slowly learned to stop and ask Guy's advice, not to dash full steam ahead. If the two were out dancing on Saturday night—she acknowledged that he was entitled to his kind of entertainment at least once a week—she stepped back and let him handle the coat checks even though he fumbled through every pocket or misplaced the checks entirely. She encouraged Guy to show Tim how to use a hammer and saw, to help Harry with his homework, even though she thought privately (and, perhaps, correctly) that she could do better.

Now, to take up Guy. He yearned to be accepted by other men as a regular fellow, a yearning that largely explained his interest (quite superficial) in the ladies. What Guy sought from both men and women was admiration, acceptance, approval. Unfortunately, he didn't know how to be a regular fellow. Petticoat-dominated from his boyhood, he had no masculine model, no hero to follow and emulate. Deprived of his father as a pattern, Guy adopted his mother's ideas of what a man should be, eventually discarded her standards as too rigid and unworkable . . . and then became really confused. Until he got out from under his mother's influence it was most unlikely he would ever develop either self-confidence or wisdom. A suggestion, rare in counseling, was proposed to him. Guy went to his mother, explained his family situation, confessed in plain words his own culpabilities. Then he told her that neither he nor Gail required further advice from relatives, and after this courageous step he began to loose the bonds and fears that tied him to the past. . . .

Most of my work was done with Gail. After weeks of self-examination, she came to realize that her suspiciousness, her deep-lying resentments (a childish leftover of her resentment of her doll-like sisters) had to be excised if her marriage was to be successful. She conceded that she had suspected Guy of philandering on more than one occasion when he was innocent. She also admitted the probability that her moodiness and depressions could be just as hard on her sons as was Guy's neglect.

At this stage—about midway in our counseling—something happened. Six-year-old Harry, whose progress at school had continued to deteriorate, was sent to a psychiatrist. An encephalograph established that the child had suffered a slight brain damage at birth and should be placed in a special school. . . . Curiously, this news was a relief to both Gail and Guy. They stopped blaming each other for Harry's backwardness, and accepted the hard facts of his handicap as inevitable.

In the course of this conference on ways and means, Guy disclosed hitherto withheld statistics about his income. It developed that the special school where tuition was $100 a month was too expensive for their budget. With some trepidation, Gail suggested she take a part-time job. Guy was enthusiastic. Guy was offered an opportunity to become a partner in a small greenhouse and nursery. . . . There was a long anxious consultation and Gail, characteristically conservative, dragged her feet a little. In the end, however, she agreed that Guy should give up sales work and take the gamble. This story has no fairy-tale ending. It wasn't to be expected that Gail and Guy could turn their personalities inside out. Nor did they. As they gained insight they became happier in their marriage and in themselves and they became better parents.

2   Analysis of Thirty "Can This Marriage Be Saved?" Columns from the Containment Era, 1953–1966

Division of Labor[1]

Couple's Description of Marriage	Keep as is	Counselor's Advice (offered in 16 of 30 cases)			
		Wife should start paid work	Wife should quit paid work	Husband should be more domestic	Husband should be less domestic
Wife domestic work; husband paid work	9				
Wife domestic work; husband paid & domestic work					4
Wife paid & domestic work; husband paid work			1		
Wife paid & domestic work; husband paid & domestic work	2				

[1] The numbers in this table tell us that in nine of the sixteen cases, the couples said that the wife engaged in domestic work and the husband in paid work, and the counselors said that arrangement should not be changed. In the four cases where the couples said that the husband engaged in some domestic work, the counselors said he should do less of that; in the one case where only the wife engaged in both paid and domestic work, the counselor advised that she quit her paid work. But in two cases where both husband and wife engaged in both types of work, the counselors advised them to keep that arrangement.

Source: Jason Stohler, "How Was This Marriage Saved? Thirty-five Years of Advice from 'Can This Marriage Be Saved?'" Senior thesis, Grinnell College, May 2000.

Decision Making

Couple's Description of Marriage	Counselor's Advice (offered in 27 of 30 cases)		
	Husband sole decision maker	Husband primary decision maker	Shared decision making
Husband sole decision maker	3	12	
Husband primary decision maker	4	3	1
Shared decision making			
Wife sole decision maker	2		1
Wife primary decision maker	1		

Sexual Satisfaction

Couple's Description of Marriage	Counselor's Advice (offered in 18 of 30 cases)				
	Wife responsible for sexual happiness	Both responsible; wife more	Husband responsible for sexual happiness	Both responsible; husband more	Both should be responsible
Wife dissatisfied		4	1	1	
Husband dissatisfied	4	1		1	
Both dissatisfied; wife more dissatisfied	1	3	1		
Both dissatisfied; husband more dissatisfied		1			

3 *"Phil Doesn't Do Anything with the Children,"* December 1976

Julie and Phil had married in 1967, just a few months before the air force shipped him to Vietnam. Julie was already pregnant with their first child, Beth, and she became pregnant with their second child, Jimmy, shortly after Phil's return from a year-long, battle-scarred tour of duty. Phil admitted to some initial hope that his wealthy father-in-law would be an asset in advancing Phil's career as an industrial sales engineer, but he soon felt

Source: Can This Marriage Be Saved?, *Ladies' Home Journal,* December 1976, pp. 20, 24, 28, 64.

dominated by Julie's "arrogant" father, especially after their second child was diagnosed with a severe hearing impairment and Julie's father financed the child's enrollment in a private school for the deaf. Julie complained that "for the last three years I've felt as if I were raising two fatherless waifs" and predicted the virtually sexless marriage would end if Phil could not "be a father to both our children as well as a husband to me." Phil conceded that "I'm the bad guy in my marriage, but frankly, I didn't want to be a father. I didn't even want to be a husband." Phil feared winding up like his own father, who had spent his life attending to his ever-sickly mother; he complained that Julie was "too soft with both our kids"; insisted that "sex was never the be-all and end-all for me"; and expressed real worry that Julie's wealthy background left her with "no sense of money. . . . I'm up to my ears in debt."

Jimmy's deafness definitely complicated this marriage, but Julie and Phil were in trouble long before Jimmy's birth. They began marriage ignorant of the other's wants, needs and personalities.

Julie was a "rescuer." She needed to please everyone all the time. Choosing to live with her father [after her parents divorced] was a clear example: Daddy looked "sad and lonesome" and needed her. Although aware that [her father] exploited her outrageously, Julie felt helpless to fight him out of fear of hurting his feelings.

Phil subconsciously regarded all women with a mixture of anger and dread. Domesticity frightened him and so did sex — "the sex trap" was his phrase. He felt that all women were whining hypochondriacs like his mother.

Phil was drawn to Julie because she was a loving, caring person who was not in a greedy search for attention. He wanted a wife who was devoted to his interests but one who would let him be free. He wanted a patsy — and he didn't want to share his patsy with anyone, including his own children.

In counseling, Julie began to realize the vital importance of her approach to Phil. Once she understood his inner feelings, she softened her requests for assistance. Frequently, if there were numerous requests, she made written lists, which he was able to study later in a more relaxed mood. She came to understand that sharp demands inevitably swept Phil's emotions back to his boyhood past. Phil felt his mother's constant demands had virtually emasculated his father and, as a result, left Phil himself forever wary of female domination.

With Julie's consent, Phil closed her charge accounts and he now pays their bills. Once his needs and anxieties were considered, Phil was able to interest himself in the needs of Julie and the children. . . . Phil was reluctant to accept individual counseling, especially in the sexual area. In group counseling, though, he met other couples with complex sexual difficulties — and he and Julie were able to discuss their own problems without false notions of delicacy. As a result, their sexual relationship was resumed on a much improved basis. *[The marriage counselor concluded this column by reporting that Phil had bought a small business and moved the family to New Mexico without his father-in-law's help or interference. "All four of us," Julie reported to the counselor, "are feeling fine."]*

4 *Analysis of Forty-eight "Can This Marriage Be Saved?" Columns from the Uprising Era, 1967–1978*

Division of Labor

Couple's Description of Marriage	Keep as is	Counselor's Advice (offered in 36 of 48 cases)			
		Wife should start paid work	Wife should quit paid work	Husband should be more domestic	Husband should be less domestic
Wife domestic work; husband paid work	10	3		1	
Wife domestic work; husband paid & domestic work	2				1
Wife paid & domestic work; husband paid work	10		2	3	
Wife paid & domestic work; husband paid & domestic work			1		2
Wife paid work; husband paid work	1				

Decision Making

Couple's Description of Marriage	Counselor's Advice (offered in 37 of 48 cases)		
	Husband sole decision maker	Husband primary decision maker	Shared decision making
Husband sole decision maker	4	6	14
Husband primary decision maker	1		3
Shared decision making			2
Wife sole decision maker			3
Wife primary decision maker			4

Source: Jason Stohler, "How Was This Marriage Saved? Thirty-five Years of Advice from 'Can This Marriage Be Saved?'" Senior thesis, Grinnell College, May 2000.

Sexual Satisfaction

Couple's Description of Marriage	Counselor's Advice (offered in 34 of 48 cases)				
	Wife responsible for sexual happiness	Both responsible; wife more	Husband responsible for sexual happiness	Both responsible; husband more	Both should be responsible
Wife dissatisfied	3	6	3	2	
Husband dissatisfied	5	4	1	3	
Both dissatisfied; wife more dissatisfied		3			2
Both dissatisfied; husband more dissatisfied	1			1	

 ### *"My Husband Wanted to Call It Quits,"*
November 1984

> Jack and Lynn met while working in the same factory. After marriage, Lynn stayed home while Jack learned masonry and launched his own business in Florida. Jack worked round-the-clock, striving to be a successful bread-winner for his three children. Suddenly, it all seemed pointless, and he wanted out. Lynn had told the marriage counselor that Jack was "a con-scientious provider, a loyal and loving husband, and a devoted father." She also said, "Jack is the head of the household, and I make sure he knows it. Although his long work hours do set limits on our sex life, I don't make an issue of it. And I never let outside activities interfere with my role as a wife and mother." Jack, meanwhile, had told the counselor: "I'm ashamed to admit this, but there are times when I bitterly resent Lynn for not helping out financially. I know this is unfair, because I made it clear at the start that I considered her homemaking a full-time job. But the truth is, I'm too exhausted from carrying the full responsibility for our finances to worry about whether I'm behaving fairly. Lynn prides herself on being unde-manding, yet she depends on me for everything. Even when it comes to our sex life, she expects me to make all the decisions. She never initiates lovemaking, and though she doesn't refuse me, I never can tell if she's really in the mood or is just accommodating my desires."

My first major challenge was to get them to rediscover themselves as individu-als. Jack had to realize it was *okay* for a good worker-husband-father to be self-indulgent at times. Lynn had to know that a good housewife and mother could have an identity beyond that.

Source: Can This Marriage Be Saved?, *Ladies' Home Journal*, November 1984, pp. 14, 16, 18, 20.

Lynn's moment of truth was a dramatic one: One month into therapy Jack moved into his own apartment. Heartbroken, Lynn faced this situation with an amazing show of strength and determination. Weighing her talents she pinpointed the one that was most marketable and started her own small business—cleaning houses. At first, Jack assumed that isolating himself from his family would relieve him of tension. This did not prove to be true. Six weeks of loneliness were enough to convince him that life was empty without the supporting framework of the family unit. To the relief of all concerned, he moved back home.

But things had changed there in the short time he had been gone. Jack was surprised to find that his wife's new business was doing extremely well. Lynn was busy doing light housekeeping for elderly and disabled people. She already had five or six regular customers for her services, and she was averaging eight dollars an hour. She was also enjoying the company of the women for whom she was working and considered several of them friends.

Now that Lynn's earnings lightened their financial burden, Jack felt comfortable cutting back on his own work hours. With Lynn's encouragement, he used some of his free time to reinvolve himself in the activities he had enjoyed as a youngster—fishing, camping and motorcycle riding.

Realizing that she, too, needed breathing space, Lynn began to take some private time for herself. One significant step she took toward reducing her dependency upon her husband was to join a local health club, which offered her an opportunity to make new friends, as well as get some physical exercise. As she gained self-confidence socially, Lynn became more confident in private also and, much to Jack's delight, started to assume a more aggressive role in lovemaking.

As the tension in their lives eased Jack was able to analyze the motivation behind his obsession to achieve. He realized that, subconsciously, he had been attempting to prove himself to his father. Once he recognized this, he was able to reassess his personal value system. He and Lynn discussed their priorities and agreed that the acquisition of material possessions was of far less importance to them than the enjoyment of a simple, unpressured lifestyle.

This couple terminated therapy after eight months, feeling good about themselves and about their marriage. One year later, when contacted for permission to use their story for this article, Lynn reported that things were "still going great, and Jack's like a whole different person." Jack could not come to the phone, since he had just returned from a four-day camping trip and was shaving off his beard before taking the whole family out for cheeseburgers.

"I Wanted to Quit to Have a Baby,"
May 1985

Wendy and Michael had been married a little over three years when they turned to a marriage counselor in White Plains, New York, to help them resolve their conflict over starting a family. Wendy wanted to quit her high-powered job with a management-consulting firm, where she had worked since receiving her MBA five years earlier. Now she wanted to have a baby and spend her days in the Dutch Colonial house that she and Michael had just bought. Michael, a psychiatric social worker in private practice, argued that their new mortgage meant this was not the time to "throw away sixty-five percent of the family income!" Wendy feared Michael's resistance meant they would never have children; Michael feared that full-time domesticity would transform his energetic wife into a woman like his mother. "Mom always complied with my father's wishes, seemed depressed much of the time, and never really initiated *anything* on her own," Michael told the counselor. He tried to tell Wendy about how his mother was always "moping around in an apron and slippers because my dad wouldn't let her get a job."

Wendy and Michael were facing a painful clash of expectations typical of many couples we've seen in the past few years. As old assumptions about the wife's role bump up against new choices, these couples are finding that they have to reexamine some deep-seated values as well as re-think decisions they made at an earlier point in their marriage. Interestingly, this problem—which is not uncommon today—was rarely seen before this generation. For years, men like Michael's father were ashamed to let their wives work; now many men, like Michael, not only expect but depend on a wife's paycheck to help maintain their standard of living.

While at first an immediate compromise—for instance, keeping the status quo for two or three years and then having a baby—might have seemed to make sense, both Wendy and Michael shook their heads when I proposed it. Wendy's wish to trade her career for a baby—and Michael's frank refusal to let her—were bound together with many other feelings that needed to be sorted out. Besides, when they came for counseling they were involved in a power struggle: Each purported to have the only grown-up point of view.

Wendy saw only two alternatives: Either be an aggressive, ambitious ca-reerist like her father, or a happy homemaker, as she perceived her mother and sister to be. When she found herself burning out at work, Wendy felt she had to shift directly from her father's style to her mother's without considering the middle ground. On the other hand, Michael feared that if Wendy stopped working, she would automatically become idle and glum, like his non-working, deeply frustrated mother. He was afraid, too, of becoming saddled, like his father, with the full burden of the family finances.

Source: Can This Marriage Be Saved?, *Ladies' Home Journal*, May 1985, pp. 10, 12, 17.

Wendy and Michael had also been guilty of what I call partner deafness. Though both thought they were listening to their spouse, in fact they were hearing only what they wanted to hear. First, I had them practice a three-step listening exercise, in which one partner listens to the other for two minutes without interrupting and without tuning out. Then the listener repeats what he or she thinks has been said and the speaker can say, "Yes, that's what I said" or "No, it's a little different; what I really meant to tell you was . . ."

This simple technique worked beautifully for Michael and Wendy. As Wendy calmly described her unhappiness at work, Michael realized that all along he had tried to fix her problems with sweet words and backrubs, and had been ignoring her real wish to leave her firm and find another job. At the same time, Wendy realized that though Michael had spoken disparagingly of having a baby, she wrongly assumed that he meant "never," when in fact he meant "not just yet."

I also asked Wendy to talk with her sister to see if Anne's day-to-day life [as a full-time mom] was as idyllic as Wendy imagined. Much to her surprise, she discovered that Anne had her share of pressures and problems; in fact, Anne actually had many agonizing afternoons of envying Wendy's financial independence and freedom. When I suggested that perhaps Wendy didn't have to give up work to find happiness, she began to take a hard look at her skills and interests. She discovered that she really did love her work, but perhaps her current job in such a high-powered firm was preventing her from experiencing any real and lasting satisfaction. During one session, Wendy sheepishly admitted that some of her urgency to have a baby might have been an attempt to find an instant career change, and that perhaps she also would prefer to wait a year or so before plunging full-time into motherhood. . . .

I also suggested to Wendy that along with a new job, she needed to adopt a calmer approach to her work. . . . Just last week, Wendy accepted a consulting job with a small new firm. She's extremely happy with the decision she's made, and to celebrate, Michael gave her a Siamese kitten with a card promising "another bundle of joy when we're both ready."

Wendy and Michael came only for short-term therapy—ten sessions. Today, they are happily renovating their house, and though Wendy is still a very busy woman, she's learned to trade in the old I-must-be-Superwoman tensions for the fun and closeness of spending a whole Sunday morning in bed with Michael reading the paper and *really* talking. When they do have a baby, I'm certain they will be wonderful, loving parents.

"My Husband Was Ashamed of Me,"
February 1986

Ken moved out of the home he shared with Marie and their two young daughters because he was furious at his overweight wife for drinking too much and dancing too provocatively at his law firm's office party. After eight years of marriage, during which Ken went to college and law school and Marie took care of the house and babies, these high school sweethearts had grown apart. When Ken joined a big law firm, Marie felt her husband was "totally out of my league, and he made me feel self-conscious and stupid. The funny part was, anytime I made a move to look for a job that would challenge me, Ken reminded me of chores that had to be done at home." Marie's reaction to the situation was to become depressed and overeat, and whenever Ken yelled at her, she would faint. Ken told the marriage counselor in Brooklyn, New York, of his frustration that Marie "can't understand the importance of keeping a neat and orderly home. When I try to instill a sense of pride, she takes it as an insult. I just don't see how running a house and taking care of two nice kids is so difficult. . . . She can't even stick to a diet. . . . Marie is not a stupid woman, but she did play more than she worked in high school. I thought I could influence her, but even now she refuses to use her mind. Lots of women today juggle careers and kids, but Marie doesn't even have time to read a good book. No wonder she has nothing to talk about at parties."

I shocked them both when I praised Ken's decision to move out. This, I told them, would be their chance to discover who they really were, without the pressure of struggling to be what each thought the other needed.

One of my first goals was to help Marie get back on her feet, so I suggested that Marie and Ken see me separately for a few sessions. Right away, I urged Marie to stop thinking negatively about herself. I reminded her of her many positive qualities—not the least of which was the impressive energy and resolve she had shown in managing to raise two daughters. When Marie said she longed for a more challenging job but did not want to spend years getting her college diploma, I reassured her that many interesting jobs do not require a degree. . . .

By the third week, Ken had gotten over his initial outrage, but he seemed agitated, demanding to know the details of Marie's life. I told him she was doing fine and that it was time he stopped focusing on his wife's helplessness and tried instead to rekindle his original feelings of love and admiration.

Ken was very surprised when I pointed out that his dependency needs were less obvious but just as strong as Marie's. He *needed* Marie to be weak so he could feel strong. For example, whenever Marie had mentioned looking for a job, Ken had been quick to squash her initiative by reminding her of chores that needed to be done. Time and again he had thwarted Marie's attempts to grow by criticizing her. . . .

Source: Can This Marriage Be Saved?, *Ladies' Home Journal*, February 1986, pp. 16, 19–20.

We spent a lot of time exploring this macho-protector role of Ken's. . . . I pointed out, it was Ken, not Marie, who needed to do some growing up emotionally. He had to start accepting Marie as a separate person with strengths and weaknesses of her own.

After four weeks, Ken and Marie started to come for counseling together. By this time, Marie had found a job as a recreation aide in a hospital for children with terminal illnesses. She adored her work . . . [and] Marie's supervisor had recently offered to pay for a hospital-sponsored night course that would open the way for more money and swift advancement. Ken was clearly amazed. I asked the couple how it would work if Ken babysat the two evenings a week that Marie would be at school. At first Marie balked—the children had always been her domain. Finally, she agreed. What's more, the new arrangement gave Ken a chance to get to know his daughters better as well as an opportunity to see just how tough a job it was to run a home and take care of two growing girls. Ken confessed that when he found himself putting the girls to bed an hour and a half past their bedtime—with math homework still to be completed and the smoke from burned hamburgers still hanging heavy in the grease-blackened kitchen—that Marie had been doing a super job. By that time, Marie was feeling so much better about herself that she joined Overeaters Anonymous. The program helped her realize why her previous attempts at dieting had failed: She had lost weight not for herself but for Ken. Then, [when] she was angry with him, she sabotaged herself by gaining back those lost pounds. . . .

Once Ken and Marie felt stronger as individuals, they were able to talk honestly about their feelings. . . . Ken moved back home [and] they both have new confidence in their own abilities as well as a healthy respect for each other's needs. Ken and Marie started out as two very young, incomplete people looking to each other for the missing pieces. Now, they are two *whole* people, better able to love each other and make their marriage work.

8   *"My Husband Is So Bossy,"* March 1987

Arlene and Jack were both in their late thirties, had been married for sixteen years, and were living in Sherman Oaks, California, when conflicts with their teenage sons forced them to face problems in the marriage. Arlene had always deferred to Jack but had come to feel that his intimidating control over the family was causing their sons to become rebellious at home and at school. Concern for her sons emboldened Arlene to challenge Jack's authority. Having always been the family's sole breadwinner, Jack felt entitled to authority. He told the marriage counselor, "I've taken the responsibility for making decisions and running the house. I

Source: Can This Marriage Be Saved?, *Ladies' Home Journal,* March 1987, pp. 14, 20, 22.

> want to know how my money is being spent and that my sons are fulfilling their responsibilities. It's not that I don't care what Arlene thinks or wants, but I don't think she even knows what that is."

Although this marriage looked successful on the surface, it had been in trouble for a long time. The most obvious symptom was Jack's unending need for control. But the real issue went far deeper. Neither Jack's nor Arlene's emotional needs were being met because this couple was afraid to share and trust.

At the core of their problems was the fact that Jack and Arlene had each come into marriage carrying a lot of unresolved feelings from the past. . . . because her mother and father had made Arlene feel that her problems were not important, she had never learned to trust her feelings. Instead, she looked to others to tell her what to think or want. . . . Jack saw work as the only way to feel good about himself. And because he had been taught that he couldn't count on others to come through for him, he never learned how to give or how to consider the needs of anyone but himself. . . . Jack wanted someone who wouldn't challenge him, and Arlene was looking for someone to tell her what to do, and the pattern solidified over the years.

It wasn't until Arlene saw how Jack's behavior was affecting their sons that she realized what had been happening in their marriage. Finally, she began to fight back, although in an indirect way. . . . Our major goal in therapy was to teach Jack and Arlene how to be intimate. But, first, they both needed to discover and understand Arlene's emotional needs. To do this, I told Jack to practice listening to Arlene without judging her and then repeat what she'd said. If Jack became critical, I instructed Arlene to stand up for what she needed. And if she slipped back into her old pattern of giving up, she was to start the whole process all over again. . . .

Consequently, as Arlene got in touch with her needs, she realized that she did have rights within the marriage. She felt manipulated, and she became very angry—the legitimate product of years of frustration. . . . Once this couple's problems were addressed and old patterns started to dissolve, we had to determine how they would run their household now that Jack was no longer in charge. First, we decided that Arlene and Jack would have equal say in any important family decisions. Then we divided household tasks.

Because Arlene was better able to deal with the children, she became the sole disciplinarian. If Jack did not like something the boys did, he was to go to Arlene and let her deal with it. This was very hard for Jack at first, but it was also very effective. Having their parents speak as a united front made the boys perceive both as stronger . . . Once the boys were given some real room, their behavior improved. And for the first time, Jack began to establish a real relationship with his sons. As Jack became more responsive to Arlene, their relationship became stronger. Knowing that she has the right to her own needs and feelings has given Arlene more self-esteem. And as a result of becoming more aware that his wife *does* have needs, Jack has learned to be more sensitive with other people.

9

"My Husband Is Never There for Me,"
August 1987

At twenty-nine years old, Joyce had been married for eleven years and had four daughters but was so lonely in her marriage that she was tempted to have another affair. Her first fling had gotten the attention of her husband, Henry, and caused him to stop drinking and become sexually interested, at least for a while. Joyce and Henry turned to a marriage counselor in Sarasota, Florida, because Henry's sixty-hour-a-week job as a chef meant he played little role in family life, leaving Joyce to handle all household affairs and child rearing. Years earlier, Henry had decided on his own to move the family to another state so he could attend culinary school, and Joyce had felt forced to take a part-time job as a nightclub hostess while Henry attended school. It was then that Joyce had her extramarital fling. Now that Henry was a chef, he was "pleased that Joyce doesn't have to work anymore. She's so good at running a home; those kids don't need their dad for anything other than his paycheck. That's just as well, because girls are a foreign breed to me. . . . my five ladies have developed their own ways of doing things. I try not to interfere." But Henry's absentee style was not good enough for Joyce; "on the few occasions he is home, he hovers on the edge of the family like a reluctant visitor. . . . Now, when he comes home from a night of carousing, he either goes straight to the television or wants to have sex. I refuse to make love to a drunk."

Without realizing it, both Henry and Joyce were using Henry's drinking as an explanation for their unsatisfactory relationship. By doing this, they were overlooking the main issues. Henry obviously had a problem, though his drinking was less habitual than it was stress related. His increased drinking over the last few years indicated he was far less happy than he was willing to admit.

Henry had been drawn to Joyce because of her nurturing personality and her desire for the kind of home life he had never known. In theory, he agreed with her ambition to be full-time mother and have a large family. However, when his wife set out to make her dream a reality, Henry found he had let himself in for more than he had bargained for. As his financial pressures mounted, Henry had to push his long-term dream of owning a restaurant further into the background. Even worse, he was unable to reap any tangible reward for his sacrifice. The more hours he spent working, the less time he devoted to family activities—until he felt like a visitor in his own home.

Henry and Joyce's problem was a classic case of lack of communication. Though these two people had been married a long time, they were completely out of touch. Joyce especially found it impossible to talk about her feelings. She had been brought up in a family in which the parents never aired their differences. All couples disagree and fight, I told her, adding that her parents never allowed her to see that you could argue, settle your differences and move on. In

Source: Can This Marriage Be Saved?, *Ladies' Home Journal,* August 1987, pp. 14, 16–17, 19.

an effort to entice Henry to spend more time at home, Joyce had shielded him from family problems. Unfortunately, this merely caused Henry to feel uncomfortable and unneeded. . . .

When Henry first heard Joyce speak resentfully about living like a single parent, he was astonished; he quickly expressed his willingness to take over more parenting duties. The fact that he worked evenings and weekends, however, presented a very real problem. Even so, when they set their minds to it, Henry and Joyce came up with innovative ways to foster family togetherness. He volunteered to break up his workday and come home between his lunch and dinner shifts. This allowed him to greet his daughters when they got home from school and help chauffeur them to their extracurricular activities. . . . He then decided to give his daughters cooking lessons. . . . The girls were happy to have so much more contact with their father. . . .

Joyce's goal was to learn to air her feelings. To encourage this, she and Henry agreed to set aside time to talk right after he got home from work. During these sessions, Joyce shared her concerns about household and child-raising problems. Once when they were discussing some unpaid bills, Henry immediately offered to take over that responsibility, thereby freeing Joyce from an unwanted burden and giving himself a more active role in running the family.

Joyce and Henry were highly motivated to strengthen their relationship. Within two months, they had made enough changes in their life together to let them both feel their marriage had vastly improved. Henry also followed through on his promise to cut down on his drinking. Though he didn't give up alcohol completely, he set himself a cut-off point of two beers and confined his drinking to social occasions with Joyce.

Within the next several years, Henry plans to open a part-time culinary school out of their home. If that is as successful as they hope, they will expand their business to include a homestyle, family-run restaurant. Being involved in the planning of this enterprise has boosted Joyce's self-esteem, allowing her to see herself not just in the role of wife and mother but also as a partner in an exciting venture.

 ### *"My Husband Couldn't Handle My Success,"* June 1988

Kathryn and Paul had met eight years earlier, soon after she graduated from high school and went to work as a salesgirl in the Dallas, Texas, department store where Paul was the assistant manager of the shoe department. Since then, they had married and had one son. Kathryn had gotten an associate's degree in business and become a manager at the department store, while Paul had gotten a degree in civil engineering but failed to hold onto a job.

Source: Can This Marriage Be Saved?, *Ladies' Home Journal*, June 1988, pp. 14, 16, 20.

When they finally saw a marriage counselor, Kathryn reported that she had shouldered most of the household duties in the first years of their marriage, even though both were working. After Paul was laid off from his fifth job, he stopped looking for work and stayed home with their son for eight months, "doing a bad job of housekeeping and watching TV wrestling matches." Kathryn admitted that she "nagged him" to take an unsatisfying but steady job as a foreman in a warehouse, and she stated that "the only communication he's interested in is sex, and I'm so furious I'm totally turned off. I can't fake it, either." Paul expressed resentment at "being pressed into maid service" while his wife "was out there being Wonder Woman," getting raises and promotions while he was continually losing jobs. "She had such a good time ordering people around all day, she kept right on giving orders when she got home. I never heard a word of thanks for doing the housework, just complaints that I wasn't bringing home a paycheck."

Paul and Kathryn presented a classic example of how past events can color and shape the present. . . . Kathryn had not had any respect for her father, an irresponsible man who had not provided adequately for his family. Therefore, one of the qualities she had hoped for in a husband was that he be a good provider. When they met, Paul was that man. But when his job options disintegrated, she panicked, thinking he was following a pattern all too familiar. Her automatic reaction was to nag her husband in the same way her mother had nagged her father. She had just as little success, for Paul had been conditioned by his own father to respond to such accusations by closing his ears. . . .

Paul felt cheated. Having grown up under the thumb of a domineering mother, he had fallen in love with Kathryn because she was docile and submissive and made him feel important. When his bride suddenly began expressing opinions, making demands and making her own decisions, he was stunned. Even harder to take was the fact that she was out in the world achieving at exactly the time he was shoved onto the sidelines. . . .

Initially, I worked with Kathryn alone to help her find a way to break her habit of nagging and making accusations. Her constant verbal assault on Paul created a tension that made real communication impossible. . . . When Kathryn explained in a nonjudgmental way how frightened she was that family history was repeating itself, Paul quickly reassured her. "I'm not going to cop out on you and Gary," he promised. "I'm just confused and discouraged and, well, threatened. I'm in a holding pattern, and you're going full speed ahead. I feel like I'm nothing but a failure; I'm scared I'll never catch up."

That confession melted Kathryn completely. She immediately reassured Paul that she had faith in his abilities and would help him in every way. Together they worked out a plan for Paul to make an all-out effort to find work in his chosen field. If he failed to accomplish this, Kathryn agreed to take on extra projects on a free-lance basis so Paul could devote his time to going back to school.

Paul's new job search, undertaken with renewed self-assurance because of Kathryn's encouragement, was more successful than either had anticipated. In the course of checking out jobs at an employment agency, he happened upon a listing for an engineering spot in an area of the business with which he was unfamiliar. . . . he asked for an interview though he knew he was underqualified. He was turned down, but several weeks later, when he noticed the ad was still posted, he drove back and reapplied for it. Impressed by Paul's tenacity, the interviewer hired him and agreed to train him.

Reestablishing himself as a wage-earner did much for Paul's ego. No longer threatened by his wife's success, he was more than happy to do his share of the housework. As the hostility between them eased, their sex life became vital and exciting.

Paul and Kathryn ended counseling after nine months, confident in their love for each other as well as their ability to talk things through if new problems cropped up.

Analyzing the Source

REFLECTING ON THE SOURCE

1. Looking over the tables for the containment and uprising eras (Sources 2 and 4), and your own analysis of the columns from the 1980s, where do you see the most decisive changes? What categories were slow to change? What did you find surprising in the patterns apparent from these tabulations?

2. The percentage of married women working outside the home, part-time and full-time, increased from 65 percent in 1980 to 77 percent in 1990. As a historian, would you say that some elements of popular culture, such as *Ladies' Home Journal,* caused this change or reflected it? How might the tabulations for "Division of Labor" in the uprising era and your own tabulations for the 1980s be of use in thinking about cause and effect?

3. Now that you've read a few columns from the 1980s and categorized the counselors' advice, do you think it's accurate to call this decade an era of "accommodation" between feminism and traditional gender roles? Would you use a different term to characterize this era's gender attitudes?

MAKING CONNECTIONS

4. One of the basic principles of the second-wave feminist movement was that male and female behavior is shaped more by culture than nature. Where do you see that principle reflected in these excerpts from "Can This Marriage Be Saved?" Where do you see the assumption that the female role is naturally different from the male role?

5. How would you compare the attitudes toward male and female roles evident in the 1980s advice offered in "Can This Marriage Be Saved?" to the attitudes you encountered in Vicki Ruiz's chapter on the 1920s, "Flappers in the Barrio," or in the post office murals painted during the New Deal of the 1930s?

Beyond the Source

The families profiled in "Can This Marriage Be Saved?" are usually those that have choices. The women in these stories are, by definition, married women whose male partner typically earns an income. Consistent with general trends in the 1980s, the couples in these stories often found that family tensions and husbands' stresses could be greatly reduced if the wife went to work, and *Ladies' Home Journal* marital advice came around to the view that shared responsibility for family support was healthy in a marriage. The fact remains, however, that the majority of wives in these columns are of an economic class that allows them to choose whether to combine work with motherhood, and a much-applauded noneconomic reason for these wives working is that husbands can become more involved as parents. In other words, the couples in "Can This Marriage Be Saved?" represent those fortunate Americans who can choose whether to combine work with motherhood, who can afford to pay for private child care, and who have two parents to share at-home care of children.

The second-wave feminist movement has made great gains for this population of married mothers. So, too, the movement has achieved tremendous progress for single women who have no children. By successfully tapping into Americans' belief in individual rights, the modern women's movement has established that women are individual human beings with aspirations and talents that qualify them for positions of independent authority. Those individual women whose education, class status, marital status, or childlessness positioned them to take advantage of new job opportunities have been beneficiaries of the feminist emphasis on women's individual rights and capacities.

This emphasis on individual achievement as the route to gender equality fit with the political climate of the 1980s and 1990s in which there was more enthusiasm for progress through individual prosperity than through collective, government efforts. Thus, at the start of the twenty-first century, feminist activism is most robust in those areas that emphasize the individual's right to reproductive choice, to equal pay for equal work, to one's personal sexual preference, to educational and athletic opportunities, to job training and promotion, and to legal protection from physical violence.

There is an irony in this individualistic aspect of feminist success, however. In applauding the independent woman who can earn her own living or the wife whose job makes her a better partner, this individualistic focus has overlooked the fact that women continue to be children's primary caregivers and women continue to earn just seventy cents for every dollar a man earns. For many mothers who do not have an adult male partner to help with income or child rearing, access to jobs and child care is scarce and children are quickly impoverished. This is more true for black women than for white women and more true for less-educated women than well-educated women, but it happens to divorced women without child support just as surely as it happens to women who bear children out of wedlock.

The women's movement of the 1970s envisioned a society in which child care was as common as public school and in which men as well as women, and neighbors as well as family members, pitched in to ensure that all children in the community had the support they needed, regardless of the whereabouts, wherewithal, or willingness of fathers. This vision was obscured in the antigovernment, antitaxes climate of the 1980s and 1990s, and feminism came to mean each individual woman's private management of her own work and family duties. Women's new freedom to work outside the home meant that those single mothers who could not earn sufficient wages to afford child care were stigmatized as lazy for staying at home. The poor wages in women's traditional service jobs combined with the lack of progress in community child care and the increase in single mothers due to divorce, lack of access to or knowledge of family limitation methods, and men's desertion, unemployment, or imprisonment resulted in the "feminization of poverty" in the 1980s. This really meant the maternalizing of poverty, since it was mothers and their children who were disproportionately poor.

Ladies' Home Journal offers evidence that, by the 1980s, American popular culture was ready to embrace the notion of wives working alongside husbands to provide for children within a traditional family structure where there was sufficient income to either pay for child care, have dad take some time from work for child care, or have the mom stay home temporarily until the children entered school. Public policy in the 1980s and 1990s, however, made clear that Americans were less willing to raise the minimum wage or expand public services like child care to a level that would enable women raising children on their own to work outside the home. The welfare reform act of 1996, for example, ended the federal government's six-decade commitment to aid single mothers. This "Personal Responsibility and Work Opportunity Reconciliation Act" embraced the feminist notion that women are capable breadwinners, but did not recognize the feminist claim that mothers must have access to child care if they are going to work outside the home.

Successive waves of feminist activity in the United States will undoubtedly fuel the debate over whether gender equality is to be achieved in a society where women continue to be primary caregivers and individual women make private arrangements for their family and work lives, or if gender equality and reduction of child poverty require more fundamental changes in how Americans define responsibility for children. We can all watch for signs in the popular culture, including *Ladies' Home Journal*, for which way the winds of change in gender roles seem to be blowing.

Finding and Supplementing the Source

Many public and university libraries have bound volumes of popular magazines, such as *Ladies' Home Journal*, going back to the late nineteenth century. In addition, many periodicals, including *Ladies' Home Journal*, have been copied onto reels of microfilm, and it is often possible to borrow, through interlibrary loan, specific reels for specific dates if your own library does not own the issues you want to examine. To celebrate the fiftieth anniversary of "Can This Marriage Be Saved?," Margery D. Rosen and the editors of *Ladies' Home Journal* published *Seven Secrets of a Happy Marriage: Wisdom from the Annals of "Can This Marriage Be Saved?"* (New York: Workman Publishing, 2002). Articles from various women's magazines are collected in *Women's Magazines 1940–1960: Gender Roles and the Popular Press*, edited by Nancy Walker (Boston: Bedford/St. Martin's, 1998).

For historians' analyses of the role and influence of women's magazines in American popular culture, see Nancy Walker, *Shaping Our Mothers' World, American Women's Magazines* (Jackson: University Press of Mississippi, 2000), which examines this aspect of popular culture from the 1920s through the 1950s. *A History of Popular Women's Magazines in the United States* by Mary Ellen Zuckerman (Westport, Conn.: Greenwood Press, 1998) analyzes magazines from 1865 up to 1998, while Helen Damon-Moore compares *Ladies' Home Journal* to the *Saturday Evening Post* in *Magazines for the Millions: Gender and Commerce in the* Ladies' Home Journal *and the* Saturday Evening Post, *1880–1910* (Albany: State University of New York Press, 1994).

Since the 1980s, American historians have been publishing interesting analyses of gender roles in married life. Five of the best books on this subject are *Homeward Bound: American Families in the Cold War Era* by Elaine Tyler May (New York: Basic Books, 1988); *The Way We Never Were: American Families and the Nostalgia Trap* by Stephanie Coontz (New York: Basic Books, 1992); *To Have and To Hold: Marriage, the Baby Boom, and Social Change* by Jessica Weiss (Chicago: University of Chicago Press, 2000); *Public Vows: A History of Marriage and the Nation* by Nancy F. Cott (Cambridge: Harvard University Press, 2000); and *Man and Wife in America: A History* by Hendrik Hartog (Cambridge: Harvard University Press, 2000).

CHAPTER 14

The Changing Profile of America

Population Statistics and the Effects of the Immigration Act of 1965

Mohamed Arabi convinced his parents to let him leave Syria to attend college in the United States in 1973. His father, once a successful tailor in the Damascus fashion world, had fallen on hard times. Mohamed argued that an American education would improve the family's economic status after he returned home to Syria. Though Mohamed's parents agreed, they feared their son would never move back to Syria—and they proved to be right.

Mohamed's first four years in the United States, spent at the University of Texas in Austin, were difficult. He struggled to adjust to the educational, social, and sexual freedoms in American culture, tried to fit in by marrying an American woman, and finally quit both school and his marriage. Legal status as the spouse of a U.S. citizen, however, had brought him a precious "green card," officially known as a "permanent resident card." This document entitles a non–U.S. citizen to live and work in the United States. It was printed on green paper in the 1940s and 1950s, and even though it is now issued in other colors, this valuable document is still known popularly as a green card.

With his green card, Mohamed was able to start anew in Houston, where he found his footing in that city's emerging Arab American community. Two years as the food and beverage manager at a large Holiday Inn allowed Mohamed to open a grocery store in the city's Arab neighborhood, offering Arab specialty foods. Out of that base he built the Arab American Communication Service, which provided Arab immigrants with translation assistance and legal advice. By the mid-1990s, Mohamed was supporting his Arab communication service through a full-time night job as a quality control officer for

Procter and Gamble. The Arab American Communication Service was never going to make him rich, but it had allowed Mohamed to talk to fellow Arabs about the value of building bridges of communication between Arabs and non-Arab Americans.

Mohamed became an American citizen in 1986 and went back to Syria in 1987 to marry the sister of his brother's wife. As a citizen operating under the U.S. immigration law established in 1965, Mohamed was able to sponsor his now-widowed mother's entry into the United States. She, in turn, was able to sponsor the legal entry of her other sons. Her sons then sponsored the legal entry of their wives and of the family's youngest sister. Mohamed's wife also sponsored the legal entry of her parents. By 1995, Mohamed had been joined by twenty-one members of his Syrian family, and he and his wife were raising their two American-born children amid Houston's well-established Arab American community. Like all immigrants to the United States, Arabs in cities like Houston have created communities that boast native-language newspapers, ethnic restaurants, religious institutions, and self-help organizations. By raising his children in an Arab American community, Mohamed has tried to shield them from the sexual freedom that he believes is undermining American family stability while at the same time providing them with the "freedom of the mind" that he has come to treasure in American life.

Mohamed's father, coming of age in Damascus in the 1930s, did not have the same freedom to immigrate to the United States. At that time, U.S. immigration policy was governed by the National Origins Act of 1924, which set rigid annual quotas for how many immigrants of each nationality the United States would accept. Each nation's quota was calculated at just 2 percent of the immigrant population from that nation living in the United States in 1890. Since very few Syrians had lived in the United States in 1890, the Syrian quota was set at just 100 immigrants per year. Hungary, which did not begin to send many immigrants until after 1900, had a quota of just 473. Germany, by contrast, which had been sending millions of emigrants to the United States since the 1830s, had a quota of 51,227.

The national origins quotas, first set in 1921 and then extended in 1924, were the first numerical limitations in U.S. immigration history. Before the passage of these restrictive laws in the isolationist era that followed World War I, immigration policy barred the admission of "all idiots, insane persons, paupers or persons likely to become a public charge, persons suffering from a loathsome or contagious disease, persons who have been convicted of a felony or other infamous crime or misdemeanor involving moral turpitude," and "polygamists." Starting in 1883, U.S. law had specifically restricted the immigration of Chinese, and all Asians were restricted from entry by 1917 legislation creating an "Asiatic Barred Zone." Before the 1920s, however, there were no broad restrictions on the number of immigrants allowed to enter the United States. The national origins acts were designed not only to limit the number of immigrants entering the United States, but also to ensure that those who did enter were more likely to be from northern and western Europe, people who were then thought to be of superior "racial stock" to immigrants from eastern or southern

Europe, the Mideast, or Africa. In deference to agricultural growers in the western states, the new quota system did not apply to the Western Hemisphere, so immigrants from Canada, Mexico, and Latin America were not limited by the 1920s restrictions.

Mohamed Arabi faced a very different U.S. immigration system in 1973 from the one his father would have faced in earlier years. In 1965, the U.S. Congress completely changed the foundations of U.S. immigration law and thereby increased the chances that a young Syrian could gain legal entry. The basic principles governing the Immigration Act of 1965 are still in place today and have resulted in dramatic changes in the profile of America's immigrant population, making the United States the most ethnically diverse nation in the modern world. Before examining the "demographic" changes—or statistical changes in the population—produced by the 1965 immigration act, it is useful to consider the historical forces that caused U.S. legislators to design such a thorough overhaul of the immigration system.

The cold war and the American civil rights movement were the two compelling reasons why the U.S. Congress, which had just passed the Civil Rights Act of 1964 and the Voting Rights Act of 1965, enacted a sweeping change of U.S. immigration law in October 1965. In the years following the Allies' victory over the Axis powers in 1945, many Americans had grown increasingly uncomfortable with their own nation's racial codes and came to view the national origins quota system as one more legacy of segregationist policies. At the same time that the civil rights movement was pressing to reform racist aspects of U.S. domestic law, the State Department was arguing that existing immigration law actually aided the Soviets' global campaign to depict the United States as a racist nation. Indeed, a 1952 immigration reform act that technically ended the Asiatic Barred Zone granted each Asian nation such paltry quotas that the communist press in Korea described the reform as "only one of many things . . . which spread prejudice among the people of the United States against Asian people."

It was not only Asian exclusion that caused headaches for those engaged in fighting the cold war. The national origins system set very low quotas for eastern Europeans, the precise population of people who were seeking refuge in the United States from Soviet control. For example, after the Hungarian crisis of 1956, when the Soviet military moved in and crushed a rebellion in Hungary, the United States government was hamstrung by immigration quotas that limited the number of Hungarian dissidents the government could rescue and bring to the United States. In the end, 15,000 Hungarian refugees were allowed in under special provisions. In fact, between 1948 and 1960, the U.S. Congress had passed so many special provisions to the National Origins Act that 700,000 "nonquota" refugees, most of them from Europe, had entered the United States. A law that necessitated the creation of so many exceptions was clearly no longer functional.

By the early 1960s there had emerged a political coalition between those legislators who were strongly committed to racial justice and those who wanted the United States to triumph over the Soviets in the hotly contested cold war being waged in Asia and Africa. Like it or not, American politicians had to face the fact that racist immigration law did not advance a global image of the United States as the champion of freedom and justice. As one U.S. diplomat put it, "the kind of immigration policy we adopt is a factor in the world struggle between democracy and totalitarianism." Because they fully endorsed that view, U.S. presidents from Harry Truman through Dwight Eisenhower and John F. Kennedy argued for immigration reform, but it was during the administration of President Lyndon Baines Johnson that Congress enacted a thorough overhaul of the system as part of LBJ's Great Society agenda.

According to the basic provisions of the 1965 immigration law (technically referred to as the Hart-Celler Act because its leading sponsors were Senator Philip Hart from Michigan and Congressman Emmanuel Celler from Brooklyn, New York) the national origins quotas were abolished. On a voice vote in the Senate and a vote of 326 to 69 in the House of Representatives, the Congress replaced yearly quotas for each nation with a yearly quota of 170,000 immigrants from the Eastern Hemisphere, with no country in the Eastern Hemisphere to receive more than 20,000 visas per year.[1] The law also set a yearly quota of 120,000 immigrants from the Western Hemisphere, but there was no one-country cap. The Western Hemisphere limit was the first-ever restriction on U.S. immigration from neighboring American countries and represented a compromise that agribusinesses in western states and congressional advocates of reform had to make with those who feared growing immigration from Mexico and other Latin nations. In 1978, the Congress combined the two hemispheric caps into a global quota of 290,000, with no country anywhere getting more than 20,000 visas per year.

Beyond this basic immigration formula, the 1965 law also created a much more significant "preference system" for admitting individuals with particular qualifications that made them exempt from any global quota. It was thanks to this system of preferential exemptions that Mohamed Arabi was able to bring twenty-one of his Syrian relatives to the United States. According to this system, top priority is "family reunification." Automatically exempt from any numerical limits are the spouses, unmarried minor children, and parents of U.S. citizens and of legal permanent residents (legal immigrants who are not yet citizens). There is, after that, a preferential ranking system that admits the adult children and siblings of U.S. citizens and legal permanent residents. There are also preference categories for certain professionals, scientists, artists, and skilled workers whose abilities are in demonstrable demand in the United States and, finally, a preference category for refugees fleeing war or persecution. Advocates for this system of nonquota preferences argued in 1965 that the system's emphasis on the individual, regardless of national origin, was in keeping with America's principle of recognizing individual rights regardless of group

---

[1] A "visa" is a government's authorization that an individual can legally enter that government's country. A person's own country issues a "passport" certifying that person's citizenship. It is up to all other countries to decide if they will issue a visa on the basis of a person's passport.

identity. Further, they argued that in establishing a system of preferences be-yond the annual numerical caps, the United States affirmed its strong commit-ment to the family and to rewarding the individual's acquisition of valuable skills.

The importance of the 1965 law's system of preferences and exemptions is evident in the simple fact that the law set a yearly numerical cap of 290,000, but the United States has received, on average, 631,000 legal immigrants each year between 1965 and 2000. Whoever was admitted beyond the 290,000-person cap was either given family reunification preference or occupational preference.

Historians today debate whether those who supported the 1965 immigra-tion act foresaw the changes it would introduce into the composition of the U.S. population. There is evidence to suggest that some legislators voted for the bill in the belief that it would bring very little change in the numbers of immi-grants or in the basically European profile of the U.S. immigrant population but would improve the United States' global image in the cold war. There is also evidence that key advocates for the bill understood that the new law would expand immigration from eastern and southern Asia, Africa, and the Mideast but did not view this as a negative outcome.

Research on the expectations that accompanied passage of the 1965 law continues to spark debate. But all historians agree that it is impossible to grasp the significance of this legislation without examining the population statistics on immigration to the United States in the last thirty-five years.

Using Population Statistics as a Source

In the last forty years, many historians of the United States have shifted their at-tention from the stories of famous heroes and villains to the stories of ordinary people whose experiences have often been ignored. The resulting works of "so-cial history" have included stories of female factory workers, African American slaves, migrant farm laborers, and, of course, American immigrants. The emer-gence of social history as a field, distinct from more traditional political or intel-lectual history, has meant an increased focus on people who, though not pow-erful as individuals, often wield enormous collective influence—or experience the greatest impact of decisions made by the elite few in powerful positions.

Because social historians often study people who were not wealthy, did not leave vast collections of letters to museums, and were not profiled in news ar-ticles, they regularly turn to population statistics to determine what common threads tied a community together, what demographic factors made an indi-vidual unique or representative. In the United States, social historians are aided in their recovery of the lives of ordinary people by the U.S. Bureau of the Census. Article I of the U.S. Constitution stipulates that an "actual enumera-tion" of the nation's population be conducted every ten years. As a result, his-torical researchers are able to access demographic data on the U.S. population going back to 1790. This material is available at three levels of detail. There is the actual "manuscript census," which are the house-to-house records, written down by census takers or mailed in by citizens; that material (for every township, county, and state in the nation) is available on microfilm in federal repository libraries. Second, there is the "published census," which collates all the household data into printed reports on everything from fertility rates to fisheries, and appears in bound volumes and on the Internet. Finally, the *Statistical Abstract of the United States*, published annually since 1878, offers a convenient summary of basic statistics on the U.S. population and various social and economic entities. It is widely available in community and school libraries, and editions published since 1995 can be accessed on the Internet.

In addition, historians of U.S. immigration can draw upon the reports of what used to be called the Immigration and Naturalization Service (INS) and is now called the Bureau of Citizenship and Immigration Services (BCIS). For decades, the INS published an *Annual Report* which, in 1978, was retitled the *Statistical Yearbook*. While the Census Bureau is the best source for demographic information on all of the foreign-born people residing in the United States, the BCIS is the place to go for information on each year's immigration into the United States. These annual compilations of statistics about immigration, coupled with the Census Bureau reports, allow historians to track trends and change over time when telling immigrants' stories.

Advantages and Disadvantages of Working with Population Statistics

The great advantage of quantitative material on a whole population is that it tells the historian whether an individual or community was typical or unusual for that time and place. When trying to reconstruct the lives of forgotten subjects, social historians often use population information to figure out if, for example, a person was part of a racial minority in their county or if a group of people formed an ethnic majority in their neighborhood. Census data can reveal if an individual's known job was typical among workers in that community; if the individual's job is unknown, census figures can suggest what were the typical sources of employment in that community. This sort of "quantitative" material can offer useful context for interpreting the bits and shards of "qualitative" material that have survived from an individual's or a community's experience. For example, if a woman's diary mentions working in a textile factory in Georgia, then quantitative data can reveal how common it was for women to do such work; if a news clipping in a shoebox tells of a Slovak marrying a Mexican in Chicago in 1910, then quantitative data can reveal how often such ethnic mixing occurred in that place at the time.

Since many of the interpretations a historian makes are rooted in the basic question of typicality, it is enormously important to position an individual story on a demographic map. By turning to the INS *Annual Report* for 1973, for example, we can determine that Mohamed Arabi was a rather unusual immigrant for his time. He was one of just 213 Syrians issued a student visa that year, giving Syrians less than half of 1 percent of the 91,000 student visas issued to all foreigners in 1973. He and his fellow students constituted just 6 percent of the 3,348 Syrians who entered the United States that year on temporary visas, but at the same time, 1,128 Syrians entered the United States as true "immigrants," people intending to make the United States their home. Syrians represented only a drop in the sea of 400,063 foreign-born individuals who entered the United States in 1973 as immigrants. The INS *Annual Report* gives us a taste of Mohamed's isolation by listing only 288 immigrants as newcomers to Austin in 1973, but the *Report* does not say how many foreigners on student visas were enrolled at the university. The national figures on Syrian immigration, however, confirm Mohamed's recollection that he was without the support of an Arab community when in Austin. It is Mohamed's personal recollection of loneliness and isolation that we find compelling, of course, but the statistics allow us to construct a solid social context for understanding that individual experience.

The INS report for 1973 holds promising information on the Syrian story in twentieth-century America. In trying to move beyond the 1973 report to trace change over time, however, historians confront the disadvantages with using the government's statistical data. In the 1980 report, for example, there is no information on student visas, and the 1997 report gives statistics on student visas from some countries but not from Syria. So, too, there are some post-1973 reports that provide data on immigrants in Austin and Houston, Texas, and some that do not; some that mention Syrians, some that do not. A historian trying to follow a particular group of immigrants by making comparisons in the size and settlement patterns of one nationality over a period of several decades quickly confronts this fundamental reality: published government population reports are designed by statisticians whose job is to provide the best data on the most pressing issues at the time the reports are being written. Unfortunately, those government reports do not offer historians consistently comparable data over decades and centuries.

Just as historians can become frustrated by the absence of demographic data on a topic, they can also feel overwhelmed by the abundance of information. Faced with rows and rows of figures on dozens of tables in any one report, it is crucial to keep careful track of the distinctions between one set of published tables and another. Consider, for example, the difference between these tables, which sample only three states:

Reports where each legal resident entering the United States in 2000 planned to live

Table A   Immigrants Admitted by State of Intended Residence, 2000

Of those who entered the United States in the year 2000

State of Intended Residence	Number of Immigrants	Percentage of All Immigrants
Alabama	1,904	0.2
Alaska	1,374	0.16
Arizona	11,980	1.4

Does not include children of the foreign-born who were born in the United States

Tells the number of foreign-born persons living in each state in 2000 and the percentage of each state's total population which was foreign-born

Table B   Nativity of the Population by State, 2000

State	Number of Foreign-Born	Foreign-Born as % of State Population
Alabama	71,000	1.6
Alaska	26,000	4.1
Arizona	630,000	12.9

Can then calculate that 87.1% of those living in Arizona in 2000 were born in the United States

Table C   Concentration of Foreign-Born in the United States by State, 2000

State	Number of Foreign-Born	Percentage of All Foreign-Born in U.S.
Alabama	71,000	.25
Alaska	26,000	.09
Arizona	630,000	2.2

Calculated by dividing 71,000 by 23,379,000, the total number of all foreign-born persons living in the United States in 2000

Each table answers a different question, each speaks to a different experience. The historian strictly interested in the choices of people coming into the United States in one single year would be interested only in Table A because it looks solely at one year's immigrant population. The historian interested in the community experience of all foreign-born residents of the United States (regardless of when they arrived) would want to use Table B because it reveals that the foreign-born are less common in some parts of the United States, such as Alabama, than in other parts of the country, such as Arizona. But Table C is of most interest for the historian who wants to find out which parts of the nation have been most affected by immigration. When using the wealth of population statistics the government publishes every year, historians have to make sure that the information on the table they are consulting is relevant to the question they are asking.

Alongside the problems with both scarcity and abundance in the government's demographic data lies an even more vexing question: who *never* gets counted? Who completely eludes the statisticians' gaze? In the case of immigration, this is a tremendous disadvantage in the source because those typically not counted are "undocumented aliens," foreign-born persons who have entered the United States without legal approval and accompanying documents. Since the 1965 law placed a limit on immigration from the Western Hemisphere, the number of undocumented aliens, referred to by some as illegal immigrants, has risen dramatically. This is simply because migrants from this hemisphere can enter the United States without having to pass through an airport or a seaport. But while we have a variety of social measures indicating a significant rise in the number of undocumented aliens, there is no way for the

BCIS to count those immigrants who do not go through official channels and no way for census takers to count those who must hide from authorities in order to stay in this country. The consequent absence of precise statistical data is a constant source of frustration for historians, social scientists, and policy-makers wanting to track this trend.

In the ongoing national debate about immigration, there are issues that our statistical data cannot settle and issues that such data can address. Population statistics cannot tell us why the Congress passed the 1965 immigration act; for that, historians turn to the *Congressional Record,* public speeches, correspondence, and news reports. But statistics can allow us to trace the effects of that law since 1965, showing how the lifting of quotas has altered the U.S. ethnic composition and showing the importance of family reunification preferences in reshaping the profile of America. So, too, official statistics cannot tell us all we want to know about illegal immigration since undocumented aliens fear the detection that could come with being counted. But statistics on legal immigration can serve as a reminder that not every immigrant is illegal and that specific provisions of immigration law can limit or expand access to the United States. As you read through the charts and tables included in this chapter, you will have the opportunity to ponder the degree and direction of change in the U.S. population since 1965. You will then have the opportunity to consider how this demographic information might be used today in a debate over immigration policy.

Working with the Source

The demographic data included on the following tables, charts, and graphs allows you to track changes in the U.S. population that resulted from passage of the 1965 immigration act. There is no great mystery hidden in this material; it will be quite obvious to you that the new law ignited change in the *composition* of the immigrant population, meaning the nationalities that make up the whole immigrant population, and in the *nativity* of the whole U.S. population, meaning that portion of the U.S. population which is native-born and that portion which is foreign-born. You will also see that the 1965 law increased differences between those places in the United States where being an immigrant is quite common and those places where it is more unusual.

Since you know from the start that the point of all of the charts, tables, and graphs included here is to illustrate population changes over time, you are free to consider three questions that historians who work with such material must ask themselves: First, what is the best way to display all of this information? Second, how do I make sure that the statistical information I am using is relevant to the question I am asking—for example, how can I ensure that I do not look at information on the nativity of the whole U.S. population in 1990 to answer a question about the composition of the immigrant population that year? Third, how might this statistical material be employed in a contemporary political debate about U.S. immigration policy? This last question is a reminder that historical data that is this modern and is on a social topic as contested as immigration is bound to be used by advocates both for and against expansion of legal immigration. As you work through the various measures of change here, consider how advocates on both sides of the debate might use this data to support their positions.

The source data is displayed here in tables, charts, and graphs to highlight the choices historians must make about how best to present quantitative information. We try to choose the form that best illustrates the story we want the data to tell. So consider the different displays as you trace this story of population change over time. Think about how a "fever chart" on overall immigration is better (or worse) than a table of population figures; consider why a bar graph works well for showing some kinds of comparisons and a pie chart is better for demonstrating other comparisons. Every choice a historian makes about how to display statistical information is driven by the question: what point am I trying to make? Do the choices made here succeed in illustrating the point about change over time?[1]

The table on page 312 is meant to help you track the connection between a set of population figures and a particular question. For each set of figures, make a check mark if it illustrates the composition of the immigrant population, the nativity of the U.S. population, or the location of immigrants in the United States. It is possible that a particular chart or graph may give relevant information on more than one category.

[1] Most of the displays in this chapter were created with the help of a simple Excel computer program that allows you to type in the appropriate categories and numbers, click on the type of chart or graph you want to use for your display, and then observe the result. Once you've typed in the numbers, it is easy to try out different forms of display. In the case of the source material in Source 2, for example, it was clear that a fever chart with two lines *could* be used to trace change in both the size of the foreign-born population and in the percentage of the total U.S. population that was foreign-born, but a bar graph display of those relationships over time was much easier to read and comprehend. Computer-assisted graphing allows us to experiment with these displays while focusing on what point we want to make with the numbers.

Source	Types of Demographic Changes Addressed		
	Composition of the immigrant population	Nativity of the U.S. population	Immigrants' geographic location
1. Annual Immigration, 1820–2000			
2. Foreign-Born Population, 1850–2002			
3. Immigrants by Region of Birth, 1955–2000			
4. Immigrants' Intended Region of Residence, 1960 and 2000			
5. Concentration of the Foreign-Born by State, 1960 and 2000			
6. Foreign-Born as Percentage of the Population in Selected Cities, 1960 and 1990			
7. Naturalization Rate of the Foreign-Born Population by Year of Entry, 2002			
8. Persons Naturalized by Decade and Selected Region of Birth, 1961–2000			
9. Distribution of Immigrants Admitted under Nonquota Preference System, 1970 and 2000			
10. Immigrants Admitted under Family Reunification Preference System, 1970–2000			
11. Population by Nativity, Age, and Sex, 1960 and 2002			
12. Refugee and Asylee Admissions, 1946–2000			

The Source: Statistics on U.S. Demographic Changes Resulting from the Immigration Act of 1965

1 | *Annual Immigration to the United States, 1820–2000*

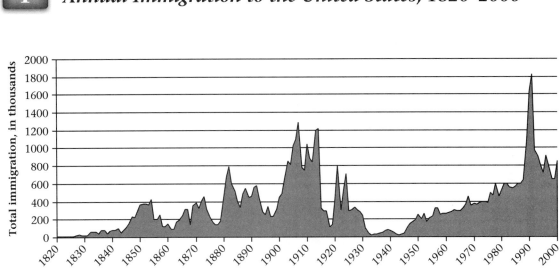

Source: "Fever chart" based on the Bureau of Citizenship and Immigration Services, *Statistical Yearbook* for 2000, Immigration Statistics, Table 1, p. 6, at **bcis.gov.**

2

Foreign-Born Population in the United States, 1850–2002

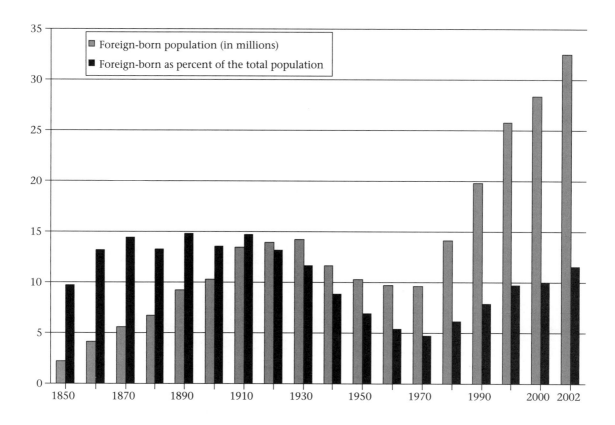

Source: Numerical data from U.S. Bureau of the Census, at **census.gov**. Bar graph derived from Census data.

Immigrants to the United States by Region of Birth, 1955–2000

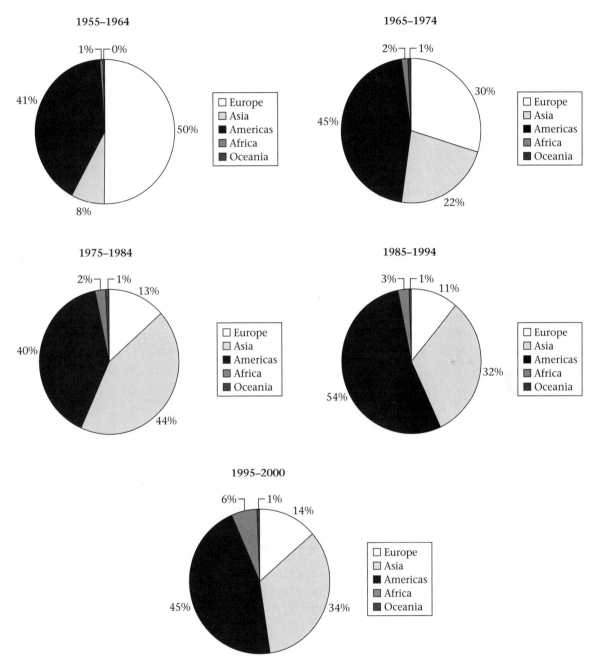

Source: Pie charts based on *Statistical Yearbook of the INS* (October 1999), Table B, p. 20, and Bureau of Citizenship and Immigration Services, *Statistical Yearbook* for 2000, Immigration Statistics, Table 3, pp. 11–14, at **bcis.gov**.

4   *Immigrants' Intended Region of Residence, 1960 and 2000*

Region	% of 1960 Immigrants Intending to Settle in Each Region	% of 2000 Immigrants Intending to Settle in Each Region
New England	8.5	4.8
Middle Atlantic	30.7	19.3
South Atlantic	7.7	19.7
South Central	6.9	9.9
North Central	15.8	11.6
Mountain	3.3	4.5
Pacific	25.9	29.7

Regions: **New England** = Maine, New Hampshire, Vermont, Massachusetts, Rhode Island, Connecticut; **Middle Atlantic** = New York, New Jersey, Pennsylvania; **South Atlantic** = Delaware, Maryland, District of Columbia, Virginia, West Virginia, North Carolina, South Carolina, Georgia, Florida; **South Central** = Kentucky, Tennessee, Alabama, Mississippi, Arkansas, Louisiana, Oklahoma, Texas; **North Central** = Ohio, Indiana, Illinois, Michigan, Wisconsin, Minnesota, Iowa, Missouri, North Dakota, South Dakota, Nebraska, Kansas; **Mountain** = Montana, Idaho, Wyoming, Colorado, New Mexico, Arizona, Utah, Nevada; **Pacific** = Washington, Oregon, California, Alaska, Hawaii.

Source: Compiled from INS *Annual Report*, 1960, p. 75, and BCIS *Statistical Yearbook of the Immigration and Naturalization Service, 2001*, Immigration Statistics, Table 17, p. 58, at **bcis.gov**.

5   *Concentration of the Foreign-Born by State, 1960 and 2000*

Creation of the maps on page 317 illustrates some of the challenges and choices that historians face in using census data. The purpose of these maps is to show where immigrants were common and where they were scarce in 1960 and 2000. The Census Bureau provided the actual numbers of all immigrants in the United States, the number of immigrants in each state, and the total population of each state. But when it calculated percentages, the Census Bureau reported the percentage of each state's total population that was foreign-born. That calculation is so skewed by the varying sizes of states that both Ohio and Kentucky reported that the foreign-born comprised 2.5 percent of their total populations, even though Ohio was home to 282,000 foreign-born people while only 96,000 foreign-born people lived in Kentucky. To illustrate that more immigrants lived in Ohio than in Kentucky, we had to calculate what percentage of all the nation's foreign-born were living in each state. The Census Bureau provided the raw numbers, but to make our point we made our own calculations. Once those calculations were made, we fed them into a mapping program that produced these illustrations of immigrant distribution around the United States.

Source: Campbell J. Gibson and Emily Lennon, "Historical Census Statistics on the Foreign-Born Population of the United States, 1850–1990," Table 13, Population Division, U.S. Bureau of the Census, 1999, at **census.gov**, and U.S. Bureau of the Census, Current Population Survey, March 2000, Table 4-1A.

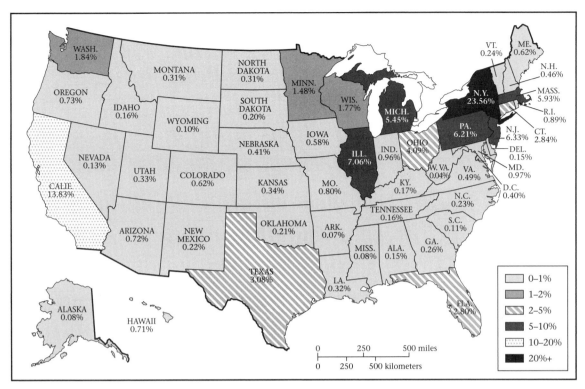

Concentration of the Foreign-Born by State, 1960

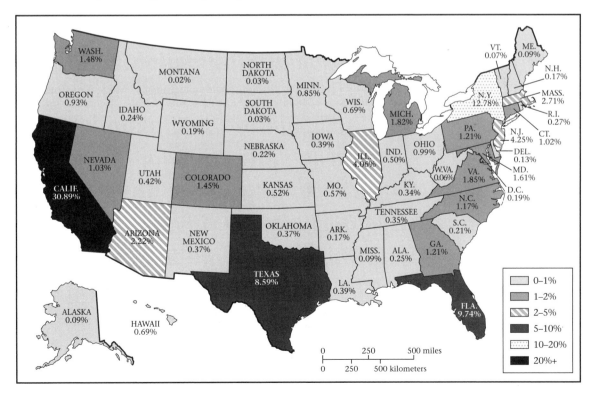

Concentration of the Foreign-Born by State, 2000

6 Foreign-Born as a Percentage of the Population in Selected Cities, 1960 and 1990

City	% of Population in 1960	% of Population in 1990
Atlanta	0.9	3.9
Boston	12.4	11.3
Chicago	9.7	11.9
Cleveland	9.7	4.5
Dallas	1.5	8.8
Denver	3.7	5.0
Detroit	9.7	5.5
Houston	2.3	13.3
Los Angeles-Long Beach	9.1	32.7
Miami	12.0	45.1
Minneapolis	4.8	3.5
New York City	17.4	26.7
Oklahoma City	1.1	3.2
Pittsburgh	6.5	2.4
San Jose	8.0	23.2
Seattle	8.1	8.4
Washington, D.C.	4.2	11.6

Source: Campbell J. Gibson and Emily Lennon, "Historical Census Statistics on the Foreign-Born Population of the United States, 1850–1990," Table 16 and Table 17, Population Division, U.S. Bureau of the Census, 1999, at **census.gov**.

7   *Naturalization Rate of the Foreign-Born Population by Year of Entry, 2002*

Naturalization is the legal process by which an immigrant becomes a U.S. citizen. To qualify for naturalization, an individual must have been registered with the BCIS as a legal "permanent resident" and must have resided in the United States continuously for five years. In addition, an applicant for naturalization must demonstrate "good moral character" by having no criminal record involving violence, drugs, drunkenness, illegal gambling, or prostitution. Finally, to gain naturalization, an applicant must pass a test that demonstrates the ability to read, write, and speak basic English as well as a basic knowledge of U.S. history and government. As the horizontal bar graph below makes clear, the longer individuals reside in the United States, the more likely they are to become U.S. citizens.

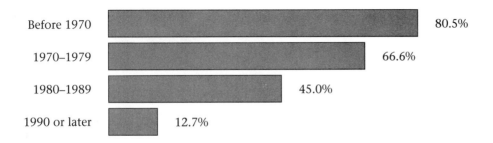

Before 1970   80.5%
1970–1979   66.6%
1980–1989   45.0%
1990 or later   12.7%

Source: U.S. Census Bureau, "The Foreign-Born Population in the United States," March 2002, p. 4., at **census.gov.**

Persons Naturalized by Decade and Selected Region of Birth, 1961–2000

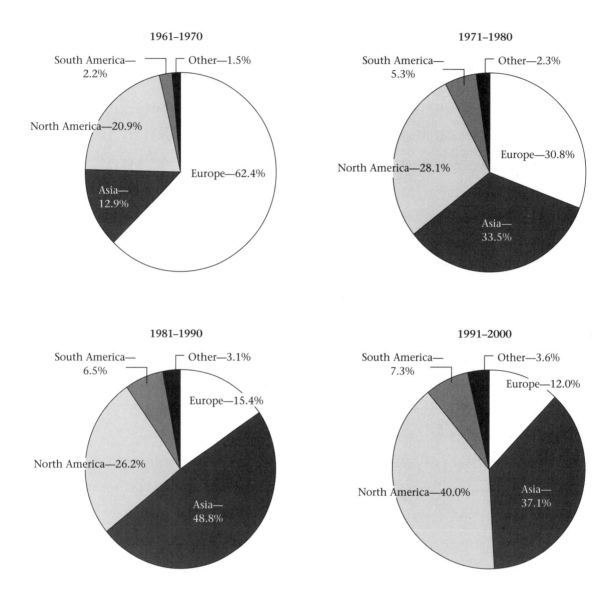

1961–1970

South America— 2.2%
Other—1.5%
North America—20.9%
Europe—62.4%
Asia— 12.9%

1971–1980

South America— 5.3%
Other—2.3%
North America—28.1%
Europe—30.8%
Asia— 33.5%

1981–1990

South America— 6.5%
Other—3.1%
Europe—15.4%
North America—26.2%
Asia— 48.8%

1991–2000

South America— 7.3%
Other—3.6%
Europe—12.0%
North America—40.0%
Asia— 37.1%

Source: BCIS *Statistical Yearbook, 2001*, Immigration Statistics, Chart M, p. 2, at **bcis.gov**.

9 *Distribution of Immigrants Admitted under Nonquota Preference System, 1970 and 2000*

	Family Reunification	Employment Preference	Refugees	Other
1970	46%	9%	14%	31%
2000	69%	13%	8%	10%

Source: INS *Annual Report*, 1970, p. 38; BCIS *Statistical Yearbook, 2001*, Immigration Statistics, "Highlights," p. 2, at **bcis.gov**.

10 *Immigrants Admitted under Family Reunification Preference System: Immediate Relatives of U.S. Citizens, 1970–2000*

This graph does not include the spouses, parents, or children of legal resident aliens, the siblings of U.S. citizens, or the married children of U.S. citizens. Figures on those legal admissions under the preference system were not uniformly reported in distinct categories from 1970 to 2000. The figures for nonquota family members illustrated here were gathered in the same period when the quota system capped immigration at 290,000 individuals per year.

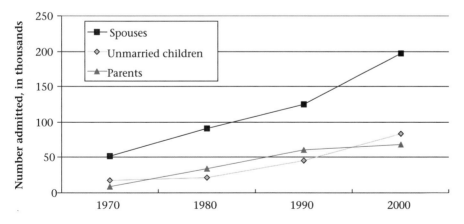

Source: Line graph based on INS *Annual Report*, 1970, p. 38; INS *Statistical Yearbook*, 1980, p. 8; INS *Statistical Yearbook*, 1997, p. 32; BCIS *Statistical Yearbook, 2001*, Immigration Statistics, Table 4, p. 14, at **bcis.gov**.

Population by Nativity, Age, and Sex, 1960 and 2002

These horizontal bar graphs from 1960 and 2002 illustrate differences between the age distribution and sex composition of the native-born and foreign-born populations in the United States in 1960 and 2002. They also show how age and sex differences in the composition of each population changed from 1960 to 2002.

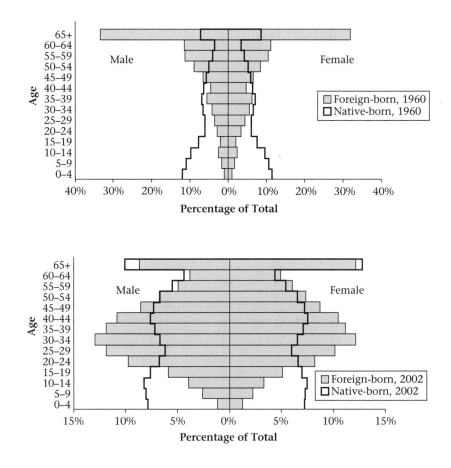

Source: Historical Statistics of the United States, Colonial Times to 1970, U.S. Bureau of the Census (1975), p. 15; Gibson and Lennon, "Historical Census Statistics on the Foreign-Born Population of the United States, 1850–1990," Table 7, Population Division, U.S. Bureau of the Census, 1999, at **census.gov**; and U.S. Bureau of the Census, "The Foreign-Born Population in the United States," March 2002, p. 3, at **census.gov**.

12 *Refugee and Asylee Admissions and Adjustments to Lawful Permanent Resident Status, 1946–2000*

According to U.S. immigration law, a "refugee" is an alien living outside the United States who is unable or unwilling to return to his or her country of nationality because of persecution or a well-founded fear of persecution. An "asylee," on the other hand, is an alien residing in the United States and unable or unwilling to return to his or her country of birth because of persecution or fear of persecution. Both categories of people must provide evidence to support their claims of persecution. If granted asylum in the United States, they are eligible to apply for permanent resident status after a year of residence.

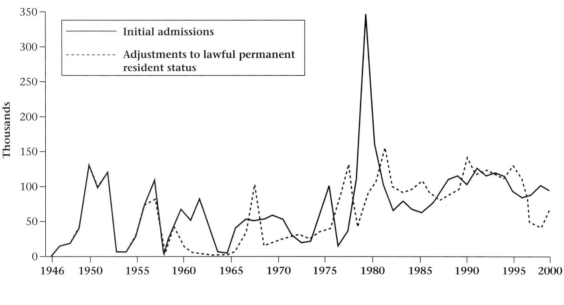

Major refugee programs

1949–53	Displaced Persons Act	1978–84	Indochinese Refugee	3/75–3/80	Indochinese refugees paroled
1954–57	Refugee Relief Act		Adjustment Act	1980	Refugee-Parolee adjustments
11/56–7/58	Hungarians paroled	2/70–3/80	Refugee-Parolees admitted		began
1959	Hungarians adjustments	1/59–3/80	Cubans paroled	4/80	Refugee Act admissions
	began	1967	Cuban adjustments began		began
1966–80	Refugee conditional			1981	Refugee Act adjustments
	entrants				began
				4/80–10/80	Mariel boatlift
				1985–87	Mariel adjustments

NOTE: For the period 1946–56, admissions to lawful permanent resident status and initial admissions were the same.
Source: Tables 23, 24, 27, and 32.

Source: BCIS *Statistical Yearbook, 2001*, Refugee Statistics, Chart C, p. 2, at **bcis.gov**.

Analyzing the Source

REFLECTING ON THE SOURCE

1. As you review the types of changes that these charts, graphs, and tables report, which set of data tells you the most dramatic story of change in the composition of the immigrant population since 1960? Which would you argue offers the *most* striking evidence of change: Source 3, Source 10, or Source 11? Explain your choice.

2. Which sources would you point to in order to discuss the effect of the 1965 immigration law on the nativity of the U.S. population? Which would you argue tells the most striking story: Source 2, Source 4, or Source 6?

3. What do Sources 4, 5, and 6 tell you about the variations around the United States in native-born Americans' experiences with immigration? What do those sources tell you about how state of residence might affect an immigrant's experience?

MAKING CONNECTIONS

4. In the always heated debate about immigration in the United States, opponents at one end of the spectrum describe immigrants as an invading horde of aliens whose extended families threaten to overrun American culture. At the other end of the spectrum, proponents argue that the size of the foreign-born population is minor compared to its large role in reaffirming a work ethic and traditional family values that form the core of American culture. How might the demographic data presented here be used by both proponents and opponents of immigration to argue their positions?

5. A central purpose of the 1965 immigration law was to advance U.S. foreign policy goals by making American practice more consistent with American rhetoric and strengthening our image with non-European peoples around the globe. Based on the demographic data presented here, would you conclude that the results of the law satisfied its framers' intentions?

Beyond the Source

Congressional passage of the Immigration Act in 1965 was not the sole cause of increased immigration to the United States in the subsequent decades. Political instability around the world and the emergence of a global economy caused worldwide migration to double between 1960 and 2000. By 2003, 150 million people, or 2.5 percent of the world's population, were residing outside their country of origin; twelve million of those people were refugees. The Immigration Act of 1965 did not cause people around the world to leave their homes, but it made the United States more accessible to those people around the globe who became migrants in the latter part of the twentieth century.

While passage of the Immigration Act of 1965 did not cause worldwide migration, it did have a significant impact on the population and the cultural life of the United States. Whether they regard the alteration in U.S. immigration policy in a positive or negative light, most historians agree that the 1965 act was the single most influential piece of legislation to emerge from the Great Society of the late 1960s. Evidence of the law's significance can be found in the fact that immigration issues and policy pertaining to cultural diversity play a much bigger part in American public debate than they did fifty years ago, when the quota system had made the United States a more homogeneous society than it is today.

Additional evidence of the law's importance can be found in the fact that Congress continues to grapple with the two main weaknesses in the 1965 legislation: its creation of a population of "illegal" immigrants and its inadequate provision for refugees from war and persecution. In 1986, 1990, and 1996, Congress passed immigration reform acts intended to address the problem of illegal immigrants who were coming primarily from south of the Mexican border. The problem was created by the 1965 law's revolutionary imposition of a ceiling on immigration from the Western Hemisphere. The law could not suppress workers' and employers' well-ingrained habit of ignoring the Mexican border when work was needed and jobs available. Overnight, a whole population of people accustomed to moving easily back and forth across the border became "illegals," and for many it made more sense to simply stay in the United States, even if they lacked a visa.

With the Immigration Reform and Control Act (IRCA) of 1986, Congress tried a two-pronged approach to the problem of undocumented workers. On the one hand, the IRCA granted amnesty to any undocumented alien who had been residing in the United States since 1982 and applied for legal status by 1988. On the other hand, the IRCA imposed sanctions on employers who knowingly hired undocumented workers. The twofold purpose of the IRCA was to choke off the underground economy, where illegal immigrants were exploited by low wages that also hurt legal workers, and to address social and health problems created when a group of people fear contact with legal, medical, or educational authorities. The IRCA legalized the status of over a million U.S. residents but did not solve the problem of illegal immigration that inevitably followed the creation of Western Hemisphere caps. Legislation in the 1990s tried a more punitive approach, with more policing of the border and harsher penalties for violations of immigration laws, but Congress also recognized the economic value of immigrants by raising the overall cap on work-related entry into the United States. So persistent is the problem of illegal immigration that some call for an end to the Western Hemisphere immigration ceiling on the grounds that it is like trying to stop a river with a sieve; others, on the other hand, argue that an unlimited flow of immigrants into the United States threatens the economic health and cultural stability of the nation.

Amidst the debate over undocumented workers, there has also been a persistent litany of problems with U.S. refugee policy. The 1965 law gave refugees a "seventh preference" after family reunification and work-related preferences, but the number of refugees allowed in under that system proved wholly inadequate to the demand created by global instability. As Source 12 indicates, the United States has had to make continual adjustments and enact numerous special provisions, just as it did in the 1950s, to cope with the needs of foreigners fleeing war and repression in their own countries. In the case of Cuban and Indochinese refugees, foreign policy and international opinion dictated that the United States open its doors. With the Refugee Act of 1980, Congress established a program for refugees entirely separate from the nonquota preference system set up in 1965. Since 1980, the president of the United States has had the authority to establish an "allotment number" for each region of the world, which caps how many refugees will be allowed to enter the United States that year. There is no lack of demand for these allotments, but funding problems with processing applications means that the quotas are often not met.

In the aftermath of the terrorist attacks on the World Trade Center and the Pentagon on September 11, 2001, Congress passed the Patriot Act, whose provisions immediately affected immigration policy. The Patriot Act expanded the Justice Department's authority to track the activities of legal aliens in the United States and increased the penalties for visa irregularities and other infractions of immigration law. The breakup of the Immigration and Naturalization Service (INS), which had been a unit of the Department of Justice, is a direct result of the U.S. war on terrorism. The new Bureau of Citizenship and Immigration Services (BCIS) is now a unit of the also new Department of Homeland Security. Ironically, longtime critics of the INS now bemoan its demise. They worry that the BCIS, because of its origin within Homeland Security, will spend more resources on policing alien activities than serving legal immigrants' needs to have family and employment petitions processed, documents issued, naturalization applications approved, and refugee papers reviewed. As was true in 1965, so it is today that the daily lives of immigrants to the United States are shaped in the most direct ways by American foreign policy and global concerns.

Finding and Supplementing the Source

Mohamed Arabi's immigration story was reported in *Fresh Blood: The New American Immigrants* by Sanford J. Ungar (New York: Simon & Schuster, 1995), pages 44–47. Ungar's book records the stories and examines the situation of modern immigrants to the United States. *First Generation: In the Words of Twentieth-Century American Immigrants* by June Namias (Urbana: University of Illinois Press, 1992), contains interviews with immigrants who came between 1900 and 1990.

There are a number of excellent histories that trace modern immigration trends and legislation affecting immigration. See, for example, Roger Daniels, *Coming to America: A History of Immigration and Ethnicity in American Life* (New York: HarperCollins Perennial, 2002); Reed Ueda, *Postwar Immigrant America:*

A Social History (Boston: Bedford Books of St. Martin's Press, 1994); and Elliott R. Barkan, *And Still They Come: Immigrants and American Society, 1920 to the 1990s* (Wheeling, Ill.: Harlan Davidson, 1996). David M. Reimers has written a close analysis of the congressional and national politics surrounding immigration legislation in *Still the Golden Door: The Third World Comes to America* (New York: Columbia University Press, 1992). A very thorough and up-to-date reference book on immigration and immigration history is the *Encyclopedia of American Immigration*, edited by James Ciment (Armonk, N.Y.: M. E. Sharpe, 2001).

Numerous books treat the national debate over immigration policy. Among the best are *Debating American Immigration, 1882–Present* by Roger Daniels and Otis L. Graham (Lanham, Md.: Rowman and Littlefield, c. 2001); *The Immigration Reader: America in a Multidisciplinary Perspective,* edited by David Jacobson (Malden, Mass.: Blackwell, 1998); and *Unwelcome Strangers: American Identity and the Turn Against Immigration* by David M. Reimers (New York: Columbia University Press, 1998).

For historical background on the U.S. census, see Margo Anderson, *The American Census: A Social History* (New Haven: Yale University Press, 1988), or Jason G. Gauthier, *Measuring America: The Decennial Census from 1790 to 2000* (Washington, D.C.: U.S. Department of Commerce, U.S. Bureau of the Census, 2002). The best source of demographic information on U.S. immigration in past decades can be found in the *Annual Reports* of the Immigration and Naturalization Service, which was retitled *Statistical Yearbook of the INS* in 1978. Now that the INS has been replaced by the Bureau of Citizenship and Immigration Services (BCIS), all statistical reports will be issued by the BCIS. Published reports from the INS and BCIS, as well as all publications from the U.S. Bureau of the Census, are available in federal depository libraries. These often are university libraries and sometimes are local public libraries. Your college, university, or community librarian will be able to direct you to the nearest federal depository library in your state. The BCIS, like the U.S. Bureau of the Census, is putting statistical data on its Web site for citizens to access before complete, bound volumes are published. You can explore their materials by going to **bcis.gov** and **census.gov**. For the most concise summary of U.S. demographic data, including immigration data, consult the annually published *Statistical Abstract of the United States* (Washington, D.C.: U.S. Bureau of the Census). The most recent issues of the *Abstract* are available on the Census Bureau's Web site.

Documenting the Source

Whenever you use another researcher's work as a source in your own writing, whether you quote the researcher's words directly or rely on the researcher's evidence and theories to support your arguments, you must include documentation for that source. This is equally true when using a map, photograph, table, or graph created by someone else. The reasons for this are twofold. First, to avoid any possibility of plagiarism, you must always include proper documentation for *all* source materials. Second, a proper citation gives important information to your reader about where to find a particular source, be it on a Web site, in a book at the library, or in an archive in your local community.

When documenting sources, historians use a standard form based on the recommendations published in *The Chicago Manual of Style*. All of the following documentation models are based on the guidelines published in the fifteenth edition of *The Chicago Manual of Style* (Chicago: The University of Chicago Press, 2003). These examples are based on the sources that appear in both volumes of *Going to the Source*. The diversity of the examples will give you some sense of the variety of source types that you may encounter in your research. For each source type, you will see a citation style that can be used for either a footnote, which appears at the bottom of the page of text, or an endnote, which appears at the end of a chapter or at the end of the whole text. This will be followed by an example of how this source type would be cited in a bibliography. Two examples are provided because footnote/endnote citation style is slightly different from bibliography citation style.

The examples provided here will help you address many of the documentation issues associated with source types that you come across in your research. However, this guide is not a comprehensive list, and as you dig further into the past, you may uncover source types that are not covered in this brief guide. For additional information about documenting sources in the *Chicago* style, please see **bedfordstmartins.com/resdoc.**

Documentation Basics

The question to keep in mind when you are wondering what to include in a citation is this: what does my reader need to know in order to *find* this source? When citing sources internally, you should use the footnote or endnote style. Footnotes and endnotes are used to document specific instances of borrowed text, ideas, or information. The first time you cite a source, you need to include the full publication information for that source—the author's full name, source title (and subtitle, if there is one), and facts of publication (city, publisher, and date)—along with the specific page number that you are referencing.

> 1. David Paul Nord, *Communities of Journalism: A History of American Newspapers and Their Readers* (Urbana: University of Illinois Press, 2001), 78.

If you refer to that source later in your paper, you need to include only the author's last name, an abbreviated version of the title, and the page or pages cited.

> 4. Nord, *Communities of Journalism,* 110–12.

A bibliography is used in addition to footnotes or endnotes to list all of the works you consulted in completing your paper, even those not directly cited in your footnotes. The sources included in your bibliography should be listed alphabetically, so the citation style for a bibliographic entry begins with the author's last name first.

> Nord, David Paul. *Communities of Journalism*: *A History of American Newspapers and Their Readers*. Urbana: University of Illinois Press, 2001.

BOOKS

■ *Standard format for a book*

The standard form for citing a book is the same whether there is an editor or an author, the only difference being the inclusion of "ed." to indicate that an editor compiled the work.

FOOTNOTE/ENDNOTE:

1. Tim Johnson, ed., *Spirit Capture: Photographs from the National Museum of the American Indian* (Washington, DC: Smithsonian Institution Press, 1998), 102.

BIBLIOGRAPHY ENTRY:

Johnson, Tim, ed. *Spirit Capture: Photographs from the National Museum of the American Indian*. Washington, DC: Smithsonian Institution Press, 1998.

■ *Book with two or more authors or editors*

When citing a source from a book with two or three authors or editors, you need to include the names of all of the authors (or editors) in the order that they appear on the title page. If a work has more than three authors, you need to include all of the names in your bibliography. However, in your footnotes or endnotes, you need only include the name of the lead author followed by "and others" or "et al.," with no intervening comma.

FOOTNOTE/ENDNOTE:

2. Graham Russell Hodges and Alan Edward Brown, eds., *"Pretends to Be Free": Runaway Slave Advertisements from Colonial and Revolutionary New York and New Jersey* (New York: Garland, 1994), 58.

BIBLIOGRAPHY ENTRY:

Hodges, Graham Russell, and Alan Edward Brown, eds. *"Pretends to Be Free": Runaway Slave Advertisements from Colonial and Revolutionary New York and New Jersey*. New York: Garland, 1994.

■ *Edited book with an author*

Sometimes a book will have an author and an editor. In that case, you need to include both the author's and editor's names.

FOOTNOTE/ENDNOTE:

3. Hilda Satt Polacheck, *I Came a Stranger: The Story of a Hull-House Girl*, ed. Dena J. Polacheck Epstein (Urbana: University of Illinois Press, 1991), 36.

BIBLIOGRAPHY ENTRY:

Polacheck, Hilda Satt. *I Came a Stranger: The Story of a Hull-House Girl*. Edited by Dena J. Polacheck Epstein. Urbana: University of Illinois Press, 1991.

■ *Multivolume book*

If you are referring to a specific volume in a multivolume work, you need to specify which volume you used. This information should come before the page reference toward the end of the citation.

FOOTNOTE/ENDNOTE:

4. Bernard Bailyn, ed., *The Debate on the Constitution: Federalist and Anti-Federalist Speeches, Articles, and Letters during the Struggle over Ratification* (New York: Library of America, 1993), 2:759–61.

BIBLIOGRAPHY ENTRY:

Bailyn, Bernard, ed. *The Debate on the Constitution: Federalist and Anti-Federalist Speeches, Articles, and Letters during the Struggle over Ratification.* 2 vols. New York: Library of America, 1993.

Sometimes individual volumes in a multivolume work have separate volume titles. When citing a particular volume, you should include the volume title first followed by the name of the complete work.

FOOTNOTE/ENDNOTE:

5. Robert M. Yerkes, *Psychological Examining in the United States Army*, vol. 15, *Memoirs of the National Academy of Sciences* (Washington, DC: Government Printing Office, 1921), 145.

BIBLIOGRAPHY ENTRY:

Yerkes, Robert M. *Psychological Examining in the United States Army.* Vol. 15 of *Memoirs of the National Academy of Sciences.* Washington, DC: Government Printing Office, 1921.

■ *Book with an anonymous author*

Many books printed in the nineteenth century were published anonymously. If the author was omitted on the title page, but you know from your research who the author is, insert the name in square brackets; if you do not know who the actual author is, begin the citation with the work's title. Avoid using "Anonymous" or "Anon." in citations. As originally published, the author of *The Mother's Book* was listed as "Mrs. Child," so this citation includes that information along with the full name in brackets.

FOOTNOTE/ENDNOTE:

6. Mrs. [Lydia Maria] Child, *The Mother's Book* (Boston: Carter, Hendee, and Babcock, 1831), 23.

BIBLIOGRAPHY ENTRY:

Child, [Lydia Maria]. *The Mother's Book*. Boston: Carter, Hendee, and Babcock, 1831.

■ *Book-length work within a book*

Sometimes, the source that you are using may be a book-length work that has been reprinted within a longer work. In that case, you need to include both titles along with the editor of the longer work.

FOOTNOTE/ENDNOTE:

7. Zilpha Elaw, *Memoirs of the Life, Religious Experience, Ministerial Travels and Labours of Mrs. Zilpha Elaw, an American Female of Colour, Together with Some Account of the Great Religious Revivals in America (Written by Herself)*, in *Sisters of the Spirit: Three Black Women's Autobiographies of the Nineteenth Century*, ed. William L. Andrews (Bloomington: Indiana University Press, 1986), 55–91.

BIBLIOGRAPHY ENTRY:

Elaw, Zilpha. *Memoirs of the Life, Religious Experience, Ministerial Travels and Labours of Mrs. Zilpha Elaw, an American Female of Colour, Together with Some Account of the Great Religious Revivals in America (Written by Herself)*. In *Sisters of the Spirit: Three Black Women's Autobiographies of the Nineteenth Century*, edited by William L. Andrews. Bloomington: Indiana University Press, 1986.

■ *Chapter from a book*

If you want to cite a particular chapter from a book, you should include the title of the chapter in quotation marks before the title of the book.

FOOTNOTE/ENDNOTE:

8. Vicki L. Ruiz, "The Flapper and the Chaperone," in *From Out of the Shadows: Mexican Women in Twentieth-Century America* (New York: Oxford University Press, 1998), 12–26.

BIBLIOGRAPHY ENTRY:

Ruiz, Vicki L. "The Flapper and the Chaperone." In *From Out of the Shadows: Mexican Women in Twentieth-Century America*. New York: Oxford University Press, 1998.

PERIODICALS

Journals are scholarly publications that are usually published a few times a year. Popular magazines are written for the general public and are most often published on a monthly or weekly basis. Most newspapers are published daily, though some small local papers are published weekly. The following examples demonstrate the style for citing each type of periodical. If you consult an online periodical, the style for citing this source would be the same with the addition of the URL at the end of your citation.

■ *Journal articles*

When citing an article from a journal, you need to include the volume number, issue number (when given), and date of publication.

FOOTNOTE/ENDNOTE:

9. Elizabeth A. Fenn, "Biological Warfare in Eighteenth-Century North America: Beyond Jeffery Amherst," *Journal of American History* 86, no. 4 (2000): 1552–80.

BIBLIOGRAPHY ENTRY:

Fenn, Elizabeth A. "Biological Warfare in Eighteenth-Century North America: Beyond Jeffery Amherst." *Journal of American History* 86, no. 4 (2000): 1552–80.

■ *Popular magazines*

When citing material from a popular magazine, you need include only the magazine title followed by the date of publication and the page number(s) for the material. If you are citing from a regular feature of the magazine, you should include the title of the feature in the citation. If there is an author of the magazine article or the magazine's regular feature, the author's name would appear first in your citation, followed by the name of the feature.

FOOTNOTE/ENDNOTE:

10. Can This Marriage Be Saved?, *Ladies' Home Journal*, September 1961, 42.

BIBLIOGRAPHY ENTRY:

Ladies' Home Journal. Can This Marriage Be Saved? September 1961.

■ *Newspaper articles*

When citing newspaper articles, you must include the day, month, and year of publication, and the author if the article had a byline. *Chicago* style allows for page numbers to be omitted because newspapers often publish several editions each day and these editions are generally paginated differently.

FOOTNOTE/ENDNOTE:

11. John Dickinson, "The Liberty Song," *Boston Gazette*, July 18, 1768.

BIBLIOGRAPHY ENTRY:

Dickinson, John. "The Liberty Song." *Boston Gazette*, July 18, 1768.

INTERNET SOURCES

■ *Internet archives*

Because many older sources like newspapers and letters are rare and fragile, researchers often turn to Internet archives such as that of the Library of Congress through which digital copies of these documents are made available. Access to documents on the Internet also allows us to examine materials without having to travel to the archives in which they are housed. To cite a document found on an Internet Web site, you need to provide as much of the following information as possible: the author, the name of the document with original date of publication, the name of the site, the sponsor or owner of the site, and the URL. Sometimes a Web archive will include a document number; when available, you should include this cataloguing number as well.

FOOTNOTE/ENDNOTE:

12. Civil Rights Act of 1964, Document PL 88-352, *International Information Programs*, U.S. State Department, http://usinfo.state.gov/usa/infousa/laws/majorlaw/civilr19.htm.

BIBLIOGRAPHY ENTRY:

Civil Rights Act of 1964. Document PL 88-352. *International Information Programs*, U.S. State Department. http://usinfo.state.gov/usa/infousa/laws/majorlaw/civilr19.htm.

■ *An entire Web site*

To cite an entire Web site, you need include only the author of the site (if known), the name of the site, the sponsor or owner of the site, and the URL.

FOOTNOTE/ENDNOTE:

13. University Libraries of the University of Minnesota, *Sources for Ship Passenger Lists and Emigration Research*, University of Minnesota, http://wilson.lib.umn.edu/reference/shp-gene.html.

BIBLIOGRAPHY ENTRY:

University Libraries of the University of Minnesota. *Sources for Ship Passenger Lists and Emigration Research*. University of Minnesota. http://wilson.lib.umn.edu/reference/shp-gene.html.

OTHER SOURCES

■ *Published letters and other forms of correspondence*

When citing letters, memoranda, telegrams, and the like, you need to include the name of the sender and the recipient along with the date of the correspondence. Memoranda, telegrams, and other forms of communication should be noted as such in your citation after the recipient's name and before the date, but letters do not need to be specifically noted as such. The source cited in the following examples comes from *Foreign Relations of the United States* (FRUS), a valuable resource for historians published by the U.S. State Department. In citing any single document from FRUS, you need to provide the document's specific source, which is provided at the bottom of the document's first page in FRUS, along with the specific volume publication information. Note that these citations specify that the correspondence was a telegram.

FOOTNOTE/ENDNOTE:

14. Henry Byroade to U.S. State Department, telegram, August 4, 1956, from Department of State Central Files, 974.7301/8-456 in *Foreign Relations of the United States*, volume 16 (1955–1957), *Suez Canal Crisis, July 26–December 31, 1956* (Washington, DC, 1990).

BIBLIOGRAPHY ENTRY:

Byroade, Henry. Henry Byroade to U.S. State Department, telegram, August 4, 1956. From Department of State Central Files, 974.7301/8-456, in *Foreign Relations of the United States*, Volume 16 (1955–1957), *Suez Canal Crisis, July 26–December 31, 1956*. Washington, DC, 1990.

■ *Unpublished letters and other forms of correspondence*

Unpublished letters and those that have not been archived should include some indication of this fact, such as "in the author's possession" or "private collection." If the letter was found in an archive, the location of the depository would be included as well. (For information on how to cite material found in an archive, see the section "Photos and other material found in an archive or depository" on p. 338.)

FOOTNOTE/ENDNOTE:

15. Jeff Rogers to William and Adele Rogers, November 10, 1968, in the author's possession.

BIBLIOGRAPHY ENTRY:

Rogers, Jeff. Jeff Rogers to William and Adele Rogers, November 10, 1968. In the author's possession.

■ *Court records*

When citing legal cases in historical writing, the name of the plaintiff appears first, followed by the name of the defendant, and both names are italicized. The first time you cite the case, you should also include the court and year in which the case was decided. Supreme Court decisions are published by the government in a series called *United States Reports.* When citing Supreme Court decisions, you need to include the name of the case in italics followed by the number of the volume that contains the particular case, the abbreviation "U.S." for *United States Reports,* page numbers, and the date of the decision.

FOOTNOTE/ENDNOTE:

16. *Korematsu v. United States,* 323 U.S. 242, 242–48 (1944).

BIBLIOGRAPHY ENTRY:

Korematsu v. United States. 323 U.S., 242, 242–48. 1944.

■ *Tables, graphs, and charts*

Whenever incorporating statistical data into your work, it is important to document your evidence. If you borrow a table, graph, or chart from another source, you must cite it just as you would quoted material in your text. Include a citation in appropriate footnote format to the source of the borrowed information directly below it. If you change the table, graph, or chart in any way (for example, eliminating unnecessary information or adding another element such as a percent calculation to it), use the phrase "adapted from" in your citation, which signals to the reader that you have altered the original. If a number is used to identify the data in the original source, that information should be included as well at the end of the citation.

FOOTNOTE/ENDNOTE:

17. Adapted from Hinton R. Helper, *The Impending Crisis of the South: How to Meet It* (New York: Burdick Brothers, 1857), 71, table XVIII.

Because you wouldn't cite any one particular table in your bibliography, you would follow the style for citing the book, periodical, or Web site where the data you consulted first appeared.

■ *Paintings*

When citing paintings that appear in a catalogue, archive, or database, it is important to include the catalogue or accession number of the piece of art if available. This documentation will allow other researchers to locate the original source more easily. Generally, specific works of art are not included in your bibliography. However, if a particular painting is important to your research, you may list it in your bibliography by the painter's name first.

FOOTNOTE/ENDNOTE:

18. George Catlin, *Shón-Ka-Ki-He-Ga, Horse Chief, Grand Pawnee Head Chief* (1832, Smithsonian American Art Museum: 1985.66.99).

BIBLIOGRAPHY ENTRY:

Catlin, George. *Shón-Ka-Ki-He-Ga, Horse Chief, Grand Pawnee Head Chief.* 1832.
    Smithsonian American Art Museum: 1985.66.99.

■ *Photos and other material found in an archive or depository*

Any material found in an archive or depository, be it a photograph, letter, or a map, needs to be cited just as published material would be. The name of the author (or photographer, in the case of photographs) should appear first, followed by the title of the image or document being cited in quotation marks, the date, and the name of the archive or depository. If a source from a collection is important enough to your work, you can mention that source specifically in your bibliography. However, if you make use of more than one photograph or other type of source from a particular collection, you need only cite them generally in your bibliography.

FOOTNOTE/ENDNOTE:

19. George P. Barnard, "Ruins of Charleston, S.C.," 1866, Beinecke Rare Book and Manuscript Library, Yale University.

BIBLIOGRAPHY ENTRY:

Photographs. Beinecke Rare Book and Manuscript Library, Yale University.

■ *Government publications*

The government publishes thousands of pages of documents every year. The format for citing these documents varies slightly from source to source depending on the format of the publication and the source being cited. For example, any testimony given before a congressional committee is usually published in a book. Here the exact name of the committee is given in the title of the work in which the testimony appears. When citing government publications in your bibliography, you would substitute the agency that published the work for the author unless, of course, a particular author has been specified.

FOOTNOTE/ENDNOTE:

20. United States Congress, *Report of the Joint Select Committee to Inquire into the Condition of Affairs in the Late Insurrectionary States,* vol. 2, *South Carolina, Part I* (Washington, DC: Government Printing Office, 1872), 25–28, 33–34.

BIBLIOGRAPHY ENTRY:

United States Congress. *Report of the Joint Select Committee to Inquire into the Condition of Affairs in the Late Insurrectionary States.* Vol. 2, *South Carolina, Part I.* Washington, DC: Government Printing Office, 1872.

Acknowledgments (continued)

Page 40 (Source 4): "Spearfishing in Glacier National Park," date unknown. Great Northern Railway Company Advertising & Publicity Department Photos, Minnesota Historical Society.

Page 41 (Source 5): "Two Guns White Calf Reading," date unknown. Great Northern Railway Company Advertising & Publicity Department Photos, Minnesota Historical Society.

Page 42 (Source 6): "Old Ration Place," date unknown. Courtesy of Montana Historical Society.

Page 43 (Source 7): "Blackfeet Performance," c. 1930. Great Northern Railway Company Advertising & Publicity Department Photos, Minnesota Historical Society.

Page 44 (Source 8): "Family at Sun Dance Encampment," 1908. Courtesy of Browning Public Schools.

Page 44 (Source 9): "Students with Their Harvest," 1912. Courtesy of Browning Public Schools.

Page 44 (Source 10): "Mad Plume Family Harvest," c. 1920. Courtesy of Browning Public Schools.

Page 46 (Source 11): "Blackfeet Girl at Glacier National Park Switchboard," c. 1920. Great Northern Railway Company Advertising & Publicity Department Photos, Minnesota Historical Society.

Page 47 (Source 12): "Sewing Class at the Cut Bank Boarding School," 1907. Courtesy of the Sherburne Collection, University of Montana Archives.

CHAPTER 4

"I Discover Hull-House," "The Oasis in the Desert," "'The Ghetto Market,'" "The University," and "New Horizons" from *I Came a Stranger: The Story of a Hull-House Girl* by Hilda Satt Polacheck, edited by Dena J. Polacheck Epstein. Copyright © 1989 by the Board of Trustees of the University of Illinois. Used with permission of the University of Illinois Press.

CHAPTER 7

Page 145: "The Flapper and the Chaperone" from *From Out of the Shadows: Mexican Women in Twentieth-Century America* by Vicki L. Ruiz. Copyright 1998 by Vicki L. Ruiz. Used by permission of Oxford University Press, Inc.

CHAPTER 8

Page 163 (Figure 8.1): William Gropper, *Automobile Industry,* 1941. Smithsonian American Art Museum, Washington, D.C./Art Resource, New York.

Page 167 (Source 1): Ben Shahn, *The Riveter,* 1938. Smithsonian American Art Museum, Washington, D.C./Art Resource, New York.

Page 168 (Source 2): Elsa Jemne, *Development of the Land,* 1938. Photograph courtesy of The Art Gallery, University of Maryland.

Page 169 (Source 3): Reginald Marsh, *Assorting the Mail,* 1936. Courtesy of the General Services Administration, Public Building Service, Fine Arts Collection.

Page 171 (Source 5): Stevan Dohanos, *Legend of James Edward Hamilton—Barefoot Mailman,* 1940. Smithsonian American Art Museum, Washington, D.C./Art Resource, New York.

Page 172 (Source 6): Xavier Gonzalez, *Tennessee Valley Authority,* 1937. Smithsonian American Art Museum, Washington, D.C./Art Resource, New York.

Page 173 (Source 7): Edward Millman, *Plowshare Manufacturing,* 1937. Courtesy of the General Services Administration, Public Building Service, Fine Arts Collection.

Page 175 (Source 8): Paul Hull Julian, *Orange Picking,* 1942. Courtesy of the General Services Administration, Public Building Service, Fine Arts Collection.

Page 176 (Source 10): Michael Lensen, *Mining,* 1942. Smithsonian American Art Museum, Washington, D.C./Art Resource, New York.

CHAPTER 12

Page 258 (Source 1): Jeff Rogers to Adele and William Rogers, November 10, 1968. Courtesy of Jeff Rogers and family.

Page 259 (Source 2): Jeff Rogers to Dale Rogers Marshall, November 24, 1968. Courtesy of Jeff Rogers and family.

Page 259 (Source 3): Jeff Rogers to William Rogers, December 7, 1968. Courtesy of Jeff Rogers and family.

Page 260 (Source 4): Jeff Rogers to Adele and William Rogers, December 30, 1968. Courtesy of Jeff Rogers and family.

Page 261 (Source 5): Jeff Rogers to Adele and William Rogers, February 18, 1969. Courtesy of Jeff Rogers and family.

Page 263 (Source 6): Jeff Rogers to Adele and William Rogers, March 14, 1969. Courtesy of Jeff Rogers and family.

Page 264 (Source 7): Jeff Rogers to Adele and William Rogers, April 20, 1969. Courtesy of Jeff Rogers and family.

Page 265 (Source 8): Jeff Rogers to William Rogers, May 24, 1969. Courtesy of Jeff Rogers and family.

Page 266 (Source 9): Jeff Rogers to Adele and William Rogers, May 31, 1969. Courtesy of Jeff Rogers and family.

Page 266 (Source 10): Jeff Rogers to Adele and William Rogers, June 10, 1969. Courtesy of Jeff Rogers and family.

Page 267 (Source 11): Jeff Rogers to Adele and William Rogers, June 23, 1969. Courtesy of Jeff Rogers and family.

Page 267 (Source 12): Jeff Rogers to Adele and William Rogers, August 28, 1969. Courtesy of Jeff Rogers and family.

CHAPTER 13

Page 282 (Source 1): Ladies' Home Journal. Can This Marriage Be Saved? September 1961, copyright © Meredith Corporation. Used with the permission of *Ladies' Home Journal.*

Page 285 (Source 3): Ladies' Home Journal. Can This Marriage Be Saved? December 1976, copyright © Meredith Corporation. Used with the permission of *Ladies' Home Journal.*

Page 288 (Source 5): Ladies' Home Journal. Can This Marriage Be Saved? November 1984, copyright © Meredith Corporation. Used with the permission of *Ladies' Home Journal.*

Page 290 (Source 6): Ladies' Home Journal. Can This Marriage Be Saved? May 1985, copyright © Meredith Corporation. Used with the permission of *Ladies' Home Journal.*

Page 292 (Source 7): Ladies' Home Journal. Can This Marriage Be Saved? February 1986, copyright © Meredith Corporation. Used with the permission of *Ladies' Home Journal.*

Page 293 (Source 8): Ladies' Home Journal. Can This Marriage Be Saved? March 1987, copyright © Meredith Corporation. Used with the permission of *Ladies' Home Journal.*

Page 295 (Source 9): Ladies' Home Journal. Can This Marriage Be Saved? August 1987, copyright © Meredith Corporation. Used with the permission of *Ladies' Home Journal.*

Page 296 (Source 10): Ladies' Home Journal. Can This Marriage Be Saved? June 1988, copyright © Meredith Corporation. Used with the permission of *Ladies' Home Journal.*

Index

Letters in parentheses following page numbers refer to:
(i)   illustrations
(f)   figures, including charts and graphs
(m) maps